Avionics In Plain English

Phil Croucher

About the Author

Phil Croucher holds EASA, UK, UAE and Canadian licences for aeroplanes and helicopters and around 8500 hours on 37 types, with a considerable operational background, and training experience from the computer industry, in which he is equally well qualified. He has at various times been a Chief Pilot, Ops Manager, Training Captain and Type Rating Examiner for several companies. He is currently Head Of Training for Caledonian Advanced Pilot Training and can be contacted at **www.electrocution.com**

TABLE OF CONTENTS

TOC

CAPT

CAPT

CAPT

INTRODUCTION

0

T he rate of change in the field of avionics is so fast that even the legislators are struggling to keep up with it. With new digital cockpits, it is getting to the stage that, if your VCR still flashes 12:00, you will have no business flying a modern aircraft!

The majority of twin-engined (and many single-engined) machines now have complex autopilots, glass cockpits and navigation equipment, possibly including Flight Management Systems (FMS). They are now even fitted to training helicopters.

This book originated with a request from the RCAF for training materials for engineers, but curious pilots whose training syllabus did not include avionics, and who would like to know a little more will find it useful as well.

AUTOMATION

The brain's limitations, in terms of speed of computation and the ability to multi-task (i.e. none!) began to be recognised as early as 1959, with the Boeing 707. This was when it was realised that pilots could soon begin to exceed their design capabilities, and that the help of various black boxes was needed. A lot of work can be done for you by computers, which are just electronic machines - the man-machine system is meant to relieve pilot workload and increase time for supervision.

But how much control should be given to black boxes? If they have too much, the cockpit becomes boring and errors can go unnoticed amongst the monotony. Although automation can conserve resources and attention, it can result in routine errors, or *slips,* such as when programming waypoints into the system (it can also reduce your flying competence). Machines can wait for infrequent information without getting bored, and can perform long-term control and set values, again, without getting bored, but people can exercise judgment, make better decisions and detect unusual conditions (smells, noises, etc.), whilst getting bored very easily.

On the one hand, automation is good, because it can take much of the routine work away from you, and flight management systems can operate an aircraft very fuel-efficiently. For example, a FADEC (fuel control thingy) has a lot of monitoring functions. On the other hand, automation can induce a feeling of *automation complacency* (too much reliance on the machine) and lead you not to check things as often as you should (*reduced vigilance*), or

push the envelope, as when using a GPS in bad weather - with much of the navigation task taken away from you, it is tempting to fly in worse weather than you can really cope with (flying in bad weather is like sex - the further you get into it, the harder it is to stop). As your visual clues decrease, your mental processes focus more on trying to see where you're going and less on flying until you lose control, when flying on instruments is no help because you are not mentally prepared for it.

You can avoid automation complacency by regarding systems as one more crew member that needs to be cross-checked. Indeed, if you change decisions during flight, you'd better tell the Flight management System as well! You can cope with low error tolerant situations (e.g. where errors could have serious consequences) by constantly complying with cross-over verification procedures (cross monitoring).

A high degree of automation may alter traditional tasks so much that your attention and competence is reduced once you are out of the loop. Thus, communication and coordination call for a greater effort from the crew. The trouble is that we rely on machines so much, and their rapidity of change adds to our stress, as described by Alvin Toffler in his book, *Future Shock.*

However, one major benefit is the integration of many sources of information and its presentation in a clear and concise manner (sometimes!), as with the glass cockpit, and providing a major contribution towards situational awareness, as long as you keep a mental plot going, as the information presented can be highly filtered. What it doesn't help with is the fact that one knob used to have one function in older systems - now several functions may be hidden at different levels, for which there is no substitute for knowledge of the menu system.

Civil Aviation Authority

European Union
United Kingdom Civil Aviation Authority

APPROVED TRAINING ORGANISATION CERTIFICATE

GBR.ATO.0129

Pursuant to Commission Regulation (EU) No 1178/2011 and subject to the conditions specified below, the UK Civil Aviation Authority hereby certifies

CALEDONIAN ADVANCED PILOT TRAINING LIMITED

Wycombe Air Centre Building	C/O Helicentre Aviation
Wycombe Air Park	Leicester Airport
SL7 3DP	Gartree Road
	Leicester
	LE2 2FG

as an Approved Training Organisation with the privilege to provide Part-FCL training courses, including the use of FSTDs, as listed in the attached course approval.

CONDITIONS:

1.   This certificate is limited to the privileges and the scope of providing the training courses, including the use of FSTDs, as listed in the attached training course approval.

2.   This certificate is valid whilst the approved organisation remains in compliance with Part-ORA, Part-FCL and other applicable regulations.

3.   Subject to compliance with the foregoing conditions, this certificate shall remain valid unless the certificate has been surrendered, superseded, limited, suspended or revoked.

Date of issue: 15 February 2013

Signed

For the UK Civil Aviation Authority

EASA FORM 143 Issue 1 – page 1/2

CAPT

ELECTRICITY & MAGNETISM

The term *electricity* comes from the Greek word for amber, *elektron*. As far as pilots (and engineers) are concerned, it is not a source of energy by itself, but a way of transmitting energy (or data, with electronics) from one point to another. For this, it has to be produced, transmitted, applied and controlled, with switches and/or computers.

As you cannot see electricity, some imagination must be used in order to understand it, but the whole process is very like the movement of water (current) in a hose. The difference is that you have to put the water into the hose, whereas the charge is already present in an electrical cable - all you have to do is set it in motion.

Some airmanship points first:

- Take care not to overheat electrical equipment when it is switched on (for checking) during a preflight check (there is no airflow to cool it)

- Do not start or stop engines with unnecessary electrical equipment switched on

- Avoid using the starter motor for too long - there is usually a limit of one or two attempts for around 30 secs each, after which you must let it cool down before trying again. Also, starters don't have fuses - make sure the warning light is out after starting!

- Check that the generator or alternator is working properly after starting, and often during flight

- Make sure the Battery Master Switch is off before you leave the aircraft after flight (many pilots leave the anti-collision light on to remind them)

ATOMIC THEORY

Matter is anything that has mass and volume. For our purposes, it exists as a solid, liquid or a gas, but it can be a plasma as well. An **element** is a substance that cannot be reduced to a simpler form by chemical means. What distinguishes one element from another is the number of protons, neutrons and electrons in the atoms it contains (an element's atoms are all of the same type). A *compound* contains 2 or more elements - one example is water, which contains 2 hydrogen atoms and one of oxygen.

However, for most purposes, the atom is the most basic building block of matter. The word derives from the Greek *a tomos* which means "not cut", or that you can't reduce (or cut) the atom into anything smaller, as you can with a molecule, which is a collection of atoms in a

chemical compound, the smallest part of an object that retains its identity. By the time Einstein came along, it had been discovered that atoms are both a lot smaller and a lot bigger than was originally thought. If you enlarged an apple until it became the size of the Earth, for example, the atoms inside would be the size of cherries (and the atmosphere would have the thickness of clingfilm). Gold leaf has the thickness of about 5 atoms - if this book were printed on gold leaf, and you multiplied it by four, the total thickness would be that of a single sheet of paper.

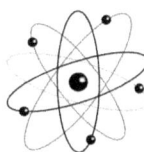

The diagram on the left is a loose depiction of the inside of an atom (the Bohr model). The large ball in the middle is the *nucleus* and the smaller ones spinning rapidly round it are a cloud of *electrons*, which are **negatively charged particles** and around 2,000 times smaller in size. The nucleus contains positive- and neutrally charged particles, called *protons* and *neutrons* (both contain quarks and other strange things). The neutrons are there to bind the protons together, as particles of a like charge are repelled. As an example of how large atoms can be, if the nucleus were the size of the apple above, the first electron would be found anywhere between 1-10 miles away, and be hardly visible at that.

In an atom, there are an equal number of electrons to protons, to make it electrically neutral, or uncharged. An atom with one extra electron is *negatively* charged, and an atom with one missing is *positively* charged, or "carrying a positive charge", which is a bit of a misnomer as all it has done is lost an electron. This is called *ionisation*, because an unbalanced (charged) atom is an *ion*, which we will come across later when we discuss the ionosphere that surrounds the Earth. Some components, like transistors, depend on the movement of electrons or holes (missing electrons) one way or the other.

None of the components of an atom are physical in nature - they are actually electromagnetic charges, or tiny whirlwinds of electromagnetic force. The negative electrons are held in place by the positive protons with *electrostatic attraction,* as particles with opposite charges attract each other. Once an electron leaves an atom, lines

CAPT

of force exist between them, to create a kind of electrical "tension" which is made use of in radio transmissions. Electrons spin round the nucleus at around 600 miles/second so, bearing in mind the relative distances above, you can see that they work quite hard! In fact, they move so quickly round a nucleus that they give the *illusion* of a more solid construction because our senses don't work fast enough to detect the difference.

So, an atom:

- is not solid

- is mostly full of nothing

Of course, Einstein proved that energy is really matter in another form with his formula:

$$e=mc^2$$

In other words, energy is equal to the mass of a body multiplied by the speed of light, squared. Matter converts into energy and back again depending on what you do with its velocity.

Electrons possess kinetic energy from their movement, and potential energy from their position. Those spinning round an atom occupy *energy levels*, or *shells*, like the orbits of the planets around the Sun, except that the planets have unique orbits. Electrons can share theirs! The first shell can hold up to 2 electrons, and the second up to 8, but it's the outer shell that is important. Unbalanced electrons in the last shell of an atom determine its valency, and are therefore called valence electrons. Valency is the property of atoms to combine with or displace others, or the number of chemical bonds that an atom can form.

Insulators & Conductors

Some atoms don't have much of a hold on their free electrons, and allow them to move around easily because their valence shells overlap. The materials made from these atoms (such as copper) are called **conductors**, and they have a low resistance to the flow of current, meaning that it flows easily. Silver is best, and copper is next by 6%, but gold is commonly used because it doesn't corrode and cause bad connections. Even a gas can conduct electricity, as with fluorescent lighting, or the ionosphere.

Insulators, by contrast, may have their shells full, and they may not overlap, so they allow no movement of electrons. This makes them useful for keeping conductors from touching each other, otherwise electricity would flow where you don't want it and create a short circuit. Examples of insulators are glass, or the plastic coating around a cable.

SEMICONDUCTORS

A substance that is normally an insulator but which can become a conductor depending on which way the current flows is a semiconductor.

As semiconductors can produce changes in circuit conditions, they are known as *active* components, as opposed to the more passive capacitors and resistors, which is why they are also called **solid state devices**, meaning no moving parts. As they have more to do with digital electronics, they are discussed under *Computers, Etc*.

ELECTRICITY
....

This involves the movement of electrons (or a statistical average of electron drift). In theory, if you line up a series of atoms in an electrical cable, and remove an electron from one end, the resulting hole is filled by a free electron from the previous atom, because the others are trying to repel each other, and so on.

That is, you have created a (very) slight difference in pressure, or potential, between each end of the cable, which causes the movement of free electrons, or an electric current, to the area with less electrons (from high to low pressure). However, this won't actually happen without a complete circuit, described later.

Although the electrical force moves at a speed close to that of light, individual electrons move relatively slowly (actually about 0.3 mph!), because they collide at random as they push each other along.

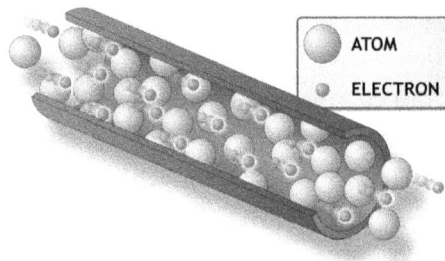

You can separate electrons from their atoms and make them move in 6 ways:

- **Heat**. The usual way of using heat is to apply it to the junction of two dissimilar metals, such as iron and copper. How much electricity you get depends on the temperature difference between the ends of the wires. The *thermocouple* is such a component that detects the heat from the back of a turbine engine. The electricity it produces drives a temperature gauge in the cockpit. As you don't need batteries for this, you have at least one gauge that works when the electrics fail.

- **Friction**. When rubbing two materials together, such as glass and silk (two insulators), electrons may be forced out of their orbits in the glass by friction and transferred to the silk, which acquires

CAPT

a negative charge of static electricity, described later. The glass acquires a positive charge.

- **Chemical Action.** Used in batteries, later.

- **Light.** Photo-electric or solar cells create reactions between two substances when exposed to light.

- **Pressure.** Certain materials, such as quartz, can produce an electric charge when pressure is applied to them. This principle is also used in carbon pile voltage regulators (described later) to control the amount of electricity fed into a battery by a generator. Applying electricity to such a substance can also make it expand or contract.

- **Magnetism.** This is the most common method, using relative motion between a coil of wire and a magnet. It is described later on in this section.

THE ELECTRONIC TIDE

Transferring electrons to a place and leaving them there sets up a stress (field) between them (the electrostatic attraction mentioned before) and the original location. It is only relieved when the electrons flow back to where they came from. The stress is the *potential difference*, but the energy behind the work needed to create it is called *electromotive force*. The problem is that they are both expressed in volts, so the terms tend to be used synonymously. In reality, emf is a cause (because it can only come from something active) and p.d. is an effect (because it can exist across a passive element).

- **p.d.** is the "pressure" difference (or energy transfer) between two points, say across a component such as a lamp, because some of the charge gets used up. Thus, the voltage measured in a circuit when current is flowing is smaller than the maximum, because of internal resistance and the work required to overcome it. Put another way, p.d. involves the conversion of electrical energy into another form, such as heat, having first been converted from, say, chemical energy to get emf. Electrons coming from a battery contain a potential charge that is used up as it goes through a component and work is done. The reason behind bonding the parts of a fuselage together is to produce a zero potential over the airframe - if the bonding breaks down, there will be a series of varying differences in potential all over the place.

The voltage coming out of a component is not the same as that going in. Kirchoff's second law (later) states that all the voltage drops in a closed

circuit equal the total voltage applied to the circuit. For example, in the picture below, the emf from the battery divides between two lamps. A voltmeter connected across the top one (in parallel) reads 3.5 volts, and one across the bottom one reads 2.5 volts. If point A has zero potential* (Earth), the p.d. at B is 2.5 volts, and at C, 6 volts. The battery is therefore a 6 volt one (3.5 + 2.5).

So, although the number of electrons (current) flowing at each point of the circuit is the same, the pressure or energy behind them (voltage) can vary.

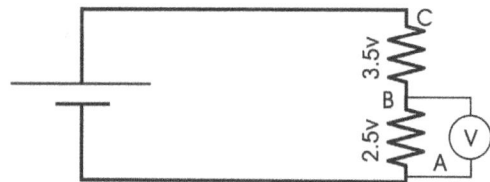

Note: The current does not flow because of the p.d. - the p.d. exists because current is flowing.

*A point of zero potential performs a similar function to Mean Sea Level. When using the term *potential difference*, from mechanics, the emphasis should be on the word *potential*, since it refers to potential energy, or the energy available due to position (a better expression is *difference in potential*).

To make this clearer, the work involved in pushing together electrons that repel each other is like pushing a large snowball ball up a hill that is getting steeper. The closer you get to the top, the more work you have to do to move it.

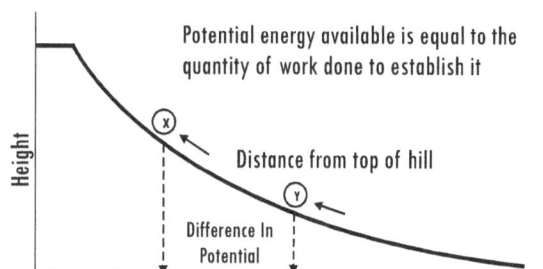

There is a greater potential at X than there is at Y, which is what creates the pressure for a current, assuming the electron at X is allowed to flow to Y.

If you take a positively charged body (one with more holes than electrons in its atoms) and bring it close to a neutrally charged one, there will be a migration of negative electrons towards the new body (the blue is the negative quality). This is an *electronic tide.*

If you move the positively charged sphere back and forth, the tide will do likewise. These are called *induced charges*, brought about by a process of *induction*, in this case electrostatic. As electrons are moving, one way or another, you now have a drift of electrons, or an electric current.

The electrons do not all rush completely to one side - the centre of the neutral body remains neutral, in that the negative charge gradually increases from the centre to the end. As the electrons have all moved over, there are holes in the atoms on the other side of the body, and there is a similar gradient from the centre to the positive end.

If you replaced the positively charged sphere with a negatively charged one, the result would be the opposite - namely, the negative electrons would be repelled and flow to the other side of the neutral body.

If you replaced the air between the two bodies with glass or mica, you could do this at a much smaller distance because you are condensing the field. See *Capacitors*.

TYPES OF ELECTRICITY

There are three:

- That which stays right where it is, or **static electricity,** although it can jump across small gaps, (this can be a problem with underslung loads on helicopters, especially in dry snow). As this force does not move, it is called *static*, meaning electricity that goes nowhere in particular, but which can build up on a point to create a charge that can be attractive or repellent (no conductor is needed).

You discharge static electricity by providing a path for the electrons to move. *Static discharge wicks* are used on aircraft for this purpose, because the airframe can develop its own static potential. They allow the charge to concentrate, then discharge to air - the visible discharge of static electricity to the air is called *St. Elmo's fire*. A conducting bead in the tyres will do the same job on the ground. Static (and sparks) are why you bond an aircraft and a refuelling vehicle together, and aircraft surfaces to each other.

- That which goes in one direction, usually at one speed and value, called **Direct Current**
- That which flip-flops back and forth, called **Alternating Current**

It is AC which concerns us when it comes to radio.

Circuits

There must be an unbroken connection between any components for electricity to flow, or a complete circuit, which is any combination of a conductor and a source of electromotive force that allows electrons to travel round it in a continuous stream. If a circuit is broken (usually with a switch), it is an *open* circuit (as opposed to *closed*), and no current flows. **With open circuits, the loss of continuity stops everything in the circuit from working.**

A cable going to a component must have one returning to the switch as an earth return, to create a *dipole circuit*. However, you can use the fuselage as a return path, which means that you only need one length of cable (the battery will be connected to the fuselage by its *negative* pole). This saves weight and space, as you don't need two cables to complete a circuit, but you do need bonding through the fuselage. Further weight savings can be made with busbars, and alternating current, both described later.

SERIES CIRCUITS

A series circuit exists when its elements are connected end to end, creating *one path* for the current to flow in, so if one fails, everything stops (as with Christmas tree lights).

Referring to the picture below:

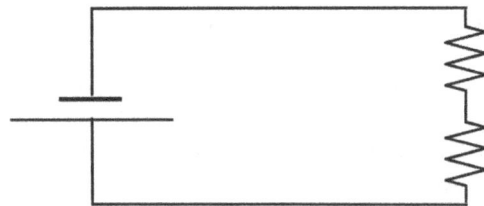

Although both lamps would have the same brightness, they would be dim, because the battery has to push the same charge through the first bulb, then the second. Less charge is flowing per second, so energy is transferred slowly from the battery.

PARALLEL CIRCUITS

In a parallel circuit, components occupy separate paths, *across* the voltage source (another term for this is a *shunt* connection). In a parallel circuit, the loss of one component does not result in a circuit failure.

CAPT

In the picture below, both lights would again have equal brightness, but this time they would be bright, as the battery can push the charge along two alternative paths. More charge can flow around the circuit per second so energy is transferred quickly from the battery.

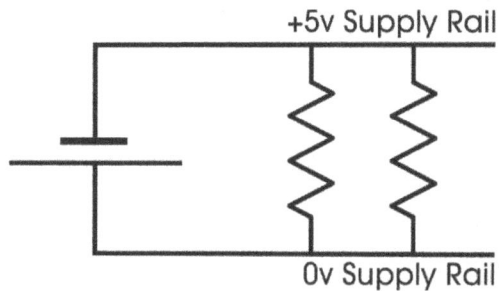

There is more energy in the 5v supply rail, so the current will naturally follow the gradient and flow towards 0.

COMPLEX CIRCUITS

Simply a circuit where the components are connected in combinations of series-parallel.

Voltage

Voltage is a measure of how much energy a charge has. It is like the head of pressure behind the movement of water in a hose. The volt is the p.d. that must exist between two points if the energy transformed is 1 joule when 1 coulomb of electricity (1 amp) passes for one second.

Current

The flow of charge (electrons) in a conductor is called the *current*. The rate of current flow is the number of electrons passing any section of the conductor in one second, expressed in terms of *amperes*, or *amps* (an ampere is the movement of 1 coulomb per second). Small currents may be measured in *milliamperes* or *microamperes*. However, one electron has such a small charge that it is hardly detectable. You need a larger unit to work with, such as the *coulomb*, which consists of 6.28×10^{18} electrons (think of a coulomb of electrons in the same way as you would a pint of beer). The symbol for a coulomb is *C*.

Remember: The rate of current flow is measured in amps, and the charge is measured in coulombs.

The more electrons that move along a wire in a given time, the higher the current that is measured, so if you increase the voltage, current will increase automatically, other things being equal. Put more technically, *current will increase with voltage if the resistance, or opposition to flow, remains constant.* It follows that to control the current, you can vary either the voltage or the resistance, discussed below.

In a series circuit, the current is the same throughout. In a parallel circuit it changes with individual values of resistance (the voltage will stay the same).

Resistance

A waterwheel produces work when it is turned, but it also slows down the flow of water. Electricity is affected in the same way. The electrical energy supplied to a circuit is changed into other forms of energy by any appliances connected to it that impede its flow or have resistance. For best economy, you must move the most current with the least waste, in a circuit with as little resistance as possible.

A conductor has a low resistance to current, and an insulator has a high one, but even a good conductor slows electrons down, because a new electron joining an atom is repelled by those already there, and some energy is lost. This increases the temperature. The more work you make electricity do, the hotter things get, which is how electric fires work. If you make it work harder, you get light as well, hence light bulbs. Each material has a specific resistance (e.g. 2.82 for aluminium) against a standard, but its actual resistance depends on cross section and length.

If your conductor is thick and short, you won't meet much resistance. If it is long and thin, on the other hand, you have to force the current along, which takes more work. Electrical energy is proportional to the difference in potential across the component (volts) multiplied by the rate of flow of the moving current, which is affected by the type of material and its cross-sectional area (resistance). In other words:

```
pd across component
current that gets through
```

The more current that gets through a component with a given p.d., the less resistance it has. It is *directly proportional* to *temperature* and *conductor length*, and *inversely proportional* to *cross-sectional area*, so the warmer, longer and thinner a cable is, the more resistance it has.

So if resistance is such a drag, why use it? The answer is that resistance can limit current, or control voltage*, for which the heat is a penalty. It is associated with the *dissipation* of energy, and power is used up (as heat) when it is present. Such power cannot be recovered.

*A switch is a very crude way of controlling current. Resistors used properly can allow much finer adjustments. For example, a volume control is a variable resistor, and combinations of switches and resistors are the basis of logic gates, described in *Computers, Etc.* A connection taken from the junction between two resistors connected in series can obtain a portion of the voltage, so you can create a specific voltage drop for a particular purpose. Indeed, this is the main use of resistors in any circuit. LEDs, for example, typically operate at around 2 volts. In a 5 volt circuit, they would need some sort of step down.

*Potential dividers*** are used in sensor circuits, where a voltage can be changed if the environment changes.

In the picture, the lower resistor is a thermistor, which is heat sensitive, in that, when it is cold, it has a high resistance and *vice versa*. Because the thermistor is on the bottom, such a high resistance allows more current to flow from R1 to the logic gate. Later on, we will see how this can be combined in a circuit to do work. If the thermistor were on top, it would block the current and the logic gate would get a low current.

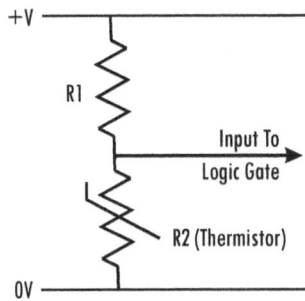

Resistors in **series act as *voltage* dividers. Resistors in **parallel** are *current* dividers.

The symbol for resistance is Ω (omega), but in diagrams the zigzag symbol given above is used. In formulae, resistance is signified by the letter R.

Note: The symbol can mean either a specific component or the amount of resistance present. A resistor slows down electrons in the *entire circuit*, not just at the resistor. In circuit diagrams, connecting lines are assumed to have no resistance.

Resistance is expressed in *ohms*. 1 ohm allows 1 amp to flow when 1 volt is applied. Thus, resistance is calculated in terms of the emf required to push a certain current through a conductor, numerically equal to the volts needed to drive 1 amp of current (volts per ampere).

For resistors in **series**, total (or *equivalent*) resistance is simply the sum of them all:

$$R_{TOTAL} = R_1 + R_2 \text{ etc}$$

This is because the same *current* flows through them all, and total resistance is always higher than any individual one, as the "conductor" is effectively longer. Thus, the current will decrease.

Resistors connected in **parallel** present a lower combined resistance because they have an increased cross-sectional area. In other words, if they all have the same value, the current divides equally between them all. As the voltage (p.d.) remains the same, and therefore so does the current through each resistor, the total current increases - it is doubled with two resistors in parallel. Put another way, the effective resistance is reduced - by half with two resistors.

If they do not all have the same value, those with *lower* resistance will draw *more* current (components are protected against excessive current with fuses and circuit breakers, described later).

Tip: Two identical resistors in parallel have half the resistance of one! To calculate the ohmic value of a pair of resistors in parallel, divide their product by their sum.

Essentially, *the resultant is smaller than the smallest resistance*, and you can often answer an exam question just by knowing that. That is, if the resistances were 3 ohms each in the diagram, they would collectively behave like a 1 ohm resistor. Individual resistors do not then have to cope with maximum current, which is useful when adding loads in a sharing situation.

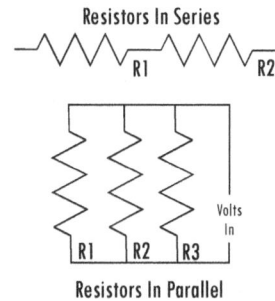

Now you find total resistance by adding the reciprocals:

$$\frac{1}{R_{TOTAL}} = \frac{1}{R1} + \frac{1}{R2} \text{ etc}$$

Instead of resistance, think of its opposite, conductance, which is simply the reciprocal. Find the sum of the conductances, then reverse it to find the resistance, as the reciprocal of the total resistance is the sum of the reciprocals of the individual resistors, which sounds a lot worse than it is. For example, with 4 resistances in parallel, of 1, 3, 8 and 15 ohms, find the unknown total R.

Turned into reciprocals, the formula would look like this:

$$\frac{1}{R} = \frac{1}{1} + \frac{1}{3} + \frac{1}{8} + \frac{1}{15}$$

The least common denominator is 120, so....

$$\frac{1}{R} = \frac{120 + 40 + 15 + 8}{120}$$

which becomes:

$$\frac{1}{R} = \frac{183}{120}$$

The non-reciprocal of which is:

$$\frac{R}{1} = \frac{120}{183}$$

As the denominator is greater than the numerator, the answer will be less than 1. This makes sense, since, if you imagined the same situation with water pipes, more liquid will flow through several pipes connected in parallel than through one, which is the same as having less resistance. If one conductor is split into two, resistance doubles in each half (because the cross sectional area is reduced), so total resistance is half that of one.

Ohm's Law

The ratio of the voltage across, and the current flowing through, a conductor is constant, and equal to the value of the resistance.

If you increase the voltage (pressure) in a circuit, you increase the current automatically. On the other hand, given a constant voltage, current flow decreases if you increase the resistance. Current flow is therefore *directly proportional* to voltage and *inversely proportional* to resistance.

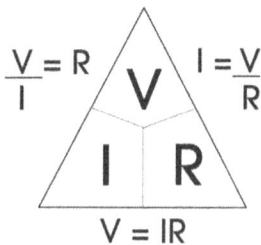

$$\frac{V}{I} = R \qquad I = \frac{V}{R}$$

$$V = IR$$

Ohm's Law describes the fixed relationship between voltage, current and resistance, and is therefore very useful for finding the unknown factor in a circuit if you know the values of the other two and have forgotten the relevant measuring instrument (actually, it's very hard to measure current, and it is most often calculated anyway). Ohm's law does not apply to all conductors, but is valid for practically all metals if their temperature remains constant.

The symbols for the elements in the formula are I for current (amps), R for resistance (ohms), V for voltage, and they come together in this formula:

        V (or PD) = I x R

or (rearranged slightly):

        I = V
            ─
            R

So, if you have a 24 volt battery, and a load has 12 ohms of resistance, there are 2 amps of current:

        24 = I(2) x 12

Aircraft systems typically use 24-volt systems because of the weight savings you get when using a higher voltage and lower current where lighter cabling is involved.

This formula can be useful in many ways - given that the resistance of an aluminium cable is about 60% greater than a copper one of the same length and cross section, you could use the formula to calculate how much larger the replacement would have to be.

Note: If you connect a heavy load to a battery, the battery's voltage will drop as it tries to satisfy Ohm's Law. If the required current cannot be produced, it pushes out as much as it can and the voltage will reduce to whatever Ohm's Law says it should be.

EXAMPLES

1. What is the current if 8v is flowing across a 2 ohm resistor? 4 amps.

2. What value of resistor needs to be connected in series with a bulb rated at 1.25V 250 mA if you want to make it work with a 5V supply?

We know that the current will be 250 mA, and that one end of the resistor will be at 5V, with the other at 1.25V. The voltage across the resistor (i.e. the potential difference) is therefore 3.75V. Dividing that by 250 gives an answer of 0.015 kilohms. You need a 15 ohm resistor.

3. Resistors R1, R2, R3 and R4 are connected as two pairs in parallel (R1 & R2, R3 & R4), connected in series. If R1 and R2 are 8 ohms each, R3 is 6 ohms, and R4 is 3 ohms, what is the total resistance of the circuit?

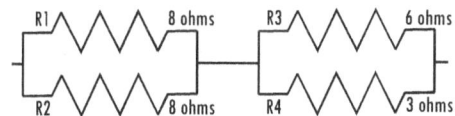

A faster way of dealing with more than two resistors is to group them in pairs, and treat the result of a pair as one.

In this example, the pair on the left are dealt with like this:

        1 + 1
        ─   ─
        8   8

which translates to:

$$\frac{8 + 8}{64} = \frac{16}{64} = \frac{1}{4}$$

The answer is 4 ohms. Do the same with the other one:

$$\frac{6 + 3}{18} = \frac{9}{18} = \frac{1}{2}$$

That gives you 2. Add the other for the answer of 6 ohms.

Note: In the right hand pair, more current will flow in the bottom resistor. The ratio of resistance is 2:3 but the ratio of current flow is 3:2.

4. R2 and R3 are in parallel with one another, and the combination of them is in series with R1. In a 6 volt circuit, if R2 has 2 amps running through it and R3 is 6 Ohms, what value is R2?

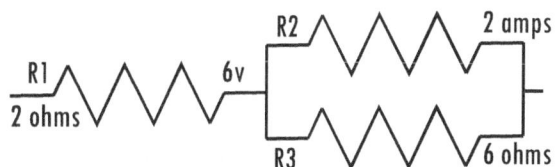

The answer is 3 ohms (6 volts divided by 2 amps).

Ohm's law often has to be combined with something like:

KIRCHOFF'S LAWS

These are generalisations that make it easier to calculate the currents involved with complex resistances.

- **First:** At any junction of resistances, the total current flowing in is equal to the current flowing out. In other words, electricity does not accumulate at any point in a circuit.

- **Second:** This is a generalisation of Ohm's Law. In any closed circuit, the sum of the products of current and resistance (drops in potential) equals the voltage applied to the circuit (emf) - the law of conservation of energy for electrical circuits.

Both are very useful in combination with Ohm's Law to find unknown values in a circuit. For example, in a circuit with two resistors that have voltage drops across them of 14 and 10 volts, the source voltage must be 24v.

BRIDGE CIRCUITS

Kirchoff's laws are the basis of the **Wheatstone Bridge**, which was invented by Samuel Hunter Christie in 1833 and improved and popularised by Sir Charles Wheatstone in 1843. It measures an unknown electrical resistance by balancing two legs of a bridge circuit, one of which includes the unknown component.

They are commonly used in Air Data Computers that use solid state capsules.

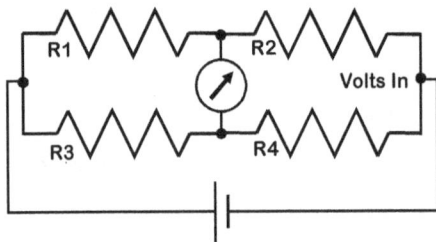

In the diagram above, a DC current flows through R1 and R2, and R3 and R4, so the potential difference across both pairs is the same. If R1 and R2 are of equal value, the p.d. across each is half the total. Equally for R3 and R4, so everything is in balance. If you have a resistance you don't know, say R4, you can simply vary R3 until the bridge is balanced again. It is the ratio between R1 and R2 that is significant rather than their values. This is why they are called the ratio arms.

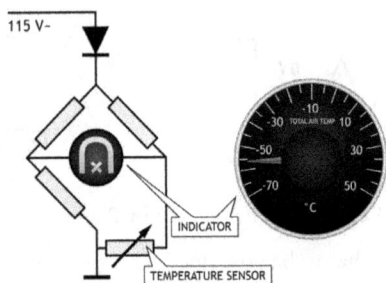

As the bridge becomes unbalanced, the varying voltage across the middle can be measured with a voltmeter. For temperature measurement purposes, for example, you can replace the voltmeter with a wiper arm that is positioned by a servo loop, and how far the arm moves is a measure of the temperature change. It will be centred at 15°C.

Power (Watts)

The *rate* at which electrons are moved about is called *electrical power*, represented by the letter P, which is measured in *Watts*, after James Watt (the Watt is the SI derived unit of power, equal to the transfer of one joule per second. 746 Watts equal 1 horsepower). However, as Watts are very small units, we tend to use Kilowatts (KW) instead, and count them in thousands (0.01Kv is 10 volts!) Power consumed (Wattage) is determined by voltage multiplied by the current (in amps):

$$P = V \times I$$

Power lost as heat is often called the *IR loss,* as the heat depends on current and resistance. The above formula (*Joule's Law*) best represents heat energy lost by a circuit.

But V is also equal to I x R under Ohm's Law. If you substitute one for the other, you only need to use current and resistance to find power:

$$P = IR \times I$$
$$P = I^2R$$

But you can also use just voltage and resistance:

$$I = \frac{V}{R}$$

To give:

$$P = \frac{V}{R} \times V$$
$$P = \frac{V^2}{R}$$

Thus, there are three formulae for calculating power, depending on the information you have to hand.

If a 240v light bulb is rated at 60W, what is its resistance?

$$R = \frac{V^2}{P}$$
$$R = \frac{57600}{60} = 960 \text{ ohms}$$

Note: This is only correct for DC.

The total power equals the sum of the power consumed by individual components. In general, for maximum power transmission, E and I (voltage and current) must be as large as possible, but the current is limited by the size of the wire and the voltage by the insulation.

CAPT

It is easier and cheaper to make a line with good insulation, so you can transmit a higher voltage, than to make one able to carry high current, as power loss is proportional to the square of the current, which should be as low as possible. This is one reason for using alternating current, as high voltages are easier to achieve with it. Sending signals down long cables is more effective when they are is based on voltage rather than current.

EXAMPLES

1. Three 24 watt navigation lights are connected in parallel and supplied with 12 volts. What is the total current?

Divide the watts by the voltage to get 2 amps, multiply by three to get 6 amps in total.

2. In a circuit with a 5 ohm resistor, and a current of 4 amps, what is the power? First, you have to find the voltage. Ohm's Law produces 20 volts. Multiply that by 4 amps for 80 watts.

3. If power is 100 watts in a circuit with 2 amps of current, what is the resistance? The voltage is 50, so the resistance is 25 ohms.

Circuit Protection

A **short circuit** exists when the full current comes into contact with the grounded part of the circuit. This can be more than the circuit is built to handle, so electrical equipment may be protected in many ways.

Note: The **Battery Master Switch** controls the power to all circuits, and others will control smaller groups of equipment, such as the **Avionics Master Switch**, for the radios and navigation aids. The Battery switch may well be in two parts, one for the battery itself, and the other for the alternator circuit, which needs DC for the electromagnet that makes it work.

Circuits will be otherwise protected by **fuses** or **circuit breakers**, which are designed to interrupt the flow of current where specific conditions that generate a lot of heat exist. One difference between the two is that a fuse will blow *before* the full fault current is reached, and the circuit breaker will trip afterwards, in which case both it and the item protected must be able to take the full fault current for a short time. Neither are designed to protect equipment as such - rather, they are there to protect the cabling and connectors which are not easy to replace and may be old and/or inaccessible if a fire starts.

Circuit protection devices should only be reset or replaced once, after allowing them to cool. Especially with the fuel system! Only reset it if the item is needed for flight safety. There are a lot of instruments in the average aircraft that do not need electricity with which to function.

FUSES

A fuse is a deliberately weak part of a circuit so, instead of replacing wiring in odd places, all you do is change the fuse. Technically, a fuse is a *thermal device wired in series with the load protected*, meaning that all the current passes through it, and it *melts* because it *overheats* from *excess current*. Fuses are placed as close to a power distribution point as possible to minimise runs of unprotected cable.

Note: As the current is large, there is no fuse protection for starter motors, which is why there is a starter warning light that must be checked after you start a piston engine.

You must carry spare fuses - EASA require the higher of 10% of the number for each rating, with at least 3.

Fuses must be replaced with those of the *correct* value. They are rated according to the number of amperes they carry, which must be a lower figure than the lowest rated equipment. As well, fuse capacity should be double the amperage requirement. So, in a 100-watt circuit using 25 volts (i.e. 4 amps), you need an 8-amp fuse. Generally, the lowest rated fuse is selected for reliable operation, but for emergency equipment (anything that will affect safety), the highest rating is used consistent with cable protection.

A *high rupturing fuse* is also known as a *heavy duty* fuse.

CIRCUIT BREAKERS

A circuit breaker is a combination of a relay and a solenoid, both described later. It is relatively slow acting, and can be used in AC and DC circuits, being a button that pops out when a fuse would otherwise break, so it is a *resettable mechanical trip device,* activated by the heating of a bimetallic strip element, where one metal expanding more than another pops it open.

Thermal trip circuit breakers show black when closed and white when they are open.

A *trip-free* circuit breaker will trip even if it is held in, and therefore does not remake a circuit, so pilots don't make the situation worse! A magnetic one is a *quick tripping response protection system.* A *flush fit* circuit breaker cannot be manually tripped or pulled.

Note: Although they are the most commonly used method of circuit protection, try not to use a circuit breaker as a switch. This cannot always be avoided, but it is still not good practice.

Generally, circuit breakers are resettable, fuses are not.

CURRENT LIMITERS

These are like fuses, but with a much higher melting point so that a higher overload current can be carried. They will limit the current to a predetermined value and are used typically to sectionalise heavy duty supply circuits.

LIMITING RESISTORS

These are used in DC circuits where initial current surges may be very high, as with starter motors or inverters.

Capacitance

Where two separate, nearby, conductors have a current flowing through them, there is an electric field flowing through the insulation (dielectric) between them. Even two wires close together can have this property. A circuit has capacitance if it can store energy as an electric field.

Whereas resistors can control the amount of current in a circuit, capacitors can control how quickly the p.d. across a component changes, so they allow you to design circuits that involve timing (see *Storage*, below). Potential energy is also associated with *elasticity*, which can be represented by a stretched spring, or a hydraulic accumulator, including smoothing fluctuations and absorbing surges. Electrically, you can do the same thing with a capacitor.

Normally, electrons cannot enter a conductor unless there is a path for an equal amount of them to leave, which is why you need a circuit. However, a conductor can hold a greater charge if it is near another one and there is an electric field in the space between them (see below).

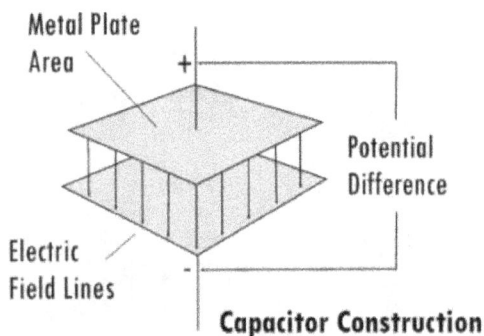

Capacitor Construction

You are concentrating the region over which the field extends, which is why capacitors were originally called condensers. The number of extra free electrons added to the conductor (or free electrons taken away) is directly proportional to the field flux between them.

STORAGE

In an electronic circuit, you often need to store small quantities of electricity for short periods for later use.

Because they can store electricity* (or energy), capacitors can make a circuit dynamic. If you had two circuits, each with a battery, a switch and a light bulb, but one with a capacitor, the capacitor can introduce a time delay before the bulb goes on or off (as can a coil, or a solenoid, for different reasons). This is because capacitors tend to resist changes in voltage drop.

*A capacitor's storage ability is not actually used much in radio - they are more useful for their ability to pass AC and block DC, as described overleaf.

Capacitance is the ratio of the stored charge to the applied voltage. The larger the capacitance, the larger the charge you can store from a given voltage. It depends on:

- the **dielectric** used. Glass, for example, has 5.1 times the capacity of dry air and fuel has double (water has 80). The reason that solids are more effective than air is that, when the charge starts or stops, a momentary flow of electrons begins or ends. This wouldn't happen if there was nothing there at all. This increase is called *permittivity* (see below). *It is the dielectric that holds the charge.*

- **distance** between the plates (they cannot touch or there would be a short circuit)

- the **parallel surface area**

Thus, capacitance is more when the conductors are nearer to each other, or larger. If they are relatively far apart, you will get more leakage from the field, which is the basis of radio transmission, discussed in *Radio Navigation*.

If you had 100 volts between two plates and introduced a third one between them, you would get two capacitors in series, with a p.d. of 50 volts each, so they have the same charge but half the voltage. To get back to 100 volts you would have to double the charge. That is to say, halving the spacing doubles the capacitance, which is inversely proportional to the spacing between the plates (it is directly proportional to the cross-sectional area).

For capacitors in parallel, the total capacitance is the sum of them (the opposite of how resistance works):

$$C_{TOTAL} = C1 + C2 \text{ etc}$$

They add up because you are increasing the plate area whilst the spacing stays the same.

Treat capacitors in series as for resistors in parallel:

$$\frac{1}{C_{TOTAL}} = \frac{1}{C1} + \frac{1}{C2} \text{ etc}$$

or:

© *Phil Croucher, 2014*

CAPT

$$C_{TOTAL} = \frac{C1 \times C2}{C1 + C2}$$

Total capacitance will be less than that of the smallest capacitor, because connecting capacitors in series has the effect of increasing the space between all the plates and reducing the p.d. across each capacitor.

The unit of capacitance is the *Farad* (F), named after Faraday. It represents 1 amp for 1 second with a change of 1 volt stored as 1 joule of energy. As it happens, this is too large to be used in most circuits (the capacitor concerned wouldn't even fit into a room), so *microfarads* (μf), representing millionths, are used instead.

CURRENT FLOW

When voltage is applied across the capacitor in the diagram, one plate becomes negatively charged with electrons leaving the battery. At the same time, electrons leave the other plate to resupply the battery, leaving that plate positively charged.

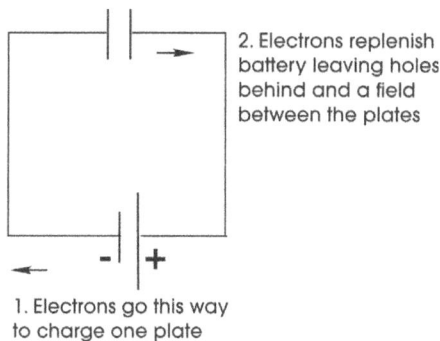

2. Electrons replenish battery leaving holes behind and a field between the plates

1. Electrons go this way to charge one plate

This effect is called *polarisation*. The current flows until the charge across the capacitor is equal to the battery emf, at which point everything stops. However, you now have more electrons and holes than you would normally have on the respective plates, which carry equal and opposite charges, attracting each other, and an electric field of force (charge) between them. There is a "strain" on the dielectric (hence the word "tension", as in *High Tension*). DC will not normally pass across the gap, unless the voltage is very high and the gap very small, in which case there may be a spark. Thus, once a capacitor becomes fully charged, it acts as an open circuit to DC because, as it reaches the maximum charge and therefore matches the supply voltage, the current becomes zero. **No current will flow if you simply charge the capacitor** (with DC).

If the source of voltage is taken away, the voltage across the capacitor stays where it is, but will leak in the reverse direction over time so, until this happens, capacitors behave like miniature batteries, since they preserve a difference of potential between the plates for a short time. This is how you can change the batteries in your mobile phone without backup power. Capacitors are also used in

computer memory cells to store information, and as suppressors on electric motors, or in magnetos.

If the capacitor discharges through a high resistance, the current will be relatively large at first, but will gradually die away, so you get a lot of current in one shot. However, if it discharges through a small resistance, the current alternates rapidly in relatively weak cycles.

Alternating current appears to pass through capacitors because the plates change between positive and negative on each cycle as the charge on them builds up and decays. The rapid change of p.d. looks like current "flowing".

If the frequency of the alternating current is high enough, the capacitor will behave as if it were a low value resistor, because it will never become charged in either direction. At lower frequencies, the "resistance" will be higher because charging can take place, and maximum at zero frequency if you ignore leakage. This quality of resistance varying with frequency is actually called *reactance*, which is useful for filtering frequencies, especially with radio.

PERMITTIVITY

The factor by which capacitance is increased when an insulator (dielectric) fills the space between the plates is called the *dielectric constant*, or permittivity of the material, which is the quality that allows it to store an electrical charge, or a measure of its ability to allow an electric flux to be established. It is the relationship between flux density and electric field strength.

A material with high permittivity can store more charge than one with lower permittivity. It is a physical quantity that describes how an electric field affects and is affected by a dielectric, or *a constant of proportionality that relates the electric field in a material to the electric displacement in that material*.

The *absolute permittivity* of a substance (or the constant for a given material) is given relative to that of a vacuum, or the *permittivity of free space*. The *relative permittivity* of a particular dielectric (i.e. the dielectric constant) is the ratio of its absolute permittivity to that of free space, or of using an insulator rather than a vacuum. The relative permittivity of air is usually taken as 1, since the difference between that and a vacuum is negligible for our purposes.

Thus, permittivity relates to a material's ability to isolate (or "permit") an electric field - as mentioned above, solids are better at being a dielectric than air, and the increased permittivity allows the same charge to be stored with a smaller electric field (and a smaller voltage), leading to increased capacitance. This is how capacitive fuel measurement takes place, using the difference between fuel and air when they are used as a dielectric.

APPLICATIONS FOR CAPACITORS

- Short term storage of DC charges

- Coupling AC circuits where no DC is wanted

- Filtering out AC where DC is wanted

- Timing circuits - with potential dividers, they can create time delays in logic circuits as they charge

- With an inductor (later), creating tuned circuits that resonate at a particular frequency

Measuring Instruments

THE AMMETER

Current is measured in series using *ammeters*, or *loadmeters*, both presenting the information in different ways. They need a low resistance so they don't affect the current they are measuring. Ammeters measure coulombs per second, and there is one per generator.

A **centre-reading** ammeter's needle (right) is typically associated with DC generators and light aircraft and should always be in the + side of the gauge (not too much!), to show a positive charge going into the battery. It is connected to the battery's positive lead. In other words, it is a two-way device that shows you what is going on between the battery and the generator. With the battery on and the engine off, the needle will show a negative reading in the minus range, or a discharge. If a discharge is shown with the engine running, the generator is not up to the job and the difference has to be made up by the battery. Switch things off until you get a positive reading.

The other type is also called a **loadmeter**. It is often associated with AC generators and/or turbine engines, and measures electrical loads rather than battery charging, so it is a one-way device connected only to the generator. The display starts at zero, and shows positive numbers, sometimes as a percentage. With the battery on and the engine off, it will read zero.

The *peak startup draw* (when the load is first applied) is always heavier than that used by a device when it is running. That is, components draw more current in the initial stages, until the flow settles down. Typically, when you switch on the generator after starting an engine, the loadmeter will read high at first, then decrease as the battery becomes topped up. Only after reaching a certain figure on its way down (say 0.7) should you switch the electrical services on.

A high rate of charge after starting an engine is only allowed for a short period.

THE VOLTMETER

A voltmeter is an ammeter that includes a multiplier resistor placed in parallel with the circuit, so the drop in voltage across the resistance is a measure of the voltage in the circuit - a high voltage is indicated if the current flow is large, and *vice versa*. *A Voltmeter is connected in parallel*, so the current does not pass through the meter instead of the circuit and affect the readings.

A good voltmeter therefore has a very high resistance.

Power Distribution (Busbars)

The lighter an aircraft is, the better, so it's impractical (if only for weight saving) to run a wire from the battery (and back) to every component it supplies. A better solution is to run a single (big) wire to a distribution point and then (via fuses or circuit breakers) to any electrical appliances, to serve all of them from the end of that line, and use the fuselage as an Earth return, which is what a busbar system is all about.

Physically, an electrical bus is a metal bar with provisions to make electrical contact with a number of devices that use electricity. Electrically, it's a conduit between components, like the memory bus in a computer. There's nothing to stop you having main buses supplying secondary ones, but the system must ensure that problems on or near it do not endanger any components connected to it, so services connected to a busbar are normally in parallel, to enable isolation and keep voltages equal.

REQUIREMENTS

There are certain requirements for busbars:

- If a power source fails, equipment must not be deprived of power unless the total demand exceeds the supply

- Earthing faults should produce the least possible fire risk and the minimum effect on systems

- Equipment faults must not endanger the supply to other equipment

The above can be met by:

- paralleling generators

- adequate circuit protection devices

- isolating faulty generators

For isolation purposes, components are graded in order of importance in an emergency: *vital*, *essential* and *non-essential*.

- **Vital** services include items that are wired directly to the battery, so they will carry on working when the generators fail (emergency lighting, etc.) The term *hot bus* or *direct bus* means that the bus is always live (i.e. it has no switches), so you must switch devices attached to it off when you close down, as with the fuel boost pumps in some aircraft. There may be a secondary battery switch for this purpose. The hot bus not only allows items to be powered if alternators or generators fail, but also allows the engine(s) to be started when they are not working anyway. All aircraft need standby electrical power systems, in case the normal one goes down. For small ones, this is usually the main battery, which is oversized for this reason. The problem is, it's time-limited to 30 minutes. Larger aircraft use an *Auxiliary Power Unit* (APU).

• **Essential** services are those needed for safe flight that can still be run by a generator or the battery.

• **Non-essential** services are things like galleys which can be isolated for load-shedding purposes.

Most multi-engined aircraft have left and right main buses, and a battery master bus for a few essential items, but there the similarity ends. There are so many variations that it's difficult to keep track, and getting acquainted with a new type of aircraft can be quite difficult, especially when the Flight Manual is less than perfect.

Essential things to know about buses are what they power, how to reroute power to them and how to isolate them, a bit like fuel systems (the bus tie does the same job as a crossfeed). It can be closed if power is lost on one side to route electricity to the other.

There are three types of busbar system:

SPLIT

Busbars can be split to protect delicate equipment from large variations in electrical power, such as found when starting. In other words, there are two separate systems that are not operated in parallel. In many aircraft, the Avionics Master Switch serves as a link between busbars.

Note: The Avionics Master Switch would also be a circuit breaker, and useful for reducing wear and tear on the switches of the radios and navaids.

Split busbars are normally found in twin engined aircraft, where each generator feeds its own AC busbar. However, they are not paralleled because this can be problematical, so they don't need advanced circuitry, and each generator can run with a slightly different frequency. If a generator fails, its circuit breaker (GCB) will close, and a bus tie breaker (BTB, or changeover relay) will connect the busbars automatically so the loads can be taken care of by the other generator. The APU is brought on line by the transfer relay, at which point the BTB will reopen. When the BTB is closed on the ground, both busbars can be served by external power or the generator on the APU.

Below is a theoretical example of a split busbar system. It shows the possible location of typical components. Each generator has its own bus with non-essential services

connected to it (passengers' coffee), or those that don't matter if it fails. Both are ultimately connected in parallel to a combining busbar which carries the essential services (pilots' coffee), so they will always have at least one source of power. Notice that the essential AC bus comes off the essential DC bus via an inverter. The battery is connected to the DC buses, so it can be charged, yet still supply essential components if both generators fail.

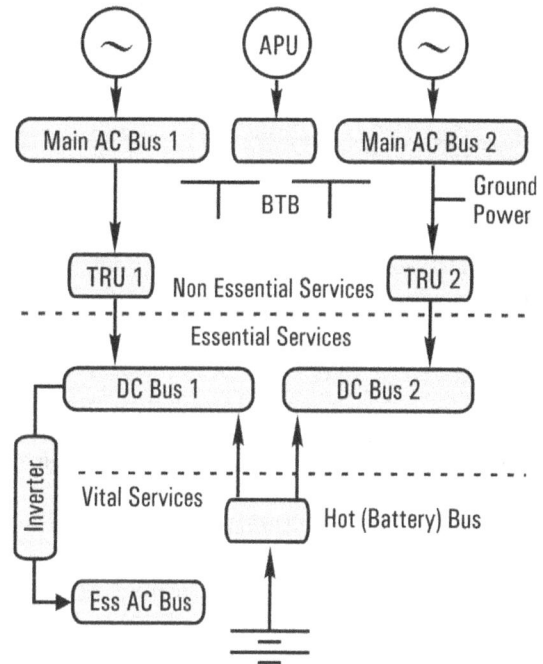

PARALLEL

Normally found on 3-engined aircraft such as the L-1011, MD-11, DC-10 and B-727*, in which all the generators are paralleled onto one bus once the engines are working. Loads can be supplied and controlled independently, so voltage must be independent of the load, but current must be proportional to them. It used to be the Flight Engineer's job to look after them, because they need careful matching before the bus tie is closed to synchronise the frequency and voltage.

*The 727 has a parallel system with a synchronising bus. This is one where several buses are connected together with bus ties (I know the 727 has 3 engines, but the picture below shows the principle):

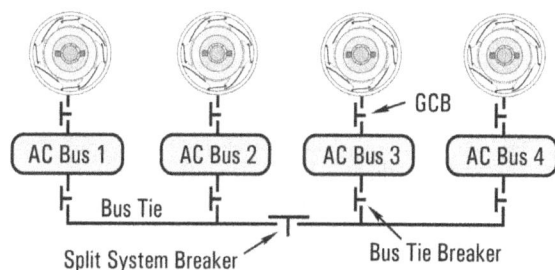

The Generator Circuit Breaker (GCB) is controlled by the generator switch in the cockpit. Bus tie breakers are normally closed, being controlled by a bus tie switch.

The split system breaker simply splits the system in half so that 1 & 2 and 3 & 4 can be separate buses in their own right. It therefore provides a measure of control and protection and system isolation. It is designed to open automatically if you try to parallel external power sources on to the bus (they cannot be synchronised). On some aircraft, you have to close it manually (with a switch) when you connect external power.

Note: On some aircraft, you cannot do this if the system is already using its own generators, or if it has the wrong voltage, frequency and phase.

SPLIT PARALLEL

Found in the B747-400, but may also be in the A-380, this is a combination of split and parallel systems. As the generators run on part loads, their life expectancy is increased. The split parallel absorbs large transient loads.

STANDBY BUSES

Some aircraft have their essential services covered through extensions that are connected to main buses through relays that are normally closed. This allows you to power those circuits from standby power sources if required, which would normally be inverters from the main battery.

MONITORING

Because the larger load is in kilowatts, the maximum load is expressed in kW in the limitations section of the flight manual. You would normally check the kW readings to ensure equal load sharing*. The kVAR reading gives you an idea of what the voltage regulator is up to.

*Frequency matching shares the real load (kW) and voltage matching shares the reactive load (kVAR).

FAULT PROTECTION

When generators are paralleled or isolated, there is some automatic control to ensure that frequency and voltage remain within limits.

Typical faults that might trip an associated circuit breaker include:

- Synchronising bus faults, which will trip a bus tie breaker.

- CSDU (see later) disconnections, or over- and undervoltages, which come from voltage regulators and will trip the GCB.

- Excitation or voltage problems, which will trip the relevant GCBs if their generators are paralleled.

- If the generator is isolated, the field breaker will trip and disconnect the voltage regulator. When the generator field breaker (control relay) trips, the voltage regulator disconnects from the excitation field and the GCB will also trip.

- A frequency problem or operation of an engine fire switch will trip the field breaker.

Batteries

Certain chemicals, when they are combined with some metals, can make electrons flow as direct current, until all the electrons disappear from the metal, causing it to eventually get eaten away - as the atoms comprising the metal lose electrons, they cease to be the same atoms and therefore cease to exist in their former state - if you could put the electrons back, you would regain your metal plate, and recharge the battery. A primary, or dry, cell, is one enclosed in a metal case which gets eaten away as the battery discharges. This process is not reversible. Primary cells are typically used in flashlights as a throwaway item.

A secondary cell can be recharged, and usually has a liquid involved in its construction.

A "battery" is a *collection* of secondary cells, which have a charge of about 2.1 volts each (lead-acid), or 1.2 (Ni-Cad), hence the need to combine them to do anything useful. Lead-Acid batteries will have 12 cells, and Ni-Cads 19 or 20 to produce the 24 volts needed for aircraft. To be the equivalent of a 12v lead-acid battery, a NiCad needs between 10-11 cells.

Note: If one cell is dead, the battery is unserviceable.

A cell consists of alternating positive and negative *plates* surrounded by a liquid called an *electrolyte*. Different materials are better or worse at this job, so you might get more or less voltage out of one type of battery compared to another. The two types used in aircraft are *lead acid*, as found in cars, and *NiCad*, as found in older portable computers, now replaced by Lithium Ion. People who use both will already understand the difference but, in simple terms, the lead acid's output tends to fall off steadily with discharge, whereas a NiCad can pump out a constant power until it can do no more, meaning that its *closed-circuit voltage* remains nearly constant until it is nearly discharged.

As well, a NiCad is more compact, has a longer shelf life, reduced charging time, recovers more quickly, and has a low internal resistance, so it's good for starting turbines.

In the early days, say, up till the 1950s, *vented* lead-acid batteries were used almost exclusively, until vented NiCads came along, with their superior performance at low temperatures, and in low voltage full discharge high-cycle applications. *Sealed* lead-acid batteries were subsequently invented, for better reliability, and are now more common, as NiCads do not perform so well in extended standby applications, such as with battery backups for IRS, etc.

An aircraft battery's purpose is to:

- maintain a power supply under transient conditions

- help with short term heavy loads

- supply total power for a short time in emergencies

- start the engines, where it also has to excite the alternators.

However, it needs the right conditions - at -30°C, a battery has less than half its power to start an engine that needs 350% more effort to get going! This is because, when it is cold, a battery's internal resistance increases (in the Arctic, you take them out at night to keep them warm).

A flat battery has maximum internal resistance, which will generate lots of heat when an attempt is made to charge it (on a bench, only a very small current is used). It is therefore not a good idea to continue a flight if your battery gets discharged! In any case, it should be replaced before the next flight. One problem is, for it to work, an alternator needs current from a battery, and your machine's electrics won't work if it isn't there.

BATTERY CAPACITY

The capacity or holding power of a battery is a measure of its ability to produce current over a specified period of time. The number of cells will determine the voltage it produces, but the area of the plates inside, the amount of active material in the plates and how much electrolyte there is determines the *ampere-hour* capacity, or amps multiplied by hours. A typical rating is 12-18 amp/hours (which rate will go down the faster you use it).

The definition of electrical current is the amount of charge flowing down a wire per second, expressed as:

$$\text{Current} = \frac{\text{Charge}}{\text{Time}}$$

Therefore current is a time-derived value. A battery delivering 45 Amps for 2.5 hours could deliver 90 Amps for 1.25 hours (double the current, but for half the time) or 22.5 Amps for 5 hours (half the current, but for twice as long). Or any combination in between. The battery's rating is therefore 112.5 ampere-hours (45 x 2.5).

Note: The minimum capacity is 80%, so a 20 amp/hour battery actually pumping out 20 amps should last at least 48 minutes, or 0.8 hours.

A battery is supposed to provide enough power for 30 minutes when fully charged, although it is never wise to rely on any battery for more than about 20 minutes.

Note: This is particularly relevant if your aircraft has an EFIS display, or a FADEC! A flat battery doesn't do warning lights much good, either.

To get an idea of your aircraft's capabilities, add up the current requirements of essential services and divide them into the amp/hour rating. So, if your devices collectively use 45 amps, and your battery supplies 45 amp-hours, you should be able to get an hours' use out of it. When faced with such an emergency, it is usual to use the navaids, for example, to get a position fix, then turn them off until you start feeling a little lost, then turn them on again until you are once more certain of your position. The same with radios. This will get a little extra time out of your battery.

POLARITY

The polarities of a battery are positive and negative, marked plus (+) or minus (-), or coloured red and black, respectively, and electrons flow from the negative (-) electrode, through the circuit the battery is connected to, back to the positive (+), because the negative end has the most electrons (the terms are indeed misleading, and the words *positively charged* even more so, but they were coined a long time ago and it's a hard thing to change).

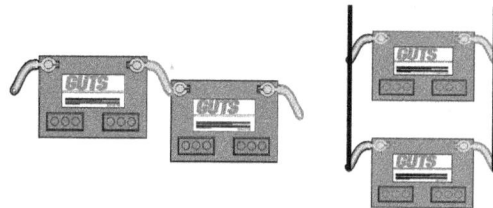

If you join batteries in *series*, that is, one after the other, with the positive of one connected to the negative of the next (left, below), you will get a voltage which is the *sum* of them both, but with the same *current capacity as one*.

If you join them in *parallel*, with the positive and negative connected to each other (right, above) you would get the *voltage* of *one* battery, but the *current capacity* of *all* of them, so you can use them for longer. This is because anything connected in series keeps the same current, and anything in parallel keeps the voltage. Since a typical aircraft runs on a 24-volt system, you would therefore connect two (12v) car batteries in series (better yet, two sets in parallel). Be aware, though, that terminals are different sizes to stop them being confused, so you need an adapter to connect them up in the middle (jumper cables may open up and spark when a load is applied).

Note: Ensure that batteries have an electrical load on them before completing a circuit. A battery condition check is best done with a load on.

In an earth return circuit, the negative pole of the battery is connected to the fuselage (negative earth).

CHARGING

When charging, the **constant voltage** method uses a reducing current as the battery's state of charge improves. This requires less time and supervision than the constant current method, which takes longer and includes a risk of overcharging. Because of the battery's internal resistance, which causes a voltage drop, the external charging voltage must be greater than that of the battery. During engine operation, the battery is recharged with a *DC or AC generator (alternator)*, using the constant voltage method via a voltage regulator. Charging a battery from an AC system requires a *Transformer Rectifier Unit* (TRU).

An AC generator alternator will charge at low RPM (a DC generator doesn't much), but some aircraft use a *starter/generator* to save space, despite this advantage. The same unit spins the engine on startup, and switched over when it's running to become a generator because their construction is the same, as we shall see later.

LEAD ACID

The lead-acid battery is made of alternating lead peroxide (+) and lead (-) plates, with separators in between, and an electrolyte made of sulphuric acid (37%) and water (63%), which can be neutralised with sodium bicarbonate (bicarbonate of soda). The oxygen in the lead peroxide has an affinity for the H_2 in the sulphuric acid and the other plate likes the SO_4, so there is a tension between the plates which would create lead sulphate on one plate and water on the other, if the battery were part of a circuit. The formation of water dilutes the electrolyte and reduces its relative density, which is why the state of charge of a lead-acid battery is measured with a hydrometer (see below). One plate turning into lead sulphate as electrons are lost is allegedly what the term *sulphated* means, which describes a fully discharged battery (it results from mistreatment).

NICKEL-CADMIUM

When uncharged, the positive electrode of a NiCad cell is *nickelous hydroxide*, and the negative is *cadmium hydroxide*. In the charged condition, the positive electrode is *nickelic hydroxide*, and the negative metallic is cadmium, meaning that the chemical reaction is in the plates. The electrolyte is *potassium hydroxide*, which is only there as a path for the current flow - it plays no part in the chemical reaction, so it will show little change over charge/recharge process. If you spill any electrolyte from a NiCad, you can neutralise it with a weak acid solution such as *dilute boric acid*.

During the latter part of a charge cycle, and during overcharge, nickel-cadmium batteries generate oxygen at the positive (nickel) electrode and hydrogen at the negative (cadmium) one (at full charge), which must normally be vented. To allow the system to be overchargeable while sealed, the battery is built with excess negative capacity so that the positive electrode reaches its full charge first. Since the negative electrode will not have reached full charge, it will not give off any hydrogen.

However, NiCads have short memories, in that if you charge them when they have only discharged a little way, they will think they have a lesser power rating which is only noticeable when you try to use all the charge, which won't be there in an emergency. To stop them causing hot starts they need regular *deep cycling* to keep them awake. Thus, although it's good practice to start an aircraft, for example, from a battery cart, to preserve the ship's battery for better reliability in remote places, occasionally a battery start is good for the system as it will help to eliminate the memory effect. The actual term is *voltage depression*, where there is a slight dip in the voltage near the end of a discharge. The dip goes below the normal output voltage, which makes you think the cell has actually discharged - a common occurrence with home movie cameras! As the battery is charged, the voltage depression point moves toward the beginning of the discharge period.

Another problem with NiCads is that they can catch fire when too much current is drawn and then replaced, a process called *Thermal Runaway*, which happens when an increase in temperature leads to a further increase because the battery's internal resistance decreases as its temperature rises. This is why some aircraft have a *Battery Temp* caution light on the warning panel which means you must land *immediately*, before the battery catches fire and takes other stuff with it, if it doesn't burn its way through the airframe and fall out. Yet another problem is that a NiCad cell will lose about 1% of its charge per day.

Note: Lithium Ion batteries, as found in most modern laptops and Portable Electronic Devices, can also overheat and burst into flame, so be wary about putting such devices in a remote baggage compartment.

CAPACITY CHECKS

Battery capacity checks should be made every 3 months. The minimum acceptable is 80%. Because the electrolyte remains unchanged, there is no way to tell the real state of a Ni-Cad's charge by checking its relative density. Checking the voltage is no good, either, because a NiCad can produce a constant voltage for some time, even when discharged, and closed-circuit voltage changes very little.

On the other hand, a *hydrometer* (see right) can be used to check the relative density and hence the state of charge of a lead-acid battery, but not when it is installed in the machine, in case the (acidic) electrolyte gets spilled (aside from corrosion, it can also create grounding paths). The relative density of electrolyte is 1.25 fully charged, and 1.3 when cold.

If you have to measure capacity whilst the battery is in the aircraft, the open and closed circuit voltages can be compared (e.g. on-load and off-load). The voltage will fall significantly as charge diminishes. Otherwise, you can use a *voltmeter* while a load is applied.

Switches

Switches control the flow of electricity round a circuit. They can be mechanical, electrical, thermo, or based on time or proximity (for doors or panels). Switches are also often relays, or based around solenoids, both discussed later.

Mechanical switches can be operated by toggle (above).

Multiple switches can be lined up in a gang of several together, like these rocker switches:

Switches can also be guarded to ensure that they are not switched off by mistake.

A button is also a (push-pull) switch. Buttons are used for short duration purposes only.

Mercury switches are typically used inside electrical gyroscopic instruments.

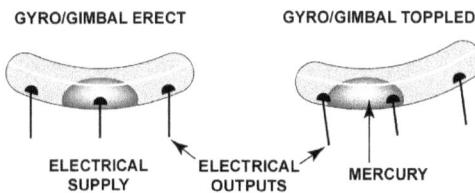

GYRO/GIMBAL ERECT   GYRO/GIMBAL TOPPLED

ELECTRICAL   ELECTRICAL   MERCURY
SUPPLY   OUTPUTS

Magnetism

Magnetism is important because, without it, we would not have electricity.

Magnetism is an invisible force which is defined as the property of an object to attract certain metallic substances, mostly ferric (iron based).

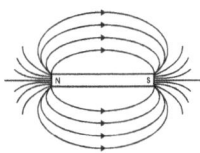

A magnet is therefore a ferrous substance, typically a soft iron bar, that has lines of magnetic force running through and around it in the shape of a *magnetic field* (the Earth is a magnet as well). The lines are called the *magnetic flux*,

expressed by the Greek letter φ (phi). The *flux density* is the number of lines within a magnetic field, and the flux is stronger when the lines are closer together (at the ends). The picture on the left is often used to show what iron filings do in a magnetic field. It is assumed that the lines of force flow from the North to the South Poles (they don't).

Magnets can be permanent or temporary, whose magnetism is lost after the magnetising force is removed. However, there is (almost) always a small amount left, called *residual magnetism*, which is useful for getting generators and motors to work in the initial stages. Even when a material is permanently magnetised, it can only be driven back to zero by a field in the opposite direction. This is called *hysteresis*, and is used widely in the recording of information on disks or tape.

Lines of magnetic flux always form closed loops and behave like stretched elastic bands, in that they are always trying to shorten themselves. This property is made use of in electric motors to turn the moving parts. As an example, the lines of flux between the North- and South-seeking poles in the bottom magnet below are as short as they can be. On the top one, however, where the two poles are the same, the flux lines are pushed out towards the sides and do not shorten.

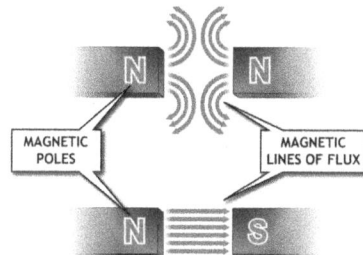

MAGNETIC
POLES

MAGNETIC
LINES OF FLUX

All magnets have a N seeking and a S seeking pole, and like poles will repel each other - unlike poles attract (parallel lines of flux moving in the same direction repel each other). If you had a bar magnet, its North seeking Pole would point towards the Earth's (magnetic) North pole. This is what a compass is all about, under *Instruments*. The thing to remember is that the South Pole is marked as North, because that's the end that points North.

Iron and steel (and nickel and cobalt, slightly) are the only elements to be attracted by a magnet, and which can be magnetised. In their non-magnetic states, the theory is that the molecules in such metals are arranged at random, and their poles cancel each other out. When stroked with another magnet, the molecules align with each other and their magnetic fields combine to create the magnet as a whole. Heat or rough treatment can destroy this effect.

Through *magnetic induction*, an unmagnetised iron bar held close to a permanent magnet will attract iron filings in its own right, without being permanently magnetised (the magnetic flux temporarily aligns the crystals in the bar).

ELECTROMAGNETISM

When a current flows through a cable, there is a magnetic field associated with it, with a clockwise* action if you look at it from the rear.

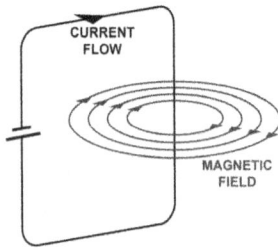

*The movement of electrons creates the field - it is nothing to do with the conductor. The flux lines do not actually rotate.

The magnetic field will become stronger if the wire is made into a coil and even stronger if the coil is placed around some easily magnetised material, such as iron, which becomes a magnet for as long as a current flows. As an iron bar has a greater permeability than air (or a lower reluctance*), it can concentrate the flux better into a smaller area.

*Reluctance with magnetism is equivalent to resistance.

In a coil, the magnetic field around the cable cuts the next loop in line. The fields merge to produce a large one through and around the whole coil, resembling that of a bar magnet (it can take up a N-S position if suspended).

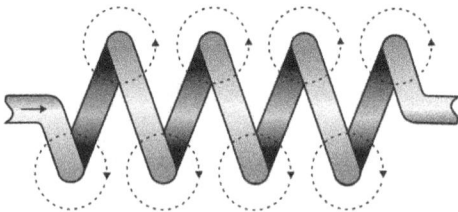

If a conductor, particularly soft iron, is moved within a magnetic field, or if a magnetic field is moved around a conductor, so that the conductor cuts flux lines, current can be made to flow in the conductor.

This is called *electromagnetic induction* (from Faraday).

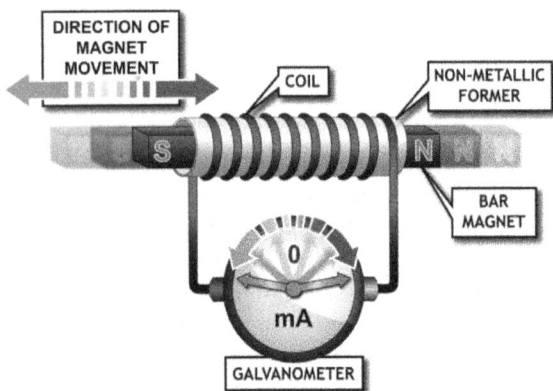

In the picture above, as the magnet moves, a current is induced in the coil and the needle moves in the relevant

direction. The maximum flux is to do with saturation. The strength of the induced emf depends on the size of the magnetic field, the number of turns in the coil or the speed the bar's movement. Induced magnetism is usually proportional to the current that creates it, but no more can be created when saturation occurs.

A changing magnetic field (as produced by an alternating current) around a stationary conductor also produces an electric current in the conductor, with the size of the voltage proportional to the rate of change of the field.

Mutual induction occurs between two coils close enough to each other to have currents induced in them. In the picture below, because there is AC flowing through the bottom coil, there must be a changing magnetic field around it, which interacts with the other coil and induces a current into it.

Mutual inductance is greatest when one coil is wound round the other, as found inside a magneto, and least when they are at right angles to each other.

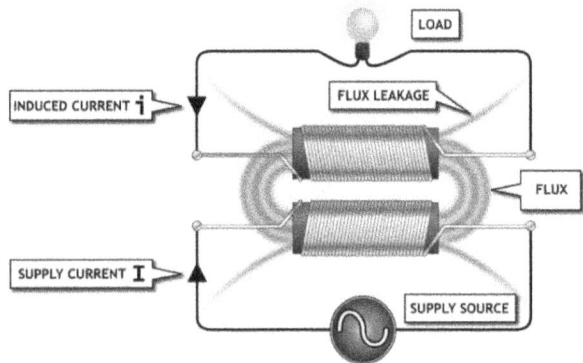

INDUCTANCE

An inductor is a coil (solenoid) of insulated wire, possibly wound over a ferrous metal former. A changing flow of current can turn the coil into an electromagnet that will induce its own current in the opposite direction (sometimes called *back emf*). Inductance is the degree of this self-induction, and it can also happen between complete circuits that are near to each other (see *Transformers,* below). Note that there is no induction if the current is steady, so if DC is used, there will only be an effect as the switch is closed and opened, and the current rises and falls, hence the use of contact points in magnetos. In this case, the coil acts merely as a resistance but, with alternating current, the constant changes set up a reverse current, or back emf. Inductance can therefore oppose a change in current flow or induce a voltage when there is a change. All conductors have this property, but for best results you need a coil.

Ordinary resistance to DC does not therefore change when a wire is coiled, but its "resistance" to AC (inductance) can be, to provide, for example, small opposition to low frequency AC and a high opposition high frequency AC, which is useful when filtering out unwanted radio signals. To produce back emf, the magnetic fields around the cable induce a current the other way, stopping the main current from rising too quickly. The effect is that, when you first apply current, the inductor appears to have a high resistance (that does not generate heat), which drops once flow becomes constant, leaving you with the normal resistance you would find in any wire. In this respect, the inductor has the opposite effect of a capacitor. Practically, an inductor slows down the rise and fall of current, and behaves like the flywheel in an engine, or a large mass, such as a locomotive - the more inductance there is, the larger is the locomotive and the effort needed to get it moving, or slow down. In an AC circuit, this acts to resist current flow. The higher the frequency, the more the "resistance".

This ability to "store" energy magnetically is due to inertia, because the current is moving as it does its work (it is like kinetic energy). Thus, the circuit discharges quicker if you apply the brakes, or add resistance. A capacitor, on the other hand, stores energy electrostatically, as nothing is moving, so the discharge rate increases when you *release* the brakes, or remove resistance.

This is proportional to the rate at which the current changes, so when it collapses to zero very quickly, as when you use the contact breakers in a magneto, the back emf will be very large, and enough to jump across a gap.

In conjunction with capacitors, inductors can produce electrical resonance at particular frequencies, which is useful when tuning radios.

The unit of inductance is the *Henry*, and its symbol is L. To find totals, treat inductance as resistance. For example, the total inductance of several inductors in series is the sum of the individual inductances. For example, 0.03 plus 0.03 results in a total inductance of 0.06 Henrys.

TRANSFORMERS

In low power circuits, you can limit current with resistors, but where large currents get involved, the heat generated could well melt the equipment. It can also be wasteful. For example, stepping 240 volts down to 24 would involve wasting around 216 volts. Coils can also restrict voltage by using their impedance (resistance), when using AC. If you can vary the inductance of a coil, you can control the voltage with very little waste.

Transformers are a special application of inductance, commonly used in magnetos to boost voltage from 24-28v to whatever is needed to jump across the gap of a spark plug, but they have other uses, such as electrical isolation, because they are able to create electricity without any wires, as mentioned in *mutual induction*, above.

They can convert alternating current at one frequency and voltage to AC at the same frequency, but a different voltage. In this respect, they work like gears. They can be used for three purposes:

- Isolating parts of circuits from others, with a *one-to-one* transformer

- Raising or lowering voltages. A *step-up* transformer has more windings in the secondary coil and will increase voltage. A *step-down* is the opposite

- Matching impedances, particularly with headphones and amplifiers (both use coils and alternating current)

A *Transformer Rectifier Unit* can convert AC to DC as well.

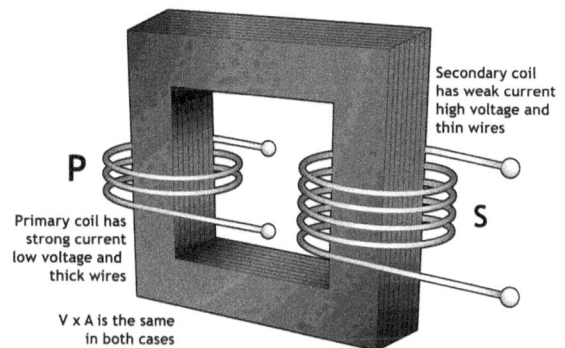

Transformers consist of electrically separate coils on a common laminated* iron core which are *magnetically coupled* when an induced emf is created in one (the *secondary*) by a change of current in the other (the *primary*).

That is, an alternating current (or fluctuating DC) in the primary coil sets up an alternating magnetic flux. Self-induction in the primary creates an opposite voltage in the secondary that is nearly the same as the original (there are some losses). The difference between the two is just enough to set up an alternating magnetic flux in the core. Mutual induction then allows a voltage to be established in the secondary. In this way, we can get an electrical current without moving conductors and magnetic fields around each other, as you would have to with a generator.

The voltage induced depends on the relative number of turns between the windings, or the *turns ratio*. For example, a transformer with 1000 turns on the primary coil and 500 on the secondary has a turns ratio of 2:1 and an output voltage that is half of the input, but Ohm's Law says that there will be more current (the power must remain constant), so the secondary windings must be thicker.

*The laminations must be insulated from each other, otherwise the core itself will behave like a one-turn coil, and will have very large eddy currents induced in it, which will cause overheating. The armature of a motor or generator is also laminated for the same reason. There are always power losses with transformers, usually as heat.

If the voltage is below the design limits, the current will increase and the transformer could overheat. Having said that, the efficiency of modern transformers is over 90%.

An **autotransformer** has part of the primary or secondary winding in common with the other, commonly used in 3-phase circuits, or radio. Autotransformers can be smaller, lighter and cheaper than standard transformers, but they do not provide electrical isolation between the primary and secondary coils.

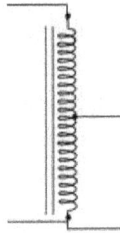

IGNITION CIRCUITS

The above principles are made use of in ignition circuits, where the current generated from a battery (in a car, as shown below) or a rotating magnet (in a magneto) is fed into a primary coil, which is wrapped within a secondary one, to make a transformer.

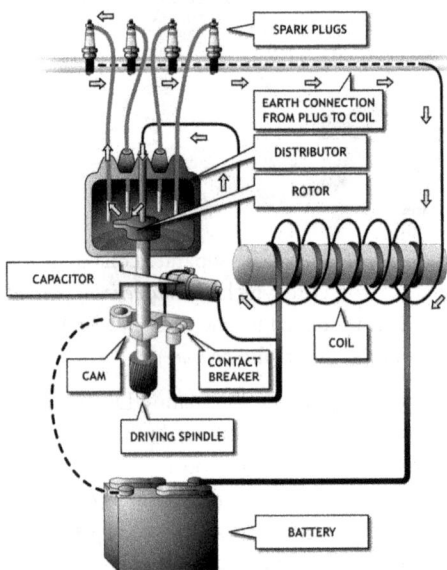

The supply to the primary coil is interrupted by contact breakers when a spark is needed, to produce varying DC. This collapses the current in the primary coil and makes the associated magnetic field flow across the secondary. Because the second coil is bigger, it produces a voltage large enough to jump the gap of the spark plug to ignite the fuel. However, although the voltage might be large (in the order of 15 000 volts), the current is reduced to keep the outgoing amount of energy the same as what went in.

The problem is that the field collapses across the primary circuit as well, and keeps the current flowing in the form of a spark across the contact beakers. A capacitor connected in parallel with the points prevents this arcing by providing a sink for the collapsing primary current. On discharging, it intensifies the current in the secondary winding by providing an opposing current for a cleaner break, as the coil slows down the rate of discharge.

THE SOLENOID

The word *Solenoid* actually refers to a coil of insulated wire, but as they are often wrapped around a moveable metal core, thus creating an electromagnet, its common usage means a *solenoid switch*, or *solenoid valve*, such as those used to operate starter motors. A speaker uses a solenoid. Some aircraft use switches in the cockpit to operate a solenoid that controls the hydraulic system. They are held on by the solenoid as long as current flows. When it stops, the switches revert to the off position. When electricity is passed through the coil, a magnetic field is created, and the core is drawn in to the centre. If the core is pulled back against a spring, when power is switched off and the magnetic field collapses, it returns to its original position.

Thus, a solenoid could be defined as a device that turns electrical energy into linear motion. It might be used to operate a starter, for example, because starters draw so much current that a normal switch would burn out (a large one can draw over 200 amps). The job of a solenoid (and the relay, to a lesser extent) is to keep heavy duty currents out of the cockpit, so you only need cables to be thick enough to operate the solenoid, thus saving weight. The cockpit starter switch therefore operates a relay which triggers a solenoid (which can handle the current) and which operates the machinery concerned. In this way, a small switch can start a large reaction in a remote location.

The strength of a solenoid can be increased by adding more turns or current, or using a soft iron core.

THE RELAY

A relay is a magnetic switch that does a similar job to a solenoid, but the only bit that moves is a contact, as relay consists of a **non-moveable** soft iron core surrounded by a coil. The force produced by the resulting electromagnet moves switching contacts back and forth.

Your microphone switch operates a relay that turns the aircraft radio from a receiver into a transmitter.

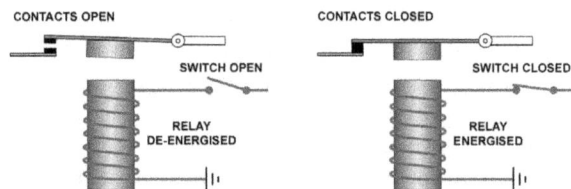

Relays are used for low-current switching or interruption of electrical current, typically used with a voltage regulator, or in conjunction with a logic gate, whose output will not be enough to drive the component concerned (the gate will, however, be able to drive a relay, which can do the work. In such cases, a protective diode will stop the logic gate being damaged when the relay demagnetises).

When a relay opens or closes, there is arcing between the movable and stationary silver alloy contacts, which causes pitting on their surfaces, and extra resistance between them. This means extra heat, plus a lower voltage under load that will need extra amperage to complete the same task. If the component controlled by the relay is also faulty, there may be more of a current draw than the relay is rated for.

The arcing occurs because there is a back emf - the coil in a relay has inductance like any other. A relay using a 6v supply can produce a spike of 100v or more when it disconnects, as the current drops rapidly to zero.

A normally open relay has its contacts open when it is de-energised. A normally closed one is the opposite. If a turbine engine starter relay fails in the open position, the starter/generator will not turn the engine. If it fails closed, the starter/generator will turn as soon as the battery is switched on, and will not switch off.

In the example shown, the relays connect various power sources to a distribution busbar. When the relevant relay is closed, that source can supply the bus.

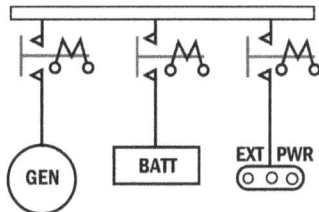

DIFFERENTIAL RELAYS

In multi-engined aircraft, these ensure that generator voltages are almost equal before they are paralleled. They allow a generator to feed the busbar when no other supplies are involved. They are controlled by the difference in voltage between them, and close when the generator voltage is above that of the busbar. They open with reverse current.

REVERSE CURRENT RELAYS

As the name suggests, these are designed to operate whenever current flows in the reverse direction, to protect components from backfeeds caused by internal faults. For example, there is often one to stop a battery discharging back through a generator or, more typically, when paralleling DC generators, preventing a weak one from being driven by the others (you could also isolate it).

Amongst other places, they are found in DC generating circuits and consist of two coils wound on a core, plus a spring-controlled armature and contact assembly. When the generator voltage builds up to a value that exceeds the battery's, the shunt winding of the relay produces enough magnetism to attract the core and close the contacts.

However, when the generator voltage falls below the battery voltage, the battery starts to discharge through the generator (i.e. the current reverses), so the current in the series-field winding, and thus the voltage across it also reverses, reversing the magnetic field. The relay armature is pulled up by its spring tension and the contacts open, to disconnect the generator from the battery.

When the reverse current cut out fails to operate, the reverse current circuit breaker should trip.

Direct Current

As previously mentioned, this is current that flows in one direction only. It can be produced in many ways, but aviators are concerned with electromagnetism and chemical action (see *Batteries*).

THE GENERATOR

The electrical equipment on an aircraft may only be run by the battery for a short while, otherwise you would have to keep stopping to recharge it. Long term, the power must come from the aircraft itself, using a self-contained generating device. For DC systems, this is a generator, or dynamo - for AC, an alternator, although the term *AC generator* is often used instead. The battery's function is really for short-term storage and to act as a buffer when the generator's output fluctuates.

Generators use magnetism to create DC. A simple one exists when a coil of wire (a conductor) is spun between the poles of a magnet to induce a current in the loop.

The magnet can be permanent*, or an electromagnet formed from battery current or the generator's own (the electromagnet produces better results and is more efficient, in that more control is available). The current so generated is actually AC, because each arm of the rotary coil cuts the flux one way, then the other. It can be converted to DC electronically with a *rectifier* (described later) or mechanically at source, in which case the slip rings are replaced with a *commutator*. To produce a current in the first place, the generator does not need help from the battery (like the alternator does) because there is residual magnetism in the field winding poles.

*Any small generator using a permanent magnet is commonly called a magneto.

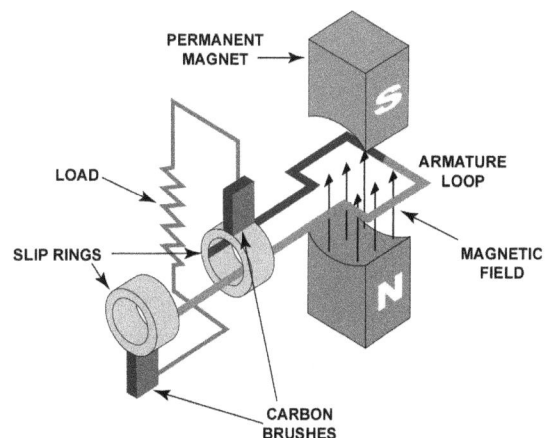

The commutator is really an adapted pair of the slip rings used in an alternator, combined and split into two halves which are placed opposite and insulated from each other, and attached to one end of the rotating loop through *brushes*, so called because the original designs used copper ones as contacts, but which have now been replaced by spring-loaded carbon blocks which simply wear out and are replaced from time to time (they need moisture for lubrication, which is a problem at high altitudes). Thus, a commutator is a *mechanical means of periodically reversing current*, or an automatic reversing switch, which is ideal for converting the AC from the loop into DC in the circuit, otherwise the current would keep reversing. As the rotor spins, the brushes contact each segment in turn, just as the current flow stops and is about to go in the other direction (actually twice per cycle). In this way, the polarity of the brushes remains constant, as does that of the commutator, and DC voltage is produced.

However, the supply in the simple generator is a series of positive pulses, which can be quite jerky (called *commutator ripple*), which can be minimised with more loops and connections, or more poles through which the coil(s) can rotate. Complex generators have several commutators to ensure a smooth output and a constant supply.

In the pictures below, the armature loop is rotating clockwise.

In position 1 (see above right), the loop is perpendicular to the magnetic field, at 0°, so the conductors are moving parallel to it, and not cutting any lines of magnetic force, so there is no emf being generated in the loop. In moving to position 2, the conductors move progressively through more lines of force until they reach 90°, where maximum current is generated. The black conductor has moved down, while the grey one has moved up. Since they are in series, the voltage across the brushes is the sum of the two emfs. Positions 3 and 4 produces the same result, but the current flows in the reverse direction.

In summary, the output of a generator depends on the:

- number of turns in the armature
- **strength of the field current**
- rotation speed of the armature, and
- supplied load

Generators are rated in Kilowatts.

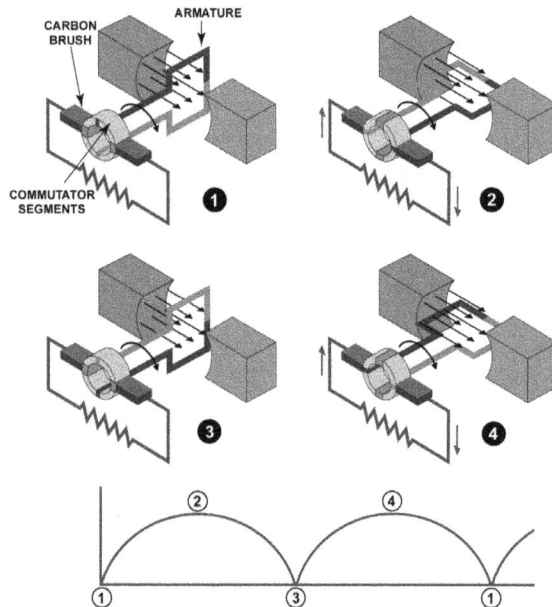

CONSTRUCTION
This is how a generator is constructed:

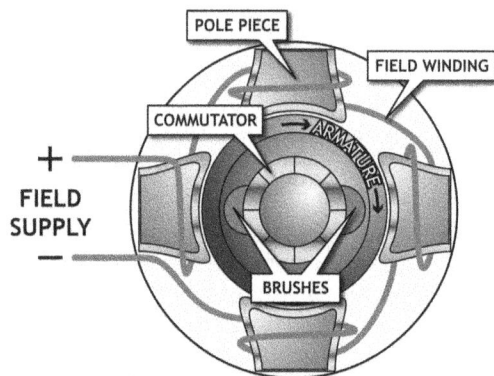

The major parts are a field frame (or yoke), a rotating armature (which includes the commutator, described below) and a brush assembly.

The field frame completes the magnetic circuit between the poles and supports the rest of the device. The above is a four pole generator frame. The poles are of alternating polarity and are usually laminated to reduce losses from eddy currents. Their function is to concentrate the lines of force from the field coils, as with any other iron core in an electromagnet (permanent magnets would work, but would make the generator too large). Because the pole

© *Phil Croucher, 2014*

pieces project out from the frame to reduce the air gap between them and the armature, they are called *salient poles*.

The armature (usually drum-type) has many coils wound on an iron core, called *windings*. The distance between each winding is the same, coinciding with the number of segments on the commutator. As the armature will rotate in the (electro)magnetic field created by the poles, it is also laminated to prevent eddy currents.

EXCITATION

When the field current is taken from the generator itself, it is *self-excited*. The types available are:

- **Permanent magnet**. Only used by small machines (i.e. magnetos).

- **Separately excited**. By DC from another source (practically all AC generators).

- **Self-excited**. Excited by current from the machine itself (e.g. with DC generators).

    - **Series wound** - the armature, field coils and external circuit (the load) are all connected, so the resistance of the load governs the

    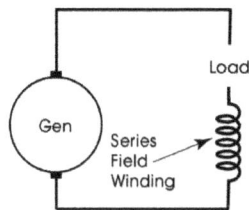

    field current (you need *few* turns of *large wire* in the field windings as the current can be large). That is, the voltage produced depends on the external load, so regulation is difficult (the terminal voltage rises as the current increases). These are not suitable for paralleling - when overloaded, they have a rising voltage profile. As, if the voltage regulator fails, the field coil will overload and overheat, they are not used in aviation

    - **Shunt** (parallel) **wound**, where the armature current is divided between the field winding and the load. In this type, emf will fall as the load

    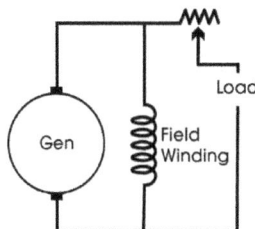

    increases and the flow through the field coils becomes smaller relative to the armature. As the field winding has a high resistance, the maximum current flows through the external circuit. This is the most common type used in aircraft, as it is stable (self righting) when load sharing. The rheostat is there to adjust the field current and the terminal voltage.

There is always *residual magnetism* in the core, enough to get the whole process started, but if it is lost or reversed, say through excessive heat or shockloading, it can be restored by briefly passing a current through it, a process known as *flashing the field*.

- **Compound wound** - one field coil in series (for the load) and one parallel with the armature (for the field). The coils carry currents in the same direction. With a light load, the machine behaves like a shunt, but as the load increases the series coil adjusts the voltage to be constant. The rising characteristics of the series and the falling characteristics of the shunt windings mean that it is hard to get a steady voltage that is independent of the load. Compound generators overcome the drop in voltage that occurs with shunt windings when the load is increased, as the series field reinforces it. Ultimately, the voltage rises slightly as the load is increased, so it is less stable for sharing.

They are used in larger aircraft, typically for hydraulic pumps that have heavy periods of use and lower periods in steady flight, plus others that use starter/generators.

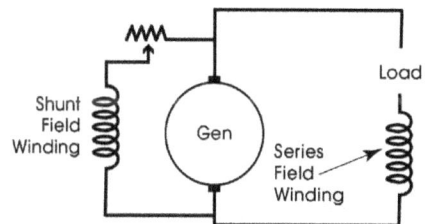

As soon as the induced current starts to flow, a generator will start behaving like a motor. This is because their construction is the same, but the motor tries to work in the opposite sense, after Lenz's law*. This is so powerful that 600-ton trains can be slowed down from 40 to 3 mph on a down gradient of 1 in 37.

*A moving magnet induces a current flow that opposes the movement of the magnet.

Speaking of motors, a **starter-generator** (as fitted to many turbine engines) has at least two sets of field windings and an armature winding, to save weight and space. A series field is used for starting, as a high torque is required. Once the engine has started, and you no longer need the starter, the other (shunt) windings are used. The back emf becomes the supply voltage on switchover.

Smaller aircraft can get their DC by using rectified output from a frequency wild AC generator, in which silicon diodes are used as a bridge rectifier (see later), but these have no residual magnetism, so they need DC from the ship's battery to self-excite.

VOLTAGE REGULATION

Problem 1 is that the generator is driven by an engine, which can run at different speeds, and Problem 2 is that the electrical loads may change, so the next step is to **vary the field current** of a generator in sympathy with the engine and/or load to keep the voltage constant.

The field current is regulated because you can't change the generator's speed independently, or the number of wires in the coil. Its output line is sensed, and the regulator tries to maintain it at a constant value. If the generator's output is low, it will increase the field strength.

Alternatively, if an overvoltage occurs, the regulator changes the resistance of the field circuit to lower the output voltage. In this case, the voltage regulator acts as a variable resistor between the external field connection and the ground. A reverse current relay between the generator and the bus stops the battery discharging through the generator, putting the generator online again as soon as its voltage rises above the battery's. It is open when everything is switched off.

Older generators that need a lot of field current use a **carbon pile** regulator. The carbon pile is a stack of carbon discs in a ceramic tube which vary their resistance when compressed. The larger the compression, the lower the resistance and *vice versa*. As resistance decreases, current through the field coils increases. The stack is biased towards full compression (least resistance) by a spring, so you can get a current straight away, and an electrical connection is made to each end of the stack so that the generator output flows through it.

Picture: Carbon Pile Voltage Regulator

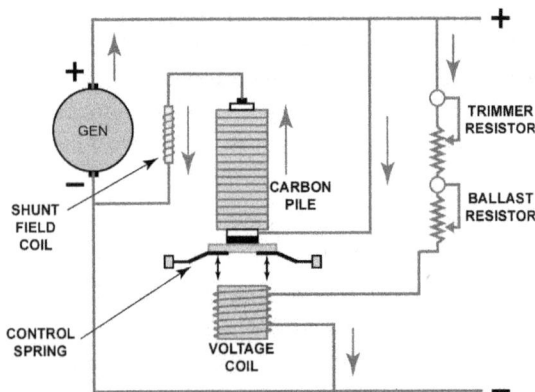

An electromagnet is placed under the stack (i.e. voltage control coil) which influences the tension of the spring against the discs, and is in parallel with the generator output, so the current flow will be proportional to the generator voltage. As the current varies in the coil, it will increase or decrease the strength of the magnetic field, to vary the compression effect of the spring. This affects the current flow and the strength of the field coil until the required output voltage of the generator is achieved.

With the **vibrating contact** version, used on lower-output systems, voltage is controlled by rapidly switching a fixed resistance in and out with an electromagnet (voltage coil) opening a pair of normally spring loaded closed contacts.

When generator output voltage is low, the current through the voltage coil is not enough to open the contact points. They open at a predetermined current through the voltage coil - when they do, field current flows through the fixed resistance causing its value to fall and produce an output voltage of the required level.

This is repeated rapidly, between 50 and 200 times a second, effectively maintaining a steady voltage while causing a lot of wear and tear. The timing of the points opening is changed as required.

Picture: Vibrating Coil Voltage Regulator

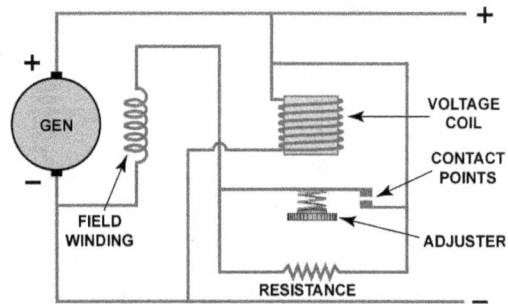

LOAD SHARING

Multiple (DC) generators are run in parallel (for maximum power) because, if the associated engine fails, there should not be an interruption in the primary power supply. In addition, the system will be able to handle the switching of high transient loads and the generators will last longer.

The downside is that you need more circuitry, mainly for protection, because a fault can otherwise affect the whole system. You also need ammeters so that the crew can check that the load sharing is being carried out properly. AC generators in parallel require matching in terms of frequency, phase and loads, which makes the process problematical. This is why bus tie breakers are used to switch busbars in and out as required instead.

DC generators are paralleled through their field circuits, and each one has a voltage regulator. Ensuring that output voltages are as near equal as possible (within about 2%) is done with paralleling coils between the voltage regulators, through which difference voltage flows. So the voltage regulators control the generator output and the voltage regulators are controlled by an equalising circuit. When the first engine is started, a current flows in the generator's field coil via its voltage regulator. The warning light goes out and the ammeter (or loadmeter) shows the current taken (the warning light indicates that the generator is undervolting or no longer feeding the busbar).

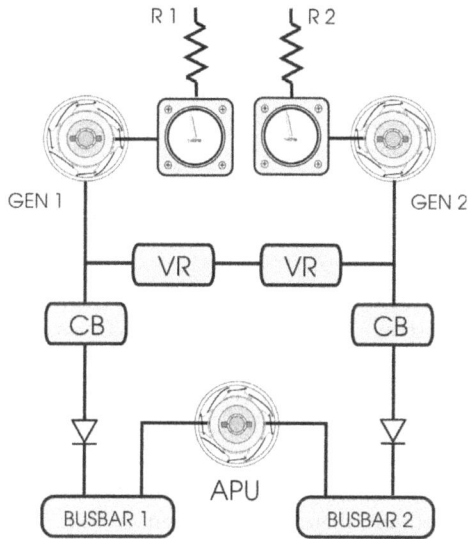

If a generator fails (in a pair), the voltage will stay the same, but the power available reduces.

The load sharing loop consists of equalising coils wound on the same core as the voltage coil in the voltage regulator). If the load is being shared equally, points X and Y will be at the same potential because the voltage drop across the resistors (R1 & R2) will be the same. As the voltage drops vary when one or the other generators takes more load, X or Y will become more negative and more current will flow to that point through the equalising circuit. The resultant magnetic fields will change the magnetic pulls on the voltage regulators to change their outputs and rebalance the system.

The relevant circuit breakers are reverse current types because a normal one will not trip if there is a short on its outgoing side. The diodes (see *Semiconductors*) protect the generators from each other.

DC MOTORS

A motor converts electrical energy into mechanical energy. It is a current carrying conductor inside a magnetic field that experiences a Lorenz/EMF force.

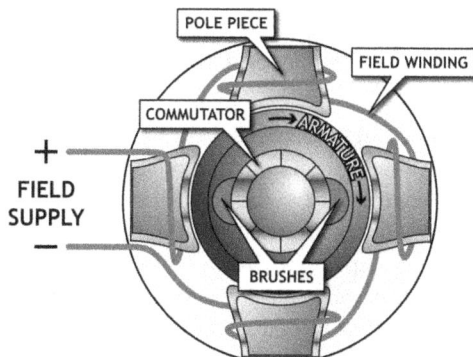

Motors are essentially the reverse of generators. As before, the field winding is carried around the inside of the casing, around pole pieces. The armature, which is magnetised and revolves inside, has a commutator, to which brushes are pressed. If many coils are used, the commutator is split into a corresponding number of pieces.

The commutator plays a very important part in the operation of a DC motor because it causes the current going through the loop to reverse just when unlike poles are facing each other, which causes a reversal in the polarity of the field, so that repulsion exists instead of attraction and the loop carries on rotating.

Since every current has an associated magnetic field, the one produced in the field winding as it is energised is repelled by the field already on the armature and the motor starts to spin. As mentioned previously, lines of magnetic flux behave like elastic bands, in that, when they are displaced, the tendency is to push back and create a force which starts the movement.

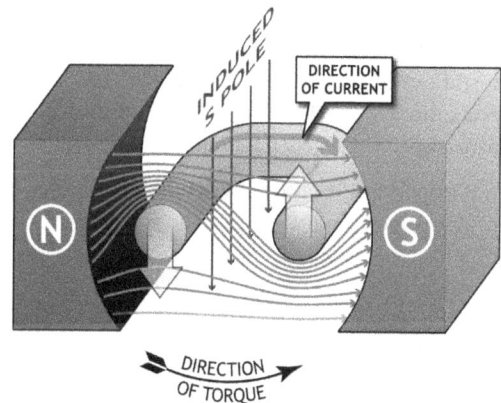

Just as the generator has a reverse motor effect, the DC motor can behave like a generator. This leads to a self-adjusting characteristic, in that, as the load is increased, the motor will start to slow down its rate of increase.

Where you use a particular type of motor can depend on its *speed* or *torque* characteristics. The turning force (or torque) that a DC motor produces arises from the interaction of the magnetic field with the armature current, so torque is the product of the main and armature currents. However, when they are first started, large DC motors have no back emf to slow things down, so a resistor may be connected in series with the armature to limit the current to a safe value, otherwise the heat generated would break down the insulation on the cables. The resistance is gradually reduced as speed builds up.

TYPES OF MOTOR

As with DC generators, DC motors are classified by the ways in which their field excitation circuits are arranged.

- **Series wound** motors have their field and armature windings in series with each other, so the same current flows through both, adding them together. As the output depends on their product, these motors have a high starting torque because, in the initial stages, there is little back emf, so all the current is used in them. As the magnetic flux is strong, the windings must be able to take a large current, so they need heavy wire (for low resistance) and a load, because the back emf will not be enough to stop the motor accelerating to destruction. Thus, series wound motors run slower with heavy loads and dangerously fast with light ones. They are commonly used as starter motors.

- As a **shunt wound** motor is wired in parallel, the back emf in the armature coil does not affect the field coil, so the only large current in the early stages is in the armature. The field winding uses relatively thin wires to keep its resistance high and the field's value to a minimum. There is a low starting torque, and the motor settles mostly at a constant speed. As well, the motor is more stable.

  Shunt wound motors are considered to be constant voltage, so they will run at practically a constant speed under normal conditions, whatever the load (within about 5%, although this could be changed with a variable resistance). As such machines have a low starting torque, they are usually started with the load disconnected.

- A **compound wound** motor can have a high starting torque, and will not overspeed. The series winding opposes the shunt winding and weakens the field as the load increases, to provide an almost constant speed (the motor runs quicker if the field weakens, as the back emf that caps the speed becomes less). If the fluxes act in opposition, the machine is known as a *short shunt*, and will behave like a series motor. If the flux is strengthened, it is a long shunt machine, with the constant speed characteristics of a shunt motor.

A *split field* motor can rotate forwards and backwards, which is useful when you want to operate something in two directions. It has two field windings in opposite directions controlled by a double throw switch to reverse the polarity as required (intended for brief operation).

To keep the weight down, DC motors often have to work hard, so they require cooling periods. For example, you may only be allowed 3 attempts at starting, with a 30-second gap between them. Then you have to wait 30 minutes before trying again.

STARTER/GENERATORS

These units combine two functions, those of a generator and a DC motor, which saves both weight and space. The DC motor function is used to start the engine, then the unit is switched over to be a generator at a predetermined speed, after a short wait (say 1 minute), to allow the system to stabilise and the battery to recover before it receives a charge. A *changeover relay* is used for the process.

Because generators don't work well at low speeds, they are usually used in turbine engines, when run at high RPM.

Alternating Current

Alternating Current is electricity that continually reverses its polarity (and direction), and magnitude. That is, the electrons flow in one direction, then back to where they came from. The quicker this is done, that is, the higher the frequency, the less distance is involved. As a result, the free electrons don't actually move very far, and the conductor length can therefore be shortened. With AC, moving half a coulomb back and forth produces the same current (1 amp) as moving 1 coulomb in one direction for the same distance. The essential point is *movement*, and many devices, such as light bulbs, only care that electrons move, and not which way they move, in order to work.

Changing the connections to a battery very quickly from one terminal to the other would achieve the same effect, but the results would be jerky, and the waves virtually square, because there would be a near 90° rise when on, and a 90° drop when off. In contrast, transitions from an alternator are smooth and like *sine waves*, as shown below (AC current is assumed to be in the form of a sine wave unless otherwise stated).

Most modern aircraft (large ones, at least) now use AC as their primary power source, employing a *Transformer-Rectifier Unit* (TRU) to get any DC they require (there are no AC batteries, so you still need DC for backup systems!) AC is typically used for flight instruments and fuel quantity systems, and its advantages include:

- **Better performance** from AC generators (more amps per unit weight), which may also be brushless, so there is less wear and fire risk. An AC generator can be even smaller (and lighter)

- **Ease of converting** voltage and current, either to different values (with transformers) or rectification between AC & DC.

- **Lighter cabling**. There is a point beyond which the size and weight of DC components become a disadvantage, as well as the power loss you get when transmitting electricity over longer cable runs. For example, with DC, you would have to have a high starting voltage to get only a relatively small one at the other end, even between the nose of an aircraft and the engine starter motor.

As an example, if you transmitted 250 volts of DC over a cable with a resistance of 1 ohm, the current would be 80 amps, if the generator had a capacity of 20 KW. This gives a voltage drop over the cable of 80 volts, so the receiving end only gets 170. The power loss would be in the order of 6400 watts (20 000 - (170 x 80). If you raise the voltage to 10,000, as you could with AC, the generator would only need to produce 2 amps of current. Ohm's Law now gives a voltage drop of 2 volts and a power loss of only 4 watts.

Aside from the lack of batteries, about the only disadvantage is that AC requires frequency control*.

AC CYCLE

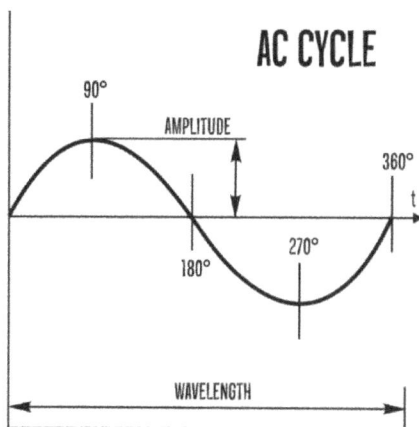

*A *cycle* is a complete set of varying conditions, in this case a transition from zero through a peak, down to a trough and back up to zero, so the more cycles you can fit into a particular time scale (the higher the frequency), the shorter the length of the wave is. One cycle per second is called 1 Hertz (Hz), and constant frequency systems on aircraft use 400 Hz as the standard. The steeper parts of the wave represent periods when the conductor cuts the most lines of magnetic flux.

Alternating currents below 20 KHz are audio frequencies (AF), and those above that are radio frequencies (RF). The value of the frequency is often as important as the supply voltage - most AC motors have their speed determined by frequency. The rate at which the frequency varies is, when it comes to radio, in millions of cycles.

After Ohm's Law, you divide the voltage by the resistance to find the current at any moment. The catch is that, as the voltage is changing, so is the current, as resistance remains constant, and current is proportional to voltage.

PHASES

The difference between the peak (or crest) and the base line of a wave is the *amplitude* (or, loosely, volume, but also power). When the *frequencies* (and hence wavelengths) of two waves coincide, that is, they pass through zero and attain their peak values in the same direction at the same time, they are *in phase* (the same amplitude is not required). When the points do not coincide, they are *out of phase* by the angle created when the second wave starts its cycle.

PHASE DIFFERENCE

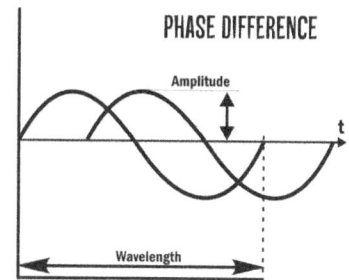

This is the basis of operation of the VOR and many other navigation aids.

Note: The word *phase* can mean the number of alternating currents being produced and/or carried by the same circuit (as in *single phase* or *three phase*), or the relationship between voltage and current in an AC circuit. There are times, when using radio, when you want them to be out of phase, and a coil or capacitor is introduced into the circuit to make current *lag* behind voltage, or *lead*.

The simplest forms of AC are good enough for light bulbs, etc., because the human eye is not quick enough to catch the flickering effect, and the bulb will stay warm anyway while the power drops and rises again, but electric motors need a more constant source of power. Aside from that, a single phase generator is uneconomical because a lot of winding space would be wasted.

Three-phase AC is essentially three AC lines running in parallel, with their peaks a third of a cycle behind each other to reduce the changeover effect. You can therefore have three separate alternating currents running down the same cable. In such *polyphase systems*, loads can draw power at a uniform rate, so a machine can run steadily under a uniform torque because the power peaks and zero values do not coincide. In addition, you can use conductors with less of a cross section, which saves weight. Using multiphase AC also means you can create a rotating magnetic field, which is handy when it comes to AC motors.

Although you can use any number of phases, most of the advantages are available with three, which is why three-phase is in general use (it was designed by the US military over 50 years ago). With it, three coils are at 120° (electrical degrees) to each other, so the voltages differ in phase by the same amount. Electrical degrees are used because there is often more than one coil per phase, and more than one electrical cycle for each geometrical cycle.

Constant Frequency AC systems run at 400 Hz (the most used frequency in aircraft). This is partly because of the effects of inductive and capacitive reactance, which both depend on frequency, and paralleling, discussed below.

Using 400 Hz (as opposed to 50 or 60) means that smaller and lighter components can be used, albeit with some induction loss, but weight savings are more important with aircraft. You need 4 sets of wiring for a 3-phase system (3 live plus a neutral), but they are smaller, so you still save weight.

The formula for calculating the frequency of an AC generator is:

$$Hz = \frac{RPM \times pairs\ of\ poles}{60}$$

So, to produce AC at 400 Hz, you need 4 pairs of poles in an AC generator running at 6000 RPM, or 3 pairs at 8000 RPM (8 poles for 6000, 6 for 8000). A generator with a 4 pole rotor must turn at 12 000 RPM.

The advantages of polyphase systems include:

- Additional phases increase total AC power as a function of the square root of the number of phases, so 115 volts multiplied by the square root of three (1.732) will give you over 199 volts from a 3-phase system, hence the 115/200 designation.

- Heating loss and the line voltage drop are less.

- Loads can draw power at a uniform rate.

- AC Generators can work in parallel.

- Phases can be connected to different loads.

- Fewer copper coils are needed to generate the necessary current, which allows for a smaller and lighter alternator.

OPPOSITION TO FLOW

Resistance, or electrical friction, affects AC in much the same way as it does DC - some of the electrical energy is converted to heat and there is a voltage drop across the component, due to the power required for the current to pass through it. In addition, as the frequency of the current increases (say up to VHF level), it concentrates more and more into the outside surfaces of the conductor (the *skin effect*), meaning that no current flows in the centre. The effect of increasing the frequency of the current is therefore to increase the resistance as the current is concentrated into a smaller area. This is why stranded cable is used on the RF (i.e. high frequency) side of a radio receiver. Otherwise, current flow is affected by real and reactive loads (capacitive or inductive, as below).

If an alternator runs below its normal frequency, inductive devices will overheat, as the current will increase as inductive reactance reduces.

REACTANCE

Reactance is the property of resisting or impeding the flow of alternating current or voltage in inductors (coils) and capacitors. It is part of the total opposition to the flow of AC, also expressed in ohms, being an extra to resistance. 400 Hz appears to cope with it best. It is overcome with reactive power from the generator.

Note: Resistors are static components, with which the current flow will be the same after the initial application of power. However, when you apply a fixed DC voltage to a capacitor, it will draw a high current as it charges up, and will appear to be a short circuit. Once it is charged, however, the current flow will stop and it will look like an open circuit. With AC, the capacitor would always be passing a current as it charges and discharges in each direction. What current you get would depend on the time it takes to charge (its capacity) and how often the AC changes (its frequency). In other words, the reactive nature of a capacitor (or an inductor) alters the relative timing of voltage and current.

There are two types of reactance:

- **Inductive reactance** is the opposition in an inductive circuit (with a coil). When you apply a voltage to an inductor a magnetic field is created that slows the current down while the voltage is allowed to build up freely. The amount of back emf depends on the rate of change of the current, in that, the larger its frequency, the larger will be the reverse current, so the effect decreases with a decrease in frequency. Any device relying on magnetism or magnetic fields to operate is a form of inductor, like motors, generators, transformers, and coils. Using an inductor in a circuit causes it to become inefficient because it makes the current lag behind the voltage or applied emf*. Resistance tempers this somewhat, because it acts in series with the coil, so the resulting phase shift will be between 0-90°. If there were no resistance (which would never happen) the phase shift would be 90°. This effect is increased by the inductance of the coil and the frequency of the current, in that the more of each, the greater the opposition to flow.

  In a circuit with resistance and inductance, the current has two components, one flowing against the resistance and one against the inductance. Thus, there are two emfs (see *Resonance*, overleaf).

  *emf is the reference, so current leads or lags on it.

- **Capacitive reactance** exists in a capacitive circuit, and it decreases with an increase in frequency. Unlike inductive reactance, changes to the current occur *before* any changes to voltage - current now *leads* the voltage because when you first apply a voltage, the current will be at its highest value, but

CAPT

the voltage will be at its lowest. A capacitor in an AC circuit builds up a charge as supply voltage rises, which opposes and reduces current flow, so that, when the maximum supply voltage is applied, current is zero. As the supply voltage falls, the capacitor starts to discharge, hitting a maximum rate when the supply voltage is zero. This means that current is maximum when voltage is zero and *vice versa*, or current leads voltage by 90°.

In the picture below, as the voltage rises rapidly at A, the current starts to flow into the capacitor, and decreases down to zero when the voltage is maximum at B.

From B to C, the capacitor is discharging in the opposite direction reaching its maximum at C, when voltage is zero, and so on.

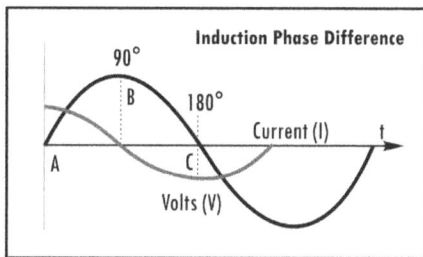

The current actually flowing is the resultant of one flowing against resistance and the other being the discharge current.

Capacitive reactance is also measured in ohms, and is inversely proportional to AC frequency, meaning that when frequency is high reactance is low, and when it is low reactance is high. Capacitors therefore act as low resistances to high frequencies and high resistances to low frequencies.

Note: The term *reactance* is only used when voltage and current are out of phase with each other. When they are in phase, the term *resistance* applies.

In summary, the effect of reactance varies with the frequency of the current, in that an increase in frequency causes an increase in inductive reactance and a decrease in capacitive reactance. Coils therefore oppose high frequencies, while capacitors oppose low frequencies. Adding a resistance reduces the lead or lag angle.

IMPEDANCE

Impedance is the total opposition to the flow of AC current, so any voltage drop is proportional to the product of current and impedance, which consists of resistance and reactance of whatever type (capacitive or inductive). Its symbol is Z, and its value is always greater than resistance, except at resonance (see below), when Z = R. *Impedance is the vector sum of resistance and reactance* - the total equivalent resistance at any given frequency, and the

square root of the squares of reactance and resistance added together. Put more simply, it is the result of RMS Volts divided by RMS amps (overleaf).

Total impedance is not simply the algebraic sum of resistance and reactance. Capacitive and inductive reactance can cancel each other out and the total (effective) reactance is then the *difference* between the two. The phase shift characteristics (i.e. whether voltage or current is leading) will be determined by the largest value. For example, in a circuit with 20 ohms of inductive reactance and 36 of capacitive, the total will be 16 ohms of capacitive reactance. Therefore current will lead voltage.

As the inductive and capacitive reactance are 90° out of phase with the resistance, and their maximum values occur at different times, vector addition must be used for calculations. Impedance matching (as used in avionics) means that a device works best when a circuit to which an input or an output is connected has the same impedance as the input or output. A low impedance circuit should not be connected to a high impedance one without allowing for power losses, hence the use of transformers (the connection between a 75 ohm coaxial TV cable and a flat TV twin lead, which has an impedance of 300 ohms has a transformer in it, with a turns ratio of 2:1).

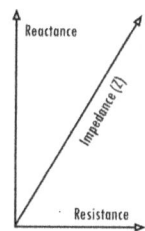

RESONANCE

We know that the frequency of an AC voltage applied to a series circuit determines its reactance or, put another way, the quicker the changes in current, the more opposition is experienced.

The current has three components:

- One flowing against the resistance, in phase with the applied emf
- One flowing against inductance which is lagging behind the emf
- One from capacitance which is leading the emf, in opposition to that flowing against inductance

If the inductive reactance is larger than the capacitive (usual for higher frequencies), the circuit is inductive and the voltage leads the current. If the capacitive is the larger reactance (for lower frequencies), the circuit is capacitive, and the voltage lags behind the current. Somewhere in the middle, the reactances will be equal and that of the circuit will be zero, meaning that impedance will be minimum, and equal to the "normal" circuit resistance (R). The voltage across the circuit and the current in it will be in phase. This condition is *series resonance* which occurs at the circuit's *resonant frequency*.

Put another way, in an AC circuit, current and emf are only in phase when either:

- the circuit contains only resistance.

- the leading effect on the current from capacitance is balanced by the lagging effect from inductance.

The second condition refers to a state of resonance.

A resonant, or *tuned*, circuit is one where the inductive and capacitive reactances (that is, concerning voltage and current) are equal, and cancel each other out because they have opposite polarity. The reactive elements (L and C) have values that cause the circuit to vibrate electrically in sympathy with the electrical supply, which can reinforce the voltage or current in the circuit. The principle is used when selecting a radio frequency, where the tuning knob is connected to a variable capacitor. This means that an alternating current is required - an inductor in a DC circuit would have no effect, aside from the normal resistance in the wire wrapped round the coil.

Circuits not containing components with resistance, capacitance, and inductance can still exhibit their effects. For example, a coaxial cable has some capacitance and some inductance whose values are very small, but not negligible in sensitive circuits. As such a circuit presents a low opposition to a voltage at the resonant frequency, the current is large, so the circuit can differentiate between voltages at different frequencies. In other words, it is *selective*. This is OK in an electronic circuit with a high resistance, but in a power circuit with low resistance it can cause damage.

RMS VALUES

As alternating current is constantly changing, how do you compare it to DC without measuring both in a circuit? Using a measuring instrument on an AC circuit is problematic because the average value is nothing, and the needle would be waving about anyway. In practice, such peak values are calculated from the RMS value and multiplied by the square root of 2 (for a pure sine wave). If AC is passed through a wire that is wound around a thermojunction, a millivoltmeter would respond in proportion the square of the AC. As both DC and AC cause wires to get hot, the *heating effect* is used to indicate the value of AC, such that a current of, say, 5 amps, always produces the same effect, AC or DC.

The heating effect is proportional to the square of the current (I^2), so here we are concerned with the average squared value*, or *mean square*, since the normal average is zero, and you need something to work on. As you don't refer to square amperes, you then need find the square root of that (the *root mean square*) to get a suitable figure.

*Taking a current that is fluctuating between 5 and 8 volts as an example, the average would be 6.5 volts, but the square of that (42.25) does not give a true measure of the heating effect. The average of the squares (25 + 64), which is the correct figure, would actually be 44.5.

The power used in an AC circuit is the average of all the instantaneous values of power (or heating) in a complete cycle. If the circuit is in phase, the power curve is entirely above the zero axis, because two positives or two negatives make a plus (the square of a negative quantity is positive).

In the diagram below, the grey sine wave is the *square* of the black one. Now its average value is not zero, but half of the maximum of the squared current.

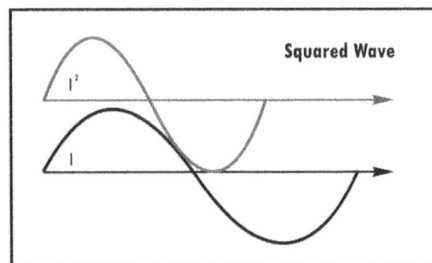

If you take a cycle and sample it 90 times (once per degree), square the values, then average them (i.e. find the mean), then find the square root of the mean, you get 0.7071 times the peak value (often called the *virtual value*).

$$RMS = \frac{peak\ value}{\sqrt{2}}$$

The peak is found by multiplying the RMS by 1.414, which is the square root of 2. If the peak to peak voltage is 400 volts, RMS is 141 volts. To convert from RMS to amplitude, divide RMS by 0.707.

In summary, as an AC waveform is not square, its peak voltage is 1.414 times that of DC to have the same energy (RMS is the effective current).

*Whenever an alternating current or voltage is specified, it is always the RMS value that is referred to.

Note: The insulation of any component must be capable of standing the peak value of an AC.

In the diagram below, the shaded area inside the curve over the square DC wave has the same energy as the shaded parts outside the curve. the horizontal straight line represents a DC voltage.

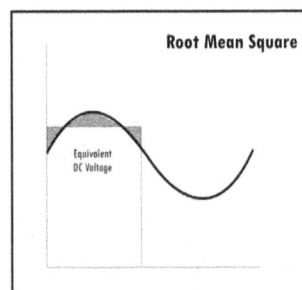

CAPT

POWER

A current that is always dying away and building up again is less effective than a steady one. For best efficiency, AC must be synchronised with the voltage and be undistorted. Electrostatic and electromagnetic forces can affect the phase relationship between voltage and current in AC circuits, which affects the power gained.

For DC, where voltage and current are always in phase, power consumed is derived simply from their product - 1 volt (E) and 1 ampere (I) *flowing in the same direction* form the Watt. However, with AC, the volt-ampere product (VA) does not necessarily give the power consumed, as a current flowing in the opposite direction puts power back into the supply. In other words, power is derived from the product of current and *that part of the voltage that is in phase with it*, so you can have current and emf without power!

For example, when the volt-ampere product is positive, as it would be when they are in phase, all the power goes to the load. When it is negative, the load returns power to the supply and can turn a motor into a generator. If the phase angle between voltage and current is 90°, the load will return as much power to the supply as it consumes, and the average power will be zero. Thus, to find out how much power you will get from an AC circuit, you must multiply amps by volts as usual, and the cosine (power factor) of the phase angle between them.

This is **True Power, Real Power,** or **Effective Power**, being that needed to drive the current loads and measured in KW. Its symbol is *P*. Put another way, components such as heaters and lights do real work and use real power, expressed in Watts and indicated on a voltmeter. Other components (i.e. transformers) use up power without apparently doing anything. This is called reactive power, mentioned below. The real load from an AC generator is proportional to its RPM and the torque supplied by its drive, both of which must be matched.

Apparent Power is simply the total of what is produced, or the RMS volt-ampere product (VAR/KVAR). Its symbol is *S*, and it has more to do with voltage regulation and field strengths. In fact, RMS values of current and emf are also called *virtual* current and emf, with their product of *virtual watts*.

So, to find the true power in an AC circuit, you find the component of emf that is in phase with the current, and multiply it by the virtual current (see *Power Factor*, below).

Reactive (Imaginary) Power (Q) is what is used in overcoming reactance (current flowing in the opposite direction), and is measured in *Volt-Amps Reactive* (VAR), and is a small value compared to the KW from real power. It is the vector sum of the inductive and capacitive currents, and voltage, representing the energy alternately stored and returned to the system by capacitors and/or inductors. Although reactive power does not produce useful work, it still needs to be generated and distributed so that enough true power is available for electrical processes to run. Because of this quality, it is also called *Wattless Power*. The more voltage and current are out of phase, the more this will be - any phase angle between 0° and 90° means that it will take more power to deliver a fixed amount of current because of the reactive losses. Thus, you will never get full power, except when everything is in phase, as with just resistance (light bulbs, etc.) or with equal values of inductive and capacitive reactance, as found in a tuned circuit.

```
kVA = kW + kVAR
```

In a loadsharing situation, the kVA and kVAR loads must be carefully synchronised.

THE POWER FACTOR

This expresses the relationship between true and apparent power. With reactance and resistance present, there is always a phase difference between current and voltage. The ratio between the actual power consumed (True Power, in Watts) to the Apparent Power (VA) that could have been transmitted if the current were in phase and undistorted is the Power Factor:

```
Power factor = KW (Real Power)
               KVA (Apparent Power)
```

Put another way, the power factor is the amount by which apparent power must be multiplied to get true power. It is the cosine of the phase angle of the circuit. Thus, the traditional **volts** x **amps** formula becomes:

```
watts = volts x amps x power factor
```

The formula for apparent power is:

```
P = EI
```

EI is RMS volts x amps.

*True power is calculated from another trigonometric function, namely the cosine of the phase angle (cos q):

```
P = EI cos q
```

The cosine of zero is 1, so in a purely resistive circuit it is ignored, which is why it is not in the first formula.

The picture on the right is a *phasor diagram* showing the relationship between Reactive, Real and Apparent Power. The Real Power equals the Apparent Power multiplied by the cosine of the phase angle between voltage and current.

In a circuit where reactance and resistance are equal, voltage and current are

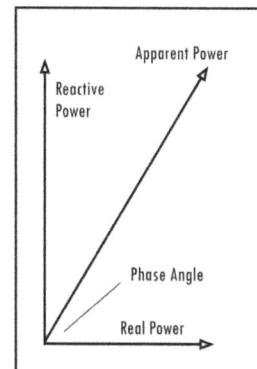

displaced by 45°, the cosine of which is 0.7071, so the power factor is 0.7071. This means the circuit has used around 70% of the energy supplied by the source and returned around 30%. This is important when you are trying to decide what size of cable to use in a circuit.

A 1.84 kW load supplied with a power factor of 0.4 would require a 20A cable, while the same load supplied at unity would only need an 8A cable.

So, the power factor determines what percentage of power is used up in Watts, and what percentage returns to the source as wattless power.

Power loss is proportional to the square of the current:

$$P = I^2R$$

The power factor is *leading* if there is more capacitive than inductive reactance, or *lagging* if they are the other way round. Electric motors result in a lagging power factor because they are more inductive than capacitive.

The type of capacitance can be found by dividing a circuit's resistance by its impedance, so, if there is 50 ohms of resistance, 50 ohms of inductive reactance and 80 of capacitive reactance, the power factor will be 0.857, or that just under 86% of the current is in phase with voltage.

A poor power factor can arise from either a significant phase difference between voltage and current, or harmonic distortion. Poor phase angles are usually the result of an inductive load such as an induction motor or a power transformer, because some current is used to create the magnetic field. This can be improved by placing capacitors in parallel with the circuits, which should actually be kept to a minimum to avoid resonance. The energy now moves between the capacitors and the inductive load, reducing the current flow from the line. That is, the capacitor catches the current and reflects it back, instead of having it flow all the way back to the generator. Capacitors reduce the lagging of the inductive component and the losses in the supply.

Typical output would be between 30-90 kVA for the largest aircraft, so, if a 90 kVA AC generator has a power factor of 0.75, what is the useful output? 67.5 KW. Talking of big jets, they often have KW-KVAR meters that show the true power in kilowatts that the system is using. Pressing a button nearby changes the circuitry so that it will read the reactive power in kilo-volt-amps, showing how hard the alternator is working.

THE AC GENERATOR

An inverter creates AC (from DC), but so does an AC generator, which is similar in construction to a DC generator, but using *slip rings* instead of commutators, so the current reversals are not modified. Each end of the rotating loop connects to a separate ring.

There are two types of alternator, one with a *revolving armature* (shown above) and one with a *revolving field* which is more common in aviation (to save confusion, the term *rotor* means rotating parts, and *stator* means fixed parts).

The revolving armature type resembles the DC generator insofar as the armature rotates inside a stationary magnetic field. The other has the opposite - the field comes from an electromagnet rotating within a stationary armature winding (in the case) so that the output can be connected directly to the load, as opposed to going through slip rings (insulation is easier). Instead, the slip rings only need to convey the excitation current.

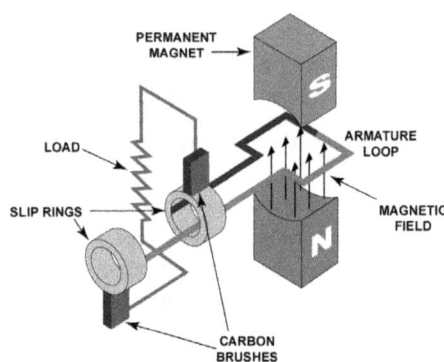

A revolving field AC generator has two main elements:

- An engine driven rotor which has the field coils wound on it. Power for the coils (to turn them into an electromagnet) comes through the slip rings and brushes from a DC source, typically the battery (hence the alternator switch next to the battery switch). This is why flying with a dud battery can be problematic. The on-off switch can isolate the alternator from the electrical system and should be turned off if the alternator fails.

- Stator windings carry three sets (or pairs) of coils (i.e. phase windings), in which the current is generated by the rotating field windings.

With only a single coil (as shown in the diagram) the output would fluctuate at twice the mains frequency. More even torque can be obtained with multiple phases. You can also save weight and utilise multiple voltages.

A 3-phase system can use the same frame, field and armature core, so you can save material and weight (in fact, you get three generators in one). In addition, transmitting a load over 3 sets of wires rather than one means less of a heating effect and less of a power drop, if only because power is drawn at a uniform rate.

With 3-phase, the windings are 120° apart and may be wired as a *mesh (delta)* or *star*. The star (on the left, below) is the most commonly found in aviation, with one end of each coil joined to a common neutral point, **with which you can get two voltages** - a *line voltage* between any two phases, and a *phase voltage* between line and neutral, as the current flows away from the centre. Line voltage is 1.73 x phase voltage, and line current is equal to phase current (1.732 is the square root of 3).

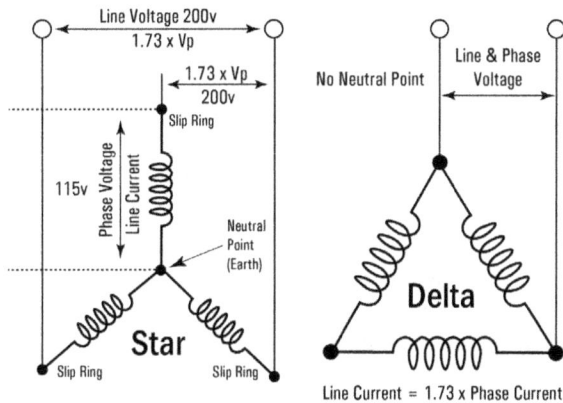

When one coil is vertical, and therefore not crossing any flux lines, and not producing any current, the others are producing equal current in opposite directions, so the algebraic sum of all three voltages is zero. Thus, you only need three slip rings, because you can interconnect the other three cables. In practice, a neutral wire is taken from the interconnected ends on the outside, with the slip rings in the middle.

The neutral wire allows you to treat the unit as three single phase systems, so you get three generators in one. The star winding can cope with unbalanced loads on different busbars, meaning that you can switch things on and off quite easily, unlike the delta, which will overheat from the extra current. If one phase becomes earthed, its voltage drops to zero. Although the other phases will still work, a protection circuit will switch the generator off.

With a mesh or delta (right, above), the three coils are in series as a closed circuit, so a short circuit will make all phases drop to zero (one terminal is earthed to the airframe). This design is only used for small motors because, unless the emfs are equal, circulating currents will exist which makes them less useful for generators. Here, line voltage is equal to phase voltage and line current is 1.73 x phase current. The difference between the two is that a star generates a high voltage at a low current (thinner cables required) and can produce a greater output for a given size. A delta generates a low voltage at a high current. You can switch between both to maximise efficiency if both are present.

The frequency of the current provided by an alternator depends on the number of **pairs of poles** and **rotation speed**, which is linked to engine RPM. In fact, many

aircraft sample the alternator output to provide the engine tachometer indication. Refer to *Induction Motors*, below.

FREQUENCY WILD SYSTEMS

Alternators are *frequency wild* if their RPM is not controlled, meaning that their voltage frequencies are allowed to vary with their speed, so they cannot be paralleled. Such items would only be used on systems that are not affected by frequency, like heating or lighting (which are purely resistive), on simple aircraft where the primary supply is DC (light aircraft usually have frequency wild bridge rectified alternators). The alternator is driven off the engine by a fan belt, so its output varies with engine RPM. Having said all that. frequency wild can be converted to stable with a TRU or inverter - that is, you can parallel the TRUs if you cannot parallel the generators.

When you switch the battery on, the busbar receives a minimum voltage, and the ammeter will show a negative value, or a discharge. There will also be a low voltage light flashing somewhere, indicating that the busbar is below its level, because the alternator is not working. The alternator switch must be selected ON to provide the initial excitation from the battery, but this will be overridden from the alternator's own output once the engine has started. When the alternator output exceeds the minimum voltage, the undervoltage light will go out and the ammeter will show a positive reading.

Fault protection includes:

- **Over/under voltage**. If the voltage goes over around 15.5 volts, the voltage regulator will break the field and lock it out, making the undervoltage light come on. You can switch the alternator off for a few seconds to reset the system, but only once. If voltage reduces, or the alternator is switched off, the warning lamp will come on, and go off when the voltage is restored.

- **Overheating**. The generator should be switched off and allowed to cool once the warning light comes on.

- **Over/under frequency.**

- **Over/under excitation**.

For larger aircraft, alternator output is typically 200 volts, 3-phase, varying in frequency between 280-540 Hz to cover the whole range of engine RPM. The initial excitation again comes from the battery (or ground power), switched in by resetting the alternator switch.

After the engine has started, and the generator warning light goes out, moving the control switch to ON allows some current to be fed back to the generator from the *Bridge Rectifier Pack*, which sits after the voltage regulator, to allow self-excitation.

CONSTANT SPEED DRIVE UNIT/IDG

To keep inductive and capacitive reactance under control, aircraft systems should be supplied with AC at a constant frequency, as almost exclusively used on large jet aircraft. The 747, for example, parallels its generators to make sure that all the systems have the power they require. If one fails, you loadshed.

The 737, on the other hand, has each generator supplying around half the load. If one fails, the other can power the whole system, with or without loadshedding, without the APU generator being brought on line. Here, the generators do not supply common busbars - they are not paralleled, so there is no need to synchronise their frequencies, although they are kept within certain limits.

As the engines cannot be relied upon to maintain a constant speed (on which the aircraft's constant AC frequency depends), there needs to be some sort of interim arrangement between the engine and its alternator.

The hydraulically operated Constant Speed Drive Unit* keeps the AC generator's rotational speed constant (usually about 8,000 RPM), for a nominal frequency of 400 Hz, ranging between 380-420. 400 Hz is low enough not to interfere with radios and high enough to allow better component designs.

*Modern technology allows systems without a CSDU. Variable output is fed to a full wave rectifier, where it is converted to DC and filtered, then chopped into square wave outputs, separated and summed for 400 Hz AC. If used in modern aircraft, the CSDU and (brushless) alternator can be combined in one unit, the **Integrated Drive Generator** (IDG). It is cooled by oil, which involves a heat exchanger.

Picture: Constant Speed Drive Unit

Otherwise, the CSDU may be cooled with ram air or its own oil supply. It is connected to the engine by a clutch (the CSD disconnect) which can be used at any RPM, but preferably at idle, to reduce loads. An electromechanical disconnect mechanism is used for emergencies.

Once a CSDU has been disconnected, it can only be reinstated on the ground, with the engine shut down.

The system uses differential oil pressure between a hydraulic pump and a hydraulic motor. The oil temperature is a function of the work being done, in that, if it rises, the load has increased. Instruments in the cockpit will show the temperature rise, which is the important value - there may be two or just one showing the IN and RISE figures. However, you can also expect an oil pressure indication in the cockpit.

The oil transfer is controlled by an eccentric swashplate whose angle of inclination is controlled by movement of a piston inside a centrifugal governor (see picture below). This may be further refined by a magnetic trim device that adjusts the flyweights in the governor. The pressure exerted on the motor piston by the pump determines the rotational speed of a centre plate, in that the higher the pressure, the faster it will rotate.

When the engine and generator speeds are equal, the system is known as *on speed*. There is no oil transfer and the governors are in the neutral position. If the throttle setting is reduced, the engine will slow down and the output of the hydraulic pump will reduce.

As the generator is now faster than the engine, an overdrive condition exists, which will be sensed by the governor, and the angle of the swashplate will be increased, as will the stroke of its pistons. For an under-drive condition, the reverse happens.

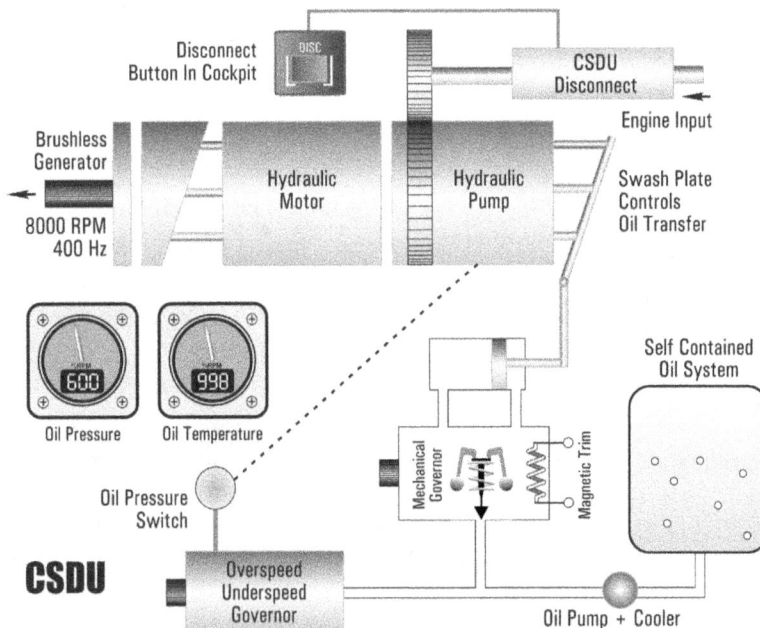

© *Phil Croucher, 2014*

If this page is a photocopy, it is not authorised!

Fault protection includes:

- **Quill Drive.** A drive shaft with a weak point that prevents engine stoppage if the IDG seizes.

- **Over/Under-excitation.** For parallel faults, a protection device trips in when the excitation to the field of one generator varies one way or the other, sensed when it takes more or less than its share of the reactive load.The fault signal has an inverse time function that trips the BTB of the over-excited generator. A voltage regulator or reactive load-sharing circuit could cause this fault. When a persistent under-excitation fault is detected on an AC generator connected to another one, the protection device opens the:

  - **Exciter Control Relay**

  - **Generator Breaker** (GCB). This closes when the generator's voltage is greater than the battery's, and opens when the opposite is true

  - **Bus Tie Breaker** (BTB). Used also when there is a phase imbalance

  When under excitation occurs, the exciter relay doesn't always trip, but the generator does. This is sensed when the under-excited generator takes less than its share of reactive load, and a fault signal causes the BTB to trip in a fixed time (3-5 sec). This could be caused by a fault in a reactive load sharing circuit, a generator, or a voltage regulator.

- **Over/Under voltage.** Protection is given when the line voltage goes over around 225v, or when high currents occur (i.e. undervoltage and overheating, where burning out is a possibility). This device operates on an inverse time function, which means that the voltage determines the time in which the offending generator is de-energised by tripping the GCR and GCB. The GCR de-energises the field, and the GCB trips the generator off the busbar. A detector, set to operate within 3 volts of 100 or 130 v, sends a signal via a time delay to two solid state switches (the delay allows the CSDU to react in time). On detecting a persistent overvoltage fault on an AC generator, the exciter and generator breakers are opened.If voltage reduces, or the alternator is switched off, the warning lamp comes on, and goes off when the voltage is restored. For undervoltage, the GCR and GCB are tripped in a fixed time (3-5 seconds), resulting in the generator shutting down.

- **Overheating.** The generator should be switched off and cooled once the warning light comes on.

- **Differential Protection.** Differences between the generator and busbar are sensed by transformers and the field automatically de-excited.

- **Over/Under Frequency** (Over/Under speed). If this is left unchecked, the inductive loads can be damaged. Older systems use a pressure switch in the CSDU, but modern system detect changes in frequency. Overspeeding causes the GCB to trip and the CSDU goes into underdrive. The GCB still trips for an underspeed, but the generator is removed from the busbar. As the heaviest loads are inductive, under frequency is most hazardous.

- **IDG (CSDU) Disconnect**. Oil pressure and temperature are monitored in the cockpit and you can disconnect if there is a problem, but the system can only be reset with engines stopped.

- **Bearing Failure.** If there is too much clearance in generator bearings, a warning light will come on.

- **Negative Sequence Voltage Protection**. This detects line-to-line or line-to-earth faults after the protected zone and makes the BTBs trip.

Time delays allow any protection devices to trip before equipment is removed from busbars. Warning lights include excessive temperature and low oil pressure.

The phrase *generator with another generator* refers to a parallel busbar and the tie breaker needs to be tripped, plus something else for the generator (usually the exciter and generator relay). *Modern twin jet/twin engine* means a split busbar and the tie breaker should not be closed. A single generator is on its own, so there is no tie breaker.

BRUSHLESS GENERATOR

A brushless generator minimises the normal losses from slip rings and brushes. The assembly is in three parts, starting with a pilot exciter that uses a permanent magnet (PMG) to generate single phase AC that is fed into a voltage regulator, from where it comes out as DC (having been rectified) into a stator coil in the Main Exciter.

A current is induced into each of three coils in the main exciter field producing a three-phase current, which is again full-wave rectified to DC which ends up in the Main Generator's rotating field rotor. The six diodes are kept cool with ram air directed down the shaft. The exciter field resistance is temperature compensated by a thermistor which keeps a nearly constant resistance at the regulator output terminals. As the field coil rotates it induces current in the stator output windings. Some of the output is fed back to the voltage regulator to help control the field excitation. On starting, in a brushless AC generator with no commutator rings, the generator is activated by a set of permanent magnets.

VOLTAGE REGULATION

Alternator output is regulated by varying the current to the field windings. A voltage regulator senses the output and adjusts the field current when the voltage rises above a set value (typically 28.5 v). The current is cut off around 2000 times a second.

LOAD SHARING

Sharing AC generators is problematical because, if two, or more, become out of balance, a current will flow between them, and those with lower voltages are driven, causing a stress on their drive shafts, which may break, as they have a deliberate *weak link*, the mechanical equivalent of a fuse.

As frequency wild systems cannot be paralleled, *their phase relationship is unimportant*. Constant frequency systems, on the other hand, are designed to be paralleled, typically using a *split* or *parallel busbar* system, described previously.

A split busbar ensures that the supplies never actually meet. Each generator has its own busbar and, if one fails (as detected by a voltage controller), the load is transferred to the other with the help of a changeover relay (bus tie).

An alternator working with others must have its excitation, speed (voltage, frequency) and phases adjusted. The process uses a *synchroniser*, which is simply a couple of small transformers. One has its primary across the busbars and the other is across the terminals of the alternator. The secondaries are connected in series with each other. When the emf of the alternator is in phase opposition to the p.d. on the busbar, the emfs of the secondaries are added together to drive a voltmeter to its highest reading.

In a paralleled 3-phase AC system, with varying loads, the most efficient generator would be compound wound.

Note: Parallel systems have the same advantages (and disadvantages) as paralleled DC systems, but they are not suitable when independence is required, as with ETOPS. The Boeing 737, for example, uses a *non-parallel* 115/200 volt, 3 phase AC from two 40 KVA generators. A third generator is driven by an APU. In a *parallel busbar* system, all AC generators can be connected to one distribution busbar, so voltages, frequencies and phases (as well as real and reactive loads, mentioned below) must be kept within very strict limits by *phase discriminators*.

REAL LOAD SHARING

The real load (in KW) is the useful power available, and reactive power (in KVAR) is the resultant of the inductive and capacitive currents and voltage in the system.

Real load sharing is determined by the rotational speeds of the generators and hence the voltage phase relationships. Generators are synchronous, so they lock together with respect to frequency when they work in parallel. The system frequency ends up as that of the generator with the highest output, which means it is carrying more of the load. The imbalance is overcome with an error detector which senses current change in a load sharing loop. The signals are sent to the electromagnetic coil in the governor of each CSDU to restore the balanced condition.

Real loadsharing control is effected by adjusting the torque at the output drive shaft. The field from the coil interacts with permanent magnet flyweights to produce a torque which, together with centrifugal force, allows fine adjustment of the governor control valve and CSD output speed.

Picture Below: Brushless Generator

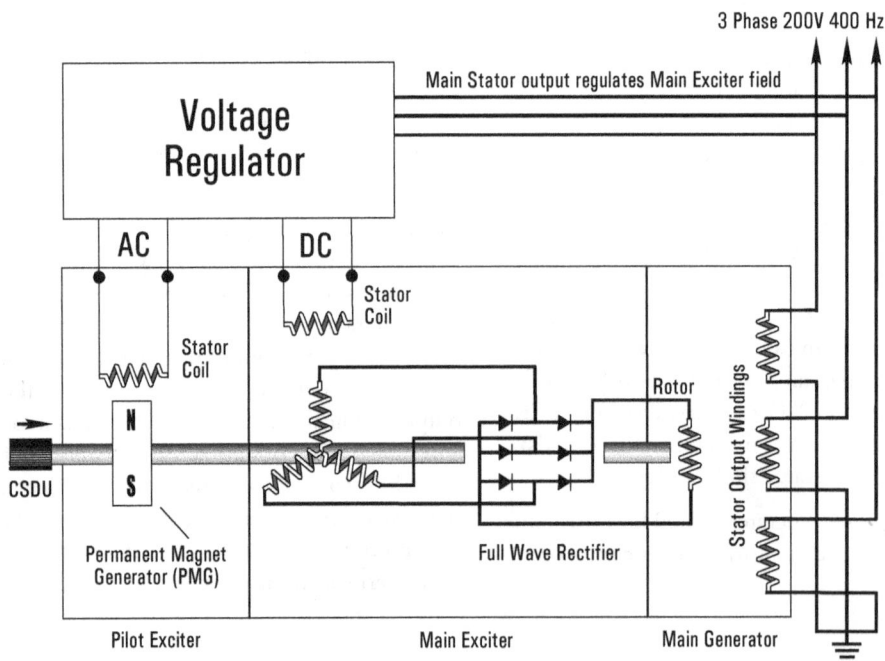

Pilot Exciter | Main Exciter | Main Generator

REACTIVE LOAD SHARING

This depends on the relative sizes of the output voltages, which depend on the settings of the relevant *voltage regulators* and field excitation current. The circuitry is similar to that for real load sharing, but the current transformers are connected to the primary windings of mutual reactors, which only deliver signals proportional to the generator's reactive load.

In a paralleled AC system, the reactive load is borne by the voltage regulators.

POWER CONVERSION

DC FROM AC (RECTIFIERS)

AC is used when it comes to generating large amounts of power, but most radio and computer equipment uses DC, and 12v at that. That part of the problem is easy - a transformer can be used to step the voltage down (or up) as required. Then a *rectifier* is used to convert the AC into DC by extracting the peaks from the AC waveform. Put another way, the alternating current is only allowed to flow through a series of diodes in one direction and every second half is turned upside down.

The diode can be a *half-wave* rectifier*, in which current will flow only on alternative half-cycles (left, below):

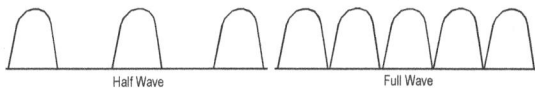

Half Wave   Full Wave

*A halfwave rectifier for a single phase requires one diode, but the lost half cycles are used in trying to drive the current in the reverse direction, and are therefore wasted as heat. To use those cycles, four diodes (*anti-phase*) allow full wave rectification. You need 3 diodes for a half wave rectifier on 3 phase, and 6 for a full wave.

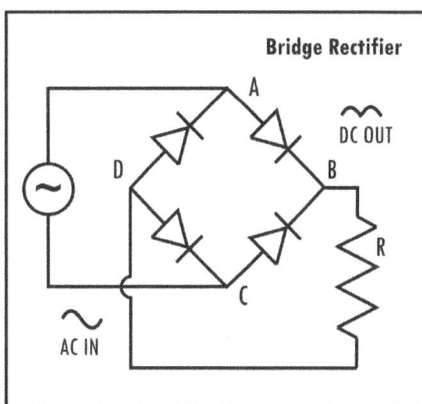

Bridge Rectifier

In the diagram, when A is positive against C, current will flow from A to B, through R (the load), then D to C. When it is negative, current will flow from C to B, through R, D to A.

However, the current is still not steady, even though it is now flowing in one direction (you can detect it with a suitable instrument). A capacitor smooths the final result, inside a *filter circuit*. There might be a *bleeder resistor* of a very high value across the capacitor's terminals to ensure it discharges when the power is switched off.

AC FROM DC

Inverters produce AC from DC. This might be because an older aircraft using DC has new equipment that requires AC. For example, you may not get any fuel indications until you switch the inverters on, because the capacitive fuel indication system requires AC with which to work.

A rotary inverter is a DC motor driving an AC generator. A static inverter is electrical, with no moving parts containing a signal generator and amplifier producing a square or sine wave.

AUXILIARY POWER UNIT

Before the engines are started, power can be supplied from a Ground Power Unit (GPU), but more typically from an Auxiliary Power Unit, which is more able to meet large power demands. The APU is usually a small axial flow gas turbine that usually sits in the tail* (behind a firewall) and which drives the same type of AC generator that is fitted to the main engines (supplying 115v, 400 Hz power after the engines have been started). The generator will be driven through an accessory gearbox.

*It will be high to stop it ingesting anything nasty. In fact, it is usually covered by a door which naturally must be opened (electrically) before you operate the APU. This is mostly automatic.

The APU also has a compressor that can supply bleed air to the pneumatic system (used for starting the main engines) and the air conditioning. The APU can still be used when the main engines are operating, especially to replace a failed generator. As the APU runs at a constant speed, it does not need any sort of speed regulation.

In emergencies, a Ram Air Turbine can drop down from the fuselage, to spin in the airflow. There may even be a generator driven by the hydraulic system.

In large aircraft, the ship's battery will only be used to start the APU, and to provide limited DC power in real emergencies. The APU otherwise has its own battery.

Picture: Typical Power Sources

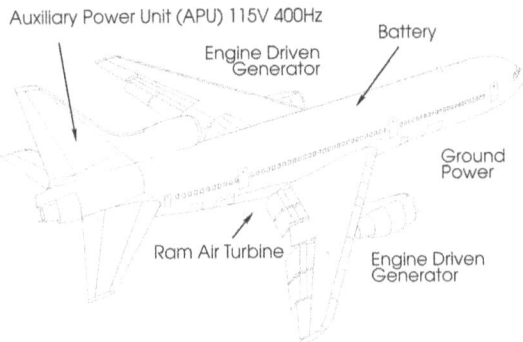

The fuel for the APU will come from the main tanks, and will normally be delivered under pressure from an AC driven pump, but there is a DC one if AC is not available. The DC pump will run off the ship's battery, as will the fuel valve, which will open when the APU is started and close automatically on shutdown.

Below is a typical control panel for an APU:

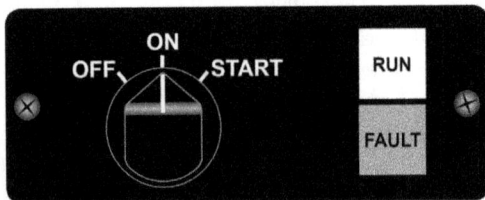

The RUN light is white, and will be illuminated when the APU is at its proper running speed. The FAULT light is amber, and it will tell you when the APU has shut down due to a fault, or when the fuel shutoff valve is not in its commanded position.

The OFF selection closes the APU bleed valve and initiates the shutdown cooling cycle after it has closed. The ON position is for normal operations. It opens the bleed valve and the door, arms the bleed valve and energises a fuel pump. The start sequence will commence when the door is fully open.

The START position is spring loaded and is used to initiate the automatic start sequence, before returning to the ON position.

The instruments that tell you what an earlier APU is up to might include RPM, EGT and oil indicators. Modern ones use the EICAS/EICAM displays.

AC MOTORS

There are three main types of AC motor - the *synchronous*, the *induction* (asynchronous), and the *series*, or *commutator* motor, which is more commonly found in domestic appliances. We are only concerned about synchronous and induction motors.

There are also three sizes of motor:

- **Large**, with an output of at least 3 KW, which are normally 3-phase

- **Medium-Small**. The output starts at 50W, mostly based on single-phase operation. Those below 750W are also called *Fractional Horsepower*

- **Miniature**. Below 50W, in instruments and servos

AC motors use a rotating magnetic field. 3-phase currents setup magnetic fields that can be resolved into a single field revolving in the air gap between the rotor and stator. At 400 Hz, this will be 24 000 RPM. By using a stationary winding with a rotating field, you only need two slip rings, which makes construction easier and reduces losses.

INDUCTION MOTORS

Induction motors are often called *squirrel cage motors*, because the rotor that spins in the middle is based on those things that hamsters run around in (their proper name is just the *cage*, or *short-circuited rotor*).

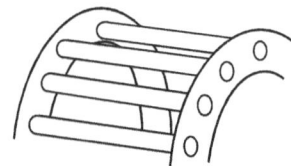

The bars are copper or aluminium, shorted together by rings at each end (apparently you can get better starting and quieter running if the bars are slightly skewed). There are no connections to or from the rotor, or moving parts, aside from the rotor itself when it is made to spin. As a brush or commutator is not required, or slip rings, there are less parts to wear out and less interference with radios.

The rotating magnetic field induces large currents in the spokes of the squirrel cage (because of the short-circuiting), which produces a magnetic field that interacts with the outer rotating field, in the opposite direction, after Lenz's law, making it spin.

As the field rotates through one revolution over each AC cycle, at 50 Hz, you will get 3000 RPM.

However, the rotor will never turn at the synchronous speed of the rotating field, or there would be no induced current. The difference between the speed of the rotor and the rotating field is *slip*. At full loads, it is around 4%.

You can obtain the speed from the number of pole pairs and the frequency of the AC supply:

$$RPM = \frac{Hz \times 60}{pole\ pairs}$$

CAPT

The speed of a 4 pole motor at 400 Hertz is 12 000 RPM.

If a phase is lost while it is running, the motor will still run, at about half speed, but it cannot be restarted (if it is not running, it will refuse to spin and probably blow the fuses in the other phases). When the load on an induction motor becomes so great that it cannot be carried by it, the motor will stop. This is the *pullout point*. To change the direction of rotation, you just swap two cables round.

The squirrel cage is simple and cheap, so it is used in smaller motors, but it takes a large starting current and has a relatively low starting torque (unless it has a high resistance, but that is inefficient). It therefore doesn't like starting against heavy loads and often must be run up to speed first. In fact, it has similar characteristics to a DC shunt wound motor*. As a result, the greatest torque on an induction motor is at start up. Gyroscopes based on such motors should not be used in the speeding up phase.

*You can run some DC motors from AC, if the same supply is connected to the armature and field. The torque direction on the armature will remain the same.

Although the most common winding (in the rotating element) is the squirrel cage (i.e. short circuited), another type has coils in the rotor slots, to produce a *wound rotor*, in three sections, out to three slip rings, so that starting resistances can be included in the rotor circuit. They are gradually cut out as the rotor speeds up until the slip rings are short-circuited.

A two-phase motor has two windings 90° apart, but their voltages come from different sources. One is the *reference* phase, and the other a *control* phase. By varying the phasing and amplitude of the currents in the control phase, you can control the direction of rotation and the speed. Such motors are not as smooth or powerful as 3-phase motors, so they are used in lesser roles, such as servo motors.

Split-phase motors also have two windings 90° apart, but one is capacitive and the other is resistive, connected in parallel across a single phase AC supply. The current in the capacitive winding leads that in the resistive winding by around 90° (called *phase splitting*). These motors are also used in lesser roles, as they operate like 2-phase motors.

SYNCHRONOUS

Synchronous motors are particularly suited for constant speed operation, since their rotors only run at the same speed as the rotating magnetic field, which is determined by the *frequency* of the AC supplied.

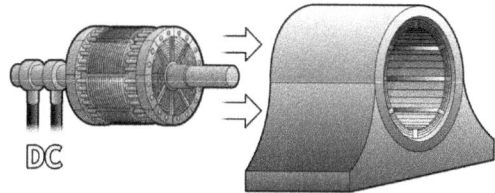

In a synchronous motor, the squirrel cage is replaced with a magnet, either permanent, for low power requirements, or an electromagnet for higher outputs. There, the rotor is supplied with a DC current (from a generator or a rectifier) that creates an electromagnet with North and South Poles to line up with the opposite poles in the rotating field.

As long as the pull between the magnets is large enough, the rotor will run at the same speed as the rotating field. If the load exceeds the maximum torque, the rotor will stall and stop.

Without complex electronics, these are essentially constant-speed motors (from no-load to full-load), after the frequency of the 3-phase input, so they are useful where a constant speed is important, such as within gyros (assuming the frequency remains constant).

Synchronous motors cannot start without being driven, or having their rotor connected as a self-starting circuit. That is, since the field is already rotating at the eventual speed, it rushes past the rotor poles so quickly that the rotor does not have a chance to get started, so the rotor is repelled first in one direction and then the other (in other words, inertia plays a part). Thus, the motor must be accelerated before it can synchronise, so it may need a separate starting mechanism. This is done mostly with a small induction motor, often called a *pony motor*.

Once the rotor is near to synchronous speed, the rotor's DC field is energized by a mechanical switch that operates on centrifugal force. This makes it lock the rotor in step with the rotating field. Full torque is developed, and the load is driven.

COMPUTERS, ETC

You can represent and store information electrically in many ways - a capacitor, for example, can store an electrical charge which can be measured and related to a mathematical value that can be used for calculations in an analogue computer. However, capacitors leak over time - as the mathematical values would therefore change by themselves, and measurements would become less accurate (assuming the mechanism was adequate in the first place), a better way of using those charges is to detect the presence (or not) of a signal, regardless of its strength, which is how digital circuits work (see *Bits & Bytes*, below).

Note: As with all computerised equipment, a digital aircraft (such as the AB/AW 139) must be grounded when not flying to guard against static damage!

There are many computers in modern aircraft, and they all work in pretty much the same way, although they won't all have a keyboard and screen. Essentially, a Central Processor (CPU), which is the brains and does all the work, is connected to memory and other peripheral chips (that may control instruments, screens, keyboards, etc.) over various buses that control memory or data. The CPU itself consists of an Arithmetic and Logic Unit (ALU), a control and timing unit, and registers.

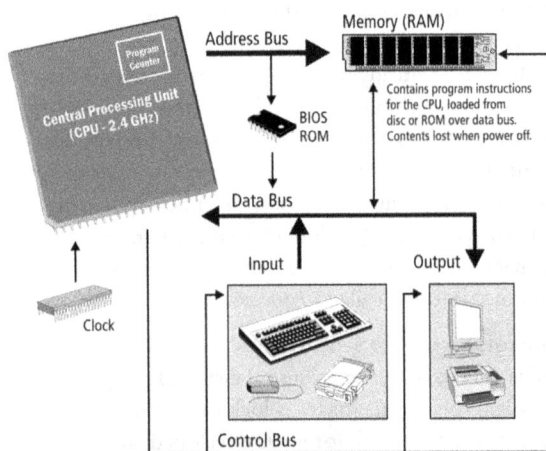

Some systems use multiprocessors that can run several tasks in parallel.

If any part of the computer needs attention, it *interrupts* the CPU, which is more efficient than having the CPU poll each device in turn, and wasting cycles when the device(s) are quite happy to be left alone, thank you very much.

Hardware

The term *hardware* covers the physical aspects of a computer, such as keyboards, screens, hard drives, etc. Keyboards and mice are *input* devices, and screens and printers do *output*.

INTEGRATED CIRCUITS

These are now found in a wide variety of equipment - not just computers. An integrated circuit is essentially a complete piece of electrical equipment inside one chip, including resistors, transistors, wiring, etc., which are therefore very small indeed.

The picture on the right is of an EEPROM, or *Electrically Erasable Programmable Read Only Memory*, which is simply a chip that can be cleared with a small voltage and reprogrammed. Such chips are used in Flight Management Systems, for example, to contain navigation or performance databases. You cannot normally change the contents, but an engineer can with special equipment when it's time for an update.

The integrated circuit inside is very small, and it has to interface with the rest of the world, which is why it is in a bigger chip so that we humans can manipulate it.

The transistor (later) prompted the development of integrated circuits. As it is able to move electrons through solid material instead of requiring the vacuum in a valve, the transistor has a much lower internal resistance and uses a lot less power. Cost is therefore reduced and, most important for aviation, weight, while increasing reliability.

The most useful application of integrated circuits is within computers, which use large numbers of identical logic circuits to make yes/no decisions. In other words, switching. If you operated five switches in their various binary combinations, you could obtain any number between 1 and 31. Adding one more switch (for 32) allows any number between 1 and 63. With only 46 switches, you can get any number between 1 and 100 trillion! The ability to check this number of switches at once is one reason why computers are fast, aside from the fact that they are run at high clock speeds anyway.

MEMORY

Memory contains the instructions that tell the Central Processor what to do, as well as the data created by its activities. As a computer works with bits that are either on or off, memory chips work by keeping electronic switches in one state or the other for as long as they are required (since they are capacitors, which leak their charges, memory cells are refreshed every other cycle). Where these states can be changed at will or, more properly, the operating system is able to reach every part of memory, it is called *Random Access Memory*, or RAM, which comes from when magnetic tapes were used for storage, and information could only be accessed sequentially; that is, not at random. A ROM, on the other hand, has its electronic switches permanently on or off, so they can't be changed (by pilots anyway), hence *Read Only Memory*. ROMs are *non-volatile*, meaning that data inside isn't lost when the power is off. System memory, on the other hand, is volatile, so it is vulnerable to power loss.

Memory is counted in K, which is actually 1024 bits, as opposed to 1000, because of the binary counting used by computers, so you get 4096 instead of 4000.

More permanent storage is provided by magnetic materials (such as the coating on floppy or hard disks), or optical means, such as DVD-ROMs, or flash memory.

Virtual memory is space used on a permanent medium (typically a hard drive) to store data that is too much for system memory to hold. The process of moving data from one to the other is called *paging*, because memory is dealt with in pages.

BUSES

A bus is a shared connection between devices, of which a computer has several; for example, the *processor bus* connects the CPU to its support chips, the *memory bus* connects it to memory.

So, buses are electronic pathways between the various parts of a computer, which could be 8-bit, 16-bit, 32-bit, depending on how much data is transferred around at once. The problem with the average desktop PC is that the rest of the machine, in terms of bus width and speed, won't necessarily have the same capability as the CPU, so you might get data bottlenecks. For example, the CPU may be running at 2000 mph (2 GHz), but the screen and hard drive, the busiest components, are sitting in the PCI bus, running at 330 mph (33 MHz). The memory bus will be somewhere in between. A fast CPU won't mean a thing if the rest of the machine is crippled, as with a Celeron.

Some computerised devices in aircraft are better designed than this, but many use purpose built chips that contain the same CPU and support chips as a PC in one. The FADEC in a Bell 407 uses a single-board computer which transmits data to the engine with the RS 232 protocol, which is quite old. Some components, such as an EGPWS or a GPS, will use a PCMCIA bus to get data in and out, which is just as old.

THE BIOS

The instructions that turn a computer into a useful machine come in three stages, starting with application programs, which are loaded by an operating system, which in turn is loaded by a bootstrap loader in the BIOS (the

Basic Input/Output System). There may be several BIOSes, a good example being the one on the video card that controls the interface between it and the computer. However, more important to the machine as a whole is the *System BIOS* which is a collection of assembly language routines that allow programs and the components of a computer to communicate with each other at the hardware level. It therefore works in two directions at once and is active all the time your computer is switched on. In this way, software doesn't have to talk to a device directly, but can call a BIOS routine instead.

Software

The term *software* refers to programming instructions that make the hardware work together. There are two types:

OPERATING SYSTEMS

A computer is only a machine, so it needs instructions to run itself. For example, it can only put letters on the screen after you press a key if it's told to. However, it's a waste of time including those instructions in every application program, which is why computers have operating systems. These are *collections* of programs that perform standard housekeeping tasks, such as translating keypushes into screen displays, changing colours on the screen, or simply moving data from one part of the computer to another. Other (application) software is then written up to the operating system level, without worrying about what sort of hardware it's dealing with. This saves programmers producing the same code that everyone uses over and over again.

Every computer has an operating system, and they ultimately all do the same job. Some are more user-friendly, though (on the Macintosh), and some are downright user-hostile (like Unix). That used on IBM-compatibles is commonly called Windows, and mostly lies somewhere in between.

A multitasking operating system switches rapidly between several running tasks.

APPLICATIONS

This is software that turns the computer into something useful, such as wordprocessors, or spreadsheets, or in the case of aviation, that runs the FADEC, or even the complete aircraft (there can be 150 computers in the average jet transport). It is so important these days, that checking the software version is part of the checklist.

Firmware

This is a cross between hardware and software, when programs are contained within Read Only Memory, or a chip, as opposed to being kept on a hard drive, so such software loads quicker and cannot be erased.

Electronic Systems

"Normal" electronic equipment consists of components such as capacitors, resistors, transistors, etc., which can be assembled into just a few basic circuits, like amplifiers. Electronic *systems* are composed of such circuits, which are used as building blocks, so you can deal with larger systems in concept form rather than getting involved with detail, especially since the introduction of integrated circuits, where the distinction between circuits and systems is much less clear cut. Now, you only need to know what a "black box" does, rather than how it works.

Two main types of circuits are used - linear (analogue) or digital. Linear circuits handle signals that change smoothly over a range of values. That is, the output will be an exact copy of the input, but larger, so there is a linear connection between them - doubling the input would double the output, for example.

An analogue signal is *analogous* to whatever it represents, and relatively smooth; the voltage over a telephone line, for instance, rises and falls in sympathy with the loudness of your voice - the fluctuating size of the signal is what's actually measured. Compare this with a digital signal, which is jerky, and like tapping on a pipe to get a message through rather than using the flow of material through it (the word *analogue*, is often taken to mean *non-digital*).

Digital electronics involves electronic manipulation of, or by, numbers, to obtain economy, reliability and speed. For convenience, only two numbers are used, and a state of On or Off is called a *Binary Digit*, or *Bit* for short.

ANALOGUE VS DIGITAL

The digital on-off signals that a computer generates as bits arise from switches (that is, transistors) making and breaking contact several million times a second, forming electrical pulses in the shape of square waves, with a very sharp rise as the connection is made, a plateau as the switch is held on and a sharp fall as the contact breaks. An *On* condition is recognised once the pulse reaches a certain threshold, and Off when it drops below. As further protection against spurious signals, the computer will only react to signals of a certain duration.

Digital systems are *discrete state* systems, in which only a fixed number of states are allowed, in our case, two.

Imagine the difference by comparing a normal light switch with a dimmer. You might get more choice with analogue, but it is more expensive to create and maintain.

An analogue system is therefore a *continuous state* or *continuously variable* system, which is able to cope with any value within certain limits. With all the variables involved, the accuracy of transmission can be as low as 0.1%. Digital signals can get quite distorted before you lose the ability to detect what they mean, since you are only dealing with the presence or absence of a signal rather than its value.

An *Analogue-Digital converter* (or *Digital-Analogue*) is simply a device that converts between digital and analogue signals, since there may be occasions when you want to take advantage of the benefits of either system.

NUMBERS

The decimal system is useless for counting numbers in this case, since you need to be able to discriminate between 10 levels of voltage. For example, say you had the answer to Life, The Universe and Everything*, which is 42. To calculate it, you must multiply 6 by 7, so you start with 7 volts. Now you have to feed it into an amplifier with a gain of 6 to get 42 volts. Easy enough, but if you start multiplying by thousands, you will soon have problems!

*from *The Hitchhiker's Guide To The Galaxy*.

Using only 2 numbers is a lot better, hence the use of the binary system, mentioned below. Now, all you need to do is find out whether a voltage exists or not, rather than how large it is, and use more wires for the bigger numbers, or put them in memory and use them in a sequence. A bit is represented on paper by a 1 for On or 0 for Off (the same as on power switches for electrical appliances). To place one character on the screen takes eight bits (a byte), so when a machine is spoken of as being eight- or sixteen-bit, it's effectively dealing with one or two letters of the alphabet at the same time - a 32-bit computer can therefore cope with 4 characters in one go. 2 bytes are called a *word*, 4 bytes (32-bits) are a *double word* and 16 bytes are a *paragraph*. 4 bits are a *nybble*.

Because it uses multiples of 8, a computer will also count to a base of 16, or hexadecimal, which uses letters as well as numbers, and the order is 0 1 2 3 4 5 6 7 8 9 A B C D E F, as numbers run out after 9. However, older systems, including transponders, use an octal system, from 0-7.

BINARY MATHEMATICS

With the decimal system, the numbers run from 0 to 9, and when you go past 9 you return to zero but place a 1 to the left of it (a *carry*, in the next column) to indicate that you have gone through the sequence once. Once you go past 19, the 1 is changed to 2, for twice round, and so on.

With binary, you do the same, by starting with 0, progressing to 1, then returning to 0 but with a 1 to the left of it. However, this is not ten, but rather one-zero, meaning 2 in the decimal system. 11 (one-one) is 3, and so on. You naturally end up with long sequences, but computers can handle this with ease.

As a bit has only two possible values, 0 or 1, there are only four possible combinations of inputs, which are:

```
0 + 0 = 0
0 + 1 = 1
1 + 0 = 1
1 + 1 = 10
```

CAPT

The fourth line shows that you need to account for two output bits when two input bits are added: the sum and a possible carry. Put another way, if you need a quantity larger than 1, the symbols will just repeat themselves. As with decimals, the least significant digit is on the right.

The first figure represents 2^0, which actually means 1, and the second (from the right) is 2^1, the third 2^2, and so on:

Digit	5th	4th	3rd	2nd	1st
Power	2^4	2^3	2^2	2^1	2^0
Decimal	16	8	4	2	1

The binary system doubles every time, so a binary number of 11001 really means $1 + 0 + 0 + 8 + 16$, which equals 25 (all you do is add the powers).

To convert decimal to binary, divide each successive number by 2 and take note of the remainders.

SEMICONDUCTORS REVISITED

The main reason as to whether a substance is an insulator, a conductor or a semiconductor is the spacing of its energy bands. With semiconductors, the size of the gap between the top of the highest full energy band (the *valence* band) and the bottom of the next empty one (the *conduction* band) is quite small, so some electrons, given some heat energy, can jump more easily to the conduction band (with metals, resistance increases with temperature, but it *decreases* with semiconductors because the number of charge carriers increases). Electricity can flow one way and not another (i.e. resistance is higher in one direction), depending on how you apply the current. The most common semiconductor material is either germanium (Ge) or silicon (Si), whose atoms will link up to share their valence electrons. In those materials, each atom shares one electron with another in a *covalent bond* which is so strong that it takes a lot of energy to break. As all the outer electrons form covalent bonds, and cannot move, the resulting crystal is a good insulator. However, you can add an impurity by doping the main material with another that may have more or less electrons in its outer shell, which degrades it and adds electrons or holes. For example, as silicon has four valence electrons, you can add phosphorous (which has 5) to create N-type material (N=negative). Adding Boron, with 3 valence electrons, makes a P-type (positive).

THE DIODE

The "orbit" of an electron is not the same as any other at the same level, because it might not have the same energy. This means that an energy shell will not necessarily be a precise line, but a slightly fuzzy band consisting of several orbiting electrons. The fuzziness is increased because you only know the position of any electron within a certain probability range. The degree of fuzziness depends on the temperature - normally, absolute zero is used.

Another name for a shell would therefore be an energy band, so the outside one is the valence band, which is the only one that may not be completely full. The gap between bands is called the *forbidden gap*. When an electron jumps, it leaves a hole in the valence band. Although holes can give the illusion of movement, this happens only in the valence band. Electrons move in the conduction band, which is an empty band beyond the valence band, where electrons that manage to escape are assumed to go. In an insulator, there is no forbidden gap between them. In a conductor, there is quite a large one* (in electronic terms). Any increase in energy will move an electron into the gap, where it can't exist, so it hops back into the valence band. In a conductor, the electron can hop easily to the conduction band where it is free to roam.

*In germanium, the gap between the valence and conduction bands is quite small, so you only need a little heat to close it enough to allow an electron to jump over. As it is nearly a semiconductor in its own right, it is known as an *intrinsic semiconductor*.

An *extrinsic semiconductor* is a substance like silicon that is doped with phosphorous or boron to produce a material that has one more electron or one more hole, respectively. These would be known as *n-type* or *p-type*. N and P refer to the type of chemical used to dope pure silicon.

The surface where one type changes to the other is a *junction*, and it is the key to modern solid-state electronics.

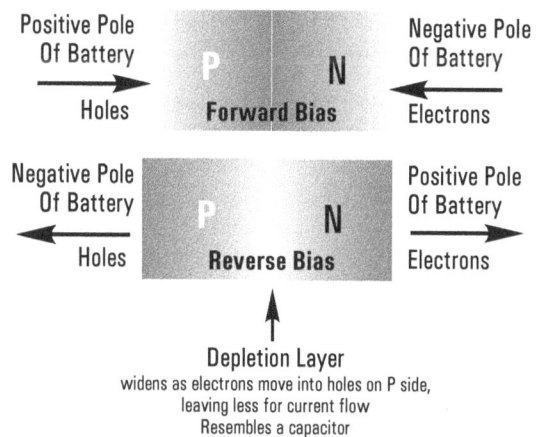

Depletion Layer
widens as electrons move into holes on P side,
leaving less for current flow
Resembles a capacitor

In the top picture above, of a junction diode, holes and electrons are repelled from the battery and interact as normal, allowing electrons to pass to the positive side of the battery and holes to pass to the negative side, so the *n* side loses energy and the *p* side gains it. There are no holes or free electrons in the junction because they diffuse into each other (and cancel each other out) at the atomic level over the junction (the depletion region). Essentially, when electrons hit the junction, they become valence electrons, so they can move through the holes in the P type material.

The electrons and holes are forced away from the power supply *toward* the junction, and the depletion region is compressed until it disappears. The barrier is broken and current can flow through the device. This is known as being *forward biased*, and the *forward voltage drop* is almost constant (0.7v for silicon, 0.3v for germanium), regardless of the current, assuming normal temperatures. Resistance is low in the forward direction.

In the lower example, a positive voltage is applied to the n-type material and electrons start filling the p-type material. Holes and electrons are pulled *away* from the junction, so the depletion region expands to take up the entire structure, which allows very little current flow (the *reverse leakage current*). This is *reverse biasing*, where the junction behaves like a capacitor. If the voltage gets too much, a reverse breakdown occurs, which fries the diode. You now have the electrical equivalent of a non-return valve.

Types of diode include:

- **Signal diodes** which pass small currents of 100mA or less. They are used with relays to protect transistors and integrated circuits from the brief high voltage produced when the relay coil is switched off. The diode is connected "backwards" so that it normally does not conduct. Conduction only occurs when the relay coil is switched off, where the current tries to continue flowing through the coil and it is diverted through the diode. Without it, no current could flow and the coil would produce a damaging high voltage spike in its attempt to keep the current flowing

- **Rectifier diodes** which can pass large currents. They are used in power supplies to convert AC to DC, and used where a large current must pass through. Rectifier diodes are made from silicon and have a forward voltage drop of 0.7V.

There are also LEDs and Zener diodes.

THE ZENER DIODE

Diodes have been used as rectifiers for a long time to produce pulsating DC from relatively large alternating currents, but the maximum safe reverse voltage is low.

A Zener Diode allows current to flow in the reverse direction if the voltage is larger than a *breakdown voltage*. As the voltage dropped is known and fixed, the Zener diode can maintain an output voltage within a fraction of a volt, while the input voltage can vary over a range of several, so it is typically used to maintain a fixed voltage, if there is a resistor to limit the current. If the output voltage rises due to a reduction in load current, the Zener takes current from the supply to keep the output constant. It is therefore useful for *voltage stabilisation*.

Below is an example of a lighting circuit:

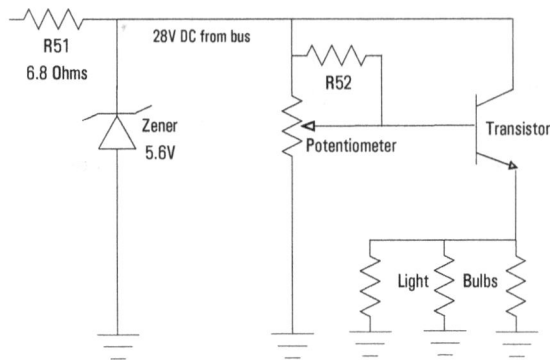

It is a simplified version of that used in the Bell 206. Between them, the Zener Diode, transistor and resistor R51 regulate the amount of voltage to the instrument lights. R51 protects the circuit from excess current in conjunction with the Zener Diode, which is set to pass current when the voltage across it exceeds 5.6 volts.

Using Ohm's Law, when the current through R51 exceeds around 3.3 amps, its rating of 6.8 ohms means that the voltage drop across it will be about 22.4 volts. If you subtract that from the 28v on the bus, you are left with the 5.6 volts setting of the Zener Diode, which therefore acts like a pressure relief valve - any current more than 3.3 amps is fed to Earth through it.

As the potentiometer is rotated (on the overhead console), the voltage applied to the base of the transistor varies, and so does the voltage applied to the light bulbs.

Zener diodes are always reverse biased.

THE TRANSISTOR

The transistor is essentially two diodes back-to-back, one forward biased and the other reverse biased. Transistor action is the turning on (and controlling) of a large current through the high resistance (reverse biased) collector-base junction by a small current through the low resistance (forward biased) base-emitter junction. This is how the name arises, as *transistor* is a contraction of *transfer-resistor*, as in transferring resistance. Essentially, the emitter injects charge carriers at one end and the collector absorbs them at the other. The base controls how fast they go.

Thus, you can have more electrons (or holes) flow one way or the other for a given input, depending on the transistor's construction, either P-N-P or N-P-N. On the right is the symbol for an NPN bipolar transistor, which is the easiest one to understand because it works just like the triode valve - the base is equivalent to the grid, the emitter is the cathode and the collector is the anode. The arrow

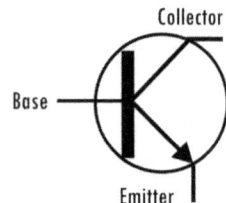

indicates conventional current flow, which is opposite to the electron flow. As the *n* material is more heavily doped* than the *p* material, it has more free electrons.

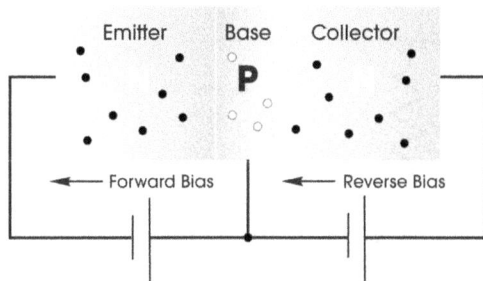

*The Collector is moderately doped, the Emitter is heavily doped and the Base is significantly less doped, so there are relatively few free holes in the picture above of an NPN transistor. When the base is made positive with respect to the emitter (i.e it gains more holes), current will flow in the base. If the collector is more positive, some of it is attracted into the collector-emitter circuit, so there is a gain in current due to the difference in resistance between the input and output (low when forward biased, high the other way). As power derives from the square of the current multiplied by the resistance, the current varies only slightly, but there is a large transfer of power.

In other words, as a weak signal (perhaps a voice wave) increases or decreases the emitter-base voltage, the emitter-collector voltage varies in sympathy, and the transistor can be thought of as a controlling device, especially when the forward biasing of the base current is done with a variable resistor, such as a volume control or a dimmer switch, as we have seen already.

So, a small amount of voltage from the base can regulate a large amount across the emitter-collector, in the order of 20 - 1 000, depending on the device. This is why transistors are used for either switching or amplification.

Whereas the NPN depends on the movement of electrons, the PNP depends on the movement of positively charged holes, so the polarities of the applied voltages must be reversed to get the same effects. The base will therefore be made negative with respect to the emitter, and the collector made negative with respect to the base and emitter.

TRANSDUCERS

Transducers (as used in Air Data Computers) change energy from one form to another so that electronic components can communicate with the outside world. Examples include microphones, LEDs, speakers, CRTs.

THE THYRISTOR

This is a semiconductor that is mainly used for rectification and switching, particularly as a relay with no moving parts. It has four layers to the transistor's three

(NPNP or PNPN), but the third layer is always the controlling one. It is known as the *gate*.

When reverse biased, it behaves like a normal diode and allows no current through. When forward biased, the current does not flow until the bias voltage reaches a *breakover value*. The voltage at which breakover occurs is varied by changing the size of the current at the gate, otherwise known as *firing*.

A thyristor could be used for detecting momentary over-temperatures when starting a jet engine, because once current flow is initiated, it will continue until the forward bias voltage is reduced to a very low value. Instead of coming on momentarily, and risking not being seen, now the overtemperature light will stay on until it is reset.

LOGIC GATES

Two-state components are often called *logic elements*, which ultimately form complete *logic systems* or *circuits*. When the voltage to be detected is above a certain level, it is called a **Logic 1**, and when below, a **Logic 0** (this could also be *High* or *Low* or *True* or *False*). A logic gate could be seen as a simple two-position switch.

For mathematical operations with only two states to work with (i.e. yes or no), you need elements which have two binary inputs and one binary output - the three from which all binary logic may be constructed are the AND, OR, and NOT gates, which combine logical input signals in various ways to produce the desired outputs, and which may be found in various chips all over a computer (there are also three combinations, discussed below):

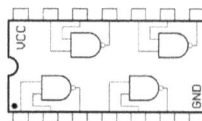

All arise from the requirements of *Boolean logic*, originally developed by George Boole in 1854 in an effort to express complex ideas in a simple fashion. With Boolean mathematics, there is no such thing as subtraction, because that implies negative numbers (since division is compounded subtraction, that is not allowed either). However, multiplication is valid, and is the same as in real algebra: anything multiplied by 0 is 0, and anything multiplied by 1 remains unchanged.

The reason you need logic gates can be shown by an example. To a computer, it is not enough to say that if you operate the On switch of a radio, it will come on. It needs more information, because it is intrinsically stupid and needs to be told precisely what to do. For example, you or I would know what to do if instructed to leave a room, but a computer would need to be told:

- Stand up

- Walk forward two paces

- Stop

- Put out hand

- Grasp door handle

- Turn door handle

- Pull door

- Check to see if door hits foot

- If yes, move foot

- If not, pull door further open

You get the picture.

In the above case, *if* the On switch is operated, *and* the radio is serviceable, *and* there is power, it will turn on.

Now, after Boole, you can say:

```
Radio Call = Switch x Radio x Power
```

or, to be pedantic:

```
Radio Call = Switch.Radio.Power
```

Programmers, incidentally, have to anticipate every stupid thing that a computer (or user) might do, and create error messages for each one. Note that, in logic terms, the period (.) means + and the + sign means OR. Go figure.

Boolean algebra has three main logical operations: NOT, AND and OR, which were extended later in time:

THE AND GATE

With an AND gate, the inputs must all have logic 1 signals applied to them for the output to be a logic 1 (i.e. *True*, as opposed to *False*). If any of the inputs are logic 0 (*False*), the output will be logic 0 as well, so it acts as if all its switches were in series. Most AND gates have 2, 3 or 4 inputs, but you can actually have as many as you want - on an EGPWS, for example, you may need to test for many conditions. AND gates are certainly used in fire detection systems, where two systems in parallel must trigger for the fire to be reported, in case of false alarms. In other words, the switch must be on *and* the fuse must be unbroken for our radio to work.

This might also be useful with an autopilot, for example, which will not engage unless a certain series of conditions is met.

Also, if one input is held open, a stream of pulses could pass through the other inputs.

If you incorporate a potential divider, you can create an alarm circuit - as we used a thermistor previously, a suitable one could warn you when part of the aircraft (say a cargo hold) is getting too cold.

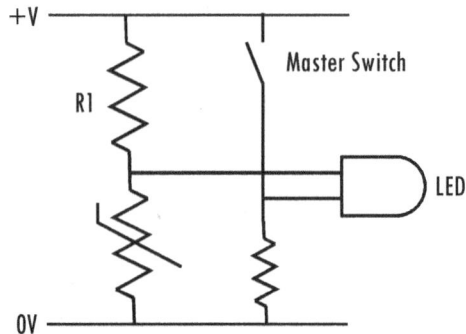

The signal from the divider to the logic gate will be high when the temperature is low, and the Master Switch will provide the other high signal required by the AND gate to issue a logic 1 to the warning LED.

Because an AND gate can only produce an output when all the inputs are at logic 1 (i.e. at the same time), it could also be known as an "all or nothing" gate.

Note: the symbols used in this book (and by the examiners) are older ones rather than the "correct" ones used by the IEC:

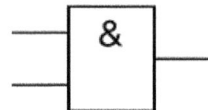

THE OR GATE

This allows the output to be true (1) if any one (or more) of its inputs are true (if the switch is off *or* the fuse is broken, the radio will not work). Put another way, the output is always 1, unless both inputs are 0. It may also be referred to as an "any or all" gate, as if its switches were in parallel.

This could be used with two baggage doors - if one is not secure it can activate a warning light.

THE NOT GATE

Otherwise known as an *Inverter*, the NOT gate has one input and one output. Whatever state is applied to the input, the opposite will appear at the output, or a signal can be produced without an input, and *vice versa*. Instead the equivalent of a relay might be energised by the 1 (On) signal to pull the other switch in the opposite direction. For a better explanation of why you might want to invert a signal, see *NAND Gate*, below.

When the small circle is on the input, it means that the signal must be low (0) for it to be an activating signal - this would be useful, for example, if you wanted to detect a current on the line that would represent a fault - a logic 0 would mean no faults. A NOT gate can be used in a generator circuit breaker control to ensure that output from the generator cannot be connected to a bus if the aircraft is receiving ground power.

THE NAND GATE

The NAND function is an AND followed by a NOT, so the result is the opposite of what comes out of an AND gate. It is called a NAND because the Boolean convention is to state the NOT first, or NOT-AND contracted to NAND.

Both inputs must have 1 signals for the output to be 0, and *vice versa* - with either input at 0, the output will be logic 1. In other words, two switches in series operate a relay to reverse the output. Essentially, with a NAND gate, the output is always 1, except when both inputs are 1.

The NAND gate is quite useful, because you can use it as a basis for making any other gate, even though it could be the long way round (in practice, the various gates can be made in easier ways). For example, with both inputs from the same source, the NAND gate becomes an inverter, or a NOT gate. Two of those feeding into another NAND gate creates an OR gate. Connecting another inverter to the output of the NAND gate creates an AND gate. This way, you could make an entire processor out of NAND gates, which themselves can be built out of two transistors and three resistors.

Below is an example of using one. You have a drinks machine, dispensing tea or coffee, both of which require money, so when you insert a coin and press either button, you will get your choice. The trouble is, you can press both buttons and get tea and coffee!

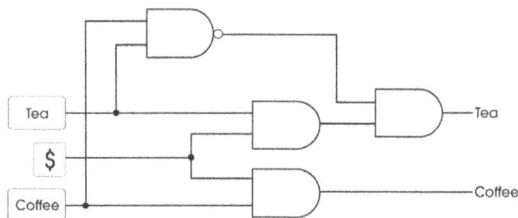

Now look at the NAND gate at the top, whose outputs are always on unless both buttons are pressed, in which case the tea choice is suppressed and you only get coffee. You can repeat it on the other side to suppress the tea.

Note: Logic gates are hard-wired, meaning that, if you want to change a function you have to add or remove or otherwise modify a component. You can change the function of a microprocessor, on the other hand, simply by changing its software.

THE NOR GATE

This is an OR followed by a NOT, or an OR with an inverted output. It forces the output to 0 when an input is true. Two switches in parallel operate the relay.

THE XOR GATE

This produces a Logic 1 signal if only one input is 1, but not both.

However, it is not in the Learning Objectives.

TRUTH TABLES

A truth table expresses all possible combinations of the inputs and outputs of a logic gate in terms of binary digits (i.e. 0 and 1). This is a truth table for an AND gate:

A (2^1)	B (2^0)	C
0	0	0
0	1	0
1	0	0
1	1	1

The number of inputs is represented by 2^n, where *n* is the number of inputs, so the table above has 2 input columns for the basic gate on the left. 2^2 equals 4, which is why there are 4 rows (you always work from right to left).

DATA COMMUNICATIONS

Every part of a computer communicates - the keyboard talks to the Central Processor, which in turn talks to the screen and other components inside, and the computer as a whole might talk to a printer or even another computer.

The whole subject of communications between computers is covered by the *International Standards Organisation* (ISO) which, in 1977, laid down standards which eventually (in 1983) defined *Open* (as opposed to closed) *Systems Interconnection*, otherwise known as OSI, so that manufacturers would make sure that people could connect their systems to others easily.

It can be likened to a philosophy of communications, which ensures that interconnection is as easy as possible. It's based on the thinking that communications can be broken down into several layers, a bit like the chart that shows how each part of a company interacts with each other (see right). You know what happens - although The Boss can talk to an equal in another company, tasks are delegated internally to executives, who sub-delegate down the line until you're the one that ends up doing everything, passing the results on to the other company where your opposite number passes them back up their system in the same way (just imagine the steps needed for one Boss to send a letter to the other one - there are many changes in modes of transport all through the process, which need not concern the people sending and receiving the messages, but only those responsible for each stage):

The problems arise when the Bosses are of different nationalities and don't speak the same language, so translators convert from one to the other.

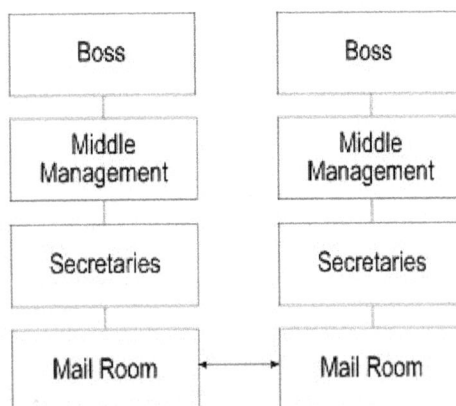

```
┌──────────────┐      ┌──────────────┐
│     Boss     │      │     Boss     │
└──────┬───────┘      └──────┬───────┘
┌──────┴───────┐      ┌──────┴───────┐
│    Middle    │      │    Middle    │
│  Management  │      │  Management  │
└──────┬───────┘      └──────┬───────┘
┌──────┴───────┐      ┌──────┴───────┐
│  Secretaries │      │  Secretaries │
└──────┬───────┘      └──────┬───────┘
┌──────┴───────┐      ┌──────┴───────┐
│   Mail Room  │◄────►│   Mail Room  │
└──────────────┘      └──────────────┘
```

Data communication is similar. At the top, the program in one computer talks to its equal in another (e.g. Boss to Boss). They agree on what they're going to send, how, when and at what speed. The data itself is passed down to the Mail Room through several levels, having been suitably prepared and converted at each stage, whereupon it's sent along the chosen channel to the next machine and the reverse procedure happens.

Actually, data undergoes a lot of conversion on its way around any system; the signals for the characters on your screen, for example, are made to go down one wire from eight, and may also be converted into sound for the telephone cable.

There are two types of signal traffic with computers:

- **low volume**, and interactive, where you might control another computer from your keyboard (maybe over the telephone system or a network)

- **high volume**, where you just transfer data from point to point, with no need for feedback

The former would tend to come and go in short bursts, and the latter, more predictably, in a continuous stream. Luckily, there are only 2 ways of sending either:

- eight bits at a time at a given signal, down eight or more wires at once (rather like a horse race), or

- one after the other down a single cable

The first is known as *parallel* communications and the second *serial*. Each has its own pros and cons, but the most common is serial, and used in FADECs and keyboards, so let's dispose of the other first.

Parallel

Parallel communications are used over very short distances; typically inside the computer itself (along buses) and to printers. The wires are very close together, and because the strength of any signal diminishes the further it goes down the line (due to the work it has to do to get past the resistance of the wire itself), there is a chance they could be interfered with when they become weak enough, giving the possibility of *crosstalk*, on top of normal attenuation, where signals from one wire are reflected in the next. This is why parallel communications are restricted to short distances unless boosters are used.

As you can send all the bits at once rather than one after the other, parallel communications are fast and accurate, because it's easy to identify which bit is which by knowing what wire it came in on, and when. Thus, because you're not carrying overheads for error checking, as with serial (below), it's possible to transfer data very efficiently, but only for short distances, as noise and signal deterioration increase rapidly with distance.

Serial

Serial transmission involves sending data bits one after the other, down one cable. This is not as standard a method as parallel, and is slower, but it is more flexible in terms of distance. It's quite possible to get away with just three wires - one to transmit, one to receive and another being a ground return path but, in practice, you need others for the same reasons as you need them for parallel; the computers have to talk to each other and co-ordinate their activities. Having said that, you very rarely need more than five, and eight at the most.

Of the various standards that were laid down to straighten things out, the best known one relating to serial communications is *Recommended Standard 232* revision C - you've probably already seen the term RS232C used somewhere. In Europe, another standard exists (V.24) which is actually based on RS232C, so to all intents and purposes they can be regarded as the same. The problem is that they were hashed out when equipment was relatively primitive, and were meant to allow you to use a computer with the telephone lines. In later years, serial transmission has been used for something it was never designed to do, such as drive a printer, run a FADEC, or pass messages between the various parts of an EGPWS. Earlier manufacturers also adapted unused pins for their own purposes, allowing many incompatibilities to creep in.

The RS232 and V.24 standards refer specifically to connections between modems and computers. In doing this, they describe two types of equipment which are a mirror image of each other, as far as wiring between them goes, anyway. The terminal (i.e. a computer or printer) is known as *Data Terminal Equipment* (DTE), as in a terminal off a minicomputer, for example, and almost everything else, like a modem, as *Data Circuit-terminating Equipment* (DCE). The DTE includes a UART (see below).

The difference is that DCE equipment terminates a line; it collects the information and passes it on to a DTE, which actually does something with it, such as put it on the screen, save it to disk or print it. In other words, a DCE will convert a DTE's signals into something suitable for whatever it wants to transmit over, and *vice versa*.

How you wire everything up depends on whether you're connecting DTE to DCE (computer to modem) or DTE to DTE (computer to computer, terminal or printer), and whether you use a male or female connector sometimes rests on the same premise (this also depends on the manufacturer of your equipment). However, if you connect a DTE to a DTE which is expecting to talk to a DCE, then there will be some confusion as transmission will try to go both ways down the same wire. Pin connections mentioned in the standards refer to DTE equipment and must be viewed from this standpoint.

Attaching anything other than a modem to an RS232 port therefore involves fooling both pieces of equipment into thinking there's a modem between them. Usually, this is done by rewiring the connection cable in such a way that it cancels the modem out, hence *null modem* (voltage from one pin may be redirected to another that is expecting such a voltage). One or two pins are therefore shorted out, but the voltage levels are such that no damage will be caused to equipment (or people) if something is cross-wired by mistake, or otherwise.

UART

The *Universal Asynchronous Receiver/Transmitter* is the device inside a computer that turns the internal parallel data stream into a serial one for transmission down one cable. It receives a character, generates an interrupt and stores it in a buffer till the next character comes, assuming the CPU is able to take it before then.

Unfortunately, the UART isn't the whole story, being only one element in the chain of components inside and outside your computer, including modems, software and overall speed of hardware.

Amplitude Shift Keying

The simplest way of representing binary information with tones is to have one volume equal to 1 and another equal to 0 but, as with AM radio, this is susceptible to noise and will only allow a rate of about 1200 signals per second over a cable.

Frequency Shift Keying

FSK is similar to ASK, except that the frequency of the signal is changed rather than the amplitude (e.g. volume), giving the same comparison as FM radio against AM. As there is less noise, the system is more robust and you can get up to 2400 signals per second. A distant cousin of this is used on cable modems.

Phase Shift Keying

PSK changes the position of a signal relative to another, so a change in phase of 180 degrees will signify a 1; no change represents a 0, producing twice the signalling rate of FSK. *Differential* PSK (as used with Microwave Landing Systems) allows 2 or more bits to be encoded per signal.

Multiplexing

This is simply the process of sending multiple signals down one channel, or even several channels down one cable, so a *multiplexer* is a concentrating device. This way, a large group of speech connections, say a hundred, can make do with something like 40 both-way circuits. Mind you, sending signals this way is a bit like driving along a congested highway - disastrous if you're not at the same speed and going the same way as the other traffic!

There are several ways of multiplexing, which vary according to whether the signals are analogue or digital.

FREQUENCY DIVISION MULTIPLEXING

Because electrical circuits (like radio) can be tuned to particular frequencies, you can send several signals along one medium without them interfering with each other. With several channels available, this is referred to as a *broadband system* (the bottom channel may be called the *baseband*). If nothing is transmitted, capacity is wasted.

When you're sending messages both ways at the same time, whatever bandwidth you have available needs to be split in half, so a *guard band* is inserted between two information-carrying frequencies to separate them and reduce the chances of overlap. They will carry no information, so will be easily identifiable. As guard bands take up space as well, the practical bandwidth for whatever channel you use is even more restricted. For example, cable TV channels have 6 KHz allocated to them, of which only 4.5 KHz is used. FDM is used for limited numbers of constantly used low bandwidth channels where cost is a factor (such as long-distance connections over the telephone, particularly with ADSL modems). It is cheaper than, but not as flexible as...

TIME DIVISION MULTIPLEXING

For multiplexing digital transmissions, bits of data are sent in succession and the time on the link is sliced in strict rotation, so that the data is interleaved in frames that occupy a strict portion of time; in other words, each chunk of data is given a time slot. A good analogy is a contraflow, where vehicles gather at the start, are forced into a single line of traffic, and spread out again at the end.

Although it sounds fraught with difficulty, TDM happens so quickly that it looks as if a constant stream of activity is occurring on each circuit. As there is no need for guard bands, the entire channel bandwidth is used for each bit. When nothing is sent, zeros are transmitted to maintain synchronisation.

Although TDM was designed for digital systems, it can be used for analogue signals with the help of *Pulse Code Modulation* (PCM), a system which converts the smooth analogue signals to digital by sampling them several thousand times a second (8000, actually).

Protocols

Having looked briefly at the signals and their carriers, we now need to establish some procedures. If you were telephoning somebody you didn't know very well, you might start by checking you've got the right number, then the right person, before saying what you need. You would also know that you're not supposed to talk to them until they've finished talking to you.

In computer terms, you would be establishing a *protocol*, or specific rules to follow when communicating (red tape, if you like). Each protocol consists of a *character set* (or *alphabet*, as used in a language) and specifies the order and priorities of the way information is exchanged using it. Protocols may also have ways of detecting and correcting errors. In other words, protocols sort out message and error handling, and status checking - even TTY (Teletype) had a protocol. Only devices using the same protocol can communicate directly with each other. Protocol of some sort is needed for all types of communication.

Transmission Schemes

The movement of information between computers is similar to sending trains round a railway system. The computers (and any equipment attached to them) are the stations, and the links (cables) between them are the tracks. The information itself behaves like the carriages, but we'll leave the engines and guards' vans alone for a moment.

The ITU-T defines:

- **Simplex** as where two way transmission is possible, but only in one direction at a time (for you railway buffs, that's "one engine in steam", with only one line available and a single engine moving the carriages either way-one engine can't go both ways at once, so control is effectively handed over to the other direction at the end of each transmission). This is like using the radio where you press a switch to talk and say "over" when finished.

- **Half Duplex** as where simultaneous two-way transmission is possible (i.e. two lines for Duplex as described below are available), but the equipment only allows it in one direction at a time (like telex, which has the wires joined up, but can't use them), and

- **Duplex** as allowing full simultaneous two-way transmission with two channels, like a radio telephone, so you can send and receive at the same time all the time.

Everyone else in the computer industry, on the other hand (in line with North America), defines *Simplex* as allowing transmission in one direction only (which seems a bit pointless as communications should be two way to be effective), and *Half Duplex* (HDX) as where two-way transmission is possible but not at the same time, because only one path is available, like ITU-T Simplex (in fact, another name for it is *Two-Frequency Simplex*).

Full Duplex (FDX), though, is the same as ITU-T Duplex. Although, on the face of it, two links are being used for transmission, there may actually be four channels, two for the data and two for ground return. These could be either separate or multiplexed, and the reason for having this many is because the whole bandwidth was designed to be used in one direction only; as there were two wires in the first place, another two were used for the opposite direction. Four-wire circuits, as they are known, will tend to be restricted to lines not generally available to the public, that is, leased lines.

Where only one channel is being used for two way transmission, a special signal is required to hand over control to the other end so that transmission can go the other way. Again, just like a radio.

Synchronisation

For computers to start exchanging information, they have to know exactly when the first bit will arrive and when the last one has been sent.

The problem with teleprinters was synchronising several motors at each end of the line, all of which had varying amounts of slack in their linkages caused by wear and design problems, which is one of the technological reasons for sticking with the Baudot Code for so long, because the chances of error with only five bits per character were so much reduced.

ASYNCHRONOUS COMMUNICATIONS

As information couldn't be sent at a constant pace, it was sent at random intervals, with each side being able to stop the other if it couldn't keep up. The arrival of each character was acknowledged by the receiver sending a receipt message, so a new character could go any time the stop bits of the preceding one had been received.

To identify characters, extra bits are added to the basic 8; *start bits* at the front and *stop bits* at the back, so now we've got an engine and a guard's van. The stop bit is actually a positive low voltage (or *mark*) on the line which indicates an idle condition, and remains in force until the next character is ready, so as soon as the start bit is received (indicated by a high voltage condition lasting for one time unit), the receiver knows it has to get its act together and synchronise with the sender to receive the incoming character, which it does by starting its own clock. The use of a stop bit is not so much to signify the end of a character (although this is useful), but to provide as much contrast as possible between it and the start bit, so the start bit is actually recognised as one.

Although the transmission speeds of sender and receiver would be the same when a character is being sent (for obvious reasons), they couldn't be said to be in continuous synchronisation, hence the term *asynchronous communications*, which actually means "not synchronised". As they are actually locked in step when a character is being sent, a better description could possibly be "self-synchronised". Even better, "start-stop" communications, which it started off as, through start/stop terminals.

The complete pattern of bits formed by start, character, parity (see below) and stop bits is known as a *frame*. The number of stop bits actually started off as 2, to allow older equipment, such as teleprinters, to allow their mechanical parts to settle down. Telex terminals could get by with 1.5 stop bits, and computers only need 1. You've probably already guessed that the closer tolerances allowed by modern technology mean that the number of bits per character can be increased from 5 (for telex) to 8, which allows computers to transmit 8-bit codes comfortably.

The main problem with adding start and stop bits is that fewer characters are actually sent in a given amount of time or, in other words, it takes longer to send your message. This isn't so important when you're at your terminal scratching your head and thinking what to say, but it could make you impatient when you want to get on with sending large volumes of previously prepared data and the telephone company is clocking up the units.

SYNCHRONOUS COMMUNICATIONS

Synchronous communications are specially geared to fast and high rates of data transfer, because they are strictly coordinated, with the computers being locked in step from the start of the transmission stream. Data is sent in blocks, between easily identifiable control characters, with checking and acknowledgement. No start or stop bits are required, although others are added for counting purposes, so it's still important to distinguish between bits, characters and complete messages. This is done by simply counting the expected bits and ticking them off as they come in. As it's difficult to distinguish between individual bits unless the clock signal is available at both ends of the system, it's sent with the data.

The advantages of synchronous transmission over asynchronous are *speed* (anywhere between 20-30% quicker) and *better detection of errors* with more effective methods (see parity, later).

Signal Distortion

Signals can be affected by *attenuation* and *crosstalk*, but there are other nasties about:

NOISE

You've probably heard it already - the crackling on the telephone line that sounds like somebody's frying eggs on it. "Noise" in electrical terms means unwanted and unpredictable impulses, breaks in transmission or extra signals, which can be thought of as extra electricity on the line, so you can see that a 0 could be made to look like a 1 if the noise level is high enough, and *vice versa*. Technically, it's any low-voltage, low current, high frequency signal causing interference with normal transmissions.

Noise is measured in decibels relative to the signal associated with it, and the comparison of one to the other is known as the *Signal to Noise Ratio* (the *decibel* is named after Alexander Graham Bell). The scale of measurement is logarithmic, so a signal to noise ratio twice as good as another is actually only higher by 3 decibels.

Noise is always present in electrical circuits and there are many types. The Man-made stuff is easily detected and is more spontaneous; crossed lines, car ignition interference, fridges turning themselves on and off, etc. Other examples include static and the clicks and pops heard when tuning between radio stations. As such, it's only predictable within certain statistical limits.

There are two types you might encounter in computers:

- **EMI**, or *Electromagnetic Interference*, generated by lights, engines, industrial tools and radar.

- **RFI**, or *Radio Frequency Interference*, which comes from microwaves and other appliances.

Ways of preventing noise include grounding equipment properly, and careful placement of (shielded) cables.

DISTORTION

You can often hear a background hiss (or "rushing" noise) in between records on a radio, even when it's correctly tuned; this is noise being generated within the circuitry itself by all the collisions between the electrons as the signal moves. The most common is a low background noise called *white noise* (or *thermal noise*) which occurs whenever there is resistance to electrical movement. It's called white noise because it covers a wide range of frequencies at a constant level, like white light. Unfortunately, amplifying the signal also succeeds in amplifying the noise. If everything were perfect, the signal would travel at 186,000 miles per second but, practically, this reduces to about 14,000 miles per second on ordinary twisted pair cable or 100,000 miles per second where microwaves are used, because of resistance.

There is a delay between sending and receipt, which can be allowed for, as the speed of transmission is known, but the length of the delay also varies with the frequency of the signal, being greater with lower frequencies.

This is OK when you're only sending one signal, but sending two at different frequencies (with the content of each dependent on the other) could mean some corruption if they're out of phase with each other at the receiving end. These constant effects can be simply calculated in accordance with known formulae and allowed for as far as possible in the design stages. Instead of merely allowing for certain effects, though, it's possible to do something about some of them. For example, one way of dealing with delays between two signals (*phase shift*) is to introduce some sort of delay equalisation.

Error Detection

Fast transmission speeds aren't everything - your information is no good if it gets there quicker but is full of errors (assuming you typed everything correctly in the first place!) Early transmission methods had no error detection. They knew very well when each part of a message had gotten through, because of acknowledgements, but these told them nothing about whether what had arrived was what had been sent ("Lead us not into Thames Station...").

Part of the process of detecting errors is guessing what the signal should have been in the first place, which is done by adding other information to the basic message from which this can be deduced. Blocks of characters are statistically analysed as they are sent, and the results of that analysis are tacked on to the end of the message and sent to the receiver, where the analysis is carried out again and the results compared.

PARITY

In addition to start and stop bits, another can be used for error checking, which is called the *parity bit* (actually not often used these days, because it used to be the eighth bit when ASCII used seven).

With parity checking, also known as *Vertical Redundancy*, the 1-bits making up a character are totalled up and, depending on whether the result is odd or even, another bit is added to make it the opposite. So, if the symbol contains an odd number of 1s, *even parity* would require another 1-bit added to make the number even (and *odd parity* would need the reverse). For instance, the character A (code 10000001) has two 1-bits. Odd parity would require the parity bit to be a 1 to make the total of 1s an odd one. C (code 10000011) having three 1-bits would have the parity bit set to 0 as the total is already odd.

The *parity generating circuit* (which is usually a dedicated chip) in the sending unit counts the number of 1s and sets the parity bit as required. The receiving unit does the same and calculates what the parity bit should be. If the two match, then no error is assumed. This works well enough, but unfortunately doesn't pick up everything - more than one error probably wouldn't be noticed, as the numbers can sometimes add up the same way, and the software rarely corrects automatically.

Both sides have to know what sort of parity is being used. The usual options are *Even, Odd* or *None*, with *Mark* and *Space* as oddballs that you probably won't come across (Mark parity is always 1, and Space always 0, a hangover from RTTY). You should set parity to *None* if you can get away with it, so if the eighth bit is used for anything strange (such as a control bit) without anyone knowing, it's left well alone, particularly when sending program, or binary, files. The parity bit must be set this way for 8-bit ASCII transfer.

CHECKSUMS AND CRCS

Checksums and *Cyclic Redundancy Codes* are based on blocks of data rather than single characters, unlike parity checking. A checksum is simply a summation of the values of every byte within a block, divided by 256 and the remainder discarded. The number is sent with the data and recalculated at the other end. If it's the same, all should be well, but you could get the same checksum for a different set of bytes. It's about 60% reliable.

CRCs include 2 bytes at the end of a block which are otherwise redundant, hence the name; we've already seen Vertical Redundancy in the shape of the parity bit.

Longitudinal Redundancy is used in synchronous systems to check the length of the message; a *Block Check Character* does this.

These values are calculated by dividing the entire numeric binary value of the block by a constant figure (called a generator polynomial - no, I don't know what it means, either, but you get the general idea). The remainder of the division is transmitted at the end of the message and recalculated at the receiver. It's about 99% reliable.

CRCs can be used in conjunction with parity.

Fibreoptics

Light rays bend, or refract, when passing from one medium to another, caused by the slowing down of the rays at one edge of the beam at the crossover point, which is why anything under water appears to be displaced when viewed from outside. Because of this, light can reflect internally along a glass fibre and bounce along the inside (like stones skimming on the surface of the sea), giving the signals a longer effective range. Every optic fibre (which is about the size of a human hair) consists of three strands, each inside the other. The centre one (the *core*) is a special low loss grade of material that has a constant refractive index; that is, its ability to bounce light along its inside doesn't reduce along its length. The next one (the *cladding*) and the outer one (the *sheath*) each have progressively lower refractive indexes (or is it indices?) which stop the light straying from the centre. The core should be made of glass for best results, but plastic-based fibre networks are used in modern cars.

As transmissions are unaffected by electrical interference and don't weaken so quickly, fibreoptics are good for long distances, especially as the transmission speeds are those of light itself - systems can carry 10 billion bits/second as standard, with *dense wave division multiplexing* able to cope with up to 160 unrelated streams of data down the same cable, each identified with a unique colour or wavelength. That's easily enough for 100 million phone conversations or half a million full-motion video streams (or, put another way, all of Canada's voice and data transmissions down 4 strands of fibre). *Repeaters* are needed, not because of attenuation (or weakening), but because the signal tends to get less concentrated, and spreads out.

AFCS (HELICOPTER)

An AFCS consists of devices that can alter or improve the stability and handling of a helicopter, or allow manoeuvres to be flown automatically. It takes place at three levels, and a system may have all three:

- **Stability Augmentation** (SAS), using rate gyros to provide rate damping and **short term** attitude hold, as used in the Bell 212, moving control surfaces only. The aircraft does not return to its original, but a similar, attitude, offset from the original flight path, so the system supports hands on flying. A SCAS, which includes control augmentation, uses a signal that is a function of stick motion to cancel out the rate gyros, so that pilot input is not interpreted as a disturbance, and the controls do not become sluggish. As a SAS would not normally move the flight controls, this is easily accomplished.

- **Automatic Stabilisation** (ATT), which uses vertical gyros to provide **long term** attitude hold, although rate damping may also be included. The aircraft will return to its selected attitude. Changes in attitude are usually accomplished through a force trim switch on the cyclic, which sets the desired attitude manually.

- **Autopilot** - functions over and above basic stability augmentation, such as altitude and airspeed hold, automatic transition and hover, and course capture and tracking. In other words, moving flight controls and surfaces.

The basic role of an autopilot (or any automatic flight control system) is to *decrease pilot workload* with *attitude retention*. In addition, AFCS systems can:

- **Overcome stability and control deficiencies**. Static stability is provided by holding airspeed, attitude and heading and coordination in turns.

- **Improve handling** or ride qualities. Dynamic stability is controlled to prevent porpoising, rocking and fishtailing.

- **Perform manoeuvres** that are difficult, maybe because of the time involved, the lack of visual cues or the accuracy required (e.g. IFR procedures)*. Pilot workload is higher in a helicopter anyway, as constant corrections are needed to maintain attitude, airspeed, and heading, and minimise oscillations.

*SAS/SCAS was originally developed for IMC flight, to provide artificial stability so that the aircraft would not wander when the pilot's attention was distracted.

Such equipment can increase SAR capabilities by providing auto-hover, automatic transition from the cruise to the hover over a point, and *vice versa*. Early auto-hover systems used Doppler velocity sensors, and later ones use Inertial systems with GPS, normally including a 2-D hover velocity indicator for the pilots. Some SAR helicopters have radio altimeter height-hold as well as barometric altitude hold. The Sikorsky S-92 has an AHAD system with 4 ring laser gyros.

Note: At least *Altitude* and *Heading Hold* are required when IFR or at night on single-pilot operations.

An automatic pilot ensures piloting and guidance in horizontal and vertical planes, stabilising and monitoring movement of the aircraft **around the C of G**. Those that control attitudes in pitch, roll and yaw are *3-axis*. A *2-axis* autopilot controls pitch and roll, and a single-axis controls roll only (the wing leveller). A 4-axis system includes the collective. Some will even handle an engine failure. An *operational autopilot* allows you to perform complete tasks, like make an approach to a predetermined point. You should be able to maintain an altitude or heading, intercept and follow a radial* or localiser and keep to a climb or descent pattern, by controlling vertical speed.

*When following a radial, the results can be unsettling to passengers, as the system doesn't anticipate the needle's movement, but keeps going past and recorrecting. A better solution is to use the heading bug and chase the needles yourself. Near the VOR cone of confusion, the roll channel temporarily switches to heading mode.

Your flight can be broken down into several phases:

- Takeoff**
- Climb to cruise altitude (including the SID)
- Cruise (including step climbs and descents)
- Descent (including STAR)
- Approach**
- Landing**

**Extreme vigilance is required!

To cover those phases, an autopilot uses display devices, sensors, comparators, computers, amplifiers and servo-actuators, plus navigation equipment, flight instruments, the Air Data Computer, and the Flight Management System. All this is supplemented by equipment on the ground, such as the ILS, runway guidance, etc.

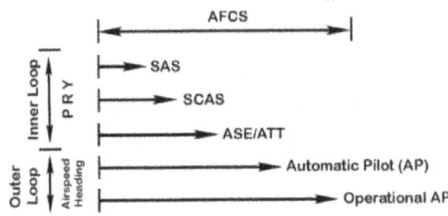

As you can see, the autopilot is just one part of a complete system. An AFCS includes the autopilot (which relates the aircraft to the outside world) and some sort of stabilisation system (see below), which operates *internally* to make the aircraft return to a previous attitude if it gets disturbed.

Typical components of an AFCS are:

- *Sensors.* Gyroscopes or accelerometers
- *Computers*
- *Output (actuators)*

CONTROL LOOPS

The **inner loop** of a system concerns itself with events internal to the aircraft, such as movement of controls, and their disturbances in pitch, roll and yaw,

so it is only concerned with stability. The loop may be closed or open according to whether the controls are moved or not.

In an **Inner Closed Loop**, there is limited authority and the controls are stopped from moving by artificial feel. If the controls are normally moved by actuators, it becomes an **Inner Open Loop**.

If external inputs are fed into the system (i.e. navigation, approach information, or airspeed and altitude), it has **Outer Loop** control. It could also be coupled to a Flight Director and become the basis for an autopilot.

ARTIFICIAL FEEL/TRIM

AFCS-equipped helicopters normally have irreversible flight controls (i.e. fully boosted), so the controls only move a selector valve as opposed to the full control. There is no feedback* unless you apply cyclic friction.

*Aside from needing a way to hold the controls in place, you typically follow up initial control inputs with secondary opposing ones so that attitude changes are made as smoothly and accurately as possible. The secondary responses are known as feedback.

An artificial feel can be built in to the cyclic and (sometimes) the yaw pedals (the collective normally only has friction). Feedback units are always installed in conjunction with, and not as part of, a system.

The artificial feel and zero force position are achieved with two opposing, pre-loaded, force gradient springs which ensure that, if the control is moved then released, it returns to the datum position. Gradient units have springs that are compressed and released as a control is moved.

© Phil Croucher, 2014

CAPT

Longitudinal cyclic force gradients are around 5-8 lbs. Lateral forces may be a bit less to allow for the relative strength of the arm in different directions.

With the AFCS engaged, if you press the trim release button to allow manual input (i.e. take over the controls), the spring units stop working so you can move the cyclic. Releasing the button reapplies the magnetic brake for a new zero force point.

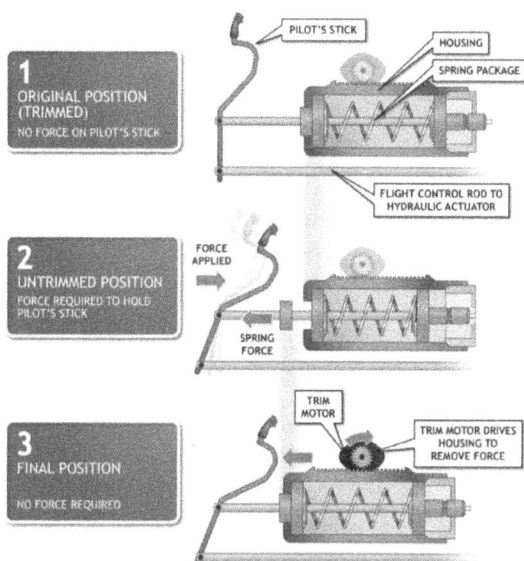

4-way beep trim switch

Coupler Disengage

Trim Release

Autopilot Disengage

A trim actuator works on the same principle as a force gradient unit, except that the cyclic is moved electrically, usually with a large 4-way beep trim on top. The actuator moves the control through the springs, then after it is released, the system works as above.

Note: Trimming is limited to a small percentage of control movement.

There are two types of trim system, which can be installed independently or together. In the first system, a magnetic brake (clutch) fixes the feel springs' anchor point to the structure of the helicopter. It contains a fluid that freezes when an electrical potential is applied to it. When the trim release button is pressed and the fluid is unfrozen, the brake is released, allowing the controls to reposition to a new zero force position. This is fixed when you release the button to re-apply the magnetic brake. In the second system an electric motor and screw jack adjusts the anchor point relatively slowly when the trim switch is used.

In addition, micro switches and/or strain gauges can sense when you are moving the controls to prevent excessive feedback opposing your input.

The system follows your movements in a synchronisation mode so there will be no snatch engagement when you re-establish the datum. The system must be working - if it isn't, you will not be able to engage the autopilot.

It should be possible to engage and disengage the AFCS at any time in flight and on the ground. On engagement, the system should come into operation smoothly, and complete disengagement should be possible quickly, safely and positively at any time, independently of all other primary services. Emergency disengagement facilities should normally be on the cyclic.

For systems that use the cyclic to hold altitude (i.e. the Puma), it should be impossible to engage the system below minimum power speed.

ACTUATORS

Actuators move the flying controls in response to signals from a computer. They may be in series or in parallel with the normal control runs. The choice of which to use is usually dictated by the complexity of the AFCS, the more involved ones using both types, either electro mechanical or electro hydraulic (as in the Puma/Super Puma - here, a small power input controls a larger output, proportional to the input, and is known as a servo mechanism.).

SERIES ACTUATOR

A series actuator is a **fast acting** linear mechanical device (usually based around a worm screw) in **series** with the control run. It gets longer and shorter as required, and moves the aerofoil surfaces for you.

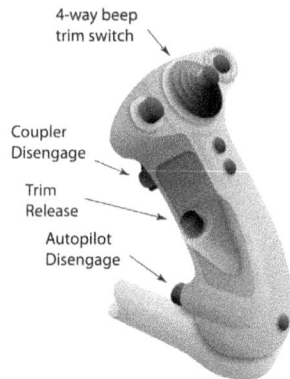

SIGNAL FROM COMPUTER TO MOTOR

MOTOR

FROM COCKPIT CONTROL

CONTROL STOPS

TO SWASHPLATE

WORM SCREW

POTENTIOMETER FOR ACTUATOR POSITION INDICATOR AND FEEDBACK TO COMPUTER

Put more technically, the actuator converts an electrical control into a displacement of its output shaft relative to its body. A neutral position is achieved when the free end of the output shaft is at mid-travel.

In a series actuator system, an attitude sensor feeds a signal to the computer, and the computer sends a demand to the actuator. The actuator, mechanically through the motor, or hydraulically, moves the control rods to the pitch change mechanism (i.e. the swash plate). The cockpit control is prevented from moving by the force gradient spring (if the force trim system is off, the actuator will

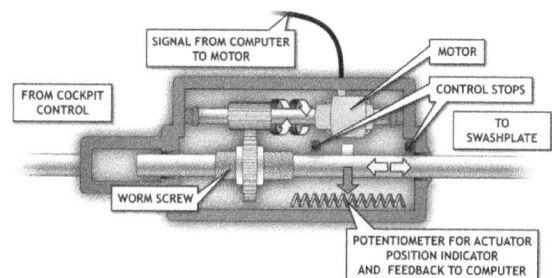

1 ORIGINAL POSITION (TRIMMED)
NO FORCE ON PILOT'S STICK

PILOT'S STICK

HOUSING

SPRING PACKAGE

FLIGHT CONTROL ROD TO HYDRAULIC ACTUATOR

2 UNTRIMMED POSITION
FORCE REQUIRED TO HOLD PILOT'S STICK

FORCE APPLIED

SPRING FORCE

3 FINAL POSITION
NO FORCE REQUIRED

TRIM MOTOR

TRIM MOTOR DRIVES HOUSING TO REMOVE FORCE

move the cockpit control and not the swash plate. For this reason the force trim must be on when using an AFCS).

The series actuator has **limited authority**, around 10-20%, according to the control and system. Thus, any failures (hardovers or attitude runaways) are not catastrophic - control is still available to the pilot.

A series actuator is be *saturated* when it goes to full travel in one direction. Thus, without any pilot input, the helicopter could go to extreme attitudes, but you can still fly with some degree of safety while re-centering the saturated actuator, or deselecting the problem channel.

In the cockpit, three small dials close together show you what the series actuators are doing (feedback from a parallel actuator is felt through the controls).

This is what they look like on the Agusta 109:

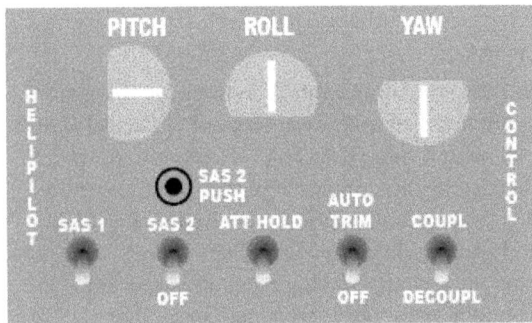

You centre the relevant API by pressing the trim release button on the cyclic and moving it in the direction shown by the API pointer.

 If you see an indication like this relating to yaw, just move the pedals to the right.

Having said all that, series actuators are not suitable for autopilots, because they need larger control movements. They are irreversible, and distorted only when electrical signals are applied to them, acting at **high speed** with **limited authority** (10% of the range of movement to protect against runaway). When the automatic pilot is not working, they have no effect and will not interfere with control movements.

PARALLEL ACTUATORS

Series actuators need constant attention to trim and re-position the controls. In a more complex system a parallel or trim actuator can provide a new datum if the series actuators get out of range. On the AS 355, they move the anchoring point of the cyclic to enhance the limited range of the series actuators. Parallel trim actuators act at **low speed*** with **high authority**, so they can *move the controls* (not just the surfaces) through their full range. They are used for *attitude retention* and *outer loop* functions, **and will provide feedback.**

An artificial feel system must be used and, to save weight, is often incorporated within the actuator.

*This so that errors and failures can be detected and corrected before hardovers or runaways can occur.

COMBINED SYSTEMS

A combination of series and parallel actuators can give good short term stabilization with long term attitude hold and autopilot capabilities.

STICK POSITION TRANSMITTER

This is a potentiometer that is used in systems where the computer needs to differentiate between auto stabilization and pilot required attitude changes.

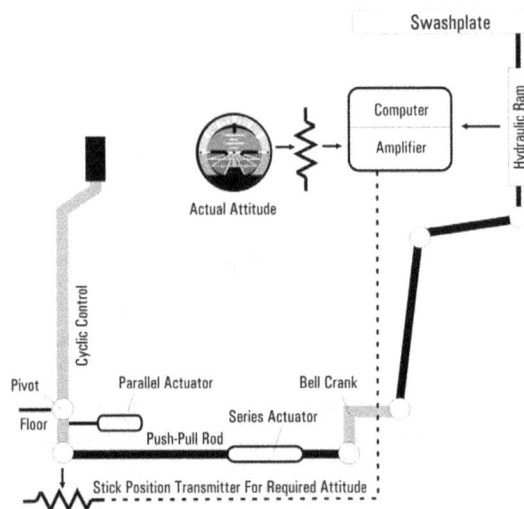

Its function is simply to tell the system where the cyclic control is.

RATE DAMPING

Everything starts here. This is the most basic type of system, which both stops things getting out of hand if a control is disturbed and makes control inputs more predictable. However, it will not help with attitude hold or augmentation during manoeuvres. For that you need.....

SAS

A *Stability Augmentation System* is used for short term control assistance, just to reduce the workload. As the name implies, it is there to help with stability* and make the helicopter easier to fly, especially with regard to wind gusts. It uses a force trim system with a magnetic clutch and springs to keep the controls in place when you let go of them for a short time.

*The primary method by which an AFCS affects static stability is through attitude hold, as rate damping is, by definition, a dynamic stability mode that generally uses series actuators. The fundamental requirement in terms of dynamic stability is to automatically suppress the nuisance modes of natural aircraft responses such as the long term

CAPT

(phugoid) or lateral/directional oscillation (Dutch roll). Autopilot modes usually operate through parallel actuators and move the cockpit controls so that the pilot can verify correct response (series actuators only move the control surfaces), preferably in conjunction with a flight director.

More advanced systems use servos to move the controls for you, with a combination of rate sensors and gyros that are quicker and more precise at detecting and correcting disturbances than humans are. They generate electrical impulses that control actuators that resist any movement of the controls from where they should be (including what the pilot does!) To stop things going out of control, there will be a *limiter*.

Any system will make for a smoother ride with a lot less twitchiness (particularly with the yaw axis). In other words, a helicopter that may be hard to control suddenly becomes nicer to handle. New pilots (especially with Robinson experience) to an aircraft fitted with SAS (Gazelle) will keep stirring the cyclic, not realising that the SAS computers are already keeping the aircraft steady. This drives them crazy! They know that the aircraft has moved without any control movement from them and react accordingly, which is an improvement on the simple rate damping mentioned above. It achieves this by providing corrective control inputs proportional to the rate of change of, and deviation from, a datum attitude.

The signals from the rate gyros can be sent to a computer and a *leaky integrator*, so called because it does not retain information for very long. The computer detects and stops the rate of control movement, and the integrator adds the information to that which it has been collecting over time, creating a notional fuselage attitude that is compared to the situation up to 30 seconds ago (this is how long the integrator remembers stuff). Then a second signal goes from the integrator to the computer to correct the attitude, so the rate of movement is controlled first, then the attitude is adjusted. Due to internal errors, the system will drift off and have to be reset with a control movement every so often. There may be a switch marked ATT (meaning attitude retention) on some systems to enable it. Minor or temporary adjustments are done by over-riding the force trim system once a new attitude is set (there is a button on the cyclic).

If you want to make a control movement, so that the system doesn't get confused, a sensor detects your inputs and cuts off the rate and attitude information signals to the integrator. Rate damping is still in progress, because the signal is still going to the computer, but there will be no attitude corrections (in fact, an attitude will only be maintained in trimmed flight, or when the controls are in a zero-force position). The influence of SAS is limited to about 10% of the control range available.

SCAS

A *Stability and Control Augmentation System* is what Bell or the US military (somewhat misguidedly) call the above. The control augmentation is there because, with a plain SAS, the controls may feel sluggish as movement of the controls by the pilot is interpreted as a disturbance, or any pilot changes are cancelled out shortly afterwards. Control movements are therefore fed directly to the actuator for a quicker initial response (on the Puma, stabilisation is disabled when the controls are moved).

The other mode used on Bell machines is ATT (Attitude), for long term attitude retention, like the ASE mentioned below. There is no rate input into the ATT system because it is handled by the SCAS computers, which must be working before ATT mode can be engaged.

In summary, SAS generates control inputs to resist rates of pitch, roll and yaw. ATT generates control inputs to maintain a particular pitch and roll attitude, so when you release the controls, they revert to the memorised datums.

ATTITUDE STABILISATION EQUIPMENT (ASE)

Aside from mechanical solutions, such as the Bell stabiliser bar, by the mid-1960s, there were two types of helicopter "autopilot", one being SAS, mentioned above, which used rate gyroscopes to return the attitude to a reference datum. Although these would drift long-term, you could at least take your hands off the controls to change a frequency without it flying drastically off course.

ASE is a progression from SAS that also detects attitude displacement, by integrating the rate gyro data or introducing a vertical gyro* per axis to the system, plus parallel actuators for long term attitude control. However, series actuators and SAS type circuits are still required to provide short term damping.

*The vertical gyro means that a stable, accurate attitude signal is available. It allows instrument flight in the cruise, but doesn't help at low speeds or in the hover.

Control mixing adds pedal movement to a collective input.

The logic of the system still needs to know when you want to change the heading, so you aren't fighting the AFCS whenever you try to fly yourself.

Attitude changes are sensed by rate gyroscopes* or accelerometers which produce an output signal proportional to the rate of change. A controller computes a corrective signal and sends it to a servo which moves the appropriate flight control and feeds back its position to the controller so the actual and required movements can be compared. As the original attitude is gradually restored, the gyroscope output and error signal are gradually removed. This is a *closed loop* system which needs feedback to work (in this case an *inner loop*, so a three-axis autopilot would have at least 3 inner loops).

The number of sensors depends on how many couple modes are in the system. Some systems have micro switches and strain gauges which sense pilot input to prevent excessive feedback forces from the system.

*Gyroscopes go unserviceable frequently, because many aircraft are moved before they have a chance to stop.

THE AUTOPILOT

Autopilots, being outer loop systems, *control* the aircraft in relation to the outside world. They have two basic modes, called *Lateral Mode* (HDA) and *Vertical Mode* (VS). A full *Autopilot and Flight Director System* (APFDS) may consist of the autopilot, auto throttle (fixed wing), yaw damper and Flight Director, described later. The *yaw damper*, which suppresses Dutch roll, controls the rudder, with the angular rate about the vertical axis as the input signal. The yaw damper indicator supplies the pilot with information about yaw damper action on the rudder. The signal for a given rate of oscillation is varied inversely with airspeed.

In a selected axis capture mode, it gives a bank attitude input proportional to the deviation between the selected heading and the current heading, but not exceeding a given value (in other words, governed to a rate of bank).

Autopilot outputs ultimately act on control servos, whose control inputs will be electronic, but the power required to do the job can be hydraulic (main controls) or electric (secondary systems, like trim). *Torque limiters* stop servos from operating control surfaces too rapidly or through too great a range. If the torque becomes excessive, a spring-loaded coupling and friction clutch will limit it.

SYSTEM PROTECTION

Fail-operational systems still function automatically after a failure, without any loss in performance. **Fail-passive** systems require manual intervention. After a failure they produce no significant out-of-trim condition or deviation of flight path or attitude.

The effects of AFCS failures come in 3 categories:

- **Soft Failures**. The system in question merely ceases to function without causing any intrinsic aircraft response. There may not be any noticeable effect in the short term.

- **Runaways**. An actuator is actively driven to an unwanted position. The extreme case is a full-scale, maximum-rate deflection known as a hardover. Runaways may occur in more than one axis at the same time.

- **Oscillatory Failures**. Oscillatory failures generally result from the failure of a component in a feedback loop and may be so severe that the pilot is only able to disengage the system using flight control-mounted devices.

To stop events such as a system runway, you can either limit an actuator's authority or the rate at which it travels.

- **Comparators** check if an attitude change is in the same sense as actuator movement, such as the nose pitching down when such a command has been given. If it is, the system is disconnected.

- **Rate Trigger**. If a rate of change exceeds a certain value (based on system runaway parameters), the system will be disconnected.

- **Multi-channel**. A *duplex system* has two lanes, each with a sensor, a computer, an actuator, and switching circuits. Outputs from the two actuators are averaged before any commands are passed to the control surfaces, so if one gets a runaway, it will be (in theory) counteracted by the other. If using comparator monitoring, this can produce *fail operational* capability. *Triplex* and *quadruplex* speak for themselves - the difference is that, if one system fails, it can be outvoted by the others and automatically disengaged. If the others have a problem, they will all disconnect and return the aircraft to the pilot in a safe, trimmed condition.

*Interlocks** stop the autopilot being used if it isn't ready, and cause it to disengage on failures. They are a series of switches and relays that ensure satisfactory engagement.

CONTROL LAWS

These are rules that the autopilot computer has to follow, determining how it interprets a performance demand against a control response, but they also determine the fundamental response of the aircraft and set safety limits for automatic flight (that is, the control law will protect the aircraft from overstress or overspeed). Put more simply, control laws allow a fly-by-wire system to position the flight controls for the most efficient response. They are electrical algorithms that figure out the proper electrical signals to be sent to the electrohydraulic actuators, so you tell the system what you want, and it figures out how best to do it.

The *Direct Control Law* represents the basic mechanical connection between input and output. In other words, the machine will obey your direct control inputs and behave the same way you would expect a normal aircraft to behave, rather than what it thinks you want.

USING AN AUTOPILOT

Typically, before takeoff, you would engage the Pitch, Roll and Yaw channels, plus the Flight Director so you can see what inputs are required (the full autopilot is not normally switched on for takeoff or landing, unless you have a suitable operational one, as used with SAR. At this stage you will actually be using the SCAS), which is available when the autopilot is on.

Engagement of an autopilot is not possible when:

- The electrical supply is faulty

- The turn control knob is not set to centre off

- There is a synchronisation fault

- There is a fault in the attitude reference unit

If you ever want to fly the machine yourself, you must use the *Disengage* button (usually on the cyclic) to release the system's grip of death on the controls, but most systems allow you to manoeuvre in pitch and roll without disengaging the autopilot, either with a panel like this one:

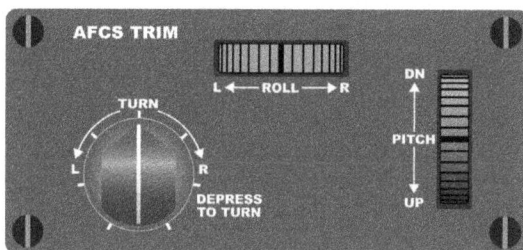

or by *control wheel steering*, which allows the controls to be moved without the autopilot dropping off line. The new attitude is held once the control wheel is released. *Touch control steering* uses a thumb switch on the control yoke, which disengages the autopilot while the controls are moved, and re-engages it once the switch is released.

The power switch for the autopilot may well be disguised as the Flight Director, with three selections:

- **OFF**, which speaks for itself

- **FDIR**. Flight Director. See *Instruments*.

- **AUTO**. The autopilot will fly the machine according to your selections below

Here is a list of some of the buttons available and their functions. Note that some will not be present on simpler autopilots, or they may be labelled differently!

- **WLV**. The Wing Leveller simply holds the wings level while you figure out what to do next. It's a handy button to punch in an overload situation and will hold the wings at the current level of bank, or level them for you if you engage it with less than a certain figure, typically 7°

- **HDG**. Heading Hold follows the heading bug on the HSI or DG. To turn, simply move the heading bug to the desired direction and the machine will follow. **Tip:** Ensure the heading bug is in place before engaging the HDG button, or the machine will seek the heading!

- **LOC**. The Localizer will fly an ILS localiser, which is more sensitive than a VOR radial, such as is used with the NAV button. Pushing this button just

arms the system - *your current HDG mode will remain in force until the localiser needle starts to move into the centre.* At that point, the LOC will go from ARMED to ACTIVE, and start flying for you, disengaging any previous modes

- **G/S**. Flies the glideslope portion of the ILS, in the same way as LOC handles the Localiser

- **ALT**. Holds the current or pre-selected altitude. If you hit this button, the system should maintain the altitude you are currently sitting at

- **V/S**. Holds a constant vertical speed. To climb or descend, push VS (*Vertical Speed*) and select the rate of climb or descent with a knob on the VSI. This will disable ALT, if selected. Once at the required altitude, reselect the ALT button to maintain

- **SPD**. Holds a pre-selected airspeed

- **FLCH**. Flight Level Change is commonly used to change altitude by allowing you to add or take away power while holding an airspeed. This is like SPD, but, if you have auto-throttle, FLCH will automatically add or take away power

- **PTCH**. Use Pitch-Sync to hold the nose at a constant pitch attitude, like the Wing-Leveller

- **VNAV**. Vertical Navigation flies altitudes from the FMS to follow route altitudes

- **BC**. The Back Course is a second *localiser* that works in the opposite sense to the proper ILS to fly along the extended centreline once you have missed the runway and have to carry out a Missed Approach. However, some airfields save money by making you use the Back Course as a proper ILS, although you won't have a glideslope. When coming back in the other way, everything is back to front. Pushing this button reverses the commands to make it look right. It does not work with an HSI

- **NAV** (or **VOR**). This keeps you coupled to a selected radial on the HSI, which must naturally be slaved to whatever navaid you are using. The problem is that it can chase the heading too much, and will overshoot and come back rather than make small adjustments to creep up on the selected heading. It is often more practical and comfortable for passengers to use HDG mode and move the heading bug yourself if time permits. In addition, you have better roll rates and maximum bank angles in HDG mode. In the cone of confusion, the last good heading is held until you get through it

In the picture below, the light behind the ALT button is illuminated, indicating that the height-keeping function has been selected. This and the HDG button are the most used functions. So much so, that these are usually the automatic selections when the thing is switched on in the first place, to maintain pitch and roll.

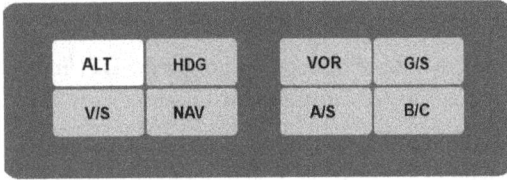

ALT	HDG		VOR	G/S
V/S	NAV		A/S	B/C

VS, FLCH and HDG all do stuff the moment they are engaged. Others, like ALT, G/S and LOC, on the other hand, sit there on standby (armed) until they intercept the altitude, glideslope or localiser required. That is, *they will not do anything until then*.

EXAMPLE
You set the machine up straight and level at 3,000 feet and push the ALT and HDG buttons. Now you can take your hands off and read the instructions, as the autopilot will maintain that level and whatever heading you set with the heading bug until you tell it otherwise. Now you want to climb to 6,000 feet, so you need to dial this figure into the altitude window (you would also set your cleared altitude before you take off).

How you want to get there determines what button you push next. You could hit the vertical speed (V/S) button, then select a rate of climb on the VSI until you get to the selected altitude.

FLCH or SPD, on the other hand, will pitch the nose up and maintain the currently indicated speed, leaving you to add power as needed. Again, this mode should disengage automatically when you get to the selected altitude.

ALTITUDE OR HEIGHT HOLDING
Altitude hold uses a barometric source. Height hold uses a radio altimeter.

Both systems can operate through the pitch channel on 3 axis systems (longitudinal cyclic) or through a collective pitch channel on 4 axis systems.

Note: The pitch channel is simpler, but can only operate down to the speed for minimum power (V_{MP}). Below that speed, if the helicopter loses altitude, raising the nose decreases the speed, to lose more altitude as there may not be an increase of power (some autopilots can cope with this). A minimum airspeed switch may therefore be incorporated or a there may be a warning placard in the cockpit and in the flight manual.

Airspeed is maintained by collective inputs. That is, more advanced systems, for helicopters that need height hold, especially at low speeds and in the hover, will operate through a collective channel.

In the hover, especially over water, the radio altimeter may try to follow the varying wave height. To avoid this there

may be some way of averaging the signal, or vertical accelerometers may be used to smooth the response.

AIRSPEED AND GROUNDSPEED HOLD
Airspeed control is provided by the pitch channel in forward flight. Groundspeed control, which is normally required at low IAS and in the hover, needs longitudinal and lateral cyclic inputs to correct for drift and attitude variations (tail rotor drift and roll). This leads to some out of balance flight conditions and cross controlling, especially when not directly into wind.

Acceleration signals are often incorporated. Also, because of poor information from the pitot static system at very low speeds, Doppler information can provide along and across track information and corrections.

HEADING HOLD
Below around 40 knots, the heading is normally controlled by the yaw pedals. Variations in power or wind velocity can have a marked effect on the heading.

A yaw channel in an AFCS will improve control in the hover, if only by damping the rate of yaw. Sensors in the yaw channel will normally include a flux detector, to sense magnetic heading, and rate or sometimes attitude gyros.

To sense the demand on the pedals, you can use:

- A micro switch on the pedals, which switches off the heading hold when you close the switch by placing your feet on the pedals. Your feet must be off the pedals when heading hold is engaged.

- A force or motion sensor which disconnects the heading hold when the pedals are moved.

- The force trim button, which disconnects the yaw channel, and the others.

In forward flight (above around 40 kts), the yaw channel operates in a similar way as it would on an aeroplane, to maintain slip indicator position. It will normally have a yaw rate sensor to compensate for the inherent side slip of the helicopter. Heading hold can also be incorporated in this speed range.

An airspeed sensor can disconnect the heading and yaw control when the airspeed falls below its set value. For a fully operational autopilot with approach to hover mode, instead of switching off, the airspeed sensor can change the control from high to low airspeed and hover control.

VERTICAL SPEED HOLD
On a 3 axis system, the ROC/ROD is controlled with the cyclic and airspeed is maintained with the collective. A 4 axis system uses the cyclic and collective channels in a more conventional sense. Transitioning from cruise to hover always need a 4-axis AFCS.

NAVIGATION COUPLING
VOR tracking is maintained through the cyclic (the roll channel) with a limit on the angle of bank of around 20°

CAPT

(depends on the type). The preferred intercept angle for radials is 30-60° and capture will occur at 5-10° (1-2 dots).

VOR/ILS Coupling

The VOR approach is the same as VOR tracking, but is optimized within 10 nm of the ground station. On the ILS, intercepts are set up automatically or manually and the system will capture the localiser then the glideslope.

AFCS (FIXED WING)

The basic role of an autopilot (or any automatic flight control system) is to *decrease pilot workload* with *attitude retention*. In addition, AFCS systems can:

- Overcome stability and control deficiencies

- Improve handling or ride qualities

- Perform manoeuvres that are difficult for pilots, maybe because of the length of time involved, the lack of visual cues or the accuracy required

An Automatic Flight Control System includes the autopilot (which relates the aircraft to the outside world).

In large aeroplanes, the autopilot is used for almost every manoeuvre except for taxying and takeoff, and landings if you don't have autoland. This is because the tolerances for navigation and aircraft separation are very tight, whether you're in a departure or arrival procedure or simply flying long distance in RVSM airspace. Probably the only time you will fly the machine completely in manual is on your initial interview!

An automatic pilot ensures piloting and guidance in the horizontal and vertical planes, stabilising and monitoring movement around the C of G. The inputs must be proportional to the rate and degree of any deviations, as you don't want them to get too large.

Those that control attitudes in pitch, roll and yaw are known as *3-axis*. A *2-axis* autopilot controls pitch and roll, and a single-axis controls roll only (the wing-leveller). Some will even handle an engine failure. An *operational autopilot* is one that allows you to perform complete tasks, like make an approach to a predetermined point.

Either way, you should be able to maintain an altitude or heading, intercept and follow a radial* and keep to a climb or descent pattern, by controlling vertical speed.

*When following a radial, the results can be unsettling to passengers, as the system doesn't anticipate the needle's movement, but keeps going past the radial and recorrecting. A better way is to use the heading bug and chase the needles yourself so you don't spill the coffee.

Near the VOR cone of confusion, the roll channel temporarily switches to heading mode.

Your flight can be broken down into several phases:

- Takeoff**

- Climb to cruise altitude (including the SID)

- Cruise (including step climbs and descents)

- Descent (including STAR)

- Approach**

- Landing**

**Extreme vigilance is required! The above are explained in excruciating detail later.

In a transport aeroplane, to cover the above phases, an autopilot comprises display devices, sensors, comparators, computers, amplifiers and servo-actuators, plus navigation equipment, flight instruments, the Air Data Computer, and the Flight Management System. All this is supplemented by equipment on the ground, such as the ILS, runway guidance, etc.

CONTROL LOOPS

The *inner loop* of a system concerns itself with events internal to the aircraft, such as movement of controls, and their disturbances in pitch, roll and yaw, etc., so it is only concerned with (positive static) stability.

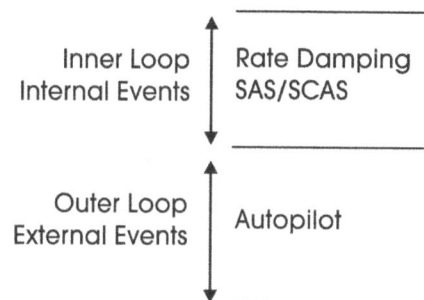

| Inner Loop Internal Events | Rate Damping SAS/SCAS |
| Outer Loop External Events | Autopilot |

The *external loop* deals with stuff affecting the machine from the outside world, including airspeed, altitude and track, so is there for *control*.

A closed loop system can measure the output from your control system and feed it back to the input side, determine the difference between what you want (input) and what you are getting (output), then tell the system to reduce or cancel the error so you end up with the output you wanted in the first place.

The average AFCS has many such loops working inside each other. The small inner loops deal with elevator angles, etc,. then more complicated ones encircle them, working up through holding specific aircraft attitudes to delivering rates of climb, speeds etc.

SYSTEM PROTECTION

For automatic landings, a concept of *system redundancy* means that multiple systems are used in such a way that a single failure has a minimal effect on aircraft performance.

When one autopilot is used in the cruise the system is considered to be fail safe, in that a disconnect will give you back a correctly trimmed aircraft within the manoeuvre envelope. The only time more than one autopilot can be engaged is for an autoland with APP selected, which brings in the redundancy factor.

- With three autopilots, the system is **Fail Active** because the other two can be used if one fails. That is, one failure leaves the overall system still working, and you can still land automatically. On the EFIS, the message **LAND 3** means that all autopilots are working. Other names include **Fail Operational** or **Fail Survival**.

- A system with only two autopilots is **Fail Passive** because you cannot autoland with only one - it would automatically disconnect at a pre-determined height and manual intervention is involved, so some sort of warning is required. A system that can fail without excessive deviation from the flight path or degrading passenger safety is fail passive, as with a single autopilot in the cruise (with only one autopilot for climbing, cruising and approach, the system is also fail-passive). Another name is **Fail Soft**.

Thus, an automatic landing system that keeps operating after a failure below alert height is *Fail Operational*, although it will then operate as *Fail-Passive*, meaning that the landing must be continued manually if something else fails. If there is a secondary independent guidance system to help with the manual landing, you have a *fail-operational hybrid* system.

To stop events such as system runaways, you can either limit the authority of an actuator, or the rate at which it can travel.

- **Comparators** check if an attitude change is in the same sense as actuator movement, such as the nose pitching down when such a command has been given. If it is, the system is disconnected.

- **Rate Trigger**. If a rate of change exceeds a certain value (based on system runaway parameters), the system will be disconnected.

- **Multi-channel**. A *duplex system* has two lanes, each with a sensor, a computer, an actuator, and switching circuits. Outputs from the two actuators are averaged before any commands are passed to the control surfaces, so if one gets a runaway, it will be (in theory) counteracted by the other. If using comparator monitoring, this can produce *fail*

operational capability. *Triplex* and *quadruplex* speak for themselves - the difference is that, if one system fails, it can be outvoted by the others and automatically disengaged. If the others have a problem, they will all disconnect and return the aircraft to the pilot in a safe, trimmed condition.

*****Interlocks** stop the autopilot being used if the system isn't ready, and cause it to disengage on failures. They are switches and relays that ensure satisfactory engagement.

CONTROL LAWS

These are rules that the autopilot computer has to follow, determining how it interprets a performance demand against a control response, but they also determine the fundamental response of the aircraft and set safety limits for automatic flight (that is, a control law will protect the aircraft from overstress or overspeed). Put more simply, control laws allow a fly-by-wire system to position the flight controls for the most efficient response. They are electrical algorithms that figure out the proper electrical signals to be sent to the electrohydraulic actuators. For example, the control law of a transport aeroplane autopilot control channel may be defined as *the relationship between the computer input deviation data and the output control deflection signals* (don't blame me, I didn't write it). Try this:

For each control channel (pitch, roll and yaw) the piloting law is the relationship between the deflection of the control surface commanded by the computer (BETA c) and the offset epsilon at the computer input. Yuk.

DIRECT CONTROL LAW

This is the basic mechanical connection between input and output - a nose-up pitch demand applied and held will initiate a nose up pitch rate. As natural stability comes in to oppose the increase in angle of attack, the pitch rate will slow to zero and the aircraft will hold a new attitude. That is, the machine will obey your direct control inputs and behave normally.

PITCH RATE DEMAND/ATTITUDE HOLD LAW

In this system, a nose-up pitch input applied and held will react as above, but the computer will continuously increase elevator deflection to maintain a constant pitch rate. With zero pitch input there will be zero change, so zero pitch input is an attitude hold condition. This means that, in a positive alpha vertical gust, attitude will not change, but the extra lift will balloon the aircraft above the intended flightpath. The disadvantage is that flightpath is not maintained under zero input and continual autopilot control inputs are needed.

G DEMAND/FLIGHTPATH HOLD LAW

This depends on level flight being a constant 1G flightpath. Increased G makes the aircraft go up, and reduced G makes it go down. In response to a nose-up pitch input, the computer initiates a demand for more G and calculates the necessary elevator angle. Thus, a pitch

CAPT

input calls for a flightpath change and zero pitch input is a flightpath hold demand. This is inherently good for maintaining a defined flightpath, but there is an inherent lag in response from gusts, which leads to sharp and rapid computed corrections, particularly at low speed.

C* LAW

This is used by the Airbus A320 series fly-by-wire system. It is basically a flightpath hold law with an element of pitch rate demand introduced at low speed to improve response on the approach.

AUTOMATIC TRIM

The function of automatic trim is to:

- Reduce to zero the hinge moment of the entire (elevator) control surface to relieve the load on the servo-actuator

- Maintain the stability & manoeuvrability trade-off in the flight envelope

- Transfer a stabilised aeroplane to the pilot during autopilot disengagement (i.e. ensure it is properly trimmed when the autopilot is disengaged)

- For pitch, cancel the hinge moment of the elevator

Automatic trimming is normally effected only about the pitch axis so the aircraft is trimmed if the pilot has to take over on disengagement.

MACH TRIM

For aircraft with a tendency to tuck under, the *Mach trim* compensates for backing up of the aerodynamic centre at high Mach numbers by moving the elevator nose-up, but only above a predetermined Mach number. The Mach number is read from the ADC, and a signal is generated that drives a screw jack which operates the elevator.

YAW DAMPER

A yawing motion (whether pilot-induced or otherwise) can lead to Dutch Roll. The vertical stabiliser and the rudder can be used to develop forces that can overcome it. Their effectiveness depends on their size and the speed of the aircraft - the yaw damper is more effective at higher speeds. A rate gyroscope provides the signals needed to start off the yaw damper actuator, which in turn activates the main actuator to the rudder.

STICK SHAKER/PUSHER

This is a device fitted to the yoke as an aid to prevent stalling - when the angle of attack, or alpha, approaches a critical value, the stick is made to shake as a warning. If it is ignored, the stick pusher applies down elevator.

SIDESTICKS

Each sidestick has a takeover button. In normal flight, simultaneous inputs from both pilots will be summed algebraically, but priority will be given to the pilot who depresses, and holds depressed, the takeover button on his stick. A green light on the glareshield tells the pilot he has

priority, while a red light tells the nonpriority pilot that his stick is dead. He can then retake control by depressing his takeover button. If he elects instead to release his stick, the green light in front of the priority pilot will go out. The priority pilot can then release the takeover button, extinguishing the red light and returning the aircraft to normal flight control.

If the non-priority pilot does not release his stick, however, because he is incapacitated, the priority pilot keeps his takeover button depressed for 30 seconds and then the dead stick is electronically latched. As soon as the obstruction is removed and the dead stick centred, it is automatically delatched.

That has proved to be one of the problems with the Airbus if you read the incident reports. There is an indicator in the panel showing the control input but it is hard to look at when you are taken by surprise. Another recurring problem has been the failure to punch the priority button when the PNF jumps on the controls in an attempt to put things right and salvage a situation.

AUTOTHROTTLE

This is a system that controls engine thrust to maintain some other value (PM, EPR or airspeed) within the design limits. It is designed to operate with an AFCS and FMS to maintain speed and a vertical flight path. Speed control is achieved by simply controlling thrust. When the vertical flight path is the parameter, speed is controlled with pitch while full (for climb) or idle (for descent) power is set.

AUTOLAND

An autoland approach is a precision instrument approach to touchdown and possibly the landing rollout. It is performed by the autopilot, which gets its position information and/or steering commands from onboard navigation equipment.

The autopilot intercepts a localiser beam at a constant heading, and vertical speed is maintained according to radio altimeter height between 50' and the ground.

Note: Autoland is intended for conditions of low visibility, meaning fog, with little wind. It is *not* designed for crosswinds over 15 kts, hand flying, or turbulence!

Semi-automatic mode with respect to landings means that the autopilot maintains the ILS and the autothrottle maintains a constant speed until DH, to disengage automatically at around 100'. *Automatic Mode* maintains the ILS until the flare, the autothrottle decreases thrust at around 30 ft, and the flare and ground roll are performed automatically.

COUPLED APPROACH

A coupled approach is an instrument approach performed by an autopilot that gets its position information and/or steering commands from onboard navigation equipment.

Coupled non-precision approaches should be discontinued and flown manually when 50 feet below the MDA, and coupled precision approaches flown manually below 50 feet AGL.

During a Cat II automatic approach, height information is supplied by a radio altimeter. From about 50 ft, vertical speed is maintained according to radio altimeter height.

On an autopilot coupled approach, Go Around mode is engaged by pushing a button on the throttles. When an automatic landing is interrupted by a go-around, the autothrottle reacts immediately upon pilot action on the TO/GA (Take-off/Go-around) switch to recover the maximum thrust, the autopilot monitors the climb and the rotation of the aeroplane, ad the pilot retracts the landing gear and reduces the flap to reduce the drag.

USING AN AUTOPILOT

Typically, before takeoff, you would engage the Pitch, Roll and Yaw channels, plus the Flight Director so you can see what inputs are required (the full autopilot is not normally switched on for takeoff or landing). In fact, engagement of an autopilot is not possible when:

- The electrical supply is faulty
- The turn control knob is not set to centre off
- There is a synchronisation fault
- There is a fault in the attitude reference unit

If you ever want to fly the machine yourself, you must use the *Disengage* button on the cyclic to release the system's grip of death on the controls, but most systems allow you to manoeuvre in pitch and roll without disengaging the autopilot, either by using the panel described above, or by *control wheel steering*, which allows the controls to be moved without the autopilot dropping off line. The new attitude is held once the control wheel is released. *Touch control steering* uses a thumb switch on the control yoke, which disengages the autopilot while the controls are moved, and re-engages it once the switch is released. The power switch for the autopilot may have three selections:

- **OFF**, which speaks for itself
- **FDIR**. The Flight Director's job is to reduce your workload by indicating the manoeuvres required to execute, achieve or maintain a flight condition. It does this by presenting data as control commands to show you the *optimal way to achieve your flight path*. In other words, the flight director gives you directions about *how to position the controls* rather than the attitude of the aircraft. This means you get no information about the flight path, for which you need a separate navigation display. When the FD bars centralise, you have only made the proper control inputs, not reached the optimum flight

path! The flight director can be used without the autopilot, although the autopilot can use the FD to tell you what it's doing.

Remember: The FD doesn't tell the aircraft what to do - *command bars* show you the control inputs. All you need to do is align them as they move.

Note: In this mode, you are doing the flying, not the autopilot!

- **AUTO**. The autopilot will fly the machine according to your selections below

Here is a list of some of the buttons available and their functions. Note that some will not be present on simpler autopilots, or they may be labelled differently!

- **WLV**. The Wing Leveller simply holds the wings level while you figure out what to do next. It's a handy button to punch in an overload situation and will hold the wings at the current level of bank, or level them for you if you engage it with less than a certain figure, typically 7°.

- **HDG**. Heading Hold follows the heading bug on the HSI or DG. To turn, simply move the heading bug to the desired direction and the machine will follow. **Tip:** Ensure the heading bug is in place before engaging the HDG button, or the machine will seek the heading straight away!

- **LOC**. The Localizer will fly an ILS localiser, which is more sensitive than a VOR radial, as is used with the NAV button. Pushing this button just arms the system - *your current HDG mode will remain in force until the localiser needle starts to move into the centre*. At that point, the LOC will go from ARMED to ACTIVE, and start flying for you, dis-engaging any previous modes.

- **G/S**. Flies the glideslope portion of the ILS, in the same way as LOC handles the Localiser.

- **ALT**. Holds the current or pre-selected altitude. If you hit this button, the system should maintain the altitude you are currently sitting at, i.e. whatever pressure is outside the aircraft. Adjusting the altimeter afterwards should make no difference unless it is linked in with the autopilot.

- **V/S**. Holds a constant vertical speed. To climb or descend, push VS (*Vertical Speed*) and select the rate of climb or descent with a knob on the VSI. This will disable ALT, if selected. Once at the required altitude, reselect the ALT button to maintain.

© *Phil Croucher, 2014*

- **SPD**. Holds a pre-selected airspeed.

- **FLCH**. Flight Level Change is commonly used to change altitude by allowing you to add or take away power while holding an airspeed. This is like SPD, but, if you have auto-throttle, FLCH will automatically add or take away power.

- **PTCH**. Use Pitch-Sync to hold the nose at a constant pitch attitude, like the Wing-Leveller.

- **VNAV**. Vertical Navigation flies altitudes from the FMS to follow route altitudes.

- **BC**. The Back Course is a second localiser that works in the opposite sense to the proper ILS to fly along the extended centreline once you have missed the runway and have to carry out a Missed Approach. However, some airfields save money by making you use the Back Course as a proper ILS, although you won't have a glideslope. When coming back in the other way, it is back to front. Pushing this button reverses the commands to make it look right. It does not work with an HSI.

- **NAV** (or **VOR**). This keeps you coupled to a selected radial on the HSI, which must naturally be slaved to whatever navaid you are using. The problem is that it can chase the heading too much, and will overshoot and come back rather than make small adjustments to creep up on the selected heading. It is often more practical and comfortable for passengers to use HDG mode and move the heading bug yourself if time permits. In addition, you have better roll rates and maximum bank angles. In the cone of confusion, the last good heading is held until you get through it.

In the picture below, the light behind the ALT button is illuminated, indicating that the height-keeping function has been selected. This and the HDG button are the most used functions, so much so, that they are usually the automatic selections when the thing is switched on in the first place, to maintain pitch and roll.

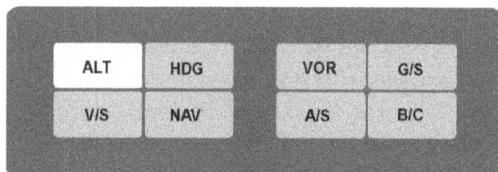

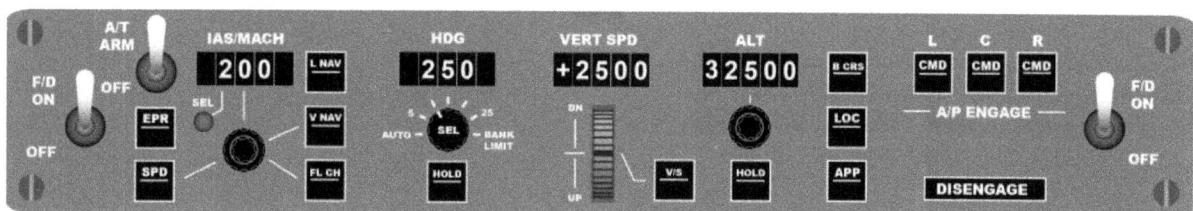

VS, FLCH and HDG all do their thing the moment they are engaged. Others, like ALT, G/S and LOC, on the other hand, sit there on standby (armed) until they intercept the altitude, glideslope or localiser required. That is, *they will not do anything until then.*

EXAMPLE

You set the machine up straight and level at 3,000 feet and push the ALT and HDG buttons. Now you can take your hands off and read the instructions, as the autopilot will maintain that level and whatever heading you set with the heading bug until you tell it otherwise. Now you want to climb to 6,000 feet, so you need to dial this figure into the altitude window (you would also set your cleared altitude before you take off). How you want to get there determines what button you push next. You could hit the vertical speed (V/S) button, then select a rate of climb on the VSI until you get to the selected altitude.

FLCH or SPD, on the other hand, will pitch the nose up and maintain the currently indicated speed, leaving you to add power as needed. Again, this mode should disengage automatically when you get to the selected altitude.

PHASES OF FLIGHT

For a large jet, before you get airborne, the AFCS should be serviceable and the FMS programmed with the lateral and vertical flight path profiles for the route and flight levels (don't forget to press the EXECUTE button!)

TAKEOFF

Line up on the runway (check the compass with the runway direction), with the Flight Director on, the autothrottle armed and set to N_1 (RPM), and with the takeoff speeds and power bugged on the instruments.

Press the TOGA (Take Off/Go-Around) switch on the throttle lever(s), which will then advance automatically while you keep straight on the runway.

At some preset speed, which is typically about 60 kts, the throttle hold will automatically be engaged and the pitch command bars will indicate a nose-up requirement. You do this at VR (rotate speed), at a rate of about 3° per second. Once you lift off, merge the flight director bars, to reach and maintain V_2 (Takeoff Safety Speed).

At around 400 ft AGL (i.e. a safe height), assuming an engine hasn't failed, you can engage the autopilot, followed by L NAV and V NAV on the MCP.

Picture Below: Boeing Autopilot Control Panel

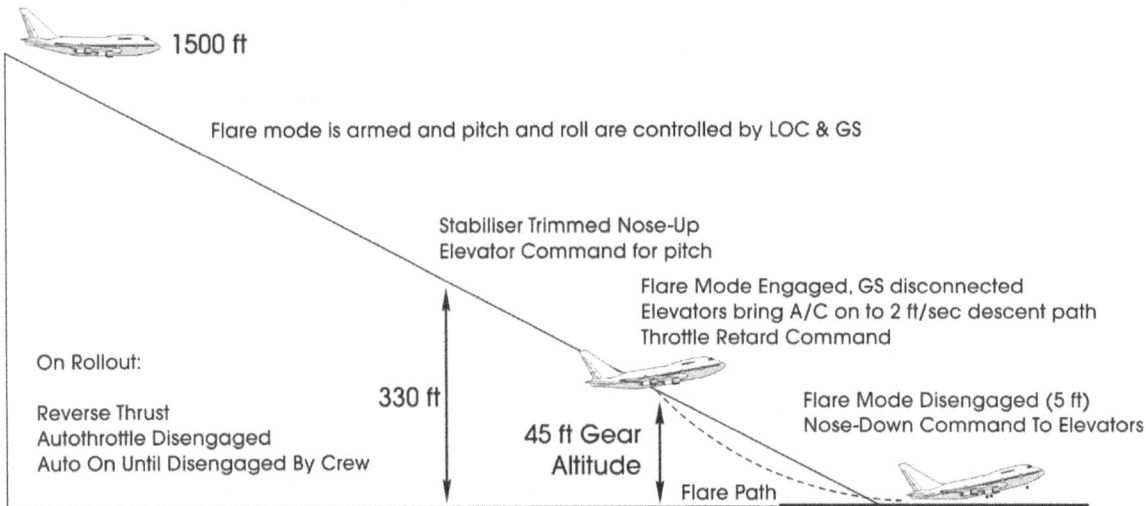

1500 ft

Flare mode is armed and pitch and roll are controlled by LOC & GS

Stabiliser Trimmed Nose-Up
Elevator Command for pitch

Flare Mode Engaged, GS disconnected
Elevators bring A/C on to 2 ft/sec descent path
Throttle Retard Command

On Rollout:

Reverse Thrust
Autothrottle Disengaged
Auto On Until Disengaged By Crew

330 ft

45 ft Gear
Altitude

Flare Mode Disengaged (5 ft)
Nose-Down Command To Elevators

Flare Path

THE CLIMB

With the gear and flaps retracted, V NAV engaged and the altitude alert system set to one above your present altitude, the autothrottle will provide maximum climb power (it knows this from the FMC). Pitch will be adjusted for the correct climb speed, also from the FMC.

When you approach the preset altitude (and assuming altitude alert is set for this level) the AFCS tells the autopilot to adjust the pitch attitude for the cruise.

THE CRUISE

The FMC generates a signal that is proportional to the required cruise speed (usually maximum economy*), leaving the autothrottle to adjust the power.

*This speed will change as you use fuel and the aircraft weight reduces, and the temperature varies. The power and pitch will be adjusted automatically.

The autopilot will use the FMC and INS to keep to the pre-programmed route, using the roll channel - L NAV must be selected for this.

DESCENT

The FMC knows the best point at which to start descending. Assuming the altitude alert is set to a *lower* altitude than your present one, the autothrottle will reduce engine power to flight idle. It then re-arms so that, if you suddenly level off, it can increase power.

The pitch angles are changed to achieve the most economical flight speed. The required radio aids are tuned and identified.

APPROACH, FLARE & LANDING

Automatic landing requires multichannel operation, so the others need to be armed (up till now, the AFCS has been operating as a single channel system, and still does, for the moment). The localiser and glideslope modes are also

armed. Altitude information comes from the radio altimeter once you get within range (usually 2500 feet).

At 1500 ft (radio altitude) the localiser and glideslope are captured, and the other armed autopilot channels engaged. Computerised control of the flare is armed, and an autoland status annunciator shows LAND 2 or LAND 3, depending on the channels voted into operation.

The pitch and roll axes are adjusted according to the requirements of the localiser and glideslope.

At 330 feet, the aircraft is trimmed for a nose-up attitude.

The **flare mode** is automatically engaged when the gear is 45 feet above the ground. This is based on the pitch attitude, radio altitude and the known distance between the gear, the fuselage and radalt antenna. Flare mode now controls the pitch for a 2 feet per second descent path.

At 45 feet, the autothrottle retards and the thrust reduces.

Flare mode disengages at about 5 feet, and the system transitions to touchdown and rollout mode. At 2 feet, the pitch reduces to 2°, and on touchdown the elevators are commanded to lower the nose so the wheels touch the runway (and stay there).

After the weight on wheel switches are energised, the autothrottle disengages after 2 seconds or when reverse thrust is applied, but the AFCS is still in charge until you deselect it, which you must do before turning off the runway or the localiser will try to keep you on it.

INSTRUMENTS

Aircraft instruments base their readings on the measurement and comparison of the different temperatures and pressures found inside and outside the aircraft. They will cover four areas of aircraft operation - *Control*, *Performance*, *Navigation*, and *Miscellaneous*, which includes voltmeters, gear position indicators, etc.

Instruments must be able to be read easily, in terms of position, lighting and clarity. They can have up to four sub-systems, not all of which will be in the same case:

- Detection (e.g. temperature probe)
- Measurement (aneroid capsule)
- Coupling (suitable linkage between measurement and indication)
- Indication (Pointer, or digital display)

At the point of measurement, a measuring body absorbs some energy and converts it to a quantity that has a functional relationship with the quantity measured. As some energy is absorbed, that quantity will never be the same as the true value. Corrections are usually included with amplification signals because the sample is small.

Displays can be *circular*, as shown on the right, or *straight* (like a tape) or *digital*, or even a combination, as with this display from an AW 139):

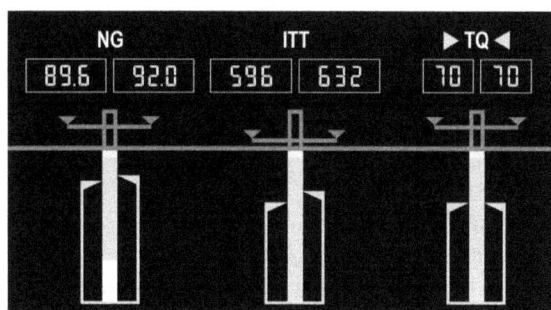

Instruments can also be classified into four groups, after the variations in properties of certain materials against variations in temperature:

- Expansion
- Vapour-Pressure
- Electrical, based on:
    - Resistance, or
    - Increase in electromotive force
- Radiation

Most will be electrical.

Right: Circular Instrument

Lighting

White lighting is usually combined with grey cockpit interiors because:

- you have unrestricted use of colour
- warning indicators become more prominent
- black instrument cases against a grey background will emphasize their size and shape

Individual instruments may be lit by:

- integral lighting, which is built into the instrument
- ring, eyebrow, or post lighting, all of which are fitted to the outside of the instrument case
- floodlighting

PRESSURE   022 01 02/02 02

In many systems, the pressure of a liquid or gas must be measured and indicated, either directly, where the source of pressure is connected to the instrument (mostly Bourdon tubes), or remotely, where it can be some distance away, with electrical signals being sent instead. Such systems would have a transmitter at the pressure source and an indicator on a panel. This means you won't have yucky fluids in the cockpit, and you don't have to carry a lot of plumbing. Indicators can be based on *synchronous receivers*, *DC* or *AC ratiometers* or *servos*.

Pressure is the *force per unit area*, or the force exerted on an area divided by the size of that area:

$$P = \frac{F}{A}$$

where F is Force (N) and A is the Area in m^2. The result:

$$\frac{N}{m^2}$$

is equal to 1 *Pascal* (Pa), which is the standard unit of pressure under the SI system, described in *POF*.

There are several types of pressure, including:

- **Absolute Pressure**, or the difference between the pressure of a fluid and absolute zero (a vacuum). It is usually measured in inches of mercury, as on a Manifold Air Pressure gauge. It would be the sum of gauge pressure (next) and atmospheric pressure, and is what forces the fuel and air charge into the cylinders of a piston engine.

- **Gauge Pressure**, on the other hand, is measured against ambient air pressure, so it is absolute pressure minus atmospheric pressure. In other words, any variance from atmospheric pressure is called gauge pressure. For example, fuel and oil pressure instruments indicate the amount that the pump has raised the pressure of the fluid above that of the atmosphere Note that it can be positive or negative. If the absolute pressure stays constant, gauge pressure varies with atmospheric pressure.

- **Differential Pressure** is just the difference in pressure between two points, as represented by the airspeed indicator. Two inlet ports may be used, with each connected to one of the sealed volumes whose pressure is to be monitored.

Pressure Sensing

Pressure is measured against a reference, such as a column of mercury, or by acting over a known area and measuring the force produced. Aneroid gauges use metallic pressure sensing elements that flex under pressure.

Aneroid means *without fluid*, or *not wet* (depends on which book you read), to distinguish between aneroid and hydrostatic gauges, which do use fluid, although aneroid gauges can be used to measure liquid pressure. The pressure sensing element may be a Bourdon tube, a diaphragm, a capsule, or bellows, all of which will change their shape in response to the pressure. The deflection is transmitted by a suitable linkage that will rotate a pointer around a graduated dial, or activate a secondary transducer that might control a digital display, the most common of which measure changes in capacitance that follow the mechanical deflection.

In order of sensitivity, you have:

DIAPHRAGMS

Diaphragms are simply circular metal discs that are corrugated to give them strength, to provide larger deflections. They are used to detect low pressures. One side of the disc is exposed to the pressure to be measured, and the other is linked to the indicating mechanism.

ANEROID CAPSULES

In gauges used for small measurements, or for absolute pressure, the gear train and needle may be driven by an enclosed and sealed chamber, called an *aneroid*, as used in aneroid barometers, altimeters, altitude recording barographs, and the altitude telemetry instruments in weather balloon radiosondes. The sealed chamber is used as a reference pressure and the needles are driven by the external pressure.

A capsule consists of two diaphragms placed face to face and joined at their edges to form a chamber that may be completely sealed or left open to a source of (absolute) pressure. They are also used for low(ish) pressures, but are more sensitive than diaphragms.

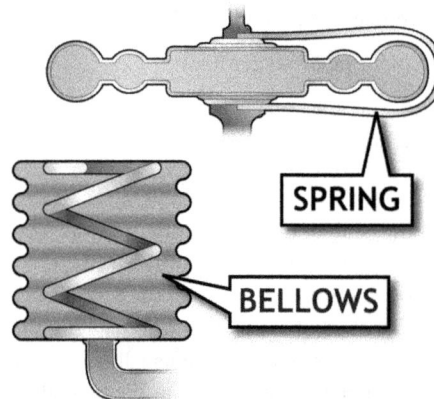

BELLOWS

Bellows are an extension of the capsule (think of them as several unsealed capsules joined together), but operate like a helical compression spring - indeed, there may even be a spring inside to increase the *spring rate* and to help the bellows return to its normal length once the source of pressure is removed. They are used for higher pressures.

THE BOURDON TUBE

The most common pressure sensor was invented by French watchmaker Eugene Bourdon in 1849, in which a C-shaped elliptical hollow spring tube is sealed at one end, with the other end connected to a source of pressure. The pressure differential from the inside to the outside causes the tube to change from an elliptical to a more circular shape, and to straighten out, rather like an uncoiling hose. Which way it moves is determined by the curvature of the tubing, as the inside radius is slightly shorter than that on the outside, and the ratio between the major and minor axes depends on what sensitivity you need - the larger the ratio, the greater it is.

CAPT

The pressure range is governed by the *tubing wall thickness* and the *radius of the curvature*.

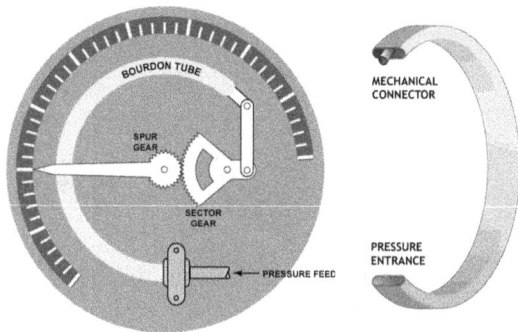

The end result is that a specific pressure causes movement for a specific distance. When the pressure is removed, the tube returns to its original shape. To do this, the material used requires a form of heat treating (*spring tempering*) to make it retain its original shape closely while allowing some elasticity under a load. Beryllium copper, phosphor bronze, and various alloys of steel and stainless steel are good for this purpose, but steel has a limited service life due to corrosion. Most gauges use phosphor bronze.

In summary, a Bourdon-based gauge uses a coiled tube which causes the rotation of an indicator arm connected to it, as it expands due to pressure increase.

MANOMETER

The term *manometer* is often used to refer specifically to liquid column hydrostatic instruments. These consist of a vertical column of liquid in a tube whose ends are exposed to different pressures, with the difference in fluid height being proportional to the pressure difference.

However, the simplest design is a closed-end U-shape, with one side connected to the region of interest. A force equal to the applied pressure multiplied by the area of the bore will force the liquid downwards until, eventually, the two levels will stand the same distance above and below the original level. If you take into account the area of the tube bore and the density of the liquid, you can calculate pressure from the difference in the levels. Any fluid can be used, but mercury is preferred for its high density and low vapour pressure, so the tube can be shorter.

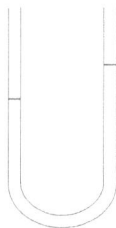

Manometers are used for calibration purposes.

TEMPERATURE
•••

Knowledge of the air temperature is needed for performance calculations, anti-ice control and calculation of true airspeed (TAS), amongst other things.

Total Air Temperature (TAT)

In the same way that we have to deal with two types of pressure (static and dynamic), there are two types of temperature (static and total). On large jets, TAT is used to determine maximum N_1 or Engine Pressure Ratio (EPR). It is displayed with OAT in the cockpit.

Whatever detects the temperature must necessarily be in the airstream. At higher speeds, compression (of the air) against the aircraft surfaces, and friction, means that whatever temperature is indicated will be a lot warmer than the Static (Outside) Air Temperature (SAT) by an amount that is proportional to TAS. At high speeds, the boundary layer can be slowed down or stopped (relatively speaking) and be affected by adiabatic compression that raises the temperature. The errors get larger as speed increases. RAM rise is negligible up to about Mach 0.3

TAT is the temperature that would be recorded if you could stop dead during flight (i.e. with nothing frictionally induced - on the ground, TAT/RAT = SAT). It is technically the maximum rise possible (SAT + 100% of RAM Rise), and can be thought of as the *indicated* air temperature, or what the aircraft feels, which is the same as the OAT plus adiabatic heating. It is not displayed in modern aircraft - TAT + SAT come from the ADC. If your system cannot measure TAT correctly, you have to include the Recovery Factor (see below).

Static Air Temperature (SAT)

Where the air has only partially been brought to rest (as it would be if you used a more basic thermometer than the Rosemount, mentioned overleaf), you don't get so much of a temperature rise. The difference is called *RAM rise*, and the indicated temperature is *RAM Air Temperature*, which is equal to SAT + a percentage of RAM Rise.

As SAT is not easy to measure in a moving aircraft, an air data computer has to calculate it from the TAT in order to get the True Air Speed needed for the Flight Management System to do its work (at low speeds, SAT = OAT). SAT may also therefore be called the *Corrected* or *True Outside Air Temperature* (COAT).

The formula used to calculate it is:

$$SAT = \frac{TAT}{(1 + 0.2\ KM^2)}$$

Where K = recovery factor (below) and M = Mach no.

The ADC does this as a function of Mach number. If you don't have one, you can obtain TAS as a function of calibrated airspeed and local air density (or static air temperature and pressure altitude which determine density) on the flight computer.

Recovery Factor

The difference between TAT and SAT is the *stagnation rise*, and the proportion of stagnation temperature that can actually be sensed by the aircraft instruments is the *recovery factor* or *K value*, which is governed by the thermometer. Thus, the recovery factor expresses the sensitivity of a temperature sensor as a percentage. It is determined by flight testing and will be found in the flight manual.

With a recovery factor of 1, a thermometer is measuring TAT, which is SAT + 100% of stagnation rise. If a thermometer has a recovery factor of 0.8, it is only measuring SAT + 80% of the RAM rise. If the recovery factor is zero, it is measuring SAT only.

For example, what is the Ram Air Temperature if the SAT is -20°C, the stagnation rise is 10°C and the recovery factor is 80%?

```
-20 + 8 = -12°C
```

With a Rosemount probe, the K factor is assumed to be 1.0, hence its other name of *Total Air Temperature Probe*.

Recovery is factored in for Mach number compressibility.

Thermometers

REMOTE BULB THERMOMETER

This consists of a bulb and a Bourdon tube filled with liquid or vapour, so the Bourdon tube could also loosely be regarded as measuring temperature (as expressed by one exam question), but it is still really measuring pressure. Expansion of the liquid causes the tube to lengthen, which moves the indicator, using the usual suitable linkage, as described above. With the vapour system, only the bulb has liquid in, which alters the pressure in the tube as it expands, with the same results, but you will get indicator errors with changes in atmospheric pressure.

RESISTIVE COIL THERMOMETER

The small, but stable, resistance of a nickel or platinum coil changes with absolute temperature. The coil is in a circuit with a fixed voltage, changes in which (from resistance) are measured with a meter calibrated in °C.

BIMETALLIC STRIP THERMOMETER

Below about 150 kts, a thermometer like that shown is good enough for getting the OAT.

The probe sticks out into the airstream, and the dial is inside the cockpit. The works consist of a helical (coil-shaped) bimetallic strip that twists as the temperature changes, and moves the pointer.

The probe cannot be shrouded from the Sun, and it is necessarily next to the fuselage skin, so its readings can be affected by kinetic heating, even at low speeds - at 150 kts, the rise can be around 3°. Being crude instruments, they

are also subject to other errors, so a professional rule of thumb is to assume an error of about 2-3°.

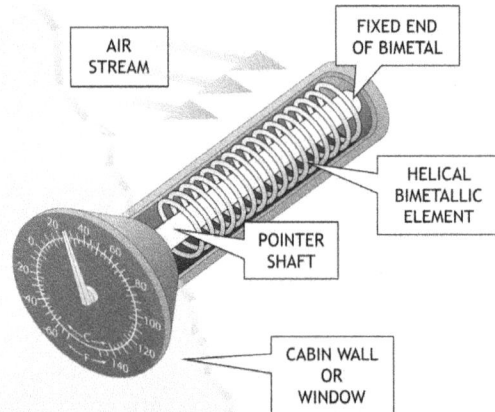

THERMISTOR

The change in resistance with these is greater than with a resistive coil, and therefore easier to detect, but you don't get the same results from one instrument to another, thus consistency is a disadvantage. The information, however, is extracted in the same way as the coil, above.

WHEATSTONE BRIDGE

This device measures an unknown electrical resistance by balancing two legs of a bridge circuit, one of which includes the unknown component. They are commonly used in Air Data Computers that use solid state capsules.

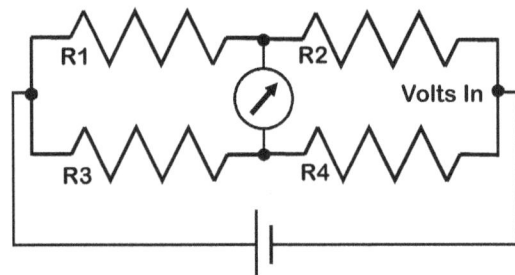

As the bridge becomes unbalanced, the varying voltage across the middle can be measured with a voltmeter.

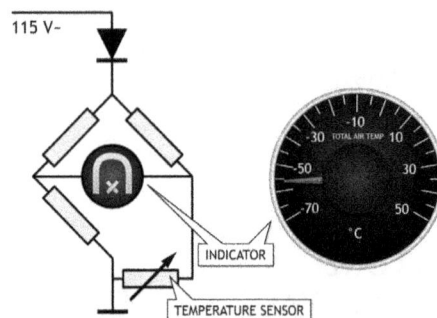

For temperature measurement purposes, you can replace the voltmeter with a wiper arm that is positioned by a servo loop, and how far the arm moves is a measure of the temperature change. It will centre at 15°C.

THE ROSEMOUNT PROBE

Otherwise known as the *Total Air Temperature Probe*, this has a small (i.e. quick reacting) platinum* based resistance coil inside concentric cylinders, mounted on a streamlined strut around 50 mm or so from the fuselage skin, which therefore has little influence on it (skin temperature can be increased by kinetic energy). The probe is open at the front with a smaller hole at the back to allow air to flow through, but it is forced through 90° to encourage water and dust particles to separate as it speeds up, so the aircraft must be moving for the probe to work. A heating element prevents icing, and is self-compensating, in that, as temperature rises, so does resistance in the element, which reduces the heater current. Although the heater affects the temperature sensed, the error is small, around 1°C at Mach 0.1 and 0.15°C at Mach 1.0, so light aircraft aren't affected anyway.

Aside from skin temperature, direct sunlight will give an artificially high reading and, when flying from cloud to clear air, readings will be low for however long it takes for moisture to evaporate from the element in the probe.

*An uncompensated instrument has one platinum sensor. A fully compensated one has 2.

Errors

Instrument error comes from the usual imperfections in manufacturing and can be sorted out by fine calibration. *Environmental error* is caused by solar heating or icing, for which the Rosemount probe has a heater. Probes are usually mounted to keep them in shadow, but the residual effects of environmental error can only be minimised, and not corrected for. Some heating is caused by compression as air is brought to rest, which is the difference between SAT and TAT, so it is only a problem when you need to find SAT. There is also frictional heating in the boundary layer, but both heating errors can be fully compensated for, either automatically or by calculation. Flat plate sensors, with their sensing element flush with the aircraft skin, are susceptible to environmental errors because of their relative lack of shielding. They are affected by frictional heating in the boundary layer (not compressibility), and instrument error.

TEMPERATURE COMPENSATION

Various methods can be used to make an instrument over- or under-read according to which way the temperature is going. For example, a thermal junction can get hot by itself, which will vary the emf it produces and give you false readings. In mechanical terms, a bimetal strip made

of invar and brass or steel can be attached to a capsule to make it expand or contract slightly, or you could arrange to vary the resistance of an electrical current.

FLIGHT INSTRUMENTS
••

Flight instruments are grouped in a *T arrangement*.

The artificial horizon is in the centre, because it is a primary instrument (it tells you which way is up), the heading indicator is below, No 1 altimeter at the top right, the vertical speed indicator below that, and the airspeed indicator at the top left with turn coordinator underneath.

The idea is to have the most important instruments as close together as possible to reduce the scanning distance.

As mentioned, instruments cover four areas of aircraft operation:

- **Control**, such as the artificial horizon and engine instruments

- **Performance**, that show you what the aircraft is doing (ASI, VSI, altimeter, compass)

- **Navigation** (VOR, ADF, DME)

- **Miscellaneous** (Warning flags, gear position indicators, pressure and temperature, etc)

A *primary instrument* is one which gives instant and constant readouts (also called *direct*). A *secondary instrument* is one that you have to deduce things from, such as the altimeter increasing, telling you that the pitch must have changed* (you might also say that the altimeter gives you an indirect indication of pitch attitude). The ASI and VSI also give indirect indications of pitch, and the HI and TC indicate bank. Note also that a primary instrument will tell you at what rate things are changing, but a secondary one will only indicate that change is taking place.

*The needle, ball and airspeed method of instrument flying refers to the Sperry turn indicator - as long as the needle and ball were centred, you were flying in a straight line. In a turn, keeping the ball centred meant you were not slipping or skidding, and holding the correct airspeed meant you were either flying straight and level or climbing or descending at a constant rate. In this case, the primary instruments were the ASI, turn and bank indicator and the VSI. However, using such slow, indirect indications was mentally tiring, as aircraft attitude had to be continually deduced, which led to the development of the artificial horizon and DGI, that gave more instantaneous readings (once gyros became more reliable!)

Instruments are further grouped under the headings of *pitch*, *bank* and *power*.

Pitch

- **Artificial Horizon** (Attitude Indicator). The most important pitch instrument, because it gives direct, instantaneous readings.

- **Altimeter**. Although it indicates pitch indirectly, it is a primary pitch instrument.

- **Airspeed Indicator.** Secondary pitch instrument, although its value becomes less at higher airspeeds, as changes are more pronounced and the range indicated by the needle is less and more difficult to read. Any given power setting has only one pitch attitude where altitude and airspeed are constant.

- **Vertical Speed Indicator** (VSI). A secondary pitch instrument, to be used with the altimeter. Don't forget that it will give a brief reverse indication if you jerk the controls.

Bank

- **Artificial Horizon** (Attitude Indicator). Also the most important bank instrument, for similar reasons under *Pitch*, above.

- **Heading Indicator.** An indirect instrument, because if you change heading, bank must be involved somewhere.

- **Turn Coordinator**. Shows a rate of turn (3°/sec for rate 1), so it is an indirect indication of bank.

Power   022 01 03

Power instruments are not strictly in the traditional T, but you have to check them anyway. The Airspeed Indicator is a secondary power instrument, as it changes in relation to power application.

Engine and temperature instruments have already been covered under *Aircraft General Knowledge*.

FUEL GAUGES

Fuel quantity is measured by the level in the tank, but may be shown as volume or weight. The measurement can be done by *float type* (resistance) or *capacitive* contents gauges.

Note: Although many fuel gauges are accurate, they should never be relied upon as the final guide to what you have in the tanks, especially if they are calibrated with lbs or kg - fuel weight (per gallon) varies with specific gravity and temperature, so instrument readings will vary as well. Reading the book *Free Fall*, about the Gimli Glider is very instructive about this - a 767 had to make a dead stick landing at Gimli (in Manitoba, Canada) after running out of fuel in the cruise, from a combination of circumstances, including misleading fuel gauges and confusing lbs for kg (the whole episode is very instructive about CRM).

Fuel system indications available to the pilot normally consist of contents, fuel low, pressure, flow, transfer status and filter condition.

FLOAT TYPE (RESISTANCE)

This consists of a resistive circuit using floats connected to a Wheatstone Bridge , typically powered by DC. The float may be made of specially treated cork, or a sealed lightweight metal cylinder. It is attached to an arm that is pivoted to allow angular movement to be transmitted to an electrical element consisting of a wiper arm and a potentiometer (variable resistance), so, as the fuel level changes, the float arm's movement alters the resistance. Ohm's Law determines the current flow, which is fed to an indicator. Float type indicators provide information on *volume*, whose indication varies with temperature.

One advantage of float-type fuel gauging systems is their easy construction. Neither are they affected by voltage variations (if a galvanometer is used), but they are influenced by *attitude, acceleration*, and *temperature variations*.

CAPACITANCE TYPE

Capacitance fuel systems are fitted to larger aircraft because they measure fuel mass rather than volume.

The capacity of a capacitor depends on the nature of the dielectric in which it is immersed (see *Electricity*). Fuel has twice the capacitance of air so a full tank has twice the capacitive reactance as an empty one. A simple capacitance system will consist of a variable capacitor in the fuel tank, an amplifier, and an indicator. The complete circuit forms an electrical bridge that is constantly being rebalanced around the differences between the tank and reference capacitors. The signal is amplified and used to drive a motor inside the indicator.

A *capacitance probe* that runs the full height of the tank consists of two tubes, one inside the other, with fuel between them. The two tubes are fed with AC so the "capacitor" formed by the tubes (fuel is the dielectric) charges and discharges alternately. The amount of discharge varies according to whether the dielectric is fuel or air, so the electrical signal produced is proportional to the tank's contents.

On their own, the detectors can only measure the height of fuel (volume), so a datum or *reference capacitor* compensates for *density* to ensure that weight is indicated correctly (if not told otherwise, assume you have a compensated system, as most aircraft use them).

In a compensated system, the indicated fuel weight remains the same if temperature changes.

Compensation works on the basis that variations in fuel capacitance follow permittivity, which describes how an electric field affects and is affected by a dielectric. Thus, permittivity relates to a material's ability to transmit (or "permit") an electric field. For example, in a capacitor, an increased permittivity allows the same charge to be stored with a smaller electric field (and a smaller voltage), leading to increased capacitance.

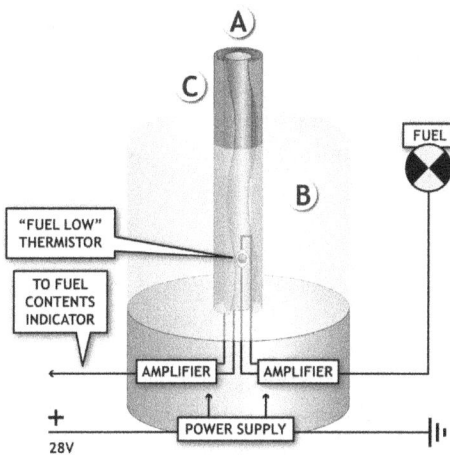

To ensure that only permittivity is measured, the compensator unit is placed in the bottom of the tank so it is always covered with fuel, which means that capacitance is not measured by fuel quantity. When temperature increases, permittivity will increase and so will capacitance, and the bridge circuit becomes unbalanced. The voltage so produced drives a motor that drives a potentiometer that decreases the resistance. As this is biased towards a full tank condition, an increase in fuel quantity is indicated. Indication errors will still be there because density also varies with temperature, but these are minor in comparison, so errors are minimised.

There are many sensors connected in parallel, because fuel has a habit of sloshing around - this ensures that a more accurate average reading is taken. There is always a zero signal which is suppressed by the signal from the probes. If it fails, your gauge will suddenly read empty, or whatever the manufacturer chooses. A test routine simulates the empty signal. If a fuel tank with a capacitive contents system has water in it, but no fuel, the gauge will be inaccurate because water has a very high dielectric constant of about 80, as opposed to 2 (fuel) or 1 (air). The reading, however will be greater than zero - possibly full, because the gauge could over-read by as much as 8000%.

PITOT-STATIC SYSTEM 022 02 01

This consists of a series of pipes around the cockpit through which air flows to feed three common instruments: the altimeter, airspeed indicator and vertical speed indicator.

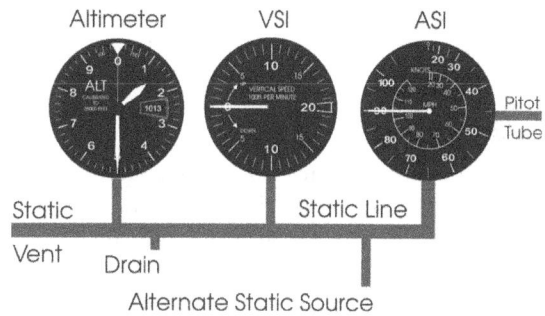

An aircraft is acted on from all directions by *static pressure*, which is fed into the system through static lines that are connected to static ports or static vents on *both sides* of the machine, to ensure that they balance out when it yaws, or performs strange manoeuvres. They may or may not be heated (generally not on smaller machines). Warning lights associated with pitot/static heating systems usually come on when the heating element or the power relay has failed, so one light can have two meanings.

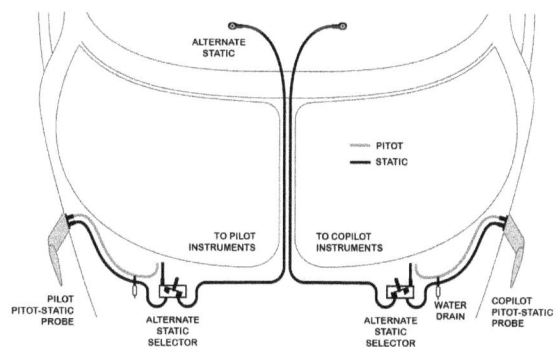

The static pressure is so called because it stays pretty much the same. It's actually the normal barometric pressure that decreases with height, so any changes in it are relatively slow. Information from the static ports may also be fed to non-flight systems, such as autopilots or flight directors.

An *alternate static source* takes its feed from inside the aircraft in case the main one starts leaking or gets blocked, either through ice, a bird strike, or whatever. When it is used, some error will be introduced into the instrument readings because the cabin air pressure is affected by the airflow over the cabin (there are also different pressure errors), so indicated airspeeds and altitudes will read *higher* than normal (that is, the altimeter and ASI will over-read).

The VSI will show a momentary climb as the alternate source is selected, then it will stabilise and produce "normal" readings. If the alternate source gets blocked, or you don't have one, smashing the VSI glass (preferably not the ASI or altimeter) will have the same effect.

Otherwise known as the *Total Pressure Probe*, the *pitot tube* (pronounced pee-toe) is used to detect *total pressure* (as mentioned by Bernoulli). It is connected to the airspeed indicator and sticks out beyond the boundary layer. Total pressure (sometimes called *stagnation pressure*) is the pressure obtained when a moving gas is brought to a stop through an adiabatic process - in this case, it includes the static pressure that affects the aircraft from all sides, and an extra element that comes from forward movement, since the pitot tube is pointed towards the direction of flight (within 5°). If the fluid (air) is an ideal one (meaning not viscous), total pressure is equal to the sum of potential energy, kinetic energy and pressure energy, but the first is ignored in a pitot tube, and the kinetic energy is converted to pressure energy anyway.

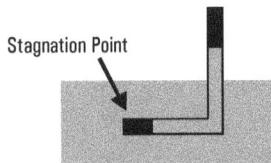

Stagnation Point

This creates an equal volume above the level of the flow, which is *dynamic pressure*, and a measure of airspeed. In simple terms, dynamic pressure of the air against the front surfaces of an aircraft (as detected by the pitot tube) is greater than the pressure of the undisturbed air sensed through the static ports. The difference is proportional to the square of the speed, so instruments can be calibrated in units of speed, such as knots.

The formula for *dynamic pressure* is:

$$\text{Dynamic Pressure} = \tfrac{1}{2}\rho V^2$$

Where ρ (the Greek letter "rho") is air density and V the true velocity. As you can see, its strength depends on the speed of the relative airflow, and its density.

You cannot measure dynamic pressure in isolation, as static pressure is always present, so you should really write:

$$q = (q + ps) - ps$$

The pitot tube may be heated to stop it icing up, so watch your hands (tell the passengers). If the pitot is not at the front, it will be in another relatively undisturbed place, parallel to the relative airflow for best effect. Sometimes, a static source will be incorporated in a pitot head, as a small hole or series of holes around the side of the base.

A pitot tube failure will affect the ASI. A static system failure affects the ASI, VSI and altimeter.

If the static system fails:

- The ASI will over-read in the descent and under-read in the climb

- The altimeter will read the same in the climb or descent

- The VSI will read zero

If the pitot system fails:

- The ASI will under-read in the descent and over-read in the climb

Pitot-static systems are checked during regular maintenance, usually something like every 2 years for IFR machines. Preflight checks will be simpler, usually just making sure that nothing is blocking the holes (take the red covers off!) and that the heating works. Do not blow into the holes, at least, not with instruments connected (or with the pitot heat on!)

Errors

Errors in measurement will affect displayed speed, height and vertical speed. Accuracy depends on the shape of the probe and where it is placed. The total *pressure error* comes in two categories, *position* or *configuration error* (inherent from the design), and *manoeuvre error*, from the way you handle the machine, which mostly affects the VSI. Position error is defined as the *amount by which the local static pressure differs from that in the free stream airflow*. The ASI and altimeter can develop positive or negative position errors.

Configuration errors will have been established during flight testing, and can be displayed on calibration cards or programmed out by electronics, if you have them. Standby instruments, however, will not have the luxury, and will have uncorrected errors given on a calibration card.

The greatest pitot-static system errors are found when manoeuvring. If the left static port becomes blocked, the altimeter over-reads when sideslipping to the left but is otherwise OK.

Air Data Computer

The traditional pitot-static system uses a lot of pipes from the air data instruments (altimeter, ASI and VSI) to get its work done. The ADC was developed in an attempt to reduce the plumbing and improve reliability and accuracy, by allowing the instruments to be operated electrically from remote places. It is a "black box" in a central location that receives inputs from the usual sources (especially TAT, plus static and dynamic pressures, and angle of attack) and translates them into electrical equivalents for transmission to the relevant indicators, which have no pressure sensing elements, so they can be

CAPT

simpler (and cheaper) to make. Each module is a *servomechanism* (described later) whose output signals are fed through a *transducer* (such as the E & I bar used in a servo altimeter) before being transmitted to their associated indicators.

The data can also be fed to the autopilot and Flight Director, Flight Management System, GPWS, area navigation aids, instrument comparison systems, and the EFIS symbol generators to be converted for electronic display. Standby instruments use the pitot-static plumbing.

There are two ADCs in most modern air transport aircraft to provide redundancy.

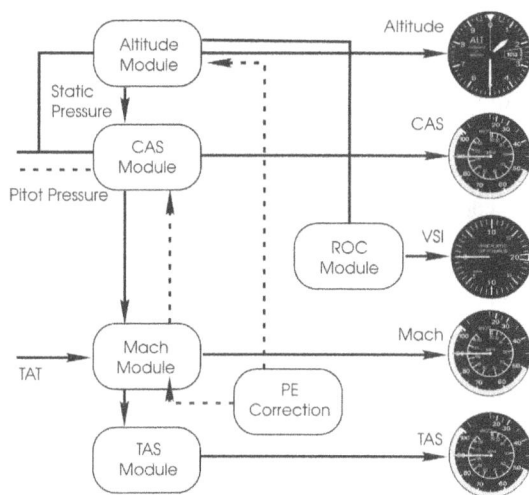

The most significant advantages of an air data computer (ADC) are:

• Position error correction, so the ADC puts out CAS, not IAS. The correction is done by the angle of attack sensor

• Remote data transmission capability

THE ALTIMETER

Static pressure is inversely proportional to altitude, so if you know the static pressure, you can figure out how high you are (in the standard atmosphere).

The altimeter is a barometer with the scale marked in feet rather than millibars. It does not measure the true height, but the weight of the air above the aircraft, which compresses the capsule inside. As you go up, pressure is less, so the altimeter translates air pressure into an *estimate* of altitude, although it will be better sealed than a barometer, so that air pressure in the cockpit doesn't affect it - the only pressure that should be there is static pressure from the pitot-static system. The readings could be inaccurate due to temperature and pressure variations from standard.

Inside a *sensitive* altimeter are *two* aneroid capsules (vacuums), which are corrugated for strength and kept open with a large leaf spring (a *simple* altimeter is a little more basic, with only one capsule - they are commonly used as cabin altimeters on pressurised aeroplanes since, at high altitudes, the capsule's movements are difficult to detect). The capsules' movements as you go up and down are magnified through the spring by a "suitable linkage" that connects directly to the pointer, using jewelled bearings. If the capsules expand, as they would when you go up, the pointer increases the reading. There is also a temperature compensation system to correct any spring and linkage tensions. Outside, there is a small knob, linked to a subscale which is visible through a small window. Rotating the knob causes the subscale to move and adjust the instrument to an *altimeter setting* (see *Meteorology*).

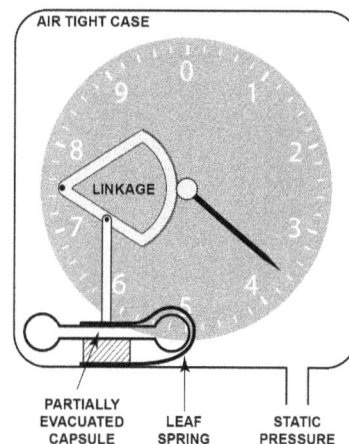

Caution: The three-needle display (on the right, below) can be easily misread:

The dials work like a clock. The long, thin pointer indicates hundreds of feet and the short, wide one, thousands. A very thin one, maybe with an inverted triangle at the end, as above, shows feet in ten thousands.

Only in standard ISA conditions will the true altitude be indicated directly. When it is extremely cold (below about -16°C), it will be a lot lower than shown, so corrections must be applied (altitudes given with radar vectors from ATC are corrected already). If this is something you need to take note of, you could perhaps mark the corrections directly on to the approach chart, next to the heights they refer to (you must recalculate *every* significant height).

Servo Assistance

The servo-assisted altimeter typically uses a digital readout and is connected to the ADC. In this instrument, the aneroid capsules are connected to one end of a pivoting magnet (an I-bar) which influences an E-bar that has windings on each of its arms.

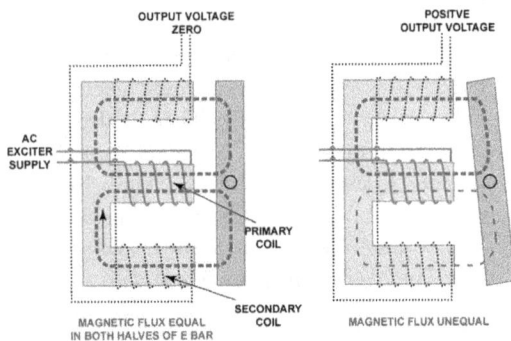

An AC current is fed to the primary winding on the centre arm, and as long as the gaps between the E and the I bars are equidistant, no voltage is induced in the coils on the other arms. The E-bars are wired in opposite directions and are connected in series to an amplifier unit - one example of the use of transformers.

Once the capsules increase or decrease in size, however, the gaps vary in size to create different magnetic fluxes and an output voltage that will be in or out of phase with the voltage in the primary coil, according to the direction of the displacement. Its magnitude will vary with the amount of the deflection.

The signal goes to the amplifier, then to the servomotor control winding so that the pointer and height counters are driven in the relevant directions (for more about servos, see *Remote Sensing & Indication*). At the same time, the servomotor gear train spins a worm gear that rotates the cam and cam follower to try and balance the magnetic fluxes at the I-bars, reaching the null point when the aircraft is levelled off and no more voltages are produced.

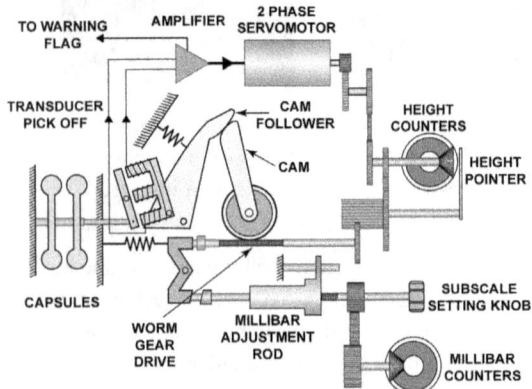

Turning the altimeter setting knob on the front drives the worm gear directly. All this complexity allows increased sensitivity at higher altitudes, as the aneroid capsules only

have to drive the I-bar and not the whole instrument. The rest is done by the servo motor, which removes lag and pressure errors, and can drive more robust displays.

If servo altimeters are used, a standby pneumatic one must be present.

Encoding Altimeter

An *encoding altimeter* is used with a transponder in Mode C so that your altitude can be shown on a radar display.

The encoding assembly is mechanically activated by the aneroid capsule. Older versions consist of a light source, various lenses and an encoder disc with a special pattern on it (in eleven concentric circles) that works like a bar code when the light is reflected from it to produce binary inputs that correspond to 100-ft increments in altitude. One turn of the disc covers the complete range of the altimeter. Naturally, there are now digital versions of the same thing that can also be fitted externally.

Note: The adjustment knob on the altimeter does not affect what ATC see on their radar screens! All encoding systems transmit your altitude corrected to 29.92 inches, or 1013.25 hPa. The ground equipment makes any regional corrections directly.

Errors

Altimeters suffer from:

- **Mechanical errors**, which include:

  - *Scale error.* The difference between the indicated altitude and the basic altitude at which the measurement is taken.

  - *Friction error.* Causes irregular or jerky movement of the needle when the inner workings are sticking together. It is fixed by gentle tapping or vibration.

  - *Position error* can arise from unusual attitudes or the behaviour of the airflow due to the shape of the surrounding fuselage as opposed to the smooth free stream. It is sometimes confused with Installation error, and is generally greater at low airspeeds as the angle of attack is abnormal, but manoeuvring doesn't help. On an aircraft with 2 altimeters, and only one compensated for position error, in straight symmetrical flight, the lower the speed, the greater the error will be between them, but an ADC should compensate (a non-compensated altimeter, however, will indicate a higher altitude). If the static source on the right gets blocked, in a sideslip to the right, the altimeter will over-read. *The error in altimeter readings caused by the variation of the static pressure near the source is position error.*

CAPT

- **Temperature error**, caused by linkages in the instrument shrinking or expanding, but this includes the temperature of the atmosphere, particularly when cold (see the *Meteorology* section). If the temperature is lower, *you* are lower! It will be around 4 ft per thousand for every degree of deviation from ISA, and the same deviation is assumed to apply for all heights. At a constant indicated altitude over a warm air mass, the altimeter reading will be less than true altitude. Going into a colder air mass, it will over-read.

- **Elastic error**, which includes:

  - *Hysteresis*, an irregular response to pressure changes (technically where changes lag behind the force that produces them) because a capsule under stress provides an imperfect response. This varies a lot with time passed at an altitude and is measured by the difference in two readings, when increasing and decreasing. Essentially, the altimeter gets used to a certain position and takes time to catch up if you move from it. The effects are negligible in slow climbs or descents, but a rapid descent will cause a delay, which is fixed with a vibrator, whose purpose is also to make the linkages work more smoothly. Indicated readings will lag behind true altitude, and the aircraft will be lower than indicated.

  - *Drift*. A slow increase in readings without an increase in altitude after levelling off from a climb - after descending the readings should return to normal. Drift should not be more than around 0.2% for every 15 000 ft change in altitude for flights over an hour long.

  - *Secular error*. The slow change over time of the entire scale error curve, mainly from internal stresses in the metal. Fixed by resetting zero.

- **Time lag** from the distance a pressure change has to travel in the pipes, at its worst during steep altitude changes. Due to lag, the altimeter will under-read in a climb, and *vice versa*.

- **Reversal error**, a momentary display in the wrong direction after an abrupt attitude change.

Between areas with different pressures, you could be at a different height than expected.

For example, flying from high to low pressure, your altimeter would over-read (from HIGH to LOW, your instrument is HIGH), so you would be lower than planned and liable for a nasty surprise, especially in the lee of a mountain wave. Conversely, going from low into high pressure, without the altimeter setting being adjusted, the altimeter will indicate lower than the actual altitude above

sea level. The same goes when you move between areas with different temperatures.

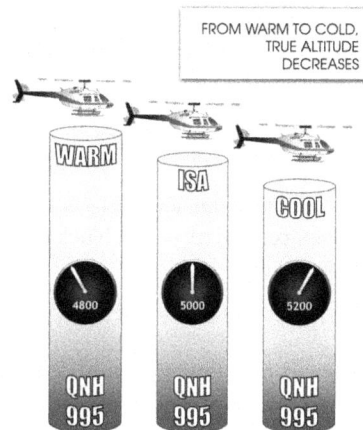

FROM WARM TO COLD, TRUE ALTITUDE DECREASES

The standard atmosphere has a temperature element that also affects the altimeter. Remembering that air density decreases as it gets warmer, a point in your imaginary column of air above a station would be higher on a warm day than otherwise. If, therefore, as is typical near the Rockies in Winter, the air is *very much* colder than standard (actually below about -16°C), you will be lower than you should be (actually, the phrase above is still valid, in that going from HIGH *temperature* to LOW, your instruments will be HIGH). A *cold low* will lower True Altitude to a point where it is dangerous to fly in mountains.

This is serious because, in low temperatures, combined with other effects from the movement of wind over ridges, you could be *as much as 3000 feet below your projected altitude* (although, with some navaids, you rely more on a radio signal than the altimeter). You could have a 150-foot difference on a published minimum of 500 feet and be too close to the ground. Normally, down to -15°C, you would apply a 4% increase for every 10°C below standard. In simple terms, when the surface temperature is well *below* ISA, correct your altitudes by:

Surface Temp (ISA)	Correction
-16°C to -30°C	+ 10%
-31°C to -50°C	+ 20%
-51°C or below	+ 25%

Another factor is the creation of a wind from a temperature difference. A cooler column has a lower pressure at a given altitude, and the warmer one has a higher pressure, causing air to move from left to right in this case so, after Buys Ballot's law, low temperature is to the left in the Northern Hemisphere with your back to the wind. The vertical distance between two pressure levels is less in cold air. Pressure in the upper levels depends on the mean temperature of the column of air beneath the point concerned.

You can refuse IFR assigned altitudes if temperature error reduces obstacle clearance limits to an unacceptable level, but once the assigned altitude has been accepted, you cannot adjust it for altimeter temperature error. When the aerodrome temperature is -30°C or colder, add 1000 feet to the MSA to ensure obstacle clearance.

The difference between True and Indicated altitude is called the D value.

A static blockage causes the altimeter to stay at the height at which the blockage occurred. A partial blockage would cause a significant time delay.

Altimetry

Altimetry is the science of measuring vertical distances in the atmosphere. The decrease of pressure with altitude depends on gravity and air density (the *hydrostatic balance*).

```
pressure = g x density x height diff
```

As vertical pressure variation follows the general gas laws, if you know the pressure on the ground and that at your height, you can work out your distance from the surface. For meteorology, 1 hPa is taken to be 27 feet in the lower atmosphere - for all other purposes, it is 30 ft.

Note: The word *height* refers to the vertical distance from a particular datum, usually the surface of an airfield (QFE, as used in Europe, is the airfield datum pressure, which makes the altimeter read your height above the airfield).

Altitude means distance above *sea level*, so the helicopter on the right has a height of 1000 feet (above the aerodrome, or QFE) and an altitude of 1500 feet (above the sea, or QNH).The difference is the *elevation* of the aerodrome.

Elevation is the vertical distance of a point on the Earth's surface from mean sea level. *Indicated altitude* is what is shown on the dial at the current altimeter setting. *Calibrated altitude* is the indicated altitude corrected for instrument and position error. *True Altitude* is the actual one above mean sea level, and is discussed later.

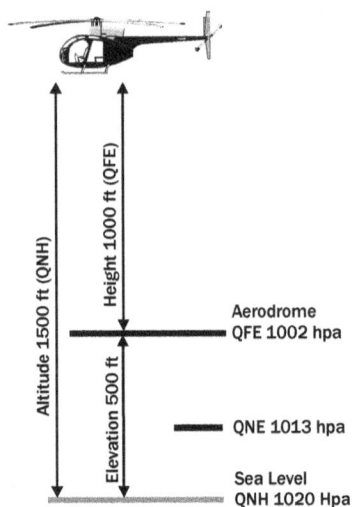

Altitude 1500 ft (QNH)
Height 1000 ft (QFE)
Elevation 500 ft

Aerodrome
QFE 1002 hpa

QNE 1013 hpa

Sea Level
QNH 1020 Hpa

CRUISING LEVELS

Cruising levels are expressed in terms of:

- **Flight Levels** - the altimeter reading with a digit knocked off the end. FL 30 means 3 000 feet when set to 1013.25. Usually, the *lowest usable FL* corresponds to, or is immediately above, the minimum flight altitude. Flight levels must be used above the transition altitude (below).

- **Altitudes**, below the lowest usable flight level, or at or below the transition altitude, based on QNH.

- **Heights** - used within the traffic pattern and based on QFE, if used, taken from the airfield elevation, but the threshold elevation is used for instrument runways if there is more than a 2 m difference, and precision approach runways.

TRANSITION ALTITUDE

A transition altitude is normally specified for an aerodrome **by the State in which it is located**. It is as low as possible, but normally at least 3000 feet in Europe, rounded up to the nearest 1000. In the USA and Canada, and other countries, it is 17999 ft. Below the Transition Altitude, vertical position is controlled by reference to altitude. Above it, Flight Levels are used, for which the altimeter must be set to 1013.

The *Transition Level* is the lowest available flight level (see below) above the Transition Altitude when the altimeter is set to 1013.2 hPa, so it would normally be FL 30 in UK, including when the QNH is more than standard.

Transition Level
Set QNH on the way down

Transition Layer
(0 - 500 ft)

Transition Altitude
Set 1013 on the way up

However, if the QNH is less than standard, the transition level will be higher than that. The Transition Level is determined **by the ATS unit concerned**, since it varies with pressure from day to day, and it is always *higher* than the Transition Altitude. The difference between transition altitude and transition level is the *Transition Layer*, which will be *more than zero and less than 500 feet*.

The change in reference between flight levels and altitudes is made, when climbing, at the Transition Altitude, and, when descending, at the Transition Level. In other words, when passing through the transition layer, report flight levels when going up and altitudes when going down. When descending to go below Transition Level, if you are cleared to a Flight Level, you must keep 1013.2 set on your altimeter. If you are cleared to an altitude, and no more FL reports are needed, set the QNH as soon as you start descending and report altitudes. Flight level zero is at the atmospheric pressure level of 1013.25 hPa. Consecutive Flight Levels are separated by intervals of at least 500 feet.

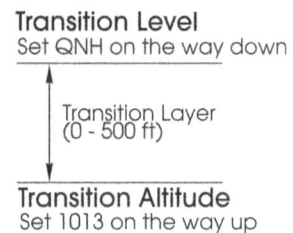

CAPT

EXAMPLE

If the QNH is 985 hPa and the transition altitude is 3000 ft, how deep is the transition layer (1 hPa=30ft)?

For this, you need to work out the pressure altitude at 3000 ft.

```
1013 - 985 = 28 hPa difference
28 x 30 = 840
3000 + 840 = 3840 ft PA
```

The next flight level is FL 40 which is at 4000 ft PA. The transition layer is:

```
4000 - 3840 = 260 ft thick
```

ALTIMETER SETTINGS

Three altimeter settings are used throughout a flight:

- **QFE** is used near an airfield, particularly in the circuit, and it indicates the your approximate height above the aerodrome reference point. At the aerodrome elevation, the altimeter will therefore read zero feet, and the QFE will be shown in the subscale. *Airfield QFE* is measured at the highest point of the airfield surface, and *Touchdown QFE* at the touchdown point.

- **QNH** is used for general transit elsewhere, below the transition altitude. It shows the approximate altitude above sea level (at the aerodrome reference point, it will show the aerodrome elevation). It is forecast for 1 or 2 (or even 3 in Australia) hours ahead over large areas, so don't expect accuracy. It is QFE reduced to MSL under ISA conditions. It should not differ from Local QNH by more than about 5 hPa although, in places like New Guinea, there could be a 10 hPa difference between the highlands in the centre as opposed to the coast.

- **QNE** is the altimeter reading at the runway threshold with 1013.25 on the subscale. It is used when the subscale does not go low enough to set QFE. It is a height, not a setting or a flight level.

QFF is the QFE reduced to MSL using long term mean conditions at the surface, including temperature and water vapour content (the temperature between there and sea level is assumed to be constant). QFF allows accurate surface charts to be drawn, as it is the basis of isobars. It is equal to QNH at sea level, regardless of temperature. When above MSL and warmer than ISA, it will be less than QNH, and more when the temperature is colder than ISA (the opposite below MSL). For meteorologists only!

The barometric pressure is constantly changing and varies from one place to another. What would happen if you departed the spot in the diagram above and returned several hours later to find the 1020 QNH above had

reduced to 995 Mb? The altimeter would be over-reading by 675 feet and you would only be 325 feet off the ground (1020 - 995 x 27 = 675, 1500 - 675 = 825 AMSL = 325 AGL). The altimeter needs constant updating as you fly.

Although altimeters are calibrated to ISA, the actual sea level pressure varies from hour to hour, and place to place. You would be very lucky to hit the standard atmosphere more than, say, 25% of the time, so you need a means of adjusting any instruments based on it to cope with the differences. To allow you to set the zero reference correctly, an altimeter has a *setting window* (also called the Kollsman window) in which you can adjust the figures of a *subscale* for the correct pressure on the ground by turning a knob on the front.

This is actually part of an important preflight check, where you make sure that if you turn the knob to the right, the height readings increase, and *vice versa*. If the subscale is set wrongly, the zero reference will be displaced by an amount proportional to 1 inch per 1000 feet, so your relative height to obstacles, like mountains, will not be maintained.

For example, if the proper altimeter setting is 29.92 inches, but you have 30.12 inches set in the subscale, the altimeter will be over-reading by 1000 feet. When flying from high to low pressure, your altimeter will also over-read (from HIGH to LOW, it is HIGH), so you would be lower than planned and liable for a nasty surprise. It's therefore much safer to be going the other way (that is, from LOW to HIGH, where your instrument is LOW).

An *increase* in pressure equals a *decrease* in altitude, so if you start with 29.92, then go to where it is 30.92, the altimeter reading would be 1,000 feet less, even though the figures themselves increase.

To convert from inches to hectopascals, start at 29.92 and find the difference between it and the current pressure. Divide the difference by 0.03" inches and apply the result to 1013. In other words, 1 hPa is about equal to 0.03". For example, if the current pressure is 30.02, that is, 0.1" above 29.92" (or 3 x 0.03), add 3 Mb and set 1016.

A more formal way is to use this formula:

$$\frac{hectopascals}{1013.25} = \frac{ins}{29.92}$$

Better yet, overleaf is a table:

hPa	Inches (of Mercury)									
(Mb)	0	1	2	3	4	5	6	7	8	9
970	28.64	28.67	28.70	28.73	28.76	28.79	28.82	28.85	28.88	28.91
980	28.94	28.97	29.00	29.03	29.05	29.08	29.11	29.14	29.17	29.20
990	29.23	29.26	29.29	29.32	29.35	29.38	29.41	29.44	29.47	29.50
1000	29.53	29.56	29.59	29.62	29.65	29.68	29.71	29.74	29.77	29.80
1010	29.83	29.86	29.89	29.92	29.95	29.97	30.00	30.03	30.06	30.09
1020	30.12	30.15	30.18	30.21	30.24	30.27	30.30	30.33	30.36	30.39
1030	30.42	30.45	30.47	30.50	30.53	30.56	30.59	30.62	30.65	30.68
1040	30.71	30.74	30.77	30.80	30.83	30.86	30.89	30.92	30.95	30.98

TRUE ALTITUDE

This is your (geometric) elevation above mean sea level, being the distance you could normally find with a tape measure, but it is impractical to throw one out of the window, so we use instruments such as the altimeter instead, to show an indicated altitude.

The only time an altimeter will indicate true altitude is in ISA conditions. As such conditions are rare, indications are almost always in error due to temperature.

The difference between true and standard (ISA) altitude is 4 feet per thousand feet per degree of deviation from ISA. That is, true altitude changes by 4% for every 10°C deviation from ISA conditions, or 2% for every 5.5°C*.

*4% is correct for the stratosphere, but it's more like 3.5% for lower altitudes. 4% for every 11°C is more accurate.

One source of error can occur when the temperature at a level might be close to ISA, when the lapse rate is not.

Note: All calculations should be rounded to the nearest lower hPa. The barometric lapse rate near mean sea level is 27 ft (8m) per hPa. Also, the airport elevation must be taken into account - that is, *only use the layer between the ground and the position of the aircraft.* In practice, true altitude is obtained from knowing the OAT at the level you are flying at, and using a flight computer. This will be reasonably accurate when the actual lapse rate is, or is near, that of ISA, i.e., 2°C per 1 000 feet, but if it's very hot, or very cold, you need further adjustments.

INDICATED ALTITUDE

Indicated and Pressure Altitudes are the same in ISA conditions.

CALIBRATED ALTITUDE

The Indicated Altitude corrected for airspeed, altitude, imperfect pressure lines, etc.becomes Calibrated Altitude.

ABSOLUTE ALTITUDE

The geometric height above terrain - what would be measured by a radar altimeter.

PRESSURE ALTITUDE

Pressure altitude is the height in the standard atmosphere that you may find a given pressure, usually 29.92" or 1013 Mb, but actually whatever you set on the altimeter - if you set 1013 on the subscale and the needles read 6,000 feet, the PA *for that setting* is 6,000 feet. So what is indicated is the height of the pressure selected. PA is a starting point for any calculations for performance, TAS, etc., and is the altimeter setting used above the transition altitude, where all altimeters must be set to 1013 hPa so that everybody is using the same standard (every country has a different transition altitude). Below the transition altitude, local altimeter settings are used.

If an altimeter is set to 1013, it is measuring Pressure Altitude with respect to Mean Sea Level. In ISA conditions, Pressure Altitude is the same as True Altitude.

If the sea level pressure is different from 1013, obstacle clearance heights and airfield elevations, etc. must be converted before using them. To do this, get the local altimeter setting, find the difference between it and 29.92 (or 1013), convert it to feet (1"=1,000 or 1 hPa=27 feet at sea level), then apply it the *opposite* side of 29.92. You could also get PA from the altimeter, by placing 29.92 or 1013 in the setting window, and reading the figures directly. The significance of this concerns performance - if the pressure on the surface is less than standard, you are effectively at a higher altitude, and your machine will not fly so well. You often need to calculate the pressure altitude of a location so you know your performance.

For example, for a strip on the side of a mountain at 400 feet above sea level, with an altimeter setting of 29.72, your PA at that location would actually be 600 feet, since the difference between 29.92 and 29.72 is 0.2, or 200 feet *added*, and where you would enter your performance charts, since they are set for the standard atmosphere (the altimeter setting is *below* the standard pressure, so your answer should be *above*). Again, you are *adding* because the sea is *lower*, and the figures ought to be higher (see the examples below).

Pressure levels with altitude are:

Height	Pressure Level
Surface	1013
10 000	700
18 000	500
24 000	400
30 000	300
34 000	250
38 000	200

CALCULATIONS

Tip: Always draw a diagram and place the numbers in order, with the large ones at the bottom. When on a local QNH for an airport, errors from variations in ISA only apply to height above the airfield elevation - local QNH (which is calculated under ISA) applies up till then.

Q: What minimum flight level will clear high ground rising to 1800 m AMSL by at least 1500 ft on a track of 225°(M), if the Regional QNH is 990 hPa? How much is the clearance at that level? (1 hPa=27 feet).

A: 1800 m is equal to 5910 ft. The difference between the QNH and QNE (1013 - 990) is 23 hPa, or 621 feet. Your minimum height is 621 + 5910 + 1500, or 8031 feet. The next applicable even flight level is FL 100, and the high ground is cleared by 3469 feet (10000 - 621 - 5910).

Q: A helicopter is flying at 2500 feet AGL near an airfield which is 350 ft AMSL. The QFE is 982 hPa. If another aircraft flies over at FL 40, what is the approximate vertical separation between them? (1 hPa = 27 feet)

A: 664 feet. 350 feet divided by 27 is 13 hPa, so the QNH is 995 (982 + 13). The difference between the QNH and QNE is 18 hPa, so sea level is 485 above the standard pressure level. Add 2500 feet to 485 and 350 to get 3336 and subtract that from 4000.

Q. A westbound aircraft is VFR at 8 500 feet. The OAT is -18°C and the altimeter is set to the nearest airport (30.22 - field elevation 2 000 ft). By how much will the aircraft clear a 7 500 ft ridge in the flight path?

A. This involves a temperature correction, with the complication that the QNH is measured at 2000 ft AMSL. ISA at 8 230 ft (the pressure altitude at 8 500 ft AMSL on the QNH of 30.22" Hg) is -1° to the nearest degree, so the deviation is -17°C. Correction is made for the difference between the elevation and aircraft altitude, i.e:

```
8 500 - 2000 = 6500
```

Adjust by 4 ft per 1000 ft per °10C:

```
4 x 6.5 x 17 = 44.2
```

The conditions are below ISA, so the true altitude is less than indicated. The aircraft is at 8 456 feet, which will be 956 feet above the ridge.

DENSITY ALTITUDE

This is the altitude in the Standard Atmosphere at which the prevailing density occurs, meaning your real altitude from the effects of height, temperature and humidity, and is used to establish performance, as it is a figure that expresses where your machine thinks it is, as opposed to where it actually is - see *Performance*. For now, it is *pressure altitude corrected for non-standard temperature* (ignoring humidity), or the true air temperature at a given level. Thus, density altitude has the same value as pressure altitude at standard temperature.

To find DA on the flight computer, set the aerodrome elevation or Pressure Altitude against the temperature in the *airspeed* window.

In the picture, the temperature is -21°C at 10 100 feet. The indicated airspeed is 350 kts, and the TAS is 396. The Density Altitude is 8100 feet - quite a difference!

If you want a formula:

```
PA ± (118.8 x ISA Dev)
```

(Multiplying the ISA Dev by 120 is usually good enough, and should be used in the exams).

Altimeter Checks

Rotating the knob through ±10 hPa must produce a corresponding height difference of about ±300 ft in the relevant directions. At a known elevation on the aerodrome, vibrate the instrument by tapping, unless mechanical vibration is available:

- Set the scale to the current QNH. The altimeter should indicate the elevation, plus the height of the altimeter above it, within ± 20 m or 60 ft for altimeters with a test range of 0-9 000 m (0-30 000 ft) and ± 25 m or 80 ft for altimeters with a test range of 0-15 000 m (0-50 000 ft)

- Set the current QFE. The altimeter should indicate the height of the altimeter in relation to the QFE reference point, with the same tolerances

- Both should be set to the aerodrome QFE and should indicate within ±80' of zero, within 60 or 80' of each other. Thus, they can misread by up to 120 or 160 feet and still be "serviceable"

- With No 1 on QFE and No 2 on aerodrome QNH, the difference should equal the aerodrome altitude AMSL, to within 80 feet

- With both on aerodrome QNH, indications should be within ±80 feet of aerodrome elevation, and 80 feet of each other

Note: No 1 is the handling pilot's primary instrument and No 2 the secondary.

According to CS 25 the tolerance for an altimeter at MSL is ±30' per 100 kts CAS.

AIRSPEED INDICATOR   022 02 06
••

To find airspeed, you need to compare the general pressure outside the aircraft (the static pressure) with the pressure created from its movement through the air, so this instrument is connected to both the static and pitot pressure systems.

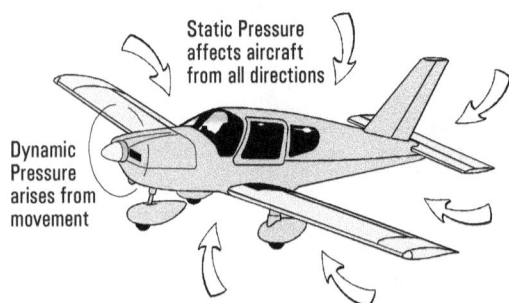

Static Pressure affects aircraft from all directions

Dynamic Pressure arises from movement

The ASI is similar to the altimeter inside, except that the capsule is fed directly with pitot pressure, and its size will vary in direct proportion to any increase or decrease. The

ASI is a pressure gauge with its dial marked in knots or mph instead of PSI. It captures **total pressure** then subtracts static pressure to get dynamic pressure. The needle is connected to the capsule through the usual suitable linkage.

Dynamic pressure varies with the square of the airspeed.

The combination of static and dynamic pressure is the *stagnation pressure*, because airflow is being brought to rest inside the pitot tube, or stagnating.

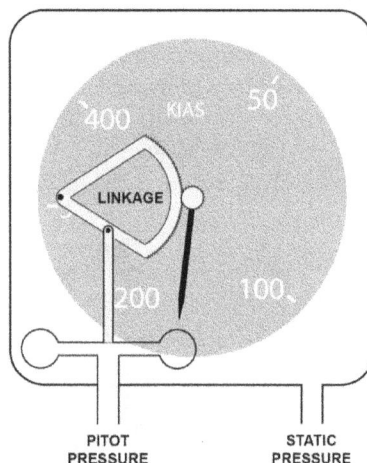

400   KIAS   50

LINKAGE

200   100

PITOT   STATIC
PRESSURE   PRESSURE

Note: Some aircraft, such as the Bell 407, have a dampened needle, which will indicate the speed you have been, and not the speed you are at.

Because the atmosphere gets less dense as you climb, the IAS must be corrected. The rate is 1.75% per 1000 feet.

There are several variations on the airspeed theme:

- **Indicated airspeed** (IAS) is the direct reading, corrected only for instrument error - turbulent flow around the pressure head accounts for 95%. Modern instruments have little error, so the direct reading is effectively IAS.

- **Calibrated airspeed** (CAS) is the IAS corrected for pressure (system) errors, which are highest at low speeds (IAS and CAS will be about the same at speeds above the cruise). It's known by older pilots as the *Rectified Air Speed* (RAS), and is a measure of the dynamic pressure at *low speeds*. Instrument and position errors can be corrected out by the Air Data Computer in modern aircraft. *An aircraft always takes off at the same CAS*.

- **Equivalent Airspeed** (EAS) is CAS compensated for compressibility, or factors arising from high speeds. It is the speed that gives the same dynamic pressure that would come from TAS at sea level. It does not consider density error, and is effectively IAS/CAS where such errors are small (below 200

CAPT

kts and 20,000 feet it will be around 1-2 kts). EAS is always lower than or equal to CAS, because, as the air is compressed inside the pitot tube, the dynamic pressure is greater than it should be, and the correction is a negative value, so it could be regarded as a form of error. The bridge between EAS and TAS is Density Altitude.

It's hardly worth working out because at the speeds and altitudes where it is significant, a constant Mach number is used anyway (see below).

- **True Air Speed** (TAS) is the CAS corrected for altitude and temperature, or density (its original calibration is based on the standard atmosphere). *It is the only speed* and the only figure used for navigation - the others are pressures and are to do with aircraft behaviour! On average, the TAS increases by 2% over the IAS for every 1,000 feet.

If air density remains constant, the relationship between IAS and TAS will remain constant so, if we double the IAS (in conditions of constant density) we will double the TAS. Dynamic pressure is proportional to the square of the TAS so, if we multiply the TAS by 2 the dynamic pressure increases by 4. With 4 times as much dynamic pressure and the same wing area, we need ¼ of the initial C_L to generate the same amount of lift.

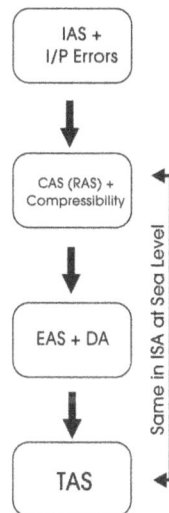

```
        ┌─────────────┐
        │ IAS +       │
        │ I/P Errors  │
        └─────────────┘
               │
               ▼
        ┌─────────────┐
        │ CAS (RAS) + │ ◄──┐
        │Compressibility│   │
        └─────────────┘    │
               │           │
               ▼           │ Same in ISA at Sea Level
        ┌─────────────┐    │
        │ EAS + DA    │    │
        └─────────────┘    │
               │           │
               ▼           │
        ┌─────────────┐    │
        │ TAS         │ ◄──┘
        └─────────────┘
```

You can find TAS from the CAS and Air Density, which can be derived from Pressure Altitude and temperature which may involve a conversion from Fahrenheit to Centigrade (and from miles per hour to knots). Thus, in ISA conditions at sea level, CAS = TAS. However, as an example, given an altimeter setting of 30.40", an indicated altitude of 3450', an OAT of 41°F and an IAS of 138 mph, let's find the TAS in knots. For the moment, take CAS as 118 kts, having converted 138 mph to 120 kts and looked it up on an imaginary graph (if there isn't one, the question will contain the information required). 41°F also converts to 5°C. The PA is found in the usual way, remembering that 1" equals 1,000'. The difference between 29.92" and 30.40" is 0.48, or 480 feet, which gives 2970' when subtracted from 3450' (29.92 is the "higher" figure in terms of distance above ground).

The TAS is 122 kts, and the Density Altitude (out of interest) is 2500'. If the TAS were over 300 kts, you have to apply a compressibility correction, which will bring TAS and CAS closer together.

If the pitot becomes blocked, the ASI will behave like an altimeter because it has only static information - its readings (i.e. your airspeed) will increase as you climb. If the static gets blocked, this will reverse.

If you maintain a constant CAS and level, flying from warm air to cold air, TAS will *decrease* as air density *increases*, and *vice versa*. In the standard atmosphere, therefore, when descending at constant CAS, TAS decreases.

If you climb at constant IAS, you will be climbing at a constant dynamic pressure, but air density decreases, so you need more V^2 to produce the same dynamic pressure.

At 40,000 ft for example, rho is about ¼ of its sea level value, so V^2 must be 4 times its own sea level value to keep dynamic pressure constant. In fact, TAS is twice the IAS.

To find out what happens to various speeds in the climb or descent, remember this picture:

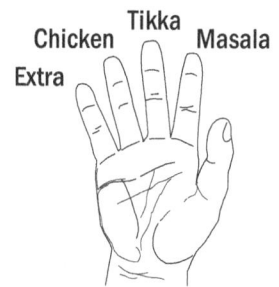

The initial letters stand for *Equivalent*, *Calibrated* and *True* airspeeds, and *Mach number*. In the climb, select which one remains constant, and the speeds to the right will be increasing, with the ones to the left decreasing. The reverse for the descent.

Above the tropopause (i.e. in an isothermal atmosphere) the Mach number and TAS will react in the same way at the same time.

Colour Coding   022 02 05

Various colours are specified for ASIs.

The *green arc* covers the range of speeds for normal operations, and the red line (in a light aircraft, anyway) is the speed not to be exceeded, V_{NE}, which varies inversely with altitude. The blue line is the single engine safety speed. A white arc represents the flap operating range. The limits are:

- Yellow scale: V_{NO}–V_{NE}
- Green scale: V_{S1}-V_{NO}
- White scale: $1.1.V_{S0}$-V_{FE}

At low levels, limiting speeds will be expressed as IAS, which is used for the takeoff and initial climb, during which the TAS increases while the speed of sound decreases as the temperature reduces. At higher levels, a Mach number is used, with the changeover point somewhere around 25 000 feet. A speed of M 0.9 at low level could be 550 kts, as opposed to 350 kts at 35 000 feet, which may be too high for the airframe.

Modern jets have a red and white striped barber pole type indicator for M_{MO}, which is a limit speed pointer that moves according to conditions, unlike the red V_{NE} line described above, which is fixed (Mach numbers depend on temperature).

Such an instrument is often called a CSI, or *Combined Speed Pointer* or even a a MASI, if it is combined with an ASI (but see also *The Machmeter*, later), because it also contains an altitude capsule that is connected to the limit speed pointer with the usual suitable linkage. The capsule expands or contracts according to altitude.

On the ground, the pointer is set to the maximum speed, where it will stay until the pressure and temperature relate to the equivalent Mach number (where V_{MO} and M_{MO} are the same, at around 27-28,000 feet).

As the IAS now decreases, the aircraft's limiting speed is referred to a Mach number and the pointer moves anticlockwise. The reverse happens on the way down. The Mach display is normally blanked at low Mach numbers.

A constant CAS and flight level produces a Mach number that is independent of temperature - i.e. it will not change.

Errors

The ASI suffers from position and attitude errors, plus those from the instrument itself, and lag. It is very susceptible to position error, which can be up to 10 or 20 kts at low speeds (check the flight manual), because the instrument will be calibrated for greatest accuracy in a particular flight condition (i.e. straight & level), otherwise the stagnation point will move to a different position.

However, density error is also important, since changes in air density affect the dynamic pressure, and make the ASI under-read at altitude (the ASI only reads TAS when density is standard, so to find it you have to apply a correction to CAS). The effect of temperature extending and contracting the linkages is fixed by a bimetallic strip that distorts to correct the expansion.

At high speeds (over 300 kts TAS, or 200 kts IAS) a further correction is made for compressibility, from air being compressed as it is brought to rest in the pitot tube.

If the pitot tube and its drain get blocked, the airspeed indicator will read high in the climb, low in the descent and not change at all when airspeed varies. This is because only the static pressure is changing, so they are behaving like altimeters (a typical icing situation). Thus, as you get higher, the instruments will over-read, and there is a danger that you will try to bring the speed back until you stall (without knowing why) which is what happened when the crew of one large jet missed the checklist item for the pitot heat. As static pressure *increases*, the ASI reading will *decrease*, and *vice versa*. If the drain hole remains open, however, IAS will read zero, as there is no differential between static and dynamic pressures, due to the drain hole allowing pressure in the lines to drop to atmospheric. A leak in the pitot total pressure line of a non-pressurised aircraft would cause an ASI to under-read.

If the static port gets blocked, the pressure inside the instrument (but outside the capsule) remains the same. The ASI will still read correctly in the cruise as long as the OAT doesn't change but, in the descent, it will over-read because the static element of pitot pressure increases inside the capsule - you will be closer to the stall than you think. In the climb, the static element of pitot pressure decreases, which causes a partial collapse of the capsule, so the instrument will under-read.

SQUARE LAW COMPENSATION

ASIs work on a differential pressure that varies with the square of the airspeed, and if you plotted the results linearly, the graph would look something like this:

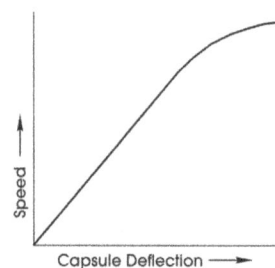

If you translated that to the instrument, you would end up with a logarithmic scale that would be difficult to read at low speed, and the whole speed range would be too big to fit in the display. To create a linear display, either the capsule or the linkage must be adjusted to produce the correct results or, rather, the indication moves at the same rate as the airspeed. Usually, the length or the point of leverage of a lever is adjusted to produce increased pointer movements for small deflections and decreased ones for large deflections. It is the *principle of variable magnification*.

V-Speeds

More in *Performance*!

Speed	Explanation
V_{LE}	Max gear extended
V_{LO}	Max gear operating
V_{NE}	Never Exceed speed.
V_{NO}	Normal Operations. 10% less than V_{NE}.
V_{MCG}	Minimum control speed on the ground
V_{MCA}	Minimum control speed in the air
V_1	Decision speed - must be greater than V_{MCG} because you need to control the aircraft
V_R	Rotation speed - must be greater than V_{MCA} because you need to control the aircraft
V_{LOF}	Lift off speed

Increasing the flap angle has no effect on V_{MCG} or V_{MCA}, but it lowers the minimum value of V_1 because it decreases V_{LOF}. However, the maximum value of V_1 is increased because drag is increased.

THE MACHMETER

Here, we are interested in the *Free-Stream Mach Number*, which is assumed to be far enough away to be unaffected by the aircraft.

In the Type A Machmeter, shown here, dynamic pressure is measured by an airspeed capsule, while the static pressure is measured by an aneroid capsule at right angles to it. A complex linkage detects their movement ratios. In other words, an ASI and an altimeter (in the same casing) feed their movements to a *main shaft*, which is connected to a *ratio arm*, then a *ranging arm*, to the *indicator* (rat ran in). When altitude decreases, the ratio arm slides to the end of the ranging arm, which reduces the ASI's involvement in the whole affair. As you go higher, it slides to the root, giving it more influence. Thus, the Mach number is found by dividing the dynamic pressure by the static pressure - *there are no temperature sensors.*

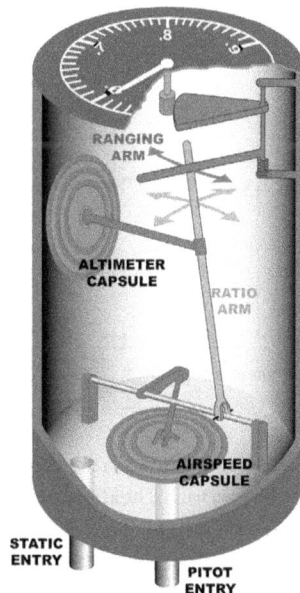

Type B Machmeters use the Air Data Computer, which does have a temperature sensor and is therefore able to correct properly for temperature rise and can display more accurate figures, usually to three decimal places.

On the flight computer, if you set the *Mach Index* opposite the temperature, you can read the speed of sound directly against the inner scale 1.0. In the picture below, the Index (a double-headed arrow) is in a window at the bottom. TAS 280 corresponds to a Mach No of 0.424.

Errors

The machmeter does not suffer from density error because it cancels out on both sides of the equation, but it is prone to instrument and pressure errors (which are actually very small, so indicated Mach number is taken as the true Mach number. Machmeter readings are subject to *position pressure error*. If the pitot source becomes blocked, the Machmeter shows the same errors as an ASI. The Mach Number will remain unchanged until static pressure changes in a climb or descent. In a climb, the airspeed capsule will have excess static pressure, so will cause the instrument to over-read (and under-read in a descent).

Blocked static sources mean that excess static pressure is trapped in the *case* and cause the instrument to under-read (in a descent it will over-read). If the static line fractures inside the pressure hull, static pressure will be too high and it will under-read. Likewise, if the pitot line leaks, the instrument will under read. At high speeds, temperature become artificially increased at speeds above about 300 kts, because of compressibility (this is already accounted for in the CR flight computer, so don't add any figures again from charts or tables).

VERTICAL SPEED INDICATOR

There is a capsule inside this, too, but it is connected only to the static system. However, there is a *restrictor*, or *calibrated leak* between the inside and outside of the capsule that makes the pressure outside it lag behind, so the VSI measures the *rate of change* of *static pressure* with height, based on pressure difference between the inside of the capsule and the inside of the casing.

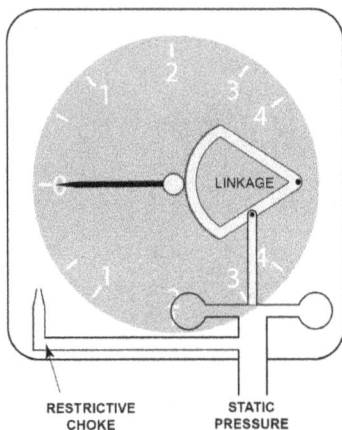

RESTRICTIVE CHOKE   STATIC PRESSURE

In other words, the difference in flow rates between two chambers is measured, with one chamber (the capsule) being inside the other (the case). Static pressure is fed in directly to the capsule so that any changes are due to movement of the aircraft. The flow through the restrictive choke, however, is constant, so the pressure inside the case is always lagging behind that in the capsule, and we are dealing with the rate of change in static pressure, as determined by vertical speed.

During level flight there is no pressure differential across the metering unit, but in a descent (for example), static pressure increases and flows into the capsule and case. The capsule will expand as normal, but the restrictor will keep the pressure inside the case relatively low and create a differential that distorts the capsule. A suitable linkage transfers the capsule's movements to the dial.

The VSI is a trend *and* a rate instrument, showing the direction of movement (up or down), and how fast you're going, in hundreds of feet per minute on a logarithmic scale, with zero at the 9 o'clock position, so it is horizontal during straight and level flight. Any movement up or down is shown in the relevant direction.

The advantage of a logarithmic scale is that, at low rates of climb or descent, the pointer movement is much larger and easier to read.

About 10% of the indicated vertical speed should be used to determine the number of feet to lead by when levelling off from a climb or descent.

Errors

A complex choke system self-compensates for temperature, density and air viscosity, using two capillary tubes to give a laminar flow and two sharp-edged orifices for a turbulent flow. Errors that result from the two types are of opposite sign and cancel each other out.

Aside from the usual position error, the VSI suffers from lag, which may last up to 6-8 seconds before the air inside and outside the capsule stabilizes. This means that, for example, once you level off and the altimeter is stable, the VSI takes a few more seconds to settle to neutral. There is also *reversal error*, which occurs when abrupt changes cause movement briefly in the opposite direction. In the hover, the VSI often shows a slight descent.

If the static source becomes blocked, pressure differentials disappear and the instrument reads zero. If the restrictor gets blocked, there is a greater difference in the rate of pressure change so the VSI will over-read. A leak in the case will make the instrument overindicate in the climb and underindicate in the descent.

IVSI

An *instantaneous (or Inertial) VSI* uses two accelerometers in the static line, or a static input to an acceleration pump, to reduce lag errors, which introduces turning errors.

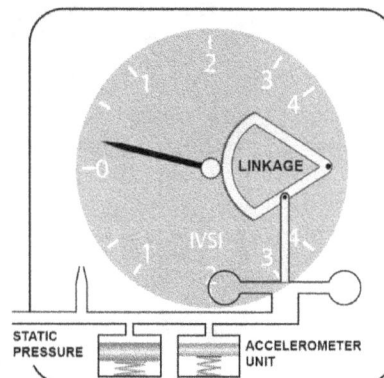

STATIC PRESSURE   ACCELEROMETER UNIT

The accelerometers are small cylinders with weights inside (they act like pistons), held in balance by springs and their own mass. The weights are centralised when stabilised in the climb or descent, but, when levelling, they act in opposing directions to sharply reduce instrument indications by puffing air into the appropriate places (inertia causes an immediate differential pressure).

When returning to level flight from large angles of bank, the IVSI will initially show a climb. If the turn is maintained it will stabilise to zero, and then indicate a descent on rollout. Thus, IVSIs should not be relied upon while initiating or ending turns at bank angles of more than about 40°

THE COMPASS   022 03/061 02

The Earth has its own magnetic field, with lines of force that are more or less parallel with the curvature of the Earth, but increasing their angle towards the Poles until they move vertically downwards in a circle surrounding the true pole.

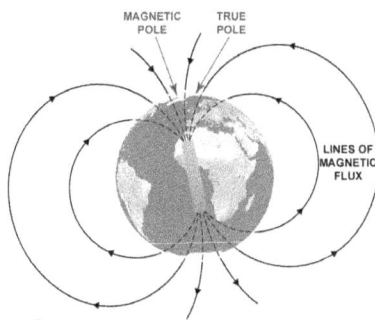

Although the origin of the Earth's magnetic field is not known, the Earth has its blue pole near the North pole and the direction of the magnetic force pointing straight down to the Earth's surface. In fact, the geographic North Pole is magnetically a South Pole, and *vice versa*, which is why the North end of a compass needle points to it.

A direct reading compass has a pivoted magnet that is free to align itself with the horizontal component of the Earth's magnetic field.

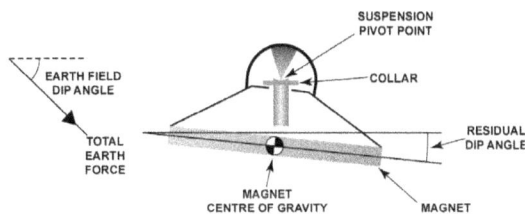

It must have certain properties to do this, namely:

- **Horizontality**. The needle must dip as little as possible, so the centre of gravity is made to lie below the pivot point, with pendulous magnets, that oppose the vertical component of the Earth's magnetic force (Z). Although there is still some dip, if it is less than 3° at mid-latitudes, it is OK.

- **Sensitivity**. This can be improved by increasing the length and/or the pole strength of the magnet. However, multiple magnets will do just as well, and they can also be employed as the weights under the pivot point mentioned above. Pole strength can be increased by using special alloys. In addition, you could use a jewelled pivot to reduce friction, and a suspension fluid which both lubricates it and reduces the effective weight of the whole assembly. Modern compasses are sensitive, down to 0.01 gauss, but even that gives excessive hunting (in fact, you need gyro assistance when the magnetic field is below about 0.06 gauss).

- **Aperiodicity**. The ability to settle quickly after a disturbance, without overshooting or oscillating, which is helped by the (transparent) suspension liquid and a wire spider assembly. The two magnets above are also useful here, as they keep the mass of the assembly near the pivot, reducing inertia. Light alloys reduce inertia even more.

Being magnetic, the compass will be affected by all the fields generated by the aircraft itself, causing a phenomenon called *Deviation*, which is discussed under *The Compass Swing*, below. To try and eliminate errors, particularly magnetic dip, a remote indicating gyrocompass may be used, which is slaved to a DGI (discussed later). The master unit is mounted near the rear of the aircraft, so it is removed from as much influence as possible (hence the term *remote*). It contains a gyroscope under the influence of a magnetic element.

The usage limits of a magnetic compass lie between 73°N and 60°S.

E2B

A typical E2B direct indicating *standby* compass, as used in most aircraft today, consists of a floating inverted bowl suspended on a pedestal in kerosene, for damping (the transparent liquid also increases sensitivity and aperiodicity). The bearings are marked on the outside of the bowl, and there are two parallel magnetised needles inside, suspended under the pivot point, as mentioned.

Here is what the insides look like:

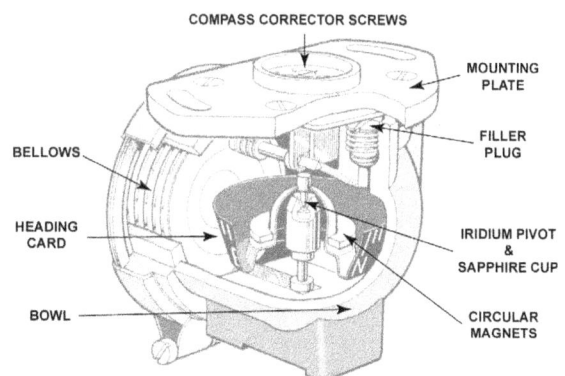

Dip

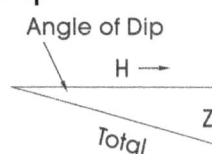

As the compass needle tries to follow the Earth's lines of force, it dips near the Poles, to where it is vertical (and unreadable), due to the vertical component of the Earth's magnetic force, which is called Z (in UK, the dip angle is around 67°). The bit we are interested in is *H*, the directive component, which is zero at the poles. At the Equator, there is no dip, so H is maximum, but as soon as you move away, the compass's Centre of Gravity becomes misaligned with its pivot point, and will move towards the Equator, or away from the nearer Pole.

H is about the same at magnetic latitudes 50°N and S.

Dip should obviously be minimised as much as possible, and is the reason why true tracks and headings are flown in Polar areas - the North and South magnetic Poles are the only places on the Earth where a freely suspended magnetic compass will stand vertical. On Northern routes, the dip effect causes a compass to turn much slower than you are used to in lower latitudes.

Magnetic dip is the angle between the horizontal and vertical forces acting on a compass needle toward the nearer pole. Its existence is why the limits of a magnetic compass lie between 73°N and 60°S (it is most effective about midway between the magnetic Poles). An *aclinic line* is a line representing points of zero magnetic dip. As the magnetic pole and lines of force do not coincide with either the true poles or lines of longitude, there is a way of accounting for any magnetic variation, discussed below.

Unfortunately, although the centre of gravity's position below the suspension point assists with minimising Z (and dip), it also gives rise to errors. Before you start relying on the compass (either to navigate or align your DGI), make sure you are in steady, level flight. Also, make turns gently, because the swirling fluid will keep the compass moving afterwards.

ACCELERATION ERRORS

These are caused by inertia on East-West headings. Because the C of G of the compass is under the pivot point, accelerating displaces the C of G behind the pivot point and makes the bulk of the compass lag behind the machine. If you were just going N-S, all you would get is extra dip, but because you are going East or West, the displaced C of G, not being vertically in line with the pivot point, creates a couple that makes the compass turn in the direction of the acceleration (clockwise when heading East) to read less than 90° during the turn. A deceleration has the opposite effect.

Acceleration errors are maximum on East/West headings and near the magnetic Poles, and nil on North/South headings, and at the Equator. The watchword here is ANDS - *Accelerate North, Decelerate South*, or SAND in the Southern Hemisphere.

In the Northern Hemisphere flying East, if you accelerate, the needle deflects to the nearest Pole (North, for an easterly deviation) and South when you decelerate.

- During deceleration after landing on runway 18 (a Southerly direction), a compass in the Northern hemisphere would indicate no apparent turn

- During deceleration after a landing in an Easterly direction, a magnetic compass in the Northern hemisphere indicates an apparent turn South

- During deceleration after a landing in a Westerly direction, a magnetic compass in the Southern hemisphere indicates an apparent turn North

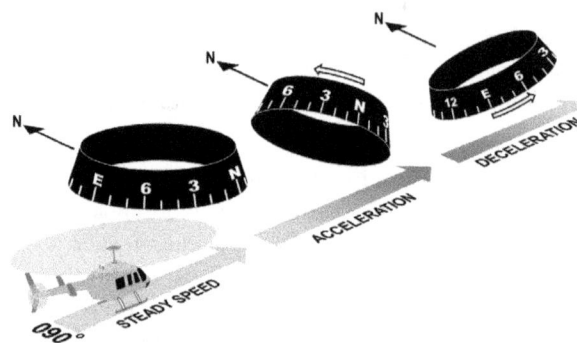

TURNING ERRORS

A Mr Keith Lucas discovered that a simple compass under-estimates turns on Northerly headings, and over-estimates them on Southerly ones in the Northern hemisphere (UNOS, and ONUS in the South).

This happens because you are banking and the compass tries to follow the lines of dip, with a little help from liquid swirl. To put it another way, to eliminate the hemispheres from the equation, during turns through the *nearest* Pole (within 35°), the compass is sluggish, so you need to roll out early. During turns through the *furthest* Pole, it will be lively, so roll out late. The errors are maximum (30°) at the Poles and decrease by 10° towards East and West, where they are nil.

Turning errors can have two elements, both of which work in the same sense:

- **Magnetic**, which depends on the angle of bank. In a turn from North to East, for example, the North-seeking end will move down towards Earth, so its readings will decrease and a turn in the opposite direction will be indicated. The more the bank, the more the error, so it is more apparent with a fast aircraft for the same rate of turn.

  Turning error actually depends on the tangent of the angle of dip multiplied by the cosine of the heading and the angle of bank. It is nil on E-W headings because the cosine is nil. For a 5° angle of bank, the error will be in the order of 30°.

- **Dynamic**, which depends on speed and the rate of turn. In a flat turn, the dip makes the C of G of the compass move toward the Equator and it moves to the outside of the turn, producing a clockwise movement as above.

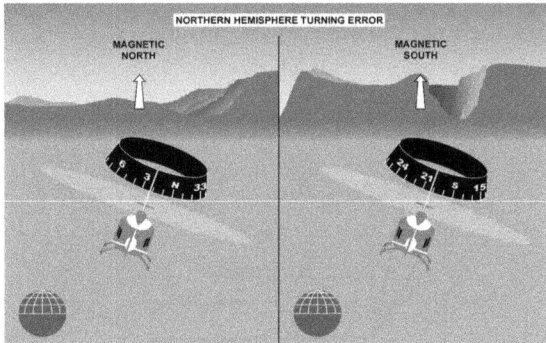

A rough calculation as to how much to overshoot or anticipate by when turning to the North or South comes from this formula:

$$\frac{\text{Bank Angle + Latitude}}{2}$$

So, to turn right on to a southerly heading with 20° bank at 20°N, you stop on an approximate heading of 200°.

In practice, just overshoot or undershoot by 20 - 30°, regardless of bank angle.

Direction

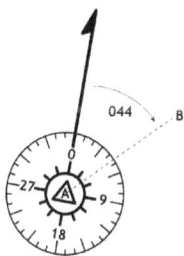

Direction (for us) is the position of one point relative to another, regardless of distance between them, measured in an angular fashion from the observer's meridian with reference to True, Magnetic or Grid North, using up to 360 numerical degrees*.

*The complete circle of direction (or *compass rose*) is split into 360 *degrees*, which are split into 60 *minutes* and 60 *seconds*, so the complete expression of an angle is in degrees, minutes and seconds - 30° 45' 53". North is 0°, so, going round the clock, East is 90°, South is 180° and West is 270° (the *cardinal* directions. NE, SE, SW & NW are intercardinal).

A *bearing* is a direction obtained by observation. It is the horizontal clockwise angle from a North baseline, or the angle between whichever North you use and any line between two points, such as that between A and B in the diagram above. The bearing is 044°, and the opposite is the *reciprocal*, found by adding or subtracting 180°, or 224°. Because you go clockwise, and the largest number is 360°, 355° is less than 010°.

Note: This is not the same as the *relative bearing* from your aircraft, which is measured from the longitudinal axis!

- **True North** is a line from any point on the Earth's surface to the North Pole (i.e. up, towards the top of the Earth), along the local meridian. Modern navigation systems such as INS/IRS output True North and their readings are changed to magnetic according to a lookup table.

- **Magnetic North** is the direction to the North *magnetic* pole, as shown by the North-seeking needle of a magnetic compass. Its usual symbol is a line ending with half an arrowhead.

- **Grid North** is a line established with vertical grid lines drawn on a map, explained later. It may be symbolised with the letters *GN* or *y*

All meridians run North to South.

MAGNETIC BEARINGS

The North *Magnetic* Pole was discovered by Soviet explorers to be the rim of a magnetic circle 1000 miles in circumference, around 600 miles from the True Pole. Both magnetic Poles move slowly around their respective True Poles, over a period of around 960 years. The North magnetic pole and various lines of force described below change their positions to the West.

That there is a True and a Magnetic North indicates that a compass will not point towards True North, since it relies on magnetism for its operation, and the two Norths (or Souths) do not coincide at their respective Poles. This is because the Earth generates its own magnetism, which may be varied by local deposits of metals under the ground, for example, which bend the magnetic flux lines. The way to Magnetic North will therefore vary across the ground from place to place, and a freely suspended compass will turn to the direction of the *local* magnetic field (the *Horizontal Component* is toward Magnetic North). As well, the lines of force will be vertical near the poles.

VARIATION

To find the direction of the geographical Pole, or True North, you have to apply a correction called variation, which is the angle between the magnetic and true meridians (that is, variation is the correction that must be applied to magnetic headings or courses (at the same place) to make them true. It is technically called *declination*.

If the magnetic meridian is to the right of the true one, variation is Easterly and has a plus (+) sign (think of what it makes the compass rose do). If it is left, it is Westerly and has a minus (-) sign So, -8 is really 8W. The **Magnetic Track Angle** (MTA) is the direction of the path of an aircraft across the Earth's surface against *Magnetic North*.

The phrase to remember is *Variation East, Magnetic Least, Variation West, Magnetic Best so*, if the variation on your map is, say, 21° West, the final result should be 21° *more* than the true track found when you drew your line.

- If you travel over many variations, use an average about every 200 miles.

- Variation on a VOR bearing is applied *at the station*, and on an ADF *at the aircraft*.

Note: Magnetic information in a Flight Management System is stored in *each IRS memory* - it is applied to the true calculated heading.

Variation can change temporarily from sunspot activity or magnetic storms. This is more of a problem in the Arctic or Antarctic areas, where the change can be ±5° for an hour or more. On a map, or chart, which would be drawn initially for True North, there is a dotted line called an *isogonal* that represents the local magnetic variation to be applied to any direction you wish to plan a flight on.

The charted values of magnetic variation normally change annually due to magnetic pole movement, causing values at all locations to increase or decrease.

When plotted, isogonals are accurate worldwide to ±2°.

An *agonic line* exists where magnetic variation is zero, or where True and Magnetic North are both the same. There's one near Frankfurt, running North/South.

The compass cannot be corrected for variation.

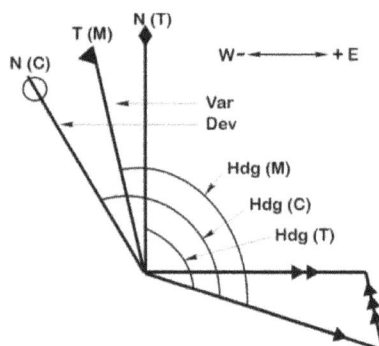

DEVIATION

Errors in the compass, plus an aircraft's own magnetism, from large amounts of metal and electrical currents, and any residual magnetism from hammering, etc. during manufacture, make the compass deflect from Magnetic North. This is deviation, which is unique to an aircraft, or even a compass position. It is applied to the compass heading to get the magnetic heading, and *vice versa*.

The net result of an aircraft's magnetic forces is represented by a dot somewhere behind the wings or rotor head. On Northerly headings, the dot lies behind the South part of the needle and merely concentrates the magnetic force. On Easterly headings, however, the dot is West of the South part of the needle and causes an Easterly deviation, and *vice versa*. It is proportional to Z and inversely proportional to H.

Deviation is the difference between a heading measured from the magnetic meridian and the same heading measured by a compass, at the same place. It is defined by the number of degrees which must be added (algebraically) to the observed reading to get the magnetic reading. Two aircraft flying in formation would have slightly different headings due to their deviations.

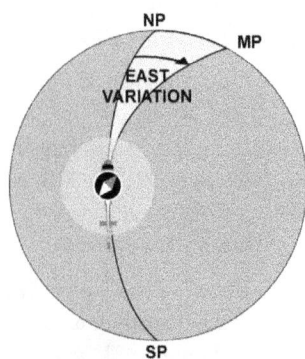

Compass needle pointing
east of true North

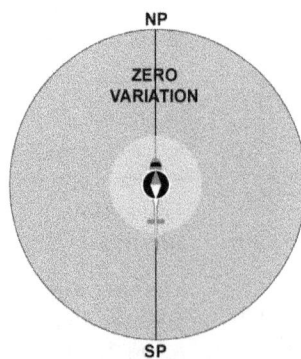

Compass needle pointing
to true North (along agonic line)

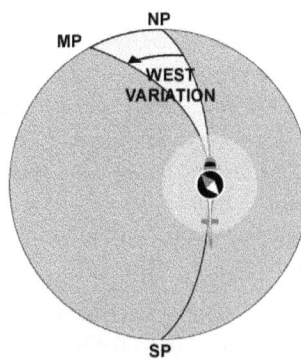

Compass needle pointing
west of true North

CAPT

When deviation is West, compass North is to the West of magnetic North. When deviation is East, compass North is to the East of magnetic North. The phrase here is *Deviation West, Compass Best, Deviation East, Compass Least,* similar to Variation. This means that if the compass is reading 005° when it should be reading 360°, the deviation is 5° West, or -5°, as it must be "added" to the observed reading to get the proper one. If it is reading 346°, the deviation is 14° East, or +14°.

Thus, positive deviations deflect the compass needle to the right, and will have a plus sign even though the heading reads less. Negative deviations deflect the needle to the left and have a minus sign, although the heading increases. The key is to realise that they are based on what the deviation does to the heading on the compass rose.

Deviation varies with the heading and its values are displayed on a correction card next to the compass (they should not exceed 1° after correction). The values are obtained after a *compass swing,* a complex procedure normally done by an engineer, described soon.

For	Steer
000	001
045	043
090	089
135	133
180	184
225	223
270	269
315	316

Allowing for deviation is called *compensation.* So:

$$HDG(T) \pm VAR \pm DEV = HDG(C)$$

EXAMPLES

1. With a compass heading of 030°, deviation of 3°W and variation of 8°E, what is the true heading?

C	D	M	V	T
030	3W	027	8E	035

The Compass Swing

The magnetic compass is incompatible with aircraft, if only because it needs to be placed where it can be seen, which is typically in the middle of any stray magnetism.

A compass swing allows you to find out by how much a compass reads differently from the proper figures on any heading, then make corrections that cancel out as many deviations as possible. Airfields have clear areas in which this can be done. The aircraft is taxied there and everything electrical that would be used in flight turned on. Then the aircraft compass is compared against a landing compass on several headings by an engineer standing out in the rain (you need to find the errors on the cardinal and quadrantal points, so the aircraft is placed on each one in turn). The deviations are reduced by adjusting the magnets inside the compass and a calibration swing is done to see what deviations or residuals, are left. Those figures are written on the deviation card. A compass swing should be done:

- on installation of the compass in the first place
- as per maintenance schedules
- whenever there is any doubt about accuracy
- after a shock to the airframe or a lightning strike
- if the aircraft has been left standing for some time or has moved to a significantly different latitude
- when major components or electrical installations change

Aircraft have built-in magnetism, whose influence on a compass can be classified broadly into 3 components, *hard iron, soft iron* and *electrical.* You can sum the individual effects and replace them with a single equivalent source.

HARD IRON

This is a more or less permanent effect that arises because the aircraft will have been on a particular heading* at a particular latitude for some time (more then three weeks or so) when it was being made, and will have absorbed some of the Earth's magnetism at that point. As such, it is the controlling factor in deviation. The effect is increased by hammering, and it will weaken when the machine starts flying, but some permanent magnetism will always remain. It is therefore unlikely to change.

There are vertical and horizontal effects, which are corrected with magnets. The field caused by such permanent magnetism is visualised as three components at the compass position:

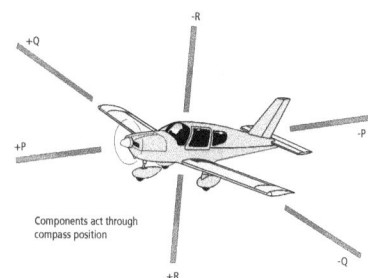
Components act through compass position

- **P** - fore and aft. It is minus if it pulls the red end of the compass needle to the rear (blue at the back), and plus if it pulls it to the front (blue at the front).
- **Q** - left to right (athwartships). Plus if it pulls the red end to starboard (blue starboard), minus if it pulls to port (blue to port).
- **R** - Up and down. Plus if it pulls the red end down (blue to the bottom), and minus if it pulls upwards (blue to the top). In level flight, it has no effect on the compass. Once it comes out of the vertical, however, the horizontal vector affects P and Q. When nose-up, for example, R will be acting forward, acting like P, so its maxima will be E-W (like Q when banking). The amount of the deviation depends on the value of R, and the angle between the longitudinal and horizontal axes. In practice, it is small enough to be ignored.

*P and Q only. If you built an aircraft at the magnetic Equator, where the Earth's lines of force are horizontal, you would get a fair amount of P and Q, and no R. If you built it facing SE in the Northern Hemisphere, you would get +PQR. R is always positive if the machine is built in the Northern Hemisphere, and negative otherwise.

Note: The capital letters represent hard iron effects. Small letters are used for soft iron effects, described below.

P is zero when facing North, but will remain attracted to North as a 360° turn is started and cause a deviation that depends on the component's polarity. It will be maximum when facing East, zero again at South, maximum again at West (in the opposite direction) and zero at North, so it is a sine relationship with the aircraft's heading. The maximum deviation from P is called *Coefficient B*, which is expressed as an angle. Coefficients are discussed overleaf.Component Q's maxima are on North and South, and vary as the cosine of the aircraft heading. The maximum deviation is resolved with Coefficient C.

In summary, hard iron magnetism is permanent, and does not change with latitude, but the deviation caused by it increases with latitude because the H force is weaker, and the compass magnets are more easily deflected.

SOFT IRON

This is a temporary influence that only appears when the metal in the aircraft is affected by the Earth's magnetic field and, to a lesser extent, aircraft electrical systems (i.e. induced magnetism). In other words, induced magnetism from ferrous metals that are not permanently magnetised. The effect of soft iron depends on the heading and attitude of the aircraft, and its geographical position.

As your heading changes, so does the soft iron magnetism.

Soft iron has a vertical element that is stronger in high latitudes because H is reduced. The horizontal element is also split further into X and Y to match the longitudinal and lateral axes of the aircraft.

Soft iron magnetism is visualised as coming from 9 soft iron rods near the compass that are affected by the Earth's magnetic field. The rods have length, but no thickness, and are *imaginary* - that is, they are simply a mathematical device that explains certain effects. You cannot use "bar magnets" as with hard iron magnetism, because of confusion as to which way the fields go in turns.

The rods are labelled with small letters (*a* - *k*) and are related to the XYZ components mentioned above like this: aX, bY, cZ, dX, eY, fZ, gX, hY and kZ.

The important ones are:

- cZ - fore and aft
- fZ - athwartships
- kZ - Vertical axes

cZ and fZ act like P and Q because they do not change polarity with heading. As Z acts vertically, it does not affect directional properties, and its sign will only change if the aircraft moved to the other magnetic hemisphere.

ELECTRICAL

Current flowing through a conductor produces a magnetic field. There can also be effects from lightning strikes.

COEFFICIENTS

Deviations from the components of hard and soft iron can be resolved into:

- **Coefficient A**, which is constant on all headings, and is found by dividing the sum of the deviations on the cardinal and intercardinal points by 8, so it is an average. It is caused by asymmetric soft iron around the compass, and is similar to a deviation caused by the lubber line being out of alignment. As the two are hard to tell apart, it is simplest just to move the compass.

  Apparent A (as opposed to Real A from soft iron) may be caused by an error in the magnetic bearing of an object used for swinging. Both are allowed for by rotating the compass by the result.

Aircraft	L/C	Result
000	352	+8
045	040	+5
090	094	-4
135	130	+5
180	172	+8
225	226	-1
270	273	-3
315	316	-1

For example, the sum of the numbers in the right hand column is 17. Divided by 8, this gives a correction of 2° to be applied to all headings (if the aircraft is headed North and the compass reads 5°, the error deviation is classed as -5°, meaning that the aircraft compass is under-reading and 5° must be subtracted to make it correct).

- **Coefficient B** is like a **fore-and-aft** magnet and is used to resolve deviations from P + cZ. It produces maximum values on East and West (zero on N-S), varying as the **sine** of the heading. It is the result of dividing E - W by 2.

- **Coefficient C** is like an **athwartships** magnet, with maximum values on North and South, varying as the **cosine** of the heading. It is used to resolve deviations from Q + cZ and is the result of dividing N - S by 2.

- **Coefficient D** is for soft iron on quadrantals*.

- **Coefficient E** is for soft iron on cardinal points*.

*D & E are not particularly important. Put another way, dealing with A, B and C is enough trouble so we leave them alone. D is not compensated for anyway as it is in the vertical plane.

- Residuals should not exceed 1° for a gyromagnetic compass and 3° for a direct reader.

- Combined changes (say from multiple electrical items) should not exceed 2°

- Deviations in level flight should not exceed 10°

- The maximum limits are ±3° for a gyromagnetic compass and ±15° for a direct reader.

Errors from B and C are corrected before those from Coefficient A (in fact, C is done first), and are minimised by equal and opposite effects to those from the aircraft.

The E2B uses *scissor magnets*, and electromagnets are used in gyro compasses.

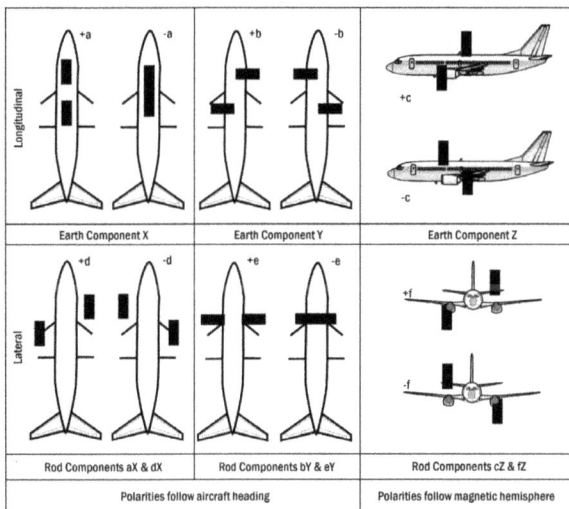

Earth Component X	Earth Component Y	Earth Component Z
Rod Components aX & dX	Rod Components bY & eY	Rod Components cZ & fZ
Polarities follow aircraft heading		Polarities follow magnetic hemisphere

GYROSCOPES

Gyros (and accelerometers) are also called *inertial sensors* because they use resistance to changes in momentum to sense angular (gyro) and linear motion (accelerometer).

The Earth itself is a gyroscope. Around the Equator it spins at around 1 000 knots, as opposed to the more typical 250 knots for man-made gyroscopes. As such, it is able to maintain its position in space to within 1° of the North Star, but another gyroscopic quality called precession (see later) makes the Earth's spin axis rotate around the North Star once every 26 000 years or so, known as the *Precession Of the Equinox*. This is because the Sun's gravity has an effect on the Earth's bulging middle, which is tilted by 23.5° anyway.

Usually, three cockpit instruments are under gyroscopic influence, the *Attitude Indicator* (artificial horizon), *Directional Gyroscopic Indicator* (DGI) and *Turn Indicator or Coordinator*. The first two are typically suction-powered and the last by electricity, but many are now all electric.

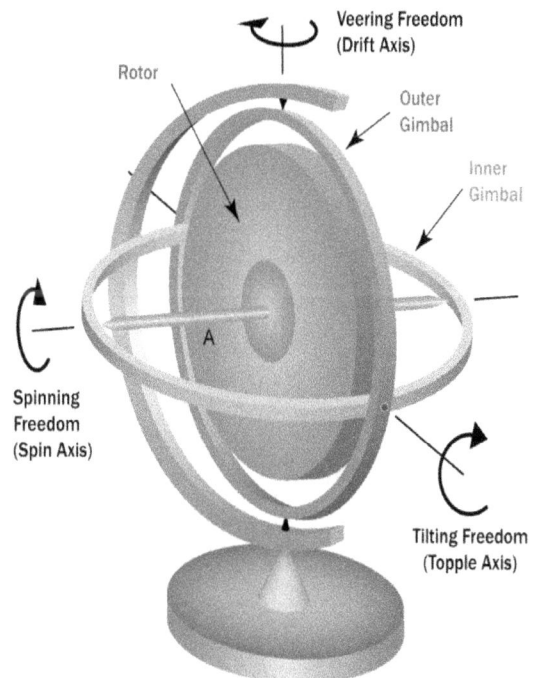

A gyroscope is a heavy rotating mass on a vertical or horizontal axis*, suspended in inner and outer *gimbals* which are in *frames*. Its operation depends on the resistance to deflection of a spinning wheel or disc, and only its Centre of Gravity remains fixed in space. The gyro is free to turn in any direction around it.

*A gyroscope's axis of rotation defines its orientation. A vertical gyro has its axis in *Earth Vertical* (as opposed to aircraft vertical) and a horizontal gyro is in *Earth Horizontal*, but more properly aligned with North.

You need a gimbal for each axis to be measured, so an artificial horizon has 2, because it measures pitch and roll.

Tip: During startup checks, pull and hold any erection or caging knobs *before* turning the power on, as the parts inside can clash against each other as they spin up (just one of those little things a pilot can do to save long-term maintenance costs).

Also, don't move the aircraft after flight until all the gyros have stopped running (takes about 15 minutes), otherwise they will go unserviceable more often. This particularly applies to autopilot equipped machines.

Rigidity

The spinning allows the gyro to maintain its own position in space, regardless of whatever it is attached to is doing. In other words, it resists attempts to displace it from its position. If you attached one to a camera in a helicopter, the helicopter could be bumping around all over the place due to wind or pilot input, and the camera would not move from where the operator put it. The same applies with the instruments mentioned above, as we shall shortly see. In fact, the gyro does not move, but the Earth moving around the gyro gives you that impression. The magnitude of this apparent movement depends on your latitude or, rather, the sine (drift) or cosine (topple) of your latitude.

Rigidity can be improved with:

- faster spin speeds
- increasing the gyro's peripheral mass
- increasing the gyro's radius

The greater the rigidity, the more force will be required to move the spinning gyro, which is an example of the *Law of Conservation of Angular Momentum*.

Precession & Wander

Any movement of the gyro's spin axis from its initial alignment is called *precession*. A force applied to a gyroscope's spinning mass is felt 90° away from where it is applied, in the direction of rotation. Put another way, pressure applied to the vertical axis is felt around the horizontal axis, and vice versa.

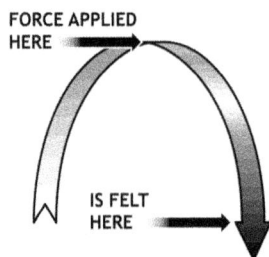

FORCE APPLIED HERE

IS FELT HERE

A mundane example comes from riding a bicycle - when you apply a force to turn one way or another, it is done at the top of the wheels, but the turning movement appears 90° later, hence the turn. More technically, precession is the *angular change in the plane of rotation under the influence of an applied force*.

The rate of precession depends on:

- the strength and direction of the applied force
- the rotor's moment of inertia (degree of rigidity)
- the rotor's angular velocity

WANDER

When a gyro moves from a preset position because of precession, it is said to wander.

The gyro is *drifting* when the axis wanders *horizontally*, and *toppling* when it wanders *vertically* (the term *topple* also refers to the tumbling that occurs when a gyro reaches a limit stop and a rapid precession occurs around a misaligned axis). Thus, a gyro with only a vertical axis cannot drift. Both are affected by real and apparent wander.

This is covered under *DGI*, where it is most relevant.

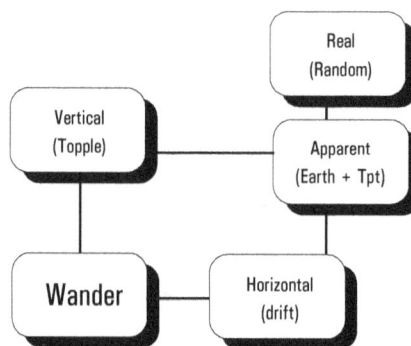

Drift occurs at 15° per hour multiplied by the sine of the latitude. Topple occurs at 15° per hour multiplied by the cosine of the latitude.

Types Of Gyroscope

3 PLANES OF FREEDOM

Gyros with 3 planes of freedom have 2 gimbals and total freedom of movement around 3 axes. There are 3 types:

- **Space Gyro**. Free to move in all directions with reference to space. Theoretical.
- **Tied Gyro**. As above, with the spin axis tied down in one local plane. 2 *degrees* of freedom (see below).
- **Earth Gyro**. As above, but the spin axis is tied *Earth vertically* by gravity.

2 PLANES OF FREEDOM

These show a rate of movement rather than a position:

- **Rate Gyro**. One gimbal, free to move around 2 axes (including the spin axis). Turn indicators.
- **Rate Integrating Gyro**. These are used in Inertial Navigation Systems.

*The fluid's viscosity is affected by temperature, so a warm-up period is required. It is so dense that the weight of the rotor and can is effectively zero.

DEGREES OF FREEDOM (GIMBALS)

A French method of classifying gyroscopes uses the numbers of axes *not* including the spin axis, so a gyro with 3 *planes* of freedom has 2 *degrees* of freedom. A degree of freedom is the ability to move around an axis, so we count the number of gimbals. The spin axis cannot precess, but each gimbal allows it to do so in one other direction.

An airborne instrument, with a gyro that has 2 degrees of freedom and a horizontal spin axis could be a DGI.

- *Spinning* freedom is about an axis perpendicular through the centre

- *Tilting* freedom is about a horizontal axis at right angles to the spin axis

- *Veering* freedom is about a vertical axis perpendicular to the spin and tilt axes

Degs	Gyro	Purpose
1°	Rate Rate Integrating	Turn Indicator Inertial Navigation
2°	Earth Tied	A/H DGI
3°	Space	Theoretical

Attitude gyros use rigidity in space for their operation, while rate gyros use precession.

Power

As mentioned, gyroscopic instruments are made to spin through suction or pressure (heading and attitude indicator) or electricity (turn instruments) although many are now all electric (even then, there should be separate and independent power supplies. If there is only one, you need suction, too).

SUCTION

With suction, air is usually *sucked out* of the casing, to create a vacuum that will be indicated on a gauge in the cockpit. It is part of the checklist before flight to ensure you have enough for the instruments to work properly, typically 4-5 inches of mercury.

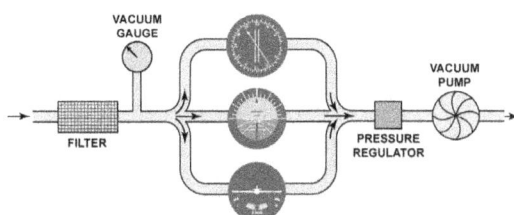

If it is reading low, the filters are blocked or equipment is worn, and the gyros will run too slowly. If the reading is too high, the gyros will run too fast.

Vanes (small bucket-shapes) on the gyro mass catch the air movement and force it to go round. at several thousand RPM. The rest of the vacuum system has a pump driven by the engine, a relief valve, an air filter, and enough tubing for the connections. Older aircraft may have a venturi tube on the side to create the initial vacuum.

ELECTRICITY

At high altitudes, suction-driven gyros can lose rigidity because they cannot produce so much vacuum. They also require large amounts of plumbing. These can be resolved with electrical gyros, whose advantages include:

- Faster spin speed, therefore greater rigidity

- Spin speed is easier to initiate and maintain, as aircraft power is regulated, and you don't need other systems running first

- The container can be sealed to keep dirt out - suction driven instruments necessarily have a hole in them to let air in

- More stable operating temperature

- The ability to work at higher altitudes

- Acceleration errors are minimised because there is no heavy mass underneath the gyro, but if there are, they will be due to the mercury sloshing around in the switches

The motor is usually a squirrel cage, using a power supply of 115v 400 Hz 3-phase AC in large aircraft, while smaller ones can have an inverter built in to produce 26 V (AC motors tend to be used in artificial horizons, while DC is used in turn and bank indicators). There must be some form of failure indication to show loss of power.

Fast erection involves giving the motors a higher error signal, which can be done in unaccelerated flight.

Ring Laser Gyros

These are used in inertial reference systems and use a partially silvered mirror (prismatic sensor) and 2 contra-rotating laser beams that go the opposite direction to each other in a precisely drilled tunnel round a triangular block of a vitro ceramic material called CERVIT that does not expand or contract with temperature (it is very hard) - any change in length produces the equivalent to real wander in a mechanical gyro (the mirror position* or the discharge current can be altered to compensate). Noise from imperfections in mirrors is the same as random wander.

The gas is used in creating the laser.

*The servo mirror can move. The collecting mirror allows a small amount of light through so one beam can be flipped around by the prism and meet with the other one that is aimed directly at the detector, which determines any fringe pattern generated by interference when the beams are out of phase. They are in phase (coherent) when there is no acceleration.

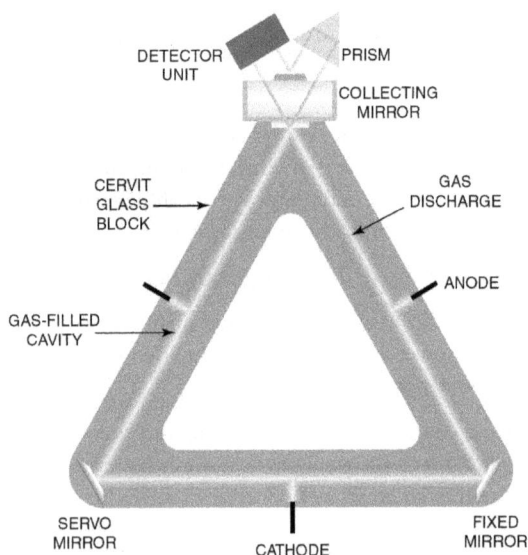

The counter-propagating waves normally beat together to set up a standing wave pattern inside the cavity. If their path length is altered artificially by movement, their frequencies change and so do their transit times.

Compared to conventional gyros, laser gyros are more accurate, and have a longer life cycle, because there are no moving parts (apart from the *dither motor* described below) and therefore no friction. They are also very quick to align, smaller and use less power.

LOCK IN

Picture: Ring laser gyros as used in an Inertial Unit:

At low input rates, the frequency differences become very near zero due to back scatter from one beam affecting the other. This makes them both synchronise.

Dithering is the name of the technique, using a piezo-electric motor, that is used to counteract it. The entire apparatus is rotated clockwise and anti-clockwise about its axis at a rate convenient to the mechanical resonance of the system, ensuring that the angular velocity of the system is usually far from the lock-in threshold. Typical rates are 400 Hz, with a peak dither velocity of 1 arc-second per second.

ARTIFICIAL HORIZON
• •

Otherwise known as the *attitude indicator*, this instrument represents the natural horizon and indicates the pitch and bank attitudes, that is, whether the nose is up or down, or the wings are level or not.

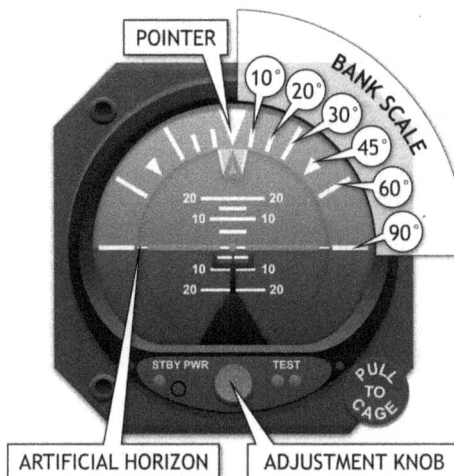

Given that a gyro tries to keep its position in space, as you move around the Earth, it needs to be kept level with the aircraft, so there is an erection mechanism, described below. The spin axis is *vertically mounted* (in line with Earth Vertical) so the housing (and the aircraft) can rotate around it. The whole assembly is inside an *outer gimbal*, which is Earth Horizontal, with two degrees of freedom.

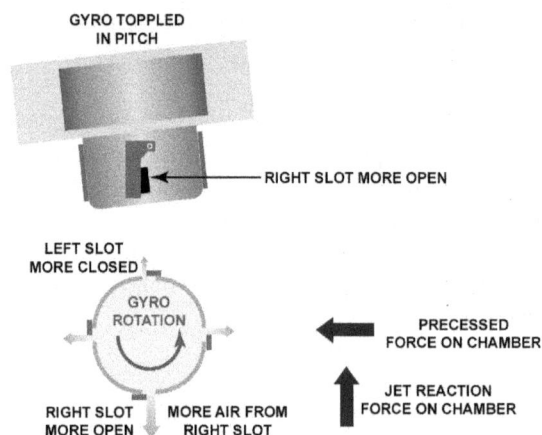

The instrument's C of G is below the suspension point, so it is nearly vertical when it is switched on, which reduces the erection time. In the suction-driven version, four *pendulous vanes* cover holes through which air tries to pass, but is blocked by the vanes as long as the instrument is vertical. When it is not vertical, the vanes, which are suspended from a pivot and kept vertical by gravity, open the hole by differing amounts to let more or less air through as required, to provide the correcting force.

CAPT

In other words, the pendulous vane stays vertical, but more of the hole is exposed as the instrument moves. As it has a slow erection speed, and is relatively slow to operate, this system is not perfect in accelerated flight. Electrical systems are more responsive.

The aircraft symbol is attached to the casing and therefore the aircraft. The *horizon bar* (which stays in line with the Earth) is connected to the rear of the frame and to the housing with a *guide pin*, so when the nose pitches up, the outer gimbal comes off the horizontal. The movement is amplified by the beam bar and the guide pin is driven down - in a descent it goes up. Rolling rotates the instrument case.

Aircraft Pitched Nose Up

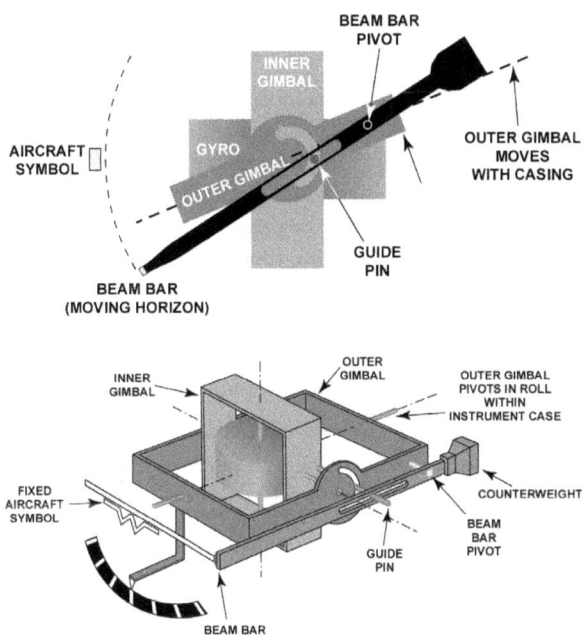

Errors

With all the rotating parts, there is bound to be friction, which will cause some errors in the readings. Others include *acceleration error*, during forward movement (as in a takeoff) which gives a false climb to the *right** - this is because of the pendulous mounting - the heavy bottom of the (suction) gyro suffers from inertia and creates an imbalance between misplaced centres of gravity (roll error) and closing one of the suction ports (pitch error) - the effect is similar to the compass. The resulting forces precess 90° away for false readings. Deceleration shows a false descent and roll to port.

*Electrical artificial horizons will show a climbing turn to the *left*, because they normally spin the opposite way.

Centrifugal force created during a turn will also displace the mass of the instrument's heavy bottom, so an instrument showing a climb to either direction indicates *pitch* and *roll* errors.

When an aircraft turns 90° with a constant attitude and bank, there will be too much nose-up and too little bank.

Electrical Version

In an electrical artificial horizon, two *torque motors* are used, one parallel to the lateral axis, and one to the longitudinal axis. The laterally mounted one detects movement in roll, and a correction from the torque motor is applied to the pitch axis. Displacement in pitch is detected by the longitudinal switch which corrects around the roll axis.

The torque motors are squirrel-cage type laminated iron rotors mounted concentrically round a stator, with two windings - one provides a constant field and is called the *reference winding*, and the other is in two parts so it can be reversible, called the *control winding*.

Levelling switches are sealed glass tubes containing 3 electrodes (one at each end and one in the middle) and a small blob of mercury. An inert gas is also present to stop any arcing as the mercury comes into contact with the electrodes. The glass tubes are set at right angles to each other on a switch block behind the gyro housing.

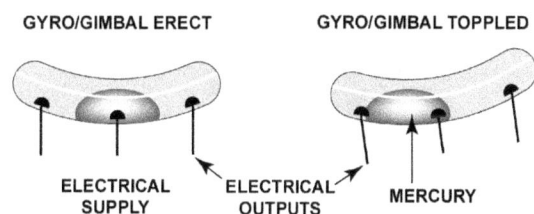

In the normal operating position, the mercury is in contact with the centre electrode, which is connected to the reference winding. If a displacement happens, the mercury makes contact with one of the side electrodes which completes a circuit to the relevant part of the control winding to apply the necessary torque correction. In fact, the voltage to the reference winding is fed via a capacitor and, as we know, this will cause the current to lead the voltage by 90°. As there is no capacitance in the control winding, it lags the reference winding by 90°. The resulting magnetic field rotates the stator in the required direction, at the same time cutting the conductor in the squirrel-cage winding and inducing a further magnetic field that makes the rotor follow the stator field. This is immediately opposed because the rotor is fixed to the case, so a reactive torque is set up to cause the required amount of precession to correct the instrument.

Remote Vertical Gyro

As older artificial horizons must be small to fit into most instrument panels, there are practical limits to the size of the gyros inside them.

A remote vertical gyro is placed somewhere on the airframe that can take the size of the gyros and the information is fed to the cockpit over electrical cables.

HEADING INDICATOR (DGI)

● ●

This is used to give a stable heading reference free from compass errors. It works in a similar way to the artificial horizon, except that the spin axis is *aircraft horizontal* in the *yawing plane*. That is, the spin axis is parallel to the surface of the Earth, so it can only turn in the horizontal plane and it will only be affected by drift.

The casing turns round a **horizontally tied gyro**, which has a compass card mounted on it, so the aircraft rotates around the compass card:

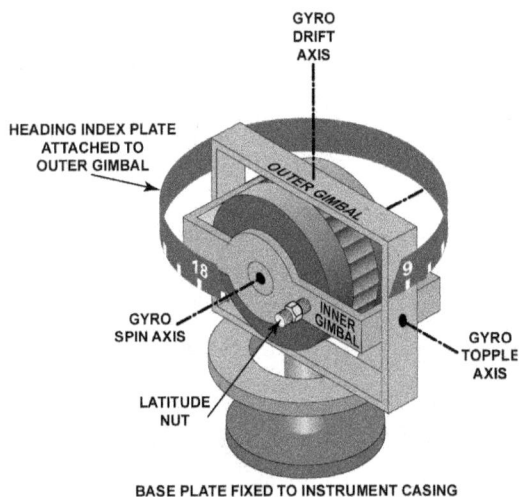

The instrument has **two degrees of freedom** with typical limits of 55° in pitch and roll. To help with re-erection after toppling, the mass of the gyro is spun at 10,000-12,000 RPM, with air jets from twin sources, very close to each other. When the gyro does not lie in the yawing plane, one jet (the drive component) will be pushing the gyro round, but the other (erection component) will strike the rim and cause a precession force at the top. This is correcting for fine topple. The caging knob deals with gross topple.

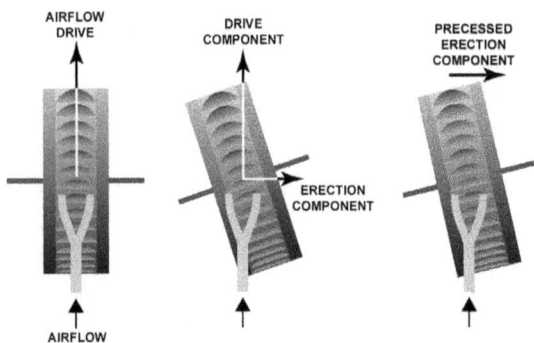

The DGI is aligned with the compass every 15 minutes or so to correct certain errors listed below (remembering, of course, to do it in level, unaccelerated flight).

DGI indications are only valid for limited periods due to:

* rotation of the Earth

* aircraft movement over the surface of the Earth

* mechanical imperfections, plus low rotor speeds

* gimbal system geometry (i.e. gimballing errors, which arise when the airframe does not move about one of the gyro axes. They are affected by banking, and go away straightening up again)

Wander

If you just sat in your aircraft (at the North Pole) and watched the DGI, you would see it change from its original setting at a rate of 15° per hour, all by itself, if you applied no compensation. This is because the gyro is trying to maintain its own position in space, and the Earth is moving. There are two main types of wander:

* **Real**, or mechanical, which comes from friction in the bearings, power fluctuations and other imperfections, although this is less than 1° per hour in modern systems and may be considered negligible. However, it is unpredictable and can be measured only by checking your heading. This is sometimes called random wander as the effect is supposed to be unintentional. A perfect gyro (in a question) has no imperfections, and no random wander., so you need not account for it

* **Apparent**, where the spin axis remains aligned to a point in space as the plane of reference changes, making the gyro *appear* to precess. It consists of:

    * **Earth Rate** (N-S), from the Earth's rotation. Although there is a vertical component, the horizontal component is meant when talking about this (assuming you are stationary). So, at the Poles, the gyro will appear to move at 15.04° per hour (in the horizontal plane) because that is the rate at which the Earth is spinning and orbiting round the Sun. The only time this won't happen is at the Equator (if the gyro's axis is aligned with a meridian and is parallel to the Earth's axis). Thus, it varies with the sine of the latitude, to the right in the Northern hemisphere and the left in the Southern hemisphere. The sign is negative in the Northern Hemisphere because the gyro under-reads as the Earth rotates. Apparent drift is corrected with a latitude nut (below).

    * **Transport Wander** (E-W). Here, the spin axis appears to move because you are crossing meridians and convergency (see *Navigation*) is added to the mix. With transport wander, flight to the West causes over-reading, and Eastward flight causes under-reading* (in the

Northern hemisphere), so if you held a steady heading of 090°, because the gyro is under-reading, you will be turning away to the *right* of earth track and your *true heading* is *increasing*. This is not normally corrected for in light aircraft, but is minimised by resetting the gyro every 15 minutes or so.

*Eastward flight increases apparent drift because the gyro is rotating faster than the speed of the Earth, and Westward flight reduces it, so errors will be more than 15° per hour, and less, respectively. N/S travel will only affect DGI readings as far as the latitude in the formula changes, so mean latitudes are used. A minor variation (**grid transport**) occurs when the great circle track curves away from a straight line track, and is proportional to the difference between convergence of the meridians as portrayed on the chart against how they should be on the Earth, and the rate at which you cross them.

LATITUDE NUT

The latitude nut (on the inner gimbal) introduces an equal and opposite precession force to counteract apparent drift - this is usually for 45° of latitude. In other words, a real wander is introduced to correct for fine drift. When wound outwards, the latitude nut exerts a greater force against the balance weight on the other side of the inner gimbal, where it is mounted. Assuming no other influence, going North of the preset latitude causes the DGI to under-read. Going South makes it over-read.

Use mean latitude for ER and TW where there is a north or south track component (**Note:** do not take mean latitude for a latitude nut - it only has one set value). Use the E or W component of groundspeed for TW calculations, taken from TAS and W/V. The formulae give you the error in degrees per hour, so interpolate for trips of more or less than one hour.

TOTAL GYRO DRIFT

This is the sum of the Earth Rate + Transport Wander + Latitude Nut + Random (Real) Wander.

- The **Earth Rate** is:

```
15° x sine latitude/hr
```

- **Transport Wander** is:

```
ch long x sine latitude/hr
```

or:

$$\frac{GS \times \tan lat}{60}$$

- The **Latitude Nut** is:

```
15° x sine of latitude setting
```

The resulting *drift budget* is the drift rate, in degrees per hour. Multiply it by the time period. The signs for the Northern hemisphere are:

- *Earth Rate* (-)
- *Latitude Nut* (+)
- *Transport Wander* East (-) West (+)

Reverse them for the Southern Hemisphere. So, for a DI with a Latitude Nut set for 40°N at 240 kts groundspeed on a Westerly heading at 50°N, you would add +9.64, -11.49 and +4.77 together to get +2.92° per hour

R	E(A)	L	T
0	-11.49	9.64	4.77

You may be given Real Drift as well (a perfect gyro has no random wander). On the DGI, *gross topple* is corrected with the *caging knob*, which grabs the gimbals and holds the gyro in one position. You can also turn the knob to move the gyro about the yaw axis, which turns the compass card so you can realign the instrument with the compass.

Note: Drift (at 15° per hour) is multiplied by the sine of the latitude, and topple by the cosine of the latitude.

EXAMPLE

What is the hourly wander rate at 49°N?

```
-15 x 0.7547 = 11.32/hr
```

The minus sign before the 15 indicates the Northern hemisphere. If this were corrected by a latitude nut, the observed drift would be zero.

Remote Sensing & Indication

Note: This is needed in order to understand gyromagnetic compasses, next.

SYNCHROS

A *synchro system* (or selsyn, to use an older trade name) is the electrical equivalent of a drive shaft, in that it can transmit motion, or information about it, electrically from one point to another. Synchros are widely used in motion and position sensing applications, although glass cockpits and transducers have reduced this somewhat.

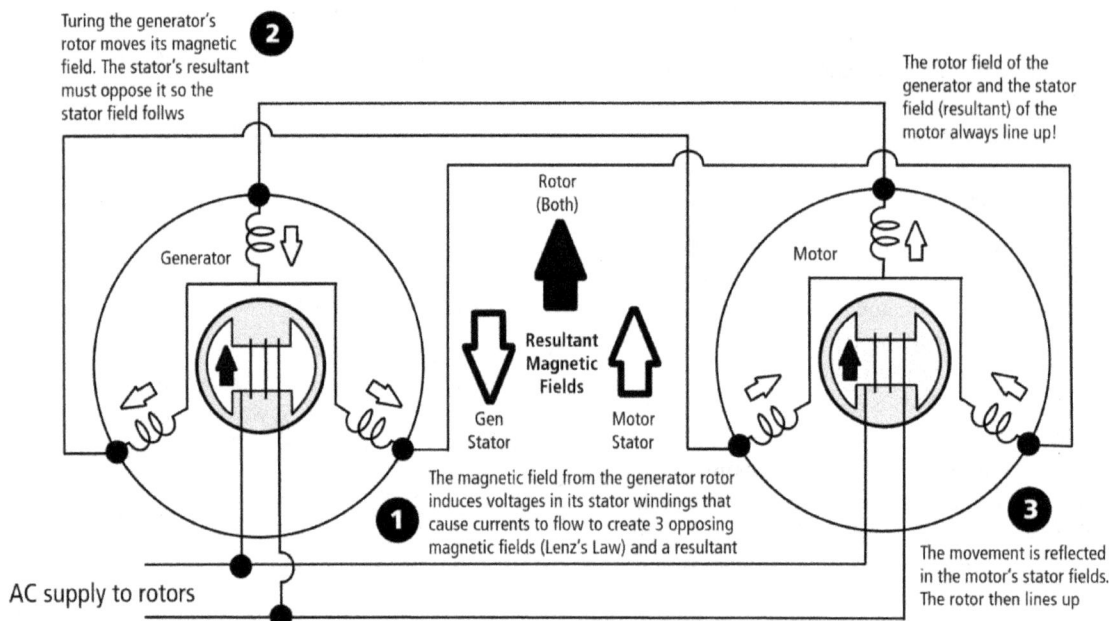

Turing the generator's rotor moves its magnetic field. The stator's resultant must oppose it so the stator field follws

2

The rotor field of the generator and the stator field (resultant) of the motor always line up!

Generator

Rotor (Both)

Motor

Resultant Magnetic Fields

Gen Stator

Motor Stator

The magnetic field from the generator rotor induces voltages in its stator windings that cause currents to flow to create 3 opposing magnetic fields (Lenz's Law) and a resultant

1

3

AC supply to rotors

The movement is reflected in the motor's stator fields. The rotor then lines up

A synchro looks just like an electric motor:

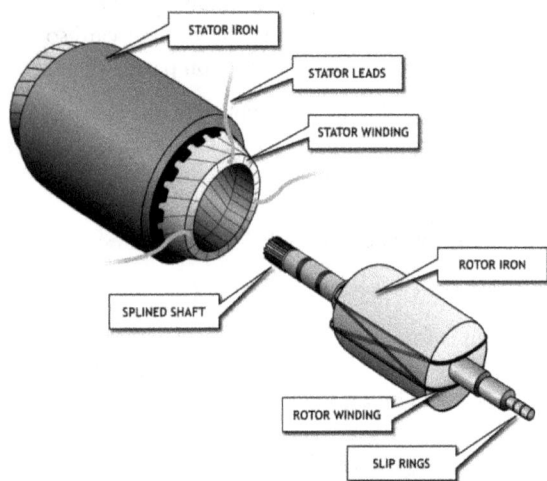

STATOR IRON

STATOR LEADS

STATOR WINDING

ROTOR IRON

SPLINED SHAFT

ROTOR WINDING

SLIP RINGS

But if you need to do more than drive simple instruments, you will need extra components in the shape of amplifiers, and motors to drive the load. This now becomes a *servomechanism*, which is described overleaf.

There are six types of synchro:

- **synchro motor**, known unofficially as an M

- **synchro generator** (G)

- **synchro differential generator** (DG). This can be either a generator or a motor. It transmits only the difference between two inputs, usually mechanical and electrical. For example, an undercarriage could be cranked mechanically with any corrections sent electrically as the sum or difference of the input signals

- **synchro differential motor** (D). Similar to the above, but the inputs are two electrical signals with a mechanical output

- **synchro control transformer** (CT). With this, an input signal produces a voltage (an error signal) rather than the mechanical movement you would get with a synchro motor. A CT normally forms part of a servomechanism in conjunction with an amplifier and a motor. After amplification, the signal can drive a motor that positions a mechanism, as with a servo altimeter. It is called an error signal because the strength and phase of the voltage represents the amount and direction that the G and CT rotors are at variance

- **resolver synchro** (CS). This is for precise angular measurements and trigonometric computations. It can convert cartesian coordinates into polar coordinates, and *vice versa*. The windings on the rotor and stator are displaced by 90° to each other rather than the 120° of other synchros. The output voltage remains constant with the rotor position but the time phase shift between input and output equals the rotor position angle in mechanical degrees. This principle may be used on navigation instruments to select the radial you wish to fly. For example, the Course Select knob on an autopilot mode control panel is usually a resolver synchro. The B737 Flap Position Indicator has a resolver synchro that monitors the outputs of two torque synchros which should always be the same. If you get an asymmetric flap condition, the synchro resolves the difference between them

CAPT

Any combination of the above is called a *synchro system*. The simplest would be a synchro generator connected to a synchro motor, which collectively is a *torque synchro system*. When the generator is turned, an electrical signal is sent to the motor, which turns the same number of degrees.

SERVOS

A servo is a machine, or a group of machines, that is capable of thinking, or at least solving particular problems within limited parameters. In other words, it can do the same thing over and over without getting bored, and could be viewed as a crude computer. A typical usage in aviation would be as an autopilot, as the follow-up mechanism to a series of synchros, since they are unable to supply the torque needed to position heavy loads. Having said that, a servo system does not need synchros to be called a servo - many are just mechanical.

A closed loop control system in which a small power input controls a much larger power output in a strictly proportionate manner is known as a **servomechanism**. Servomechanisms can correct errors from outside and from within itself. It can also figure out the difference between what should be done and what is being done, and make suitable corrections. Together with synchros, they are found in air data computers, amongst other things. As an example, you are flying East with your hands off the controls. After a while, the aircraft will drift off heading, which you notice, and conclude that you have to move the controls in the opposite direction to counteract the drift and bring you back on course.

How can you do that with a machine?

The first step is to replace your arms with an electric motor (DC) that can turn the controls in any direction, according to the position of a reversing switch.

Now you can control your heading by operating the switch, but the heading has no effect on the controls.

In other words, you need some feedback, or a mechanism that makes the heading of the aircraft activate a motor to correct the difference between actual and desired courses.

If you connect the arm of the reversing switch to the centre scale of the compass, when the aircraft drifts off heading, the compass stays where it should, but the arm will make contact with one side of the reversing switch as the fuselage rotates.

This makes the motor run and move the controls to get back on to the original heading.

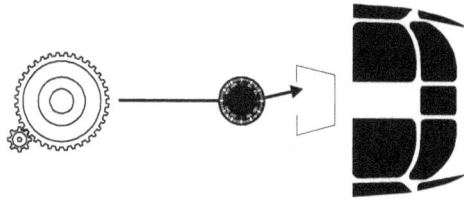

So far so good, but small movements below the minimum required to make the reversing switch operate will not be detected. More importantly, there will be a time delay between the aircraft going off course and the motor kicking in to correct things, because the aircraft has to go *past* the original heading to make the switch work in the opposite direction. The overcorrections will make the machine oscillate about the desired course. Not good for passengers' coffee!

Our autopilot, in fact, only knows in which direction to move the controls in order to correct an error, not how fast and when to stop. In other words, it lacks judgment.

So, you replace the reversing switch with a potentiometer, or variable resistance, which measures voltage differences across a wide range, and can behave like an error detector. In our case, the voltage difference will be proportional to the difference in degrees between the desired and actual headings, which can drive the motor and the controls.

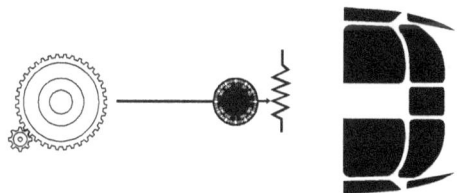

In practice, you would need something other than a potentiometer to drive the motor, because it would not be able to handle the current required. Not only that, the compass would be unable to drive the potentiometer.

However, it could operate a synchro generator, and you could replace the potentiometer with a synchro control transformer. To finish off, replace the battery and DC motor with a servo amplifier and a follow-up motor. Now, when you drift off course, the synchro G will rotate, and so will the synchro CT. The error signal from the CT will be amplified, then applied to the servo motor, which turns the controls to return back to the original heading. The above principles are used in the operation of......

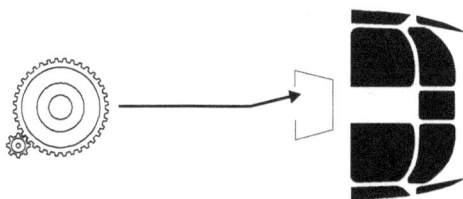

The Gyromagnetic Compass

A direct-reading compass's indications get weaker near the Poles, are subject to short term inaccuracies in the shape of turning and acceleration errors, and can only be read in one position in the aircraft. As well, it cannot drive or send information to other instruments. The Gyromagnetic Compass tries to resolve these problems by stabilising (gyroscopically) a magnetic compass and providing electrical outputs to the instruments that need to be read by the crew, or systems like IRS or INS. It is continually sampled for errors and short- and long term corrections are sent to the compass and gyro. So a gyrocompass is a DGI that keeps its own alignment. In an area with a weak magnetic flux, like the Poles, you have to disable the automatic slaving and use the instrument as a DGI.

The main components are:

- The *Gyroscope*, which provides short-term stability for azimuth reference. It will have 2 degrees of freedom and the input axis will be vertical (so the spin axis is horizontal).

- An *erection mechanism* to keep the axis horizontal.

- The *flux valve*, which is the detecting element for the Earth's magnetic field. It will be as far away from external magnetic influences as possible.

- The *Transmission and Display System* is simply the mechanism by which information is sent to the parts and instruments that need it. It includes a feedback system to keep everything synchronised.

- A *torque motor* to make the gyro process in azimuth at about 2° per minute. A dot shows in a small window on the display when the gyro is being precessed in one direction and a cross shows when it is being precessed in the other. In normal operations, they should alternate quickly. There is a manual rapid precession system.

The most significant errors are:

- *Apparent & Real Wander*
- *Gimballing*
- *Mechanical Defects*
- *Low Rotor Speed*

THE FLUX VALVE

You cannot directly measure the Earth's magnetic flux, because its H component is steady, but you can produce your own flux that changes with H, then measure and interpret the resulting voltage. This is done with a device that has three transformers at 120° to each other, with a curved horn at their ends to maximise reception.

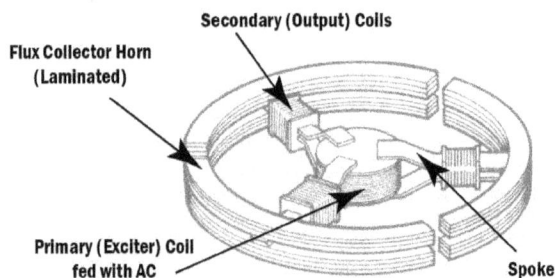

Using three spokes ensures that we know which way is North (or South). They are made of two identical parallel permalloy* strips on top of each other, with insulation between them and the transformer windings around them in series, in opposite directions.

*Permalloy loses its magnetic influence once the power is gone or, rather, it has a low hysteresis factor. It also magnetises very quickly.

The two poles of the resulting electromagnet cancel each other out and, in the absence of any other magnetic source (i.e. from the Earth), the total flux in another winding that is wound round the whole assembly is zero, as would be

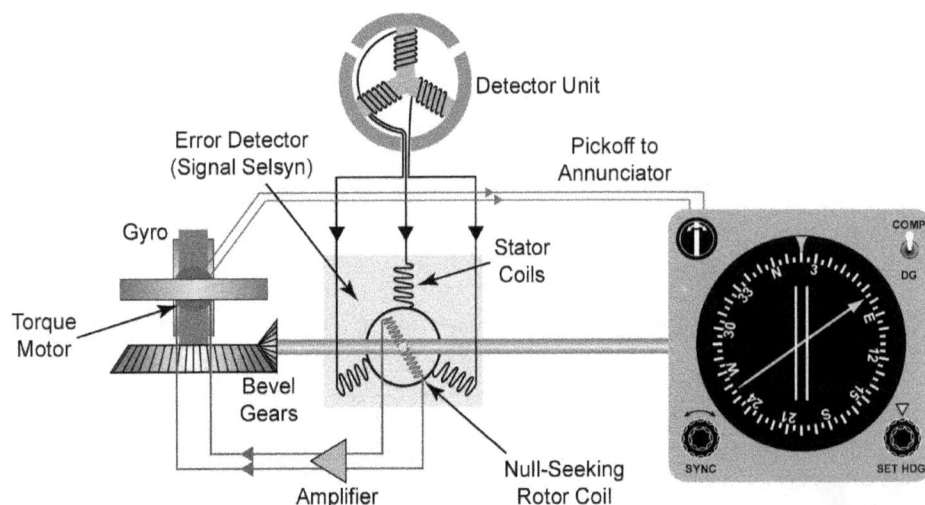

found when that spoke is at 90° to the Earth's magnetic field and both strips are detecting the same constant component of H. The maximum influence is obtained when the spoke is in line with the Earth's magnetic field, and any in between vary as the cosine.

In the picture below, a different value of H is present in each spoke, due to the angle between it and Magnetic North. The size of the field in each spoke now needs to be measured and transmitted to the rest of the equipment.

An exciter coil is placed in the centre, and fed with 400 Hz single phase AC so that a reversing magnetic field is created through the primary coil round each spoke. When the AC reaches its peaks, so much magnetism is produced that the spokes cannot deal with any from the Earth. However, as the current reverses, they become demagnetised, so current can be induced as the Earth's flux lines cut across them. As long as the aircraft is on a fixed heading, the field remains constant. When it turns, the field changes and a current is induced in the secondary coil. This varies the induction in each leg and the secondary pickoff coils produce a complex phased signal, part of which is more prone to saturation because the H element is working in the same sense. Where it is in the opposite sense, the magnetic peaks are simply reduced and can be measured.

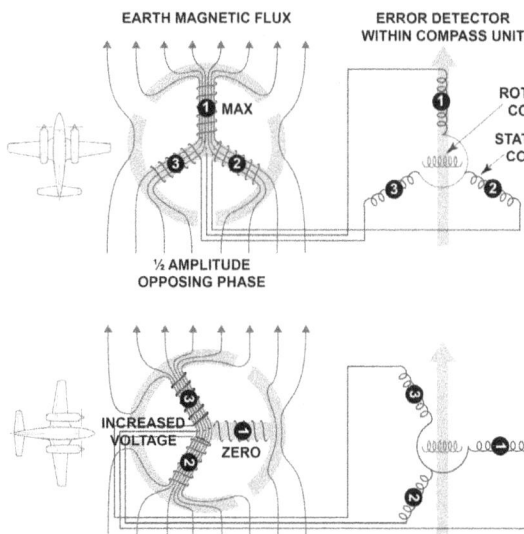

EARTH MAGNETIC FLUX — ERROR DETECTOR WITHIN COMPASS UNIT

More technically, adding magnetism from the Earth saturates a spoke before one of its AC peaks, and it won't die away for a similar period afterwards. The two fields no longer cancel each other out, and there is a blip of AC in the pickoff coil that varies with the Earth's magnetism. That is, when AC is pumped through a flux valve it produces a ripple at twice the frequency of the original current, so a sinusoidal voltage with a frequency of 800 Hz is obtained, with its amplitude directly in proportion with the Earth's magnetic field and the cosine of the magnetic heading. Thus, induction from the H component is greater

in one permalloy strip than the other, over an extended AC angle, the fields will no longer cancel out, and H will attain twice its original value. The secondary coil has converted pulses of saturated magnetism to voltage.

The flux valve assembly rotates with the aircraft. It also dangles from a *Hooke's Joint* (the technical term is *pendulous*) so it will swing within limits of around ±25°, to allow the aircraft to bank a little before it becomes inaccurate (it can switch itself off in a steep turn to avoid turning errors). The chamber that encloses the Hooke's joint also contains a viscous fluid to dampen any unwanted movement. This is to capture as much of the Earth's H force as possible, rather than the Z force which will produce turning and acceleration errors (as the DGI part uses slow acting torquers, acceleration errors are barely noticeable).

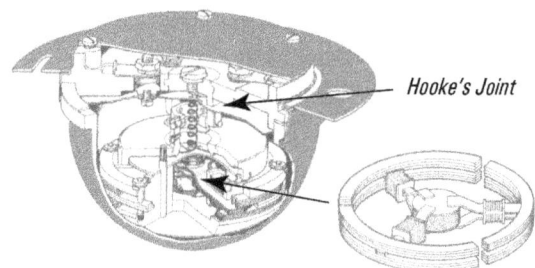

Hooke's Joint

As the system *senses* rather than *seeks*, it is more sensitive.

Heading information from the flux valve is compared to whatever the display is indicating and the results sent to an *error detector* or *selsyn unit* (self-synchroniser).

The signals then go through an amplifier to the torque motor, which precesses the directional gyro in the horizontal plane at 2° per minute. On its way, the current also flows through the *annunciator*, which is a small dial with a dot or a cross, depending on the current direction, whose purpose is to tell you that synchronisation is taking place correctly. The *synchronisation knob* is there for manual correction of gross topple in level flight. That is, it has the same function as the caging knob.

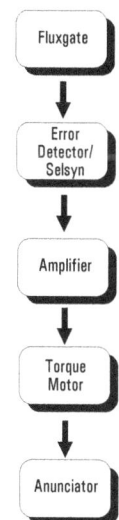

Gimballing errors arise from banking, and will disappear once a turn is complete. As deviation is corrected electromagnetically, deviation cards are not needed.

TURN COORDINATOR
●●●

This is actually a combination of two instruments, one power driven, and the other not. The idea is to measure the *yaw* rate for low *bank* rates, and since yaw and bank have to be measured, the instrument is made sensitive to both by having its axis (i.e. the gimbal ring) *tilted upwards* by about 30-35°, though it is less sensitive to roll.

The roll is sensed first, and the rate increases when the correct angle of bank is set. This is what the instrument is sensing. Displacement remains constant for a given bank, regardless of airspeed. A small aircraft tilts to indicate whether you are banking, so it is a useful backup to the artificial horizon, especially as the gyro is electrically operated and not affected if the suction system fails (although it gives you a rudimentary indication of bank, turns without the other instruments are done with timing). It becomes very useful when you are not able to use the full panel, as the amount that the wings of the aircraft move also indicates the rate of turn.

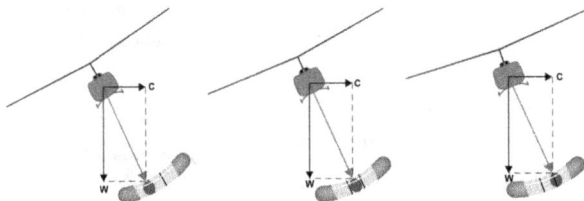

When the wings in the little aircraft hit one of the lower marks you are in a Rate 1 turn, which takes two minutes to go through 360°, making 3° per second (you can also add 7 kts to 10% of your airspeed to get a rough guide to the bank angle required). Underneath is a ball in a clear tube containing fluid, for damping purposes, called an *inclinometer*. It is subject to gravity (weight) and centrifugal force, and will be thrown one way or another if the aircraft is not in a coordinated turn. In a *slip* (left, above), the rate of turn is too slow for the bank, so centrifugal force will be less, and the ball will not be thrown out so much. It will therefore be on the *inside* of the turn (decrease the angle or increase the rate to correct). In a *skid*, the turn is too fast, so more centrifugal force causes the ball to be displaced more, to the outside of the turn (right, above).

Correction is the opposite of the slip. If you are out of balance, the instrument under-reads, so you will go past your turn.

Turn And Bank (Slip) Indicator

This instrument has a vertical needle instead of the horizontal small aircraft in the artificial horizon. As such it will only give you the *rate* of turn, since it is only sensitive to yaw., which is what is measured for **low bank angles**. It has the spin axis across the aircraft, so it spins up and away from you, with one end of the spindle held in place with a spring, so it has **one degree of freedom**. The spin rate is 10,000 RPM, and there are mechanical stops to keep it from going more than 45° either side of the centre.

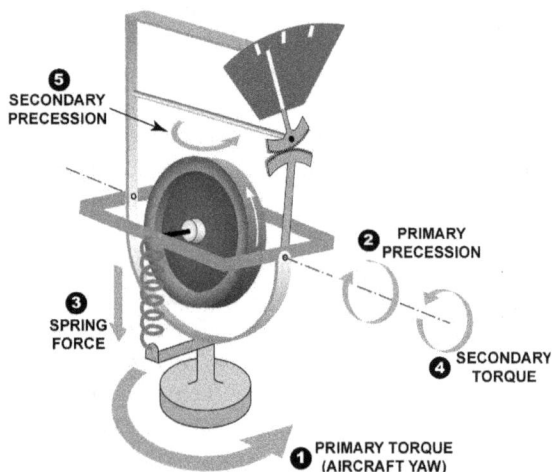

The gyro is aircraft horizontal with 2 **planes of freedom**. During normal operation, the spring keeps the spin axis horizontal so the turn pointer is at zero, and the gyro's rigidity will tend to keep it there. The yaw induced when you turn is precessed to the top and bottom of the gyro. As the springs stretch to cope with gyro movement around the longitudinal axis, they apply a force that produces a *secondary precession* equal to and in the same direction as the rate of turn. In other words, a turn makes the gyro move, to create a primary precession that stretches a spring that creates another in the same direction as the original force.

Without the spring, you would still see a turn indication, but would have no idea of its magnitude, so the spring controls the angular deflection of the gimbal ring and introduces its own precessing force. As the precession is equal to the rate of turn multiplied by the angular momentum, the force is a measure of the rate of turn.

All errors cause the instrument to under-read, except when the rate of turn is less than rate 1, when rotor speed is faster than normal, and the springs are slack. The ball is sensitive to gravity and centrifugal force.

CAPT

FLIGHT MANAGEMENT SYSTEMS

••

Understanding the FMS for your aircraft is vital for modern operations*. Luckily, they are similar between types, so that, if you understand the inner workings of the one on the Boeing 777, you can bluff your way through on the 737, 747, 757 and 767 (but not the 787). Indeed, the FMS chosen for the EASA exams is based on the 737. As the idea is to reduce pilot workload (and to make sure they don't make mistakes!), the autopilot should usually be left alone to do the job.

Managed guidance exists when the FMS controls the autpilot. *Selected guidance* exists when it controls the pilot!

*Air France 447 is one of the best known examples of why. On June 1st 2009, it was flying from Rio de Janeiro to Paris when it disappeared from radar over the middle of the Atlantic Ocean. It had flown through a thunderstorm, and there was no distress signal. The pitot tubes had frozen over in the storm, which made the autopilot disengage, and the pilots could not maintain enough airspeed to stay in the air due to the incorrect airspeed readings in the cockpit.

Basic procedures include passing everything you enter through a logic check. There should also be independent verification of entries when inputting the initial position through lat & long on the keyboard (from separate source documents). Although the idea is to enter your route before you start, it is possible to get airborne with just the first waypoints and put the rest in later when you have the time (although including the destination ICAO code at least gives it a start for calculating fuel requirements).

A Flight Management System is a mode-selectable colour flight display that can be defined as a *Global 3D Flight Management System*, whose function is to provide automatic navigation along planned routes (LNAV) and optimum flight profiles (VNAV), plus performance management for *managed guidance* by the crew. The system can manage altitude, speed, direction, multiple navigation sources and engine power, and can estimate waypoint ETAs and fuel remaining, amongst other things.

If the autopilot is not available, the FMS can at least drive the Flight Director so you can fly manually. It first arrived with the Airbus A320, to manage flight paths.

A true FMS normally consists of 2 Flight Management Computers (FMCs) and 2 (M)CDUs, one each for the Captain and First Officer (acting as Master and Slave).

A dual configuration means that the system can be used as a sole means of navigation, although backup traditional systems are usually present. With 2 systems, you have *redundancy* and *integrity*, as they can check each other out. You can also use P/RNAV airways, down to 2 nm wide, and perform FMS approaches in non-radar environments.

The data must be presented on different displays, so there is a 3-position switch that can be set to NORMAL, BOTH ON L or BOTH ON R (from that, you will deduce that there are Left and Right systems).

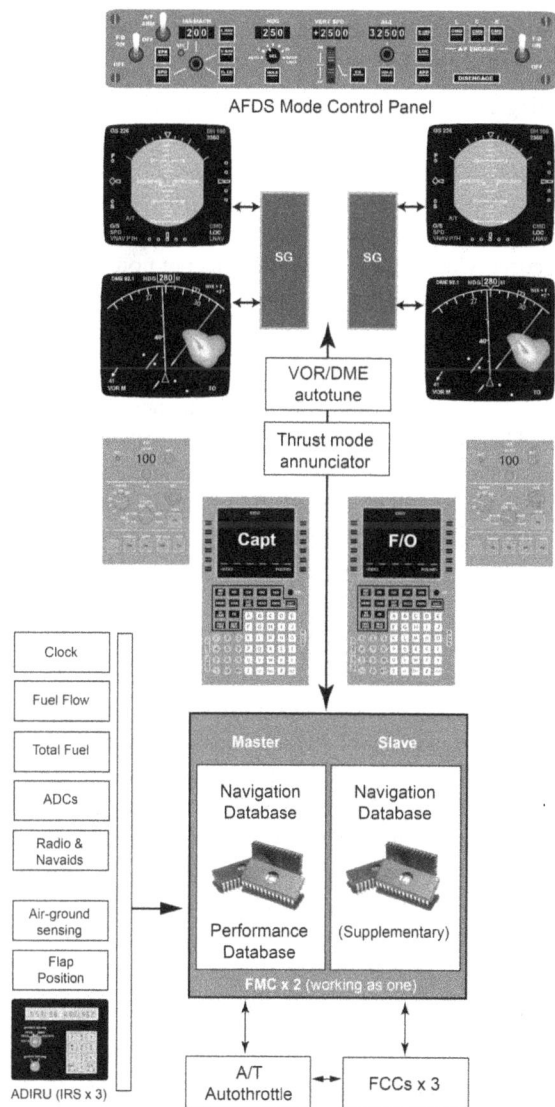

AFDS Mode Control Panel

With the switch on L or R, the system behaves like one FMC. The primary (Master) provides the guidance commands and maps the display, and the secondary (Slave) is synchronised with it. In NORMAL mode, the tasks are shared, each system effectively handling its own side of the aircraft, except that your position and velocity (and guidance) come from a weighted average. The *composite navigation solution* is a second aircraft state calculated in each FMC from both error estimates.

Single mode exists where only one FMS is operational. *Backup mode* exists when the FMC has failed in certain areas but still has limited functionality. You might have to *downmode* to Single FMC if there is a miscompare between databases on the start-up check, for example. An FMC can be *brickwalled* if there is too much of a discrepancy.

Data is combined from many sources, such as navigation systems, the Air Data Computer (airspeed, etc.), route information and operating requirements, to provide a centralised source of information and control for navigation and performance, if only to help manage fuel costs* by calculating optimum levels, etc.

*Operating costs depend not only on how much fuel you burn, but also time - it might cost a lot less if you fly slower, for example. The *cost index* is a measure of how time affects costs - that is, *direct* operating costs (insurance, etc. are fixed costs). It concerns time-related costs divided by fuel costs, which are expressed in cents per pound. If you fly slower or faster than the speed indicated by the index for that leg, costs will increase.

The 777 (and probably others) has a sliding scale of 0-9999. The higher the number entered, the higher the speed will be and the more fuel will be used - you will get maximum range by using 0! It is very rare to find an entry into an FMS of more than around 500, on the 777, at least. This is because higher speeds will be very close to some structural limits. A good average starting value might be in the 250 range. It is possible, of course, to override the set speed for timing on approaches, etc.

An *Air Data Inertial Reference Unit* (ADIRU) may supply air data (airspeed, angle of attack and altitude) and inertial reference (position and attitude) information to the EFIS displays as well as other systems, such as the engines, autopilot, etc. It acts as a single, fault tolerant source of navigational data for both pilots. The term has come to mean any integrated ADC/IRS unit, and may be complemented by a *Secondary Attitude Air Reference Unit* (SAARU), as with the Boeing 777 (see *Inertial Navigation*).

The ADIRU shows air data from the left pitot/static on the captain's side and the SAARU shows that from the right pitot/static on the FO's side.

The ADR is a small computer that corrects pitot-static information (airspeed, altitude, vertical speed) for high altitude operations. AD and IR functions are combined because some of their functions overlap - for example, the IRU knows how fast you are moving, and in what direction, and the ADR knows the TAS.

An ADIRS contains up to three fault tolerant ADIRUs, an associated control and display unit (CDU) in the cockpit and remotely mounted air data modules (ADMs). No 3 is a redundant unit that can supply data to the P1 or P2 display if the other two fail. As No 3 is the only alternate source of air and inertial reference data, there is no cross-channel redundancy between 1 and 2.

An inertial reference fault in 1 or 2 will cause a loss of attitude and navigation information on their associated PFD and ND screens. An ADR fault will cause the loss of airspeed and altitude information on the affected display. Either way, the information can only be restored by selecting No. 3.

To do its job properly, the system needs information, such as clock time, aircraft weights, fuel loaded, winds, ISA deviations, etc., particularly *databases* of waypoints, navaids, airways, procedures, airports, and other data. Most of the information for a flight can be found in the FMC. Whilst searching for it, ensure that someone is flying the aircraft!

Databases

There are two loadable databases that support the core flight management functions. These are:

- a **Navigation** database, for information relating to airports, navaids, airways, terminal procedures, and the like, along with RNP values for the associated airspace. In short, an airway manual in a chip. It does two jobs, relating to *navigation* and *flight planning*. It must be updated every 28 days (the RAC cycle) - the information, which may come from many commercial sources, is valid to the next expiry date, plus the next revisions. There is a permanent database and a supplementary one, which can be switched over at the right time.

- a **Performance** database, which is only updated when performance parameters change. It contains an average model of the aircraft and its engines, including flight envelopes and operating limits, to correct for the various conditions of flight. You can fine tune it and load defaults through the CDU, with alterations kept in NVRAM.

The system uses EPROMS for permanent storage, which cannot be changed in flight (but they can by engineers on the ground). Such NVRAM (*Non-Volatile RAM*) is Random Access Memory that keeps its contents when the power is switched off because it either uses a backup battery or flash memory ("normal" RAM, which does lose information when the power is off is called *volatile*). This allows you to update navigation data between updates.

Navigation and Performance also have their own processors, and there is a third to handle I/O (Input and Output) and the Built In Test (BIT). The information needed by them all is kept in (volatile) main memory.

CAPT

A dual system has an Inter System Bus (ISB) for communication between them. The twisted pair cable in the middle is the ARINC 429/629 data bus (the twist cancels out certain types of electrical interference). Some components are hardwired directly to the FMS, but most just wait for their data to come round.

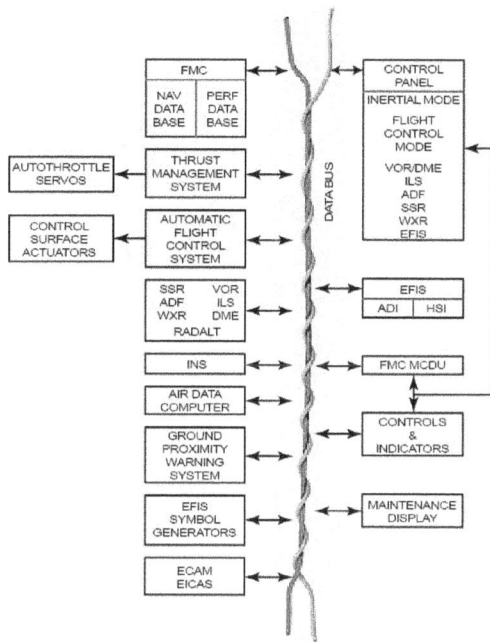

Tip: Oceanic waypoints use a 5-character naming convention (based on ARINC 424) for navigation facilities, reporting points and airway designators. The format changes North and South of the Equator and East or West of the Greenwich Meridian. For the North Atlantic, for example, take the degrees North and West and put N after them - 3060N for 30°N and 60°W. If you go over 100°, put the N in the middle- 30N60 for 30°N and 160°W (although the most you can go West across the Atlantic is around 80°W). If you have a half degree to cope with, as in 30°30' N and 60°W, the N goes at the front - N3060. Here, the N goes in the second place if you go over 100° - try 3N060.

Navigation

The FMC knows where it is from data supplied by the usual sources, plus IRS. The Best Position is generated every 5 seconds, based on the IRS, as adjusted for the Radio Position, as the FMS assumes that radio is more accurate. The new Best Position updates the System Position, which is used for LNAV (Lateral Navigation).

Operation of the FMC is based around the track to a fix and the groundspeed to get there. However, LNAV can also factor in the TAS to work out the angle of bank to fly a holding pattern (for example) and construct the dimensions of the hold each time it passes over the fix. LNAV (see *Radio Navigation*) can fly the pattern drawn on

the approach charts, based on the information entered into the Hold page and the TAS (this is a lot better than the guesstimates you fly with steam driven instruments).

Flight Planning

The basis of the flight profile is the route (or the *lateral flight profile*) you will fly from the departure point to the destination. The items making up the route are known as the *flight plan* (not to be confused with the ATC form). The information will come initially from the navigation database, and might consist of a departure airport (and runway) a SID, enroute waypoints (see overleaf) and airways, a STAR, and an approach procedure to a specific runway, although the latter two are often not selected until ATC at the destination is contacted. Once you're happy with all that, the details are assembled into a buffer where they are used for computing the lateral and vertical profiles. The data can also be transmitted from the ground via DataLink.

In Use

Central control means that you will select radio and navaid frequencies through the FMS control panel, or CDU - you should not see separate boxes in the cockpit. That is, the CDU is the principal pilot interface to the FMS and any other systems that interact with it. You enter data with the *alphanumeric keyboard* and *line select* keys, and you *must* get used to the menu system!

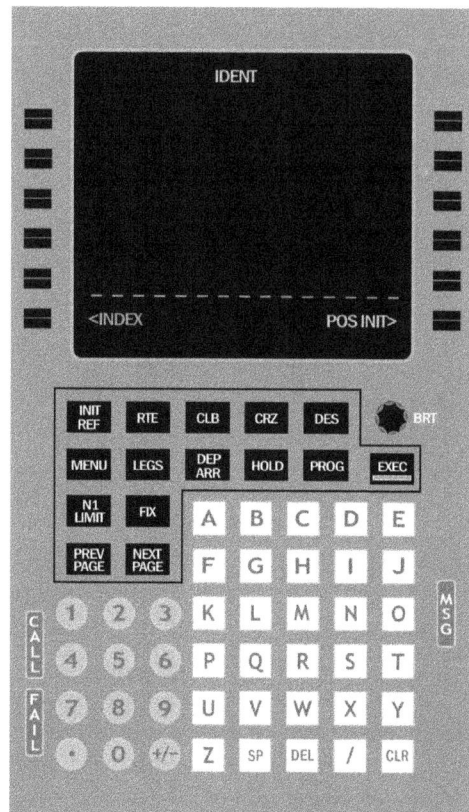

The alphanumeric keys are used to make entries to the *scratchpad*, which is actually the bottom line of the display that behaves rather like a one-line wordprocessor, in that the contents of the line can be edited in the normal way (it's also where you might get messages from the system):

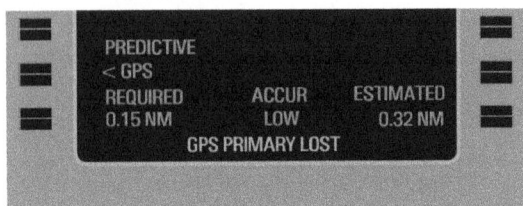

```
PREDICTIVE
< GPS
REQUIRED      ACCUR      ESTIMATED
0.15 NM       LOW        0.32 NM
        GPS PRIMARY LOST
```

It is a working area where you can enter and/or verify data before it goes into the system. For example, if you wanted to go direct to a waypoint called ANKAR you would type:

DIR TO ANKAR

Tip: Lat & Long figures are typically shortened in the main display. Pushing the button next to them brings them into the scratchpad so you can see the full readout.

Information in the scratchpad does not affect the FMS until it is moved to another line on the display. Data remains in the scratchpad over mode and page changes.

The alphanumeric keys represent the same characters as they would on any keyboard, except that the **SP** button is the space bar. The delete key clears a selected line, while the clear key deletes single characters in the scratchpad. The buttons (*Line Select Keys*) down each side of the screen represent pages that correspond to a phase of flight, or lines on a page.

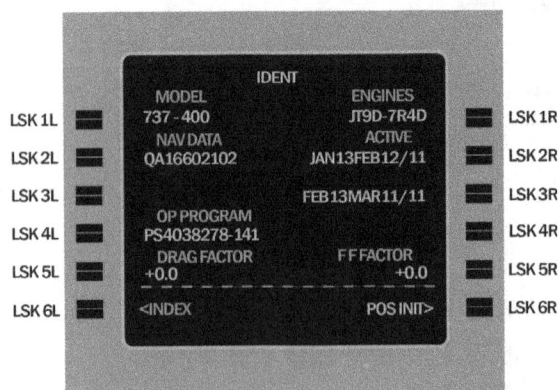

```
              IDENT
         MODEL          ENGINES
LSK 1L   737 - 400      JT9D-7R4D      LSK 1R
         NAV DATA       ACTIVE
LSK 2L   QA16602102     JAN13FEB12/11  LSK 2R

LSK 3L                  FEB13MAR11/11  LSK 3R
         OP PROGRAM
LSK 4L   PS4038278-141                 LSK 4R
         DRAG FACTOR    F F FACTOR
LSK 5L   +0.0           +0.0           LSK 5R

LSK 6L   <INDEX         POS INIT>      LSK 6R
```

Enter information on the scratchpad then press the LSK to get that information into the system. The function keys are short cuts that provide access to major functions.

The FMS starts its power up sequence right after you switch it on. You then have to tell it where you are. On the **IDENT** page, press the line select key next to where it says POS INIT. You might then get a selection of positions, such as the last known one, etc. (top right).

To enter a flight plan, the machine needs to know the destination, the route you propose to take, the alternate, the departure and the expected arrival procedure (all this should be in the database).

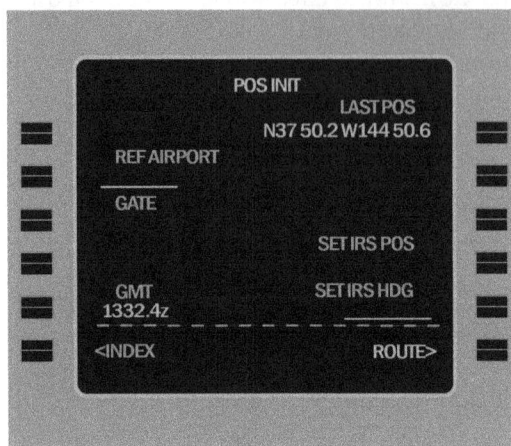

```
              POS INIT
                      LAST POS
                      N37 50.2 W144 50.6
    REF AIRPORT
    _____
     GATE
                              SET IRS POS

     GMT                      SET IRS HDG
     1332.4z
    <INDEX                    ROUTE>
```

The **ROUTE** page is the primary page for route construction. One of the buttons on the side of the display will have DEST written next to it. Enter the ICAO code into the scratchpad and push the relevant LSK (1R).

The origin will have been filled in using LSK 1L.

If there is a flight plan for the route in the database, it will be presented for your approval. Just press ACTIVATE FPL. If there is no flight plan, just enter each waypoint into the scratchpad followed by the relevant line select key.

Generally, you follow established airways until you reach a specific waypoint where you can leave the system. More often than not, this is the first waypoint associated with an approach procedure (you join the system in the first place at the last waypoint associated with a departure procedure). With just that information, the system will deal with intermediate waypoints automatically.

Eventually, you will reach the **PERF INIT** (Performance Initialisation) page. Performance data is used for many purposes, such as vertical navigation (VNAV), setting target speeds, fuel calculations, etc. Although we know the route, until the aircraft's weight is known, climb or descent profiles cannot be constructed. Neither can the optimum cruise altitude or any speeds be calculated, which is quite important on a machine like the 777 that can calculate those required for any manoeuvres in real time, which helps greatly with fuel consumption, because the flaps can be deployed at the most appropriate times.

Note: The data entered into the PERF INIT page must be correct and crosschecked!

The gross weight of the aircraft is entered using LSK 1L. 2L shows the calculated fuel and 3L shows the ZFW (normally you get this information from the loadsheet that comes from the dispatch office, but these days it comes

CAPT

over a datalink). 2L and 3L together make up the gross weight of the aircraft. In flight, you will use the FPL or PROG page while the FMS continuously computes your position from the IRS, VOR, DME and ILS as required. The priority for the most accurate fix is a DME/DME crosscut, then DME/VOR, then VOR/VOR, and IRS last. It will tune DME frequencies in sequence according to route information in the navigation database. Despite all that, you should still monitor your position carefully.

The Flight Director

The Flight Director's job is to reduce your workload by indicating the manoeuvres to execute, achieve or maintain a flight condition, particularly when things are happening quickly, as they do when close to Decision Height on the ILS (assuming you are not using the autopilot). It presents data as control commands to show you the **optimal way to achieve your flight path**. In other words, the flight director gives you directions regarding *how to position the controls* - you get no information about the flight path, for which you need a separate navigation display. You can use the flight director without the autopilot, although the autopilot can use the FD to tell you what it's doing.

The FD will be in a display which is a combination of the artificial horizon, localiser & glideslope, radio altimeter for your Decision Height and warning flags for instrument failure, so it also tells you which way up you are.

The visual guidance can come in the shape of a V-bar:

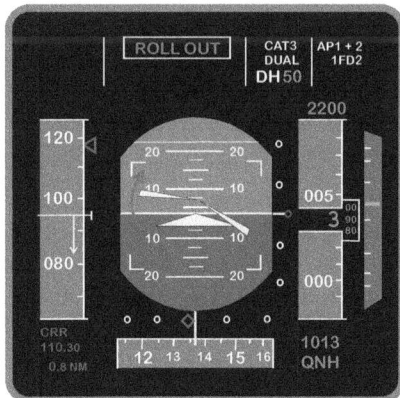

A two-cue system might use command bars. In fact, the original FD was Sperry's Zero Reader, which was a cross-pointed indicator like the modern ILS display:

The horizontal bar is for the pitch channel, and the vertical bar for roll, in terms of information about the direction and amplitude of the corrections to be applied to the controls. They will

centralise once the inputs required are enough, so the bars can be centred even when you are not straight and level. Command bars may be displayed when flying manually or when the autopilot is engaged. So, the essential components of a flight director are a *computer* and *command bars*. You engage the *heading select* mode (HDG SEL), once a heading is selected, after which the vertical bar will be centred if the bank angle is the same as the computed angle.

EFIS

Conventional instruments can go wrong, and tend to spread themselves out around the cockpit, so you need three pairs of eyes in a big machine to keep track of them all. They also have to be continually monitored. The *Electronic Flight Instrument System* replaces the traditional ones with CRT or LCD displays, or at least flat computer panels, hence the occasional reference to the *Glass Cockpit*. These have no moving parts, and can be switched to show different instruments, or duplicate information, which is helpful if one fails. In emergencies, you can isolate some instruments for closer scrutiny.

With the glass cockpit, a lot of information can be concentrated into a small space, and the associated computers can take on some monitoring tasks, so you only need to pay some of them any attention when something actually goes wrong (see *Warning & Recording*, later).

The heart of the EFIS is the symbol generator, of which there are 3 in a standard system, which receives input from the sensors around the aircraft. A third (centre) SG may be involved if the left or right unit fails. If two are used and one fails, the remaining one can supply both sides, but the information would be the same. Switching is pilot controlled. Once brightness is selected, it is automatically controlled by light sensors. Other information that can be displayed includes graphics of the aircraft systems, checklists, maps from the GPS, etc.

The technology involves small computers using solid-state (i.e. no moving parts) 3-axis gyros and accelerometers to derive altitude, magnetometers to find heading, and pressure transducers to find air data (airspeed & altitude), all displayed on flat screens, through suitable software. Because of the potential problems with software, any EFIS system will be backed up by a selection of traditional instruments, or another, separate, EFIS system.

The benefits of using EFIS include:

- Increased reliability
- The output of many instruments can be combined into one, improving situational awareness
- You can put other information on, such as checklists and weather
- Colour

EADI/PFD

The *Electronic Attitude Direction Indicator* (EADI) or *Primary Flight Display* (PFD) can combine a lot of information in one small space.

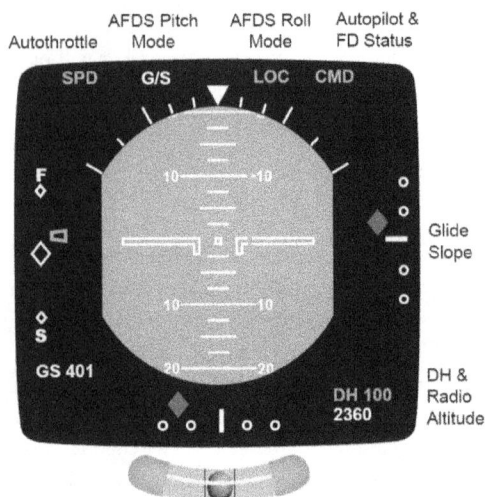

The above is the basic display. In the improved version, the Fast/Slow bar on the left is replaced by a speed tape. On the left below is a typical takeoff display, in the middle is one for the cruise, and landing is shown on the right.

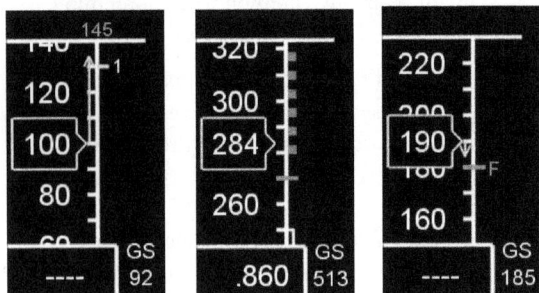

The attitude information could come from the IRS, if there is one, or more traditional gyroscopic sources. When the right equipment is switched in, you could also get ILS localiser/glideslope information, groundspeed, flight director commands, radio altitude, etc.

Between 1000-2500 ft AGL, radio altitude is shown digitally in white, with the Decision Height in green.

Below 1000 ft, it changes to an analogue presentation, namely a white circular scale in 100-ft increments which unwinds as you descend and erases above the present height. The DH is a magenta marker on the circular scale, and is set through the EFIS control panel. Radio altitude is shown digitally in the middle. At DH, the scale and marker change to amber and flash for a few seconds. There is a reset button to fix that.

If you go beyond localiser and glideslope limits during an approach, and when below 500 ft agl, the deviation pointers turn from white to amber and start to flash.

MAP

MAP mode is used for general bread-and-butter enroute navigation. It shows your position as a relationship between the current heading, navaids and actual track.

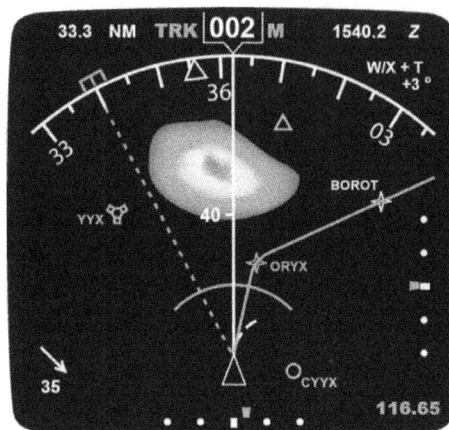

MAP Mode (Expanded)

It is oriented to the aircraft heading or track, which can be shown in True or Magnetic (True is automatically selected above 73°N and below 65°S). In expanded (ARC) mode, the arc can cover between 30-60° either side of the track. Heading information comes from the IRS.

Your (FMC) position is at the apex of the white triangle (the aircraft) at the bottom of the screen and the track is a white line extending away from it (see the Expanded version. Range markings are selected through the control panel). It normally points to 12 o'clock, except in heading mode where it will only do so in nil wind conditions.

The green circle ahead of your position is where the selected height will be reached. The white arc extending away from the triangle is a trend vector with each dash representing 30 seconds ahead. The scales on the bottom and right that look like a localiser and glideslope are there to show you deviations from LNAV and the VNAV descent path. A magenta line represents the active route, and the *active waypoint* is the one the system is currently navigating to. If you want a different heading than that chosen by the FMS, you must use the magenta heading select marker.

Fix information is a dashed green line. A dashed blue circle is a clean energy management circle. A dashed white one is a drag circle for when speed brakes are extended.

Wind speed and relative direction are in the bottom left hand corner, shown according to the compass rose. It is on Map, Expanded ILS, Full ILS and Full VOR modes. When the track line coincides with the desired track, wind influence is compensated for.

ETOs and ETAs as calculated by the FMC are naturally correct when the actual winds match the forecast winds and the FMC Mach number is the actual one. Magnetic heading is shown, but True is available via the IRS.

If a VOR receiver fails, the associated magenta deviation bar and/or pointer is removed from the display.

PLAN

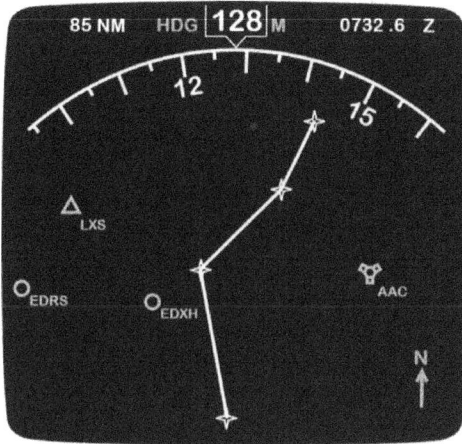

PLAN

The PLAN display allows you an overview of the whole or parts of the route, but is not displayed in real time, except for the information at and above the expanded rose.

You cannot normally display wind and weather in this mode (depends on the manufacturer). You might use it to see the effects of changes in the route before entering them into the FMC. Plan mode is always expanded, and oriented to True North (i.e. North up - watch for the arrow bottom right, though on some systems the arc may be set to N). There is also no aircraft symbol.

VOR/ILS

In full mode (also known as *centred*), you get an electronic representation of the traditional HSI. You will get wind, but not weather, information. In expanded mode, weather information is available on both EHSIs.

The full rose will change for the VOR and ILS according to the frequency selected. The full deflection is 20° for the VOR and 5° for the ILS.

OVERFLY FUNCTION

This makes the aircraft fly specifically over a waypoint, of which there are two types. A *flyover waypoint* is one whose lat & long position must be flown over before you can turn onto the next leg, typically used on departures to ensure that you don't make excessive bank angles that will interfere with performance calculations. You can fly *direct-to* any waypoint, or *direct/intercept*, where you can select a desired course to reach it. Waypoints can also have speed, altitude and time constraints (*not before*, etc.)

SYMBOLS AND COLOURS

Active flight plans and waypoints are *magenta* in MAP mode. Otherwise, general colours are:

- GREEN: Present situation, low priority info.
- WHITE: Static information, turbulence, current and armed data values.
- MAGENTA: Command information (i.e. FD bar), weather radar, turbulence, selected heading, active routes or waypoints.
- CYAN: Non-active and background information
- RED: Warnings (flight envelope or system limits).
- YELLOW: Caution or abnormal sources.
- BLACK: Off.
- BLUE: The sky.
- Tan/Brown. The Earth.

EICAS

The *Engine Indicating and Crew Alerting System* (EICAS) shows you what all the systems around the aircraft are up to. EICAS & ECAM, from Boeing & Airbus, respectively, are well known monitoring systems, but they all have an EFIS-type display at the front end.

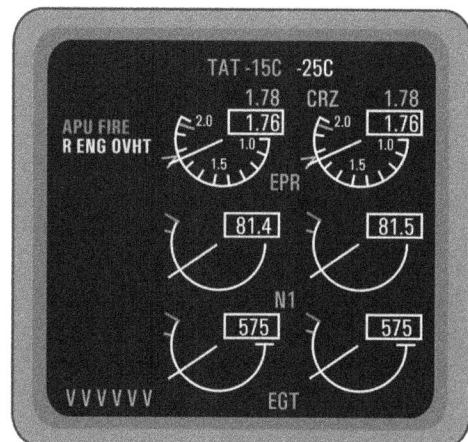

Although it primarily shows engine indications, it also acts like a central warning panel. The upper screen is the primary display, and the lower is the secondary.

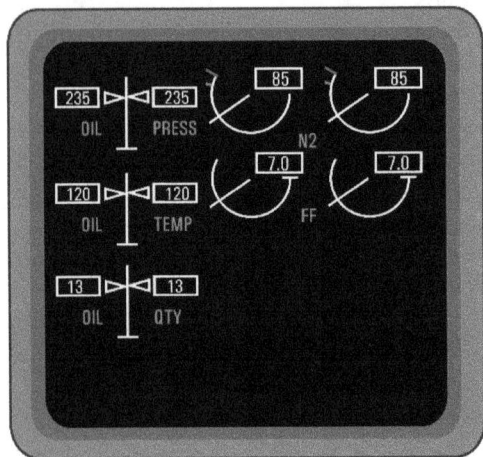

The downward pointing arrows at the bottom left of the upper screen tell you that there is information on the lower screen - if you can't see anything, it is not working.

Fly By Wire

These systems use electrical signals from a computer to control the hydraulic jacks. Transducers send signals over electrical cables to the system concerned, which will be a self-contained unit in the relevant location. There is some controversy as to whether the programmers actually talk to pilots, but the systems seem to work very well. If nothing else, they save weight, and maintenance, and improve piloting quality, plus they can create more space in various locations, particularly the cockpit, at the expense of software quality and control*. Sometimes, sidesticks replace conventional control columns, as on the A-320 Airbus. *Q-Feel* uses static and pitot inputs to prevent overstressing of powered controls. Redundancy is achieved by having multiple pathways for signals, or multiple computers for the same task, and the computers are continually self-checking.

*A military Airbus A400M was lost after its engine control software shut down three engines just after takeoff. Somebody had accidentally erased the configuration files when the software was installed, so the system was missing parameters that allowed it to monitor the power.

The disturbing thing about this (to bring up the Human Factors discussion about design) is that this extremely vital information was being loaded from external files, which is a programming practice equivalent to using virtual memory in Windows. In other words, a point of failure has been introduced, where the information could have at least been placed in the working code, i.e. in one place.

You'd think that somebody would have done an engine test before trying to take off, though.

WARNING & RECORDING

Warnings should be attention-getting without being startling, while informing you of what is going on (or not). They should also guide you to the correct actions. Systems should be reliable, meaning they should respond to genuine problems without generating false alarms.

Alerting for important failures should be fulfilled by an audio warning. Ideally, there should be a single one to alert the crew and direct their attention to a single central warning panel that announces the nature of the problem with a suitably illuminated caption.

Otherwise, the standard methods of bringing unusual occurrences to the notice of pilots include:

- **visual** (lights, gauges, displays)
- **aural** (bells, sirens, and sometimes voice)
- **tactile** (stick shakers)

The three levels of alerting are:

- **Warnings** (Level A) - Red, could be flashing
- **Cautions** (Level B) - Amber
- **Advisory** (Level C) - White

Some warnings may be turned off (or muted) so as not to be a distraction during an emergency, or a nuisance during a normal procedure. This includes the Master Caution light, which can be cancelled so you can see if another warning appears on the Central Warning Panel.

Off flags signify whether an instrument is working properly. They might come on if:

- electrical power is lost
- a gyro is at too low a speed
- the signal received by a navigation instrument is non-existent or too weak

GPWS

CAT.OP.MPA.290

A major cause of accidents is Controlled Flight Into Terrain (CFIT).

GPWS

The first attempt at stopping CFIT was the *Ground Proximity Warning System*, which is supposed to be able to give warning of your impending approach towards Terrain

Impact Mode in five areas of flight, whereas the radio altimeter relies on the crew looking at it, although it does have an adjustable height bug which acts as a rudimentary warning, if your attention is not diverted. This is why an urgent-sounding audio low height warning was also considered necessary (apart from a scream from the other pilot!) Neither, however, provide a look-ahead function, so would not help if you were about to hit a mountain. The GPWS might get its information from the radio altimeter, the ADC, the Captain's ILS receiver, and gear and flap indicators, over a range of 50-2450 feet. When fitted, *a GPWS system should be switched on and used throughout the flight,* unless it is unserviceable, *and the MEL allows it to be so.*

The GPWS will warn you in case of (amongst others):

- dangerous proximity to the ground

- loss of altitude during takeoff or missed approach

- wrong landing configuration

- descent below the glidepath

The basic installation has five modes of operation:

- **Mode 1** - *excessive* (barometric) *rate of descent*, which operates when the barometric ROD is more than 3 times greater than the radio height or the clearance available. It uses two different warnings: an advisory, or soft warning, *Sinkrate, Sinkrate*, and a hard warning of **Whoop Whoop Pull Up**, repeated twice. Both stop outside the warning envelopes of between 50-2450 feet radio altimeter (the usual operating range of GPWS). The aural alert goes off when passing the first boundary.

- **Mode 2** - *excessive closure rate*, triggered by reducing radio altitude. This can be confused with Mode 1, but you get this when the ground is coming up rather than the aircraft going down, so it may even go off in level flight. Mode 2a is sounded if the flaps are not in the landing position, and 2b if they are. If the radio altitude, speed and rate of closure are within the warning envelope, the words **Pull Up, Pull Up** after a whooping sound are heard, which cannot be inhibited.

- **Mode 3** - *negative climb rate* (for radio altitude), or *sinking after a takeoff or go-around* (i.e. height loss). If the barometric altitude lost is around 10% of radio altitude gained, the **Don't Sink, Don't Sink** aural warning will sound, with a second advisory of **Too Low Terrain** if the original radio altitude is over 150 ft AGL, then decreases by more than 25% of it. If you get a *Don't Sink* warning during takeoff or on a missed approach, you have started to lose altitude. Mode 3 activates between 30 and 667-1333 feet radio altitude (depends on airspeed).

- **Mode 4** - *approaching too close to the ground with flaps or gear up*, so this is only active during the landing phase. There are two sub-modes (4a and 4b) and three alerts, depending on the phase of flight and aircraft configuration. Aural warnings will be either *Too Low Gear, Too Low Flap,* or *Too Low Terrain* (depends on aircraft speed).

- **Mode 5** - *going too far below the glideslope* (more than 1.3 dots), assuming you have tuned the correct ILS frequency.

PULL UP

BELOW G/S

- **Mode 6** - *Miscellaneous* stuff like automatic height callout and bank angles, usually company-specific.

- **Mode 7** - *Windshear Mode*. A two-tone siren, plus the words **Windshear Windshear Windshear,** given once only, with a warning light, which are triggered if the predicted aircraft energy level falls below a safe threshold. Windshear warnings have a higher priority than other GPWS modes.

Alerts and warnings in Modes 1 and 2 are only given when you are less than 2,500 ft above local terrain, because this is in the normal operating range of the radio altimeter. Both modes are active in all flight phases.

A GPWS must generate at least one sound alarm, for which a visual alarm can be added. You can expect:

- An **alert**, which is just a caution, or

- A **warning**, which requires *immediate action*, because verifying warnings takes so long you may as well not have the device in the first place, and it takes a few seconds to get over the denial that you could be in the wrong position. Warnings could be:

  - *genuine*

  - a *nuisance* (when in a safe procedure), or

  - *false* (outside the validity area of a glideslope)

However, there are those who think that modes 1-5 have been "adjusted" so much to try to eliminate nuisance warnings that they have become ineffective. For example, to get a Mode 1 alert you need to exceed 3000 feet per minute at 500', 1200 fpm at 200' and 900' fpm at 10' - very high and very close, so the problems may well arise before the warnings! Typically, this will be for between 5-30 seconds beforehand, if at all over exceptionally rugged ground. Also, once an aircraft with GPWS has been configured for landing, there is very little protection against inadvertent proximity to terrain or water.

In summary, GPWS takes into account the aircraft's height as well as its descent rate and configuration. It has no terrain display or map, no predictive capability, and is radio altimeter based but, for all that it was a first generation attempt, GPWS marked a substantial decrease in hull loss rates in the 80s. Around 40% of fatal accidents were in aircraft without it.

TAWS

Terrain Awareness and Warning System is the generic term for altitude alerting systems of varying complexity, which includes GPWS and radio altimeters. The term therefore includes EGPWS, or Enhanced GPWS.

ENHANCED GPWS

This system is linked to all the instruments and can be updated with software. You get the basic GPWS modes but, in addition:

- **FLTA** (*Forward Looking Terrain Avoidance*), which checks for the absence of anything in the way within a preset search area (or volume, since it is vertical as well as horizontal). The search volume is curved in the direction of any turns

- **PDA** (*Premature Descent Alert*). Under normal circumstances, after the gear is lowered, if there is no ILS signal, an aircraft would be unprotected, so the internal database can be used to provide a protected area around each runway, which enhances Mode 4, described below.

To provide the FLTA function, the details in a terrain and obstacle database are compared with your GPS vertical and horizontal position, but radar helps as well, if you have it. The system also takes account of your barometric altitude and predicted flight path, so a side benefit is improved situational awareness from the advanced warning of the surrounding terrain.

As it happens, EGPWS has 32 modes! The system first identifies the stage of flight, then selects the appropriate one, with the airborne value stored in memory and kept immune from power interruptions. A system will typically go *In Air* when the weight on wheels switch indicates that you are airborne.

Note: Since the system relies on databases, they must be kept up to date! This means internal company procedures for ensuring that this is done in a timely fashion!

Note also that, to save memory space, the terrain database is only high resolution within about 16 miles of an airport - areas between them are low resolution. Beyond 60 miles, it is typically an eighth (you should be in the cruise by then). So, EGPWS is a terrain based map system, which has a predictive capability that can determine your position and flight path based on information from the FMS/GPS, Air Data System, Radio Altimeter and VOR/ILS (plus flaps and the angle of attack), comparing your altitude with its internal database and, if there is a potential threat of hitting the ground, can generate warnings well before the classic GPWS could do.

In spite of the above benefits, there are still limitations. First of all, as mentioned above, the system requires an up to date database, which may have errors and will, by definition, not know anything about mobile obstacles.

Secondly, protection will be limited if your navigational accuracy is degraded - there are still areas in which GPS reception is poor. There may also be delays in alerts being given, or even unwanted ones.

BITE

Built In Test Equipment is a press-to-test function used to do part of the prestart checks. When pressed, the GPWS system lights come on in sequence with audio alerts and warnings. If the system is not functioning, they will not be complete (pushing the **PULL UP** light tests the system and illuminates all the lights). An **INOP** light will come on if the system fails or it loses a source of input.

Radio Altimeter

A radio altimeter is a self-contained on-board safety device that indicates the *true height* of the *lowest wheels or skids* (with oleos extended) above the ground. Data supplied includes the distance between the ground and the altimeter. Radio altimeters (with audio) are required equipment over water. Low altitude radalts are used for precision approaches, with accuracy of $\pm$ 2 ft between 0-500 feet or $\pm$ 1.5%, whichever is greater, and are only active below about 2,500 ft. High altitude ones work up to 50 000 feet above the surface.

A *continuous wave* FM radio beam in the SHF band (4200-4400 MHz) is directed towards the ground in a 30° cone fore and aft, and 30° athwartships. The signal is reflected back to the aircraft. As the time delay for a pulsed signal is too small to measure properly  (and the antennae cannot switch between transmit and receive that quickly), CW (as opposed to pulse) radar eliminates minimum range problems. You need separate transmit and receive aerials.

It takes around 6.1 microseconds for a wave to be reflected back from an object around 10 000 m away. With CW radar, we can arrange for a frequency change for that time period - say from 1 000 MHz to 1006.1. The difference of 6.1 MHz therefore represents 10 000 yards. You only have to measure the difference in frequency to find the range, so the system is frequency modulated.

The transmitted frequency sweeps up and down through about 200 MHz either side of 4300 MHz. Compensation

CAPT

is made for aerial (residual) height and wiring, and to account for signal processing time, so the altimeter reads zero when the wheels touch down (placing the aerials near the gear means the radalt will also read zero when the nosewheel is on the ground). For most radio altimeters, when a system error occurs during approach, the height indication is removed.

In any case, below 1 000 feet, on an EFIS display, the readout changes to analogue.

TCAS/ACAS

CAT.OP.MPA.295

Airborne Collision and Avoidance Systems (ACAS) provide you with an independent backup to your eyes and ATC by telling you if you are likely to hit another aircraft. The system was developed after the increased use of Area Navigation systems which allowed more direct routings away from specific airways.

TCAS (the T stands for *Traffic*) is actually the system developed by the FAA, whilst ACAS is the generic name used by ICAO. Your aircraft's ACAS capability is not normally known to ATC, unless you mention it on a flight plan. Basic systems (TCAS I) just provide warnings of traffic without guidance. TCAS II, the current equipment, provides advice in the *vertical* plane, as a:

- **Traffic Advisory** (TA), or a warning, telling you where nearby *transponding aircraft* are, or a

- **Resolution Advisory** (RA) which suggests avoiding action *in the pitch plane only*.

This is because all systems depend on azimuthal accuracy, which is not all that good, and why TCAS II makes you climb or descend to avoid traffic (TCAS I leaves any avoiding action up to you). In view of this, TCAS I can be regarded as a VMC aid, and TCAS II as an IMC aid, although it is possible, of course, to use TCAS I in cloud.

The system interrogates other aircraft, so it is independent of ground facilities. It uses four antennae, a computer and a transponder to continually survey the airspace around you and predict the flight paths of likely intruders, based on Mode C (TCAS I) or S (TCAS II) transponder signals from other traffic. *It will not see obstacles or non-transponder equipped aircraft*. The problem is that, because the power is limited to reduce radio interference, the range is limited to around 45 nm to the front and a lot less elsewhere. In addition, although the system can track up to 45 aircraft, it can only display up to 45.

An *intruder* will show up on the display with a symbol representing the grade of threat, plus numbers for their relative height above or below you in hundreds of feet (+ or - signs). An up or down arrow provides a vertical trend (over 500 fpm).

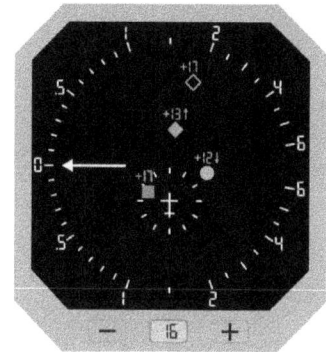

A hollow diamond (white on EFIS) indicates non-threatening traffic over 6 nm away horizontally. A shaded diamond indicates proximate traffic within 6 nm horizontally and 1 200 feet vertically. A Traffic Advisory (TA) is given when an intruder comes with 30 seconds of your aircraft (45 seconds for TCAS II), as a *potential* threat, when the symbol changes to a solid amber circle. When it becomes a red square the intruder is an *immediate* threat - red for danger and a box because if you don't follow an RA that's where you will be. An RA would normally come about 20 seconds after the TA. A *corrective advisory* calls for a change in vertical speed (or something different to what you are currently doing) and a *preventive* advisory restricts it. All RAs are corrective except MONITOR VERTICAL SPEED, which is a *preventative* RA. You should avoid deviation from the current vertical rate, but no changes should be made to that rate.

A response should be initiated immediately (not in the opposite direction), and crew members not involved should check for other traffic. Once adequate separation has been achieved, or there is no longer a conflict, you should return to your intended flight path, and inform ATC, because you have just deviated from a clearance (you are immune from enforcement action in this case). An RA may be disregarded only when you visually identify conflicting traffic and decide that no deviation is necessary. If an RA and ATC conflict, the RA wins.

Use TCAS as a keyword when telling ATC what you are up to, as in *TCAS Climb*, or *TCAS Descent*.

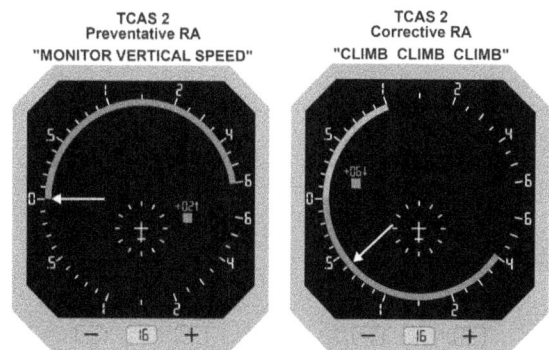

TCAS 2
Preventative RA
"MONITOR VERTICAL SPEED"

TCAS 2
Corrective RA
"CLIMB CLIMB CLIMB"

If an aircraft approaches from below, you would get an aural warning (CLIMB CLIMB CLIMB) and a visual one showing red for negative rates up to 15 fpm and green from 1500 fpm onwards (see right, above). Nuisance or false advisories should be treated as genuine unless the intruder has been positively identified and shown visually to be no longer a threat.

TCAS II can display on its own screen, on weather radar, EFIS, a variometer (VSI) with an LCD display, and others.

TCAS II can handle multiple intruders, and you could get multiple advisories when your workload is very high, which is why you can turn RAs off. Another time when you might want to do this is when operating OEI, because a climb RA could demand a higher ROC than that available. Descent RAs are inhibited anyway when below 700 ft AGL, to avoid CFIT. TAs and RAs are inhibited below 400 ft AGL.

CAPT

Radio depends on the movement of electric and magnetic waves, which depend on the movement of electricity, which ultimately depends on the activities of electrons inside an atom. If you are wondering why you need to know this stuff as a pilot, it is because it is also part of the syllabus for an amateur radio licence, of which a pilot's radio licence is a cut-down version

RADIO NAVIGATION

Alternating current is also the basis of radio waves, which we use to convey information or find our way. The sound of a rotor blade slap from 1100 feet will take one second to reach your ears, but air travelling at that speed would be ten times more powerful than a hurricane, so the sound you hear is not *in* the air - it changes the characteristics of the air instead.

The effect is like the example of electrons moving down a cable. One pushed in at one end affects the others in line until one falls out at the other, so it is easier to imagine a wave of compression pushing air particles in front of it before it affects your eardrums. If this is done too slowly, though, the air particles have a chance to get out of the way, so the effect is not noticeable below a certain rate of vibration, or *frequency*.

WAVE MOTION   062 01

A wave is a progressive disturbance in a medium that itself is not displaced permanently, although electromagnetic waves do not need a medium. Either way, waves can be transmitted without affecting matter.

The usual example is dropping a stone into water, where the water only moves up and down, but there is forward movement of energy, which comes in the first place from the loss of kinetic energy as the stone hits the water.

Making electrons move along an antenna can set an electromagnetic wave in motion in the air in the same way.

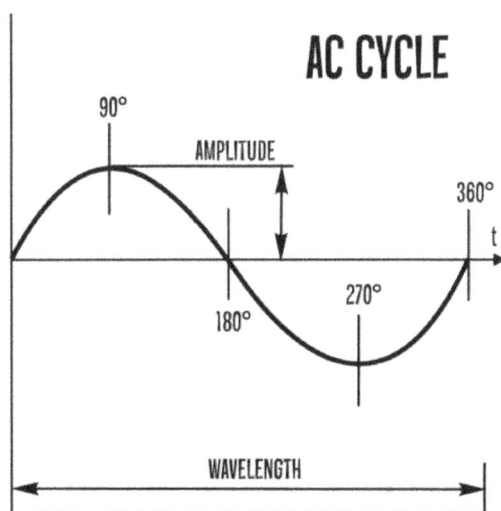

AC CYCLE

The qualities associated with any type of wave motion are:

- **Velocity**.

- **Frequency**. The rate of oscillation, or the number of waves that pass a fixed point in one second, measured in Hertz (Hz).

- **Wavelength**. The least distance between two consecutive points on two consecutive waves with the same displacement and velocity, represented by the symbol λ.

- **Period**. The time between successive waves.

- **Amplitude**. The maximum displacement of a moving particle from its mean position, labelled positive or negative. Loosely termed *volume*.

Radio waves were originally classified by wavelength, but it is more convenient to use frequency (see table overleaf).

Where the particles of the transmitting medium move at right angles to the direction of propagation (say up and down on the surface of water), you have a *transverse* wave. Where particles move back and forth in the same direction as the propagation (sound), you have a *longitudinal* wave.

Polarisation

Electromagnetic radiation is made up from E and H fields, which stand for *electric* and *magnetic*, respectively. In other words, radio waves have electrical and magnetic axes, acting at right angles to each other. The electric field arises from voltage, and the magnetic one from current.

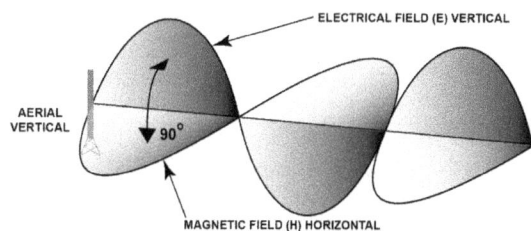

A wave's polarisation is noted with reference to the electrical field, which is parallel with its antenna, so a vertically polarised wave has a vertical electric field, which will come from a vertical aerial (for efficiency, the receiver must have the same orientation). For example, NDBs (and weather-based static) are vertically polarised, whilst VORs and ILS Localisers are horizontally polarised.

With such linear polarisation, the plane of oscillation is fixed in space, whereas with circular polarisation, the plane is rotating - the electrical and magnetic components of the wave spin about the axis of the advance at a rate equal to the frequency. Circular polarization is often used (with helical antennae) where the relative orientation of the transmitting and receiving antennae cannot be easily controlled, as with GPS, or where the polarization of the signal may change. It can reduce rain clutter with radar.

In general, polarisation does not change over short distances, but over long distances, especially at high frequencies, it can change drastically.

Calculations

In free space (or a vacuum), electromagnetic waves move at the speed of light, which is taken to be 300,000,000 metres per second, abbreviated as *C*. The number of waves that will arrive per second at a radio antenna (the frequency) depends on dividing C by the length of the wave concerned. Put another way, over 1 Hz (i.e. 1 cycle), a wave will travel for 300,000 km.

For radar purposes, this is **300 m per microsecond**. In nautical miles, try 161,800.

Frequency and wavelength are related as follows:

$$\lambda = \frac{C}{F}$$

F is the frequency in cycles per second. Wavelength is given in metres. So, to find the length of a wave with a frequency of 300 KHz:

$$\lambda = \frac{300\cancel{000000}}{3\cancel{00000}}$$

The answer is 1000 m, or 1 km.

Wavebands

The range of electromagnetic waves is quite large, but radio waves only occupy a small part of it, actually between about 3 KHz to 3,000 GHz.

This area is split up by International agreement between the people who wish to use it, and consists of frequency ranges, or bands, that share similar characteristics.

Trivia: Wavelengths below 100m (i.e. short wave, or HF) used to be thought of by scientists as useless for long distance communications until amateur operators proved them wrong!

Band	Frequency	Wavelength	Aids	Notes
VLF	3-30 KHz Kilo = Thousand	10-100 km Myriametric		This needs high power and large antennae, so it is used for long ranges, where no transmissions are required from the aircraft - the signal travels as a ground wave for several thousand miles. Has the least attenuation.
LF	30-300 KHz	1-10 km Kilometric	NDB, Decca, LORAN	Distances of around 1500 miles, with minor attenuation
MF	300-3,000 KHz	100-1000 m Hectometric		Can cover 100-300 miles over land, but the range increases at night as the ionosphere merges back into one layer. Fading and static are problems, so can be unreliable at night. Needs fairly high power and fairly large antennae.
HF Short Wave	3-30 MHz Mega = Million	10-100 m Decametric	HF/RT	Longer distances (100-2000 miles) but only after refraction from the ionosphere - it doesn't go as far by itself as LF can (i.e. 30-100 nm), but you can use a transmitter in the aircraft. This band also suffers from fading and static, and you need to choose the frequency carefully according to the time of day, season and direction of transmission. Severe attenuation. Affected by sunspots
VHF	30-300 MHz	1-10 m Metric	VOR, VDF, ILS Localiser, Marker	Line of sight, is meant for local services, say up to 50 miles. It gives more precise results, and is not really affected by static.
UHF	300-3,000 MHz	10-100 cm Decimetric	Radio Altimeter (High Alt), SSR, DME, GPS, Glidepath	Short range line of sight, but there is little interference and antennae are small
SHF	3-30 GHz Giga = Trillion	1-10 cm Centimetric	Radio Altimeter (Low Alt), MLS, Radar, AWR, Doppler	Short range line of sight, but there is little interference and antennae are small
EHF	30-300 GHz	1-10 mm Millimetric		

CAPT

HOW IT ALL WORKS

A sound wave will only travel so far by itself, which is why it needs help, in the shape of a *carrier wave*, to move over longer distances (if you could transmit a sound wave, it would be so long that huge aerials and large coils and capacitors would be needed). The carrier wave is created at radio frequency (the RF carrier), and a sound wave (the AF signal) is added to it, so that an electronic copy of the original signal is made. The process of frequency shifting is called modulation, described overleaf.

Trivia: Although Marconi transmitted the first CW signal, a Canadian, Reginald Fessenden, transmitted the first *voice* signal from Massachusetts to ships along the Eastern Seaboard. However, Nikola Tesla was ahead of them both - Marconi used 17 of Tesla's patents.

The Transmitter

Radio transmitters are based around high frequency oscillators, but applying lots of power directly to an oscillator (above about 100 MHz) reduces its stability, so a relatively weak signal is used, then amplified for the later stages. The audio signal is treated the same way. A *modulator's* job is to combine the signals from the radio and audio amplifiers by superimposing the amplified speech signal on the RF carrier with a transformer.

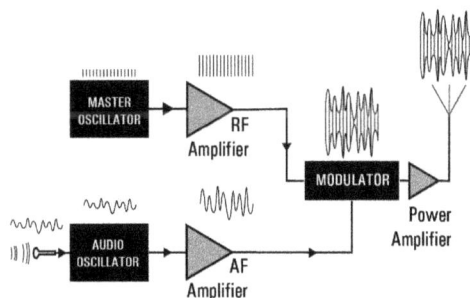

MODULATION

The information to be sent *modulates*, or varies, the carrier wave, although an unmodulated signal travels further than a modulated one for the same power.

The *Depth Of Modulation* is the extent to which a carrier wave is modulated by another frequency, as expressed by a percentage. Modulation is actually done at just below 100% (typically 90% for voice) because there is a danger of over-modulation that will cause distortion.

AMPLITUDE MODULATION (A3)

With AM, the amplitude, or power, of a carrier wave is varied according to the strength of an audio (or video) signal applied to it. Its shape changes as the AF signal distorts it.

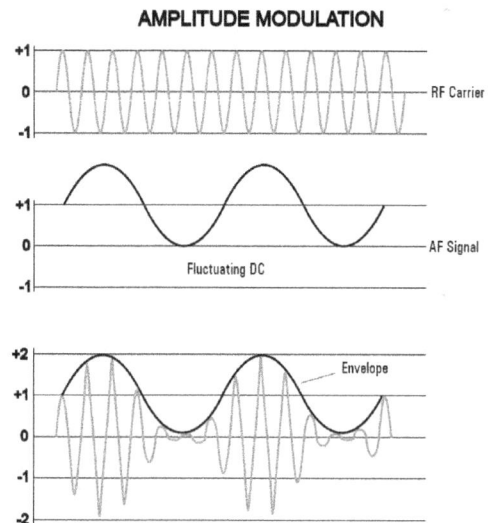

AMPLITUDE MODULATION

The top part of the picture above shows an RF carrier with alternating cycles above and below the line of nil current flow. The middle part shows a fluctuating DC waveform representing speech from a microphone (it is positive because it is all above the nil current line). When the two are merged together (in the bottom part) the RF carrier takes on the shape of the distorting AF signal.

AM suffers from two practical defects, one being noise, and the other lack of quality. Almost all natural and man-made electrical disturbances, such as atmospheric static, or electrical equipment, radiate energy with amplitude disturbances. The air gets more positively charged as you climb higher*, especially when it is wet. This may cause sudden leaks or discharges that produce electromagnetic waves called *precipitation static*, that interfere with radio transmissions, which is a factor when you want reliability in bad weather. A quick look at a rainfall map of the world will tell you where it is worst, namely the tropics. The lowest frequency where freedom from static interference can be guaranteed is 30 MHz.

*This ionisation of the air creates a layer around the Earth called the ionosphere which has less resistance to the flow of electricity. It is useful for getting longer ranges with certain frequencies (HF) and is discussed later on.

AM transmissions can therefore be noisy because the receiver cannot distinguish between the signals you want to hear and the ones you don't. This has led to the use of systems such as SELCAL (*Selective Calling*), so you don't have to listen to the background noise all the time.

Also, for a quality signal, you need to transmit all the audio frequencies in the range of human hearing. AM channels are not wide enough to do that, for historical reasons. This is why a contralto female voice is used for VOLMET - it fits the frequency spectrum better than a soprano does.

SIDEBANDS

062 01 01 03

When a carrier is modified by a frequency lower than itself, you get a band of frequencies either side of the carrier. The boundaries are effectively two extra frequencies, being the equivalent of the *sum* and *difference* frequencies of the carrier and the modulator, so you get three in total, from the carrier *plus* the audio and the carrier *minus* the audio. The extras are called *upper* and *lower sidebands*, which are exact mirrors of each other, in terms of power and information carried.

A receiver would normally need to pick up all the frequencies involved, but this can waste bandwidth (and power) as you are transmitting two identical sidebands and the carrier, which is there even if nothing is being transmitted - it is simply something to hang the sidebands on. In addition, the efficiency is limited to 33% to prevent distortion in the receiver when demodulating.

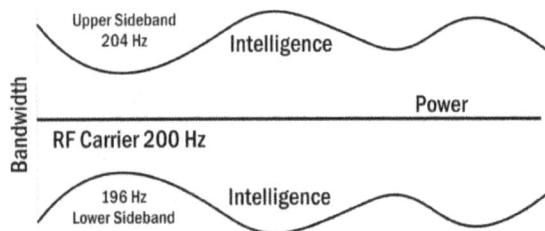

Because 80% of the power of an AM signal is in the steady carrier wave, which is essentially wasted, a neat trick is to suppress the carrier and one sideband, to transmit the other one, *adding what was taken away at the receiver.*

This means that you need less than half the power to transmit* (for the same distance), and the signal doesn't take up so much space, so you get to use more channels, although your receiver now needs an oscillator.

In effect, you can transmit with narrower bandwidths. This is *Single Sideband Transmission*, or SSB. As there is no carrier, there is no transmission unless information is being sent.

*SSB can do with 250 watts what AM requires 1000 watts for, so the ratio is 4:1, or 16 times more efficiency.

Traditionally, the upper sideband is used above 10 KHz, and the lower one below (it is a modified form of A3). HF upper sideband is used for aeronautical voice communications over the N Atlantic - soon to be replaced with satellite communications. HF VOLMET signals are also single sideband.

FREQUENCY MODULATION

Here, the frequency is changed instead of the amplitude, so FM does not suffer from man-made interference. As well, because the signal to noise ratio for FM is lower than it needs to be for AM, you don't need as much power for the same quality of reception (it is also more steady), although FM receivers are more complex to produce.

The whole audio range is covered because they were able to allocate a wider bandwidth to FM transmissions.

FREQUENCY MODULATION

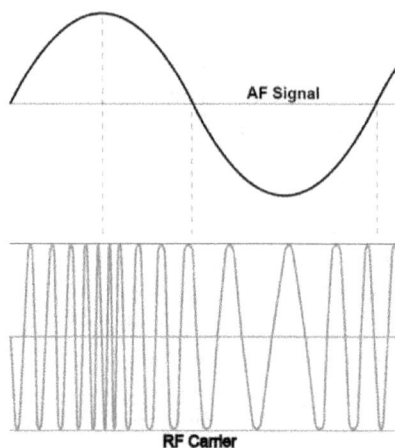

When the amplitude is positive, the frequency increases above the mean carrier frequency, and *vice versa*. The amount of change is called the *deviation*. The maximum limit is typically ±5 KHz for speech.

PULSE MODULATION

This is used for radar and is described in that section.

FREQUENCY SHIFT KEYING

For data, as used with satellites, where the carrier frequency is shifted above and below the mean (as 1 and 0) to represent bits of information.

Input is in FM with a very small deviation.

RESONANCE (TUNED CIRCUIT)

Radio waves need to oscillate at a frequency high enough to excite the air molecules surrounding an antenna. An oscillating system needs *inertia* and *elasticity*, so that energy can be stored and released. A capacitor and inductor (coil) in parallel is the simplest kind of electrical oscillating system, which behaves in a similar way to a weight on a spring, or an electrical pendulum. The problem is that, left to itself, the energy dissipates over time and the oscillations will stop. We need a way of making sure that they keep going. With a weight on the end of a spring, all you need to do is pull the weight at its lowest point by just enough to cover for the losses caused by friction. In a watch, the main spring is timed to release just enough energy to the balance wheel to keep it moving.

In our case, friction is replaced by resistance, and we have to produce undamped (continuous) oscillations. Because of their ability to amplify, transistors are very good at doing this - the amplification creates energy that can be fed back into the system at the right moments to keep it going (otherwise called regenerative feedback).

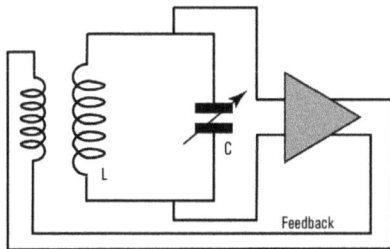

A *tank (LC) circuit* (so called because it stores energy) consists of a capacitor and inductance coil (see above). Depending on their electrical values, an alternating current can go back and forth between them in a periodic cycle.

The capacitor discharges through the coil as the excess electrons try to move from one of its plates to the other. However, back emf from the coil slows this down, and keeps the movement of the electrons going, where it would normally die away (the polarity reverses each cycle).

Current in a capacitor leads the applied voltage by 90°, while through an inductor it lags by 90°. With both in a circuit, the current flowing through the capacitor leads that in the inductor by 180°, so they cancel each other out, and only a little current is needed to keep things going. The resonant frequency is the one where reactance is zero, meaning that the circuit is operating on pure resistance. This provides a significant rise in voltage.

The coil and capacitor between them therefore behave like a flywheel and a spring. The energy is alternately stored in the electric field of the capacitor and the magnetic field of the coil, and we have an oscillator.

The Receiver

As the signal at the receiving antenna is very weak, a receiver must not only provide gain, but also be selective. The antenna picks up all the waves that are passing it, but the tuner makes the radio respond to the one you want to listen to.

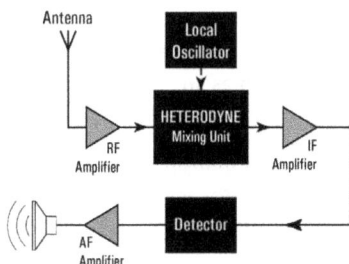

In a straight receiver (above), an RF amplifier at the end of the antenna produces a stronger copy of the transmitted signal (from about a millionth of a volt at the antenna to around a tenth of a volt). The signal is then demodulated, and amplified again on its way to the speaker.

However, early radio sets had many amplifiers and filters, which had to be tuned separately. In 1917, Edwin H Armstrong, a Major in the US Army Signal Corps, converted the received signals to a single, fixed, fairly low one (rather like mixing red and blue to get purple), at which most of the receiver's gain and selectivity could be obtained (it is easier to amplify a lower frequency). As it is between the AF and RF signals, it is called the *Intermediate Frequency*. 455 kHz has been used since the 1930s.

Frequencies were now easier to tune over a wide range and the filters could also be preset and not require tuning at all, hence one tuning knob. This was called a *superhet*, short for **superheterodyne**, or *supersonic heterodyne*, because the received and oscillator signals are mixed (heterodyned) to form a supersonic frequency. Almost every radio now is a superhet, constructed like two direct conversion receivers* in line.

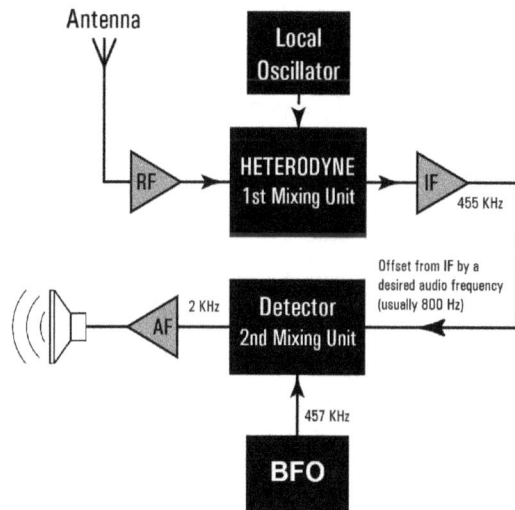

*A direct conversion receiver demodulates by mixing with a locally generated frequency. It is mainly used for SSB.

To get audio output from a direct conversion receiver, the signal is mixed with one from a Beat Frequency Oscillator.

BEAT FREQUENCY OSCILLATOR

Beat notes are created when any waves of different frequencies are mixed.

On the ADF (later), the BFO produces a small AC current which differs from the IF by around 2 KHz. The IF and BFO outputs are fed to the frequency mixer (heterodyne), where they are subtracted from one another to produce four frequencies, only one of which can be heard - the *difference* or *beat* frequency, which is amplified and fed to a loudspeaker which produces a steady AF of 2 KHz, within the human hearing range. If the incoming RF stops, no sound is heard from the loudspeaker. On modern aircraft the BFO is activated automatically.

The **squelch circuit** eliminates background noise when nothing is being transmitted. It is automatic on modern sets above a certain noise level.

DEMODULATION

Demodulation involves using a rectifier to ensure that only signal pulses moving in one direction get through.

For example, the picture below represents a very basic resonant circuit, containing a coil and a capacitor.

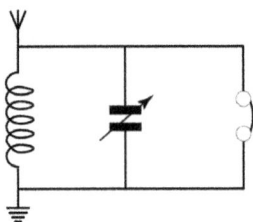

The antenna circuitry is on the left. Between them, the coil and capacitor have a natural resonance which must match that of the transmitter. In other words, the amount of inductance from the coil (L) and capacitance (C) must be the same for transmission and reception - the individual amounts can vary, but their product must be the same. The resonance can be altered by varying the inductance, but the most practical way is to adjust the capacitance (the tuning knob is a variable capacitor).

Anyhow, in its present form, the above circuit will not work, because AC has an average power of zero, meaning that the diaphragms in the earphones will simply move in sympathy with it and not actually vibrate. We need to introduce a device that only allows current to flow in one direction, namely a diode (or a "cat's whisker").

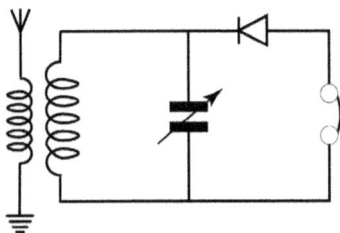

Now, the positive pulses pull the diaphragm towards the magnets, but the spaces in between the pulses (which replace the negative current) allow the diaphragm to try and spring back to its neutral position, and hence vibrate so you can hear the original speech. This is a *pulsating* direct current with a varying amplitude, with the same envelope (and effect) that was sent in the first place.

It is interesting to note that decoding an AM signal can only be done with a non linear circuit, in which the current is not directly proportional to the applied voltage - that is, it does not obey Ohm's Law.

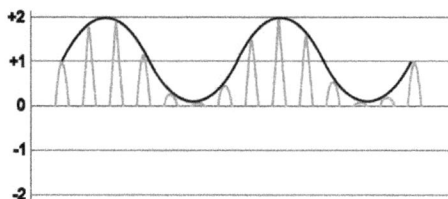

In practice, the circuit will be sensitive to a *range* of frequencies, due to the ratio of resistance to inductance, so the less resistance there is, the better the spike of voltage impressed upon the circuit. The antenna circuit can be decoupled to send its current into the circuit via a transformer, so that resistance is reduced to make the circuit tune more sharply. Notice that a step up transformer is used to give the signal a boost.

Finally, the audio-only signal goes into an audio amplifier for a quick boost before an exact copy of the original speech comes out of the loudspeaker.

Bandwidth

The "width" of any signal is known as its *bandwidth*, but a transmission medium also has a bandwidth, and here, the term is twisted slightly to mean the width it is *able to provide*, rather than the *width it occupies*. The aim, when matching signals to media, is to ensure that the signal bandwidth does not exceed that of the intended link, or that your car is not too wide for the road. So officially, the bandwidth is the difference between the highest and the lowest range of frequencies that a signal occupies. As an example, 3,000 Hz is a wide enough spread to carry voice information, and if you used it to modify a carrier wave of 3 MHz (3,000,000 Hz), your bandwidth will range from 2,997,000-3,003,000 Hz (see *Sidebands*, above). Unofficially (and more commonly), the term defines the amount of information that can be carried by any media, or signal, (that is, capacity) in a given time.

Emissions

The simplest method of transmitting information is to turn a signal on and off in a recognisable code, as used by older NDBs which break the carrier wave in a pattern matching the Morse Code ID of the station, called *Telegraphy*, or CW. This is known as an A1 transmission, whereas a carrier wave by itself would just be A0.

Otherwise, we use *telephony*, or ordinary speech, where an audio signal modifies, or modulates, a carrier wave. Sending Morse as an audio signal creates an A2 signal.

CAPT

When describing the emissions from a station, three symbols are used. The first is a letter describing the type of modulation, the second is a number for the nature of the modulation signal, and the third is a letter for the type of information transmitted.

For example, the VOR, discussed later, is A9W, because its carrier wave is frequency and amplitude modulated.

Table: Types Of Emission

Code	Modulation Type	No	Nature Of Modulating Signal	Code	Information Type
N	Unmodulated	0	Unmodulated CW	N	None
A	AM double sideband	1	Keyed CW (Morse)	A	Telegraphy (aural)
J	Single sideband, suppressed carrier	2	Modulated CW	B	Telegraphy (automatic)
H	Single sideband, full carrier	3	AM Modulated	E	Telegraphy (inc sound)
F	Frequency modulated	7	2 or more channels, Digital	D	Data
G	Phase Modulation	8	2 or more channels, Analogue	W	Combinations of the above
P	Unmodulated Pulse	9	Composite (digital/analogue)		
K	AM Pulse				

EXAMPLES

Class	Aid
N0NA1A	NDB (BFO on)*
N0NA2A	NDB (BFO on for tuning only)
A2A	NDB
J3E	HF (Communication)
A3E	VHF/VDF
A8W	ILS
A9W	VOR
P0N	DME, SSR
N0X/G1D	MLS (DPSK)

*Produces peak power all the time for better range.

Propagation

The propagation of radio waves concerns the means by which they travel between a transmitter and a receiver. They normally take the Great Circle route (see *Navigation*), but radio waves are subject to various effects described below that mean they may not necessarily do that. They can be helped along by the weather - because of a rapidly rising pressure tendency at both ends, during August 2013, NDBs in Canada were received in Europe. In a transmitter, the energy is alternately stored in the electric field of a capacitor and the magnetic field of a coil. An antenna connected to the circuit would therefore alternately radiate electric and magnetic fields. In fact, they surround the antenna at all times, as there is a crossover where each field builds up and dies down.

As electrons rush up and down the antenna (as alternating current), they form an electric field between the antenna and Earth, as the relationship between them is capacitive. The movement of the electrons also creates a magnetic field. Both radiate outwards and synchronise together about a quarter of a mile away. When a transmitter is feeding an omnidirectional antenna, the waves will spread out equally in all directions.

Picture: Typical Propagation from a vertical antenna

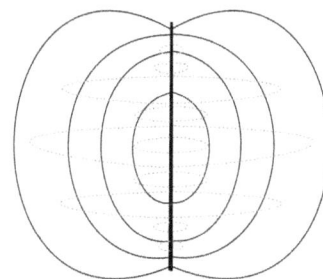

As the circumference of a wave front increases, its energy reduces per unit of length (see *Attenuation*, below). The signal strength at any point is called the *field strength*, and it is usually measured in volts. Point B in the picture is 3 times the distance from the antenna than Point A is, and the circumference is three times larger, so the field strength at B a third of A's. Field strength in volts is therefore inversely proportional to distance.

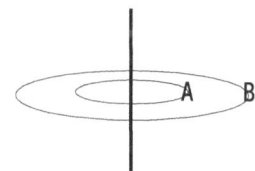

However, the signal also moves vertically and the signal has to spread out over the area of the resulting sphere. This measure of strength now is the *power* of the signal which is measured in Watts. As Point B is on the surface of a sphere with 9 times the surface area of the one at Point A, it will receive a ninth of the power. Thus, the power of a signal fades in an inverse square relationship, meaning that a signal 2 nm from its source will have a quarter of the strength of one only 1 nm away. Put another way, you need 4 times the power to double the range of transmission, as a radio wave is an expanding circle, so its area depends on the square of the radius.

This has important implications for radar, described later.

ATTENUATION

This concerns the loss of energy and velocity in various parts of a radio wave as energy is absorbed by the Earth and/or the atmosphere and ionosphere, on top of the normal decrease of power with range described above. If a signal's path is obstructed by rain, fog or a hill (for example), there will be a noticeable weakening of the signal behind the obstruction as a radio shadow is created.

The only way of combatting attenuation that we have any control over is with the frequency. The higher it is, the greater will be the attenuation.

- **Surface attenuation** increases with frequency.

- **Ionospheric attenuation** increases with a decrease in frequency.

- **Radar attenuation** increases with frequency, but is affected by water droplets which can also absorb and reflect the signal.

Radio waves generally travel pretty much in a straight line, but they may change direction because of:

- **Refraction (B)**, which is the change of speed and/or bending of a wave as it travels across different media, such as land or sea (as discussed under *ADF/NDB*, later). This also happens at the ionosphere, with HF, according to temperature, pressure and humidity. See *Sky Waves*, overleaf. The frequency does not change when refraction occurs.

- **Reflection (C)**, from a flat surface such as the Earth, or an aircraft (radar), like light off a mirror (where the initial and reflected waves have the same angle), but after reflection, a phase shift occurs, which will depend on the angle at which the surface was struck, and the wave polarisation.

- **Diffraction** (scattering). This is the spreading of a wave as it passes through a gap or round an edge, and is a problem when signals are transmitted in a narrow beam, but it is also why a radio wave follows the shape of the Earth. Diffraction increases as frequency reduces.

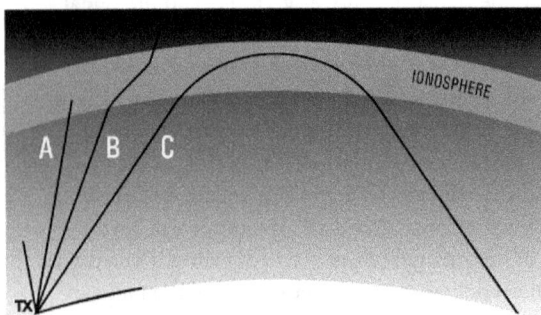

This means that, if you rely on radio waves for approaches to airfields, you should be aware that they bend at certain times of the day (e.g. dawn/dusk) and over certain terrain, such as mountains, where you could also get multipath propagation, as signals are received from many sources and will be out of phase with each other at the antenna. Such waves can cancel each other out and you end up with no guidance at all.

GROUND (SURFACE) WAVES

Ground waves are sometimes called *Surface Waves*. They are associated with LF and MF, and may go directly to their destination (if it is close enough), or curve to follow the Earth's surface, depending on the frequency.

The approximate lengths of LF/MF ground waves are 1000/500 nm, respectively. MF suffers more from atmospheric attenuation.

Ground waves must be vertically polarised to induce a current in the ground, and their range depends on:

- **Wavelength**. The lower the frequency (and the longer the wavelength), the better the reception over long distances. Below 500 kHz, you can obtain over 1000 miles just with a ground wave.

- **Type of ground**. The rate of attenuation of a surface wave is around 3 times greater over land than it is over the sea. Typical figures for maximum range are 100 and 300 nm respectively, with high power transmitters.

Contact with the surface and the widening circumference of the wave eventually weakens its power (attenuation), causes it to curve downwards and eventually be absorbed. Once a ground wave starts to die away, it does so very quickly. Over 300 miles, for example, it may only die away in proportion for the first 200 miles - then it halves its strength for each hundred miles after that.

A *ground-reflected wave* bounces off the ground on its way to the receiver (which is why Distance Measuring Equipment uses an echo protection circuit). As it is not subject to continuous absorption by the Earth, it travels further than the ground wave, but the phase can be reversed at the point of reflection.

DIRECT (SPACE) WAVES (A3E)

These are contained within the troposphere, and are otherwise known as *tropospheric, or space wave*s. Being direct, they are known as *line-of-sight*, meaning that anything in the way, like hills or buildings, will affect the transmission (direct waves will not bounce like HF waves do).

VHF/SHF/UHF reception is line-of-sight and will not curve to follow the Earth's surface, so you have to be high enough to receive your selected station at a particular distance. As an example, when crossing the Irish Sea, you must be above 3000 feet to hear either Shannon or London Information. However, when using the VOR at high altitudes, you might get station overlap and erroneous readings, so don't use VOR bearing information beyond the published protection range (see the AIP).

Air-ground transmissions are limited to 25 nm in the UK, up to 4,000 feet for tower frequencies and 10,000 feet for approach. Such limitations also mean little interference from other stations.

The (theoretical) reception range for line of sight transmissions can be estimated with this formula:

$$NM = (1.23 \times \sqrt{H}) + (1.23 \times \sqrt{h})$$

H is the height of the aircraft antenna and *h* is that of the one on the ground. Do not be tempted to combine them into one calculation - the square roots won't work.

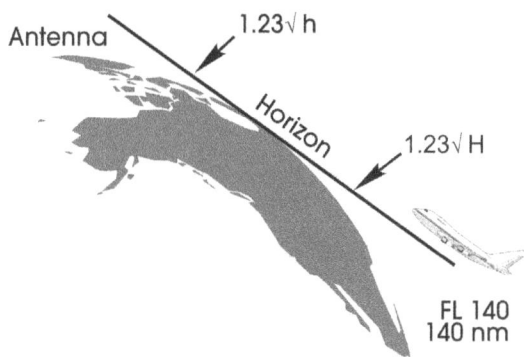

The short cut is to use Pythagoras and add a bit. In real life, however, the results will vary if the transmitter is weak, there is something in the way, or the receiver is not working properly. The actual figure is greater by around 4/3 due to diffraction. Here are some samples:

Height	Range (nm)
1 500	50
5 000	87
10 000	123

SKY WAVES (J3E)

A *sky wave* reflects off the ionosphere, where it might be reflected downwards again, if the angle is right, and reach further distances (on HF).

THE IONOSPHERE

This is a region surrounding the Earth where the Sun's rays dislodge electrons from the gas molecules, making them ionised (and therefore charged) and creating several conductive layers a couple of hundred miles thick around the Earth, starting about 60 miles up (but lower during the day) and varying with the seasons (they are not spheres, but change their shape constantly).

The ionisation stops the Sun's most violent radiation from reaching the Earth (ultraviolet light is dealt with by the production of ozone in the Stratosphere). It also makes the gases (nitrogen and oxygen) conductive. The nitrogen is ionised at the higher levels - lower down it is the oxygen. This happens mostly in daytime and is minimum just before sunrise, so air is a good insulator in the lower parts of the atmosphere, but ionisation makes it more conductive as you go up. *Recombination* is the process where electrons and atoms get back together again, starting in the late afternoon and early evening, and continuing overnight.

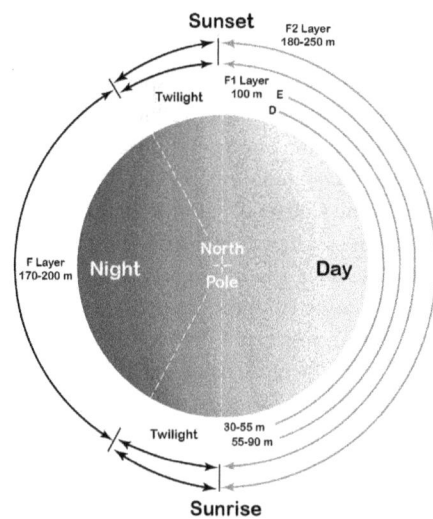

As the ionosphere depends directly on the Sun's radiation, the way the Earth moves around the Sun affects its characteristics.

Some changes are predictable, and some are not, but all of them affect radio propagation. Regular variations can be 27-day, daily and 11-yearly (from sunspots), but the daily ones have most effect on aviation. As the atmosphere is bombarded by waves with different frequencies, they produce 4 cloud-like layers of electrically charged gas atoms, between 50-300 km above the Earth: The D, E (Heaviside), F1 & F2 layers (Appleton). The first was discovered by James Van Allen in 1957, hence its naming as the Van Allen belt. UV rays with higher frequencies can penetrate deeper into the atmosphere so they create the lowest ionised layers.

- The **D layer** sits between 50-100 km high in the day. Ionisation is low because fewer UV waves penetrate to this level. The **D layer refracts VLF,** if large antennae and high power transmitters are used, **but it absorbs LF and MF waves,** so the range during daytime is about 200 miles.

- The **E layer** is higher, between 100-150 km, and almost disappears by midnight. It allows medium-range communication on **LF and HF bands,** or with waves longer than 100m.

- In daylight, the **F layer** splits into the **F1** and **F2 layers**. It is responsible for most **HF long-distance** communication (waves below 100m). During maximum sunspot activity, F layer atoms can stay ionised all night. For horizontal waves, the single-hop capability can be up to 3000 miles, and more with multiple hops.

REFRACTION/REFLECTION

Anyhow, HF waves that hit the ionosphere can be bent if the angle is right, as the side of the wave that hits one of its layers first starts to speed up, because of the reduced *dielectric constant from ionisation**, which makes it turn. The effect is similar to that of light refraction in water which makes an object appear to be displaced.

*The speed of radio waves in the atmosphere is determined by its dielectric property, which ultimately depends on pressure, temperature and relative humidity. As pressure and relative humidity decrease with altitude, so does the Dielectric Constant**, but it increases as temperature decreases. Their combined lapse rates make radio waves increase their speed with height, so that, when a radio wave moves away from the Earth at less than a 90° angle, its upper part moves faster than its lower part. In essence, as you climb, the refractive index decreases uniformly (as does the ISA lapse rate). Radio waves can therefore be bent, particularly in a downward curve towards the surface of the Earth.

**The *dielectric constant* is the ratio of the capacity of a condenser in a given medium, i.e. air, to its capacity in a vacuum. It can also be thought of as a measure of the resistance of the air to wave propagation, and vertical changes in the Dielectric Constant determine the path of a radio wave, typically following a curved path with a radius of 1.3 times the radius of the Earth. This makes the normal range of VHF/UHF (line of sight) transmissions 1.3 times the visual horizon.

The angle at which the bending of a wave first happens is the *critical angle*, or the smallest angle that will allow a wave to be reflected back to Earth. Any rays more vertical than this are *escape rays*, typically used for satellites. The *critical frequency* (at which bending occurs) depends on the density of the layer concerned. If a wave manages to pass through one, it can still be reflected from higher up if its frequency is lower than that layer's critical frequency.

The lower the frequency of a wave, the more rapidly it is reflected, and the larger will be its critical angle, but the less the distance it will travel. A 20 MHz wave will be detected further from the transmitter than a 5 MHz one. The reflection becomes less as frequency is increased, and the angle becomes too shallow.

The first wave to reach the ground after being refracted or reflected is called the *First Returning Sky Wave*, until the maximum range is reached. When a wave leaves an antenna, the ground wave will be detected until it fades, or attenuates. Between that point, and where the first sky wave comes from the ionosphere, is an area where nothing is heard, a *skip zone*, or *dead space*.

The **skip distance** is the Earth distance taken by a signal after each reflection, or the distance covered by the first sky wave. 30 MHz signals do not return because they are too high in frequency, being at the bottom of the VHF band (15-25 MHz is more typical for bouncing). You can reflect off the ionosphere and back off the ground several times for multiple hops.

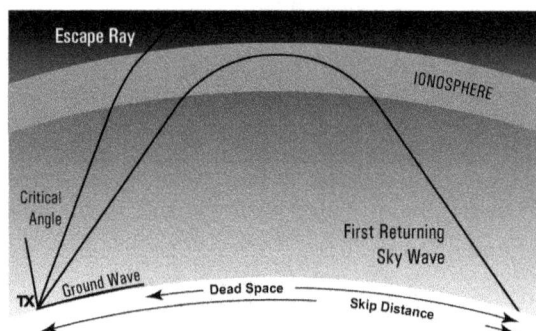

At night, if you use the same frequency, the skip distance will increase.

Ground range increases if critical angle, frequency, dead space and skip distance decrease, and *vice versa*. The skip zone of HF transmission will increase with higher frequencies and higher reflecting ionospheric layers.

What should you do if you are not getting through to a station but are receiving another from a greater distance away? Should you change to a higher or lower frequency? A lower one reduces the critical angle to make the skywave return at a shorter range and reduce the dead space.

Skip is usually best when the Sun is about halfway between you and the area you are transmitting to or receiving from. You will normally hear skip from the East in the morning and the West in the afternoon with that from the North or South at any time. *Long path skip* takes the long way round the Earth, usually because ionospheric conditions are better that way.

Thus, we depend on the ionosphere for all HF contacts beyond the ground-wave zone. It moves all the time, itself being dependent on the intensity of particle and wave emissions from the Sun, so propagation is affected considerably by the ionosphere's movement, which is why the ADF suffers from what is called *night effect* just after sunset and before sunrise when the needle swings erratically (on the other hand, during the night is when you will receive distant stations best).

Generally, HF communication is always possible when the frequency is low enough to be reflected and high enough not to be attenuated. Unfortunately, the only information we have about the above changes usually comes from statistical sources. It's not something you can work out.

Anomalous Propagation

Within the Earth's atmosphere, the velocity of a wave is less than it would be in free space, because of atmospheric conditions. Normal refractivity, which exists for around 50% of the time, will cause a wave to be bent downward from its usual straight line. It exists when moisture, pressure and temperature all decrease with altitude.

However, when lapse rates depart significantly from normal, VHF, UHF and SHF waves (particularly radar) can follow different curved paths. A rapid increase of temperature with height (an inversion) and a rapid decrease of relative humidity (a steep lapse rate) can bend the wave more toward the surface of the Earth and increase propagation distances with little attenuation (although fading can occur) for a condition of **super refraction**. This means that radar coverage, for example, can be extended for up to 50% above the normal range.

Propagation distances can reduce (*sub refraction*) with opposing conditions. Radar can also suffer from **ghosting**, or false echoes. A **shadow zone,** or **radar hole,** can allow an object be invisible electronically.

If the waves curve more than the Earth does, because conditions are more intense, radio waves can become trapped between the surface and the negative gradient causing the refraction. Because the waves also bounce off the surface, they can travel for much longer distances. Such **ducts** are associated with regions of high pressure, over flattish terrain and the sea - not normally over hilly ground. Semi-permanent ducts can be found around the Earth in the major areas of high pressure, usually in meteorological conditions associated with tropical and subtropical latitudes (i.e hot by day, and cool by night), near the Equator. In the Trade Winds, for example (see *Meteorology*), ducting over 3 000 miles can occur, off the surface and below about 5 000 feet.

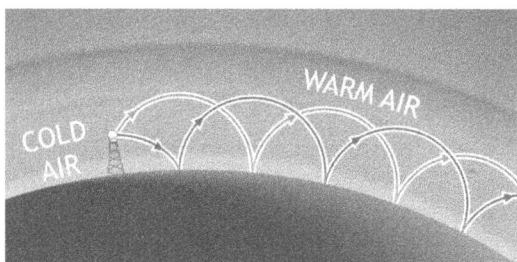

The depth of the duct required increases with the wavelength, such as 50 feet for wavelengths of 3 cm, and 600 feet for wavelengths of 1 metre, but they are normally less than 1 000 feet deep. Elevated ducts (between two layers of the atmosphere) can occur at height, so they may be present at more than one level, so if you are

experiencing radio/radar reception difficulties, you can fly towards the destination, descend, or try a lower frequency.

With radar, ducting will increase ground clutter.

- More moisture means more refraction
- Higher temperatures mean less refraction

Pressure by itself has little effect.

VLF signals can travel long distances through a similar process involving the ionospheric layers and a *conduit wave*, which is *reflected* rather than *refracted*.

FREQUENCY SELECTION

With HF, frequencies need to be higher during the day or when you are at greater range from the station. Because the ionosphere is higher at night, you can use lower ones, generally about half (that is, use *Double During Day*), which is something to be aware of when you are operating at a remote base and you use HF to keep in touch with the Operations office. Generally, you might leave for camp with a selection of five frequencies you can use depending on the time of day.

Otherwise, for successful communication on HF between two given points, there is a maximum frequency, a lowest frequency and an optimum frequency.

Optimum Working Frequency

The *optimum* usable frequency, where attenuation is minimum for the range obtained, or where you have the least number of problems, is the best theoretical frequency that brings the skywave back to the receiver. It is the one that causes the first returning sky wave to fall just short of the receiving station, so that when it drifts, the station will still pick it up. This frequency should be high enough to avoid the disadvantages from multipath fading, absorption and noise, but not so high as to be affected by rapid changes in the ionosphere. It is about 85% of the ....

Maximum Usable Frequency

The point at which refraction is no longer possible. As the level of ionisation is less in the ionosphere by night than it is by day, you have to lower the frequency to get the same type of refraction. Luckily, attenuation is reduced at night as well, so this is offset slightly. The MUF not only varies with path length and between day and night, but also with the seasons, meteor trails, sunspots, etc. This is why HF transmitters have to use a wide range of frequencies between about 2-20 MHz to get through.

Lowest Usable Frequency

This is the point below which refraction cannot start.

Antennae   062 01 02

Aircraft radios have 760 channels spaced 25 KHz apart with a power rating of between 2-25 Watts. Power won't help if you don't have a good antenna.

An antenna is a conductor (or a group of them) that can radiate or collect electromagnetic waves. Put another way, it is a device that can convert electrical energy into electromagnetic energy and *vice versa*. The relationship between an antenna and the Earth is a capacitive one, with the air between them acting as a dielectric.

A certain length of straight wire will possess a natural amount of inductance and capacitance, which will correspond to a particular wavelength, as the length of a radiated wave depends on their product. For example, a half-wave dipole for 18 MHz should be 8.33 m long. The simplest antenna for a single frequency is a single wire, just under a quarter of a wavelength long.

This means that you will be able to receive suitably strong signals on that wavelength without any extra circuitry. However, it is not practical to carry around a range of antennae, so adding a capacitor or coil to the mix will allow you to artificially adjust its natural wavelength to suit the circumstances. A normal VHF antenna would be about 15 cm long, but using complex circuitry allows you to electronically shorten it.

There are two basic types of antennae, namely *Hertz* (half-wave) and *Marconi* (quarter wave). Hertz types are also known as *dipoles*, and are usually positioned well above ground, radiating horizontally or vertically (see *Polarisation*) for frequencies of 2 MHz and above. Marconis are perpendicular to the Earth and have one end grounded to it, used for frequencies below 2 MHz.

DIRECTIONALITY (DIRECTIVITY)

Most people know they have to turn a domestic radio round in order to get the best signal. This works the other way round as well - it is possible, with simple procedures, to transmit radio waves in certain directions, which can be useful if the wave attenuates too quickly, as the power can be concentrated - using a directional aerial can boost transmission in a particular quarter and increase the gain in that direction for longer range. Some directionality can be achieved with just two elements, or dipoles.

If a second, not fed with power, and slightly longer, is placed a quarter of a wavelength behind the **driven element** (the one radiating all the power) it behaves like a resonant coupled circuit which has oscillatory currents induced in it. The currents re-radiate, and the quarter-wave spacing causes it to be in such a phasing as to cancel out the original radiation on that side, and to reinforce it on the opposite side, so the second dipole has the same effect as a reflector (see *Radar*), and gives you a marked gain in signal strength in a particular direction. The more

the number of dipoles in an array, the narrower and more intense will be the beam of radiation.

A shorter antenna called a *Director* in front of the driven element will behave like a lens which concentrates the energy. Directors and reflectors are called *parasites*, but a series of them is generally known as a Yagi array (like a TV aerial). It can create spurious side beams (or lobes) as well as the main beam.

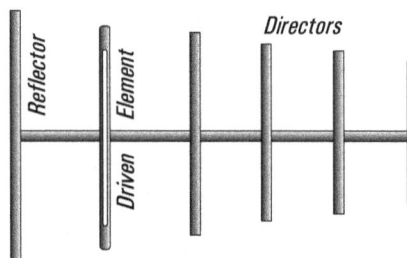

THE LOOP

Before metric and centimetric waves came on the scene, direction finding was based on the simple loop aerial, or vertical ones spaced apart (the Adcock).

Remembering that there must be a *difference* in electrical pressures between two points for electrons to flow*, the maximum signal is found when the loop is in line with the transmission (i.e. sideways-on), when the points of contact are out of phase, so a current is generated, which drives an electric motor to continually seek the null position, when the loop is square (across the signal). As the vertically polarised signal now reaches both sides of the loop at the same time, no signal is detected. The null signal point is used for direction finding because it is easier to detect (it is much more sharply defined).

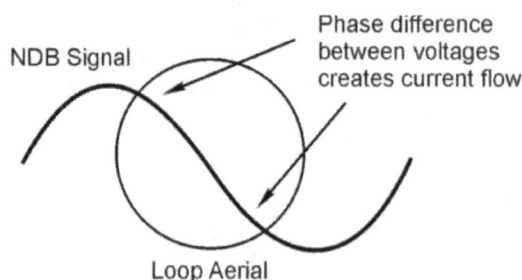

Various stages of magnification inside the receiver help this along, but they need not concern us here. Because the current flows in the opposite direction depending on the position of the loop, you also need some way of determining which end is what, otherwise you could be 180° out. A single vertical aerial called a *sense antenna* helps here - the signals are combined algebraically and the magnitude and polarity of the sense aerial arranged to be identical to the loop.

The result is a polar diagram called a *cardioid*, with only one null point:

Thus, loop aerials receive a signal, but the sense aerial is there to resolve ambiguities. It is placed vertically in the middle of the loop. By using a transformer, the electrons flowing in the sense aerial set a second stream flowing in one of the vertical parts of the loop.

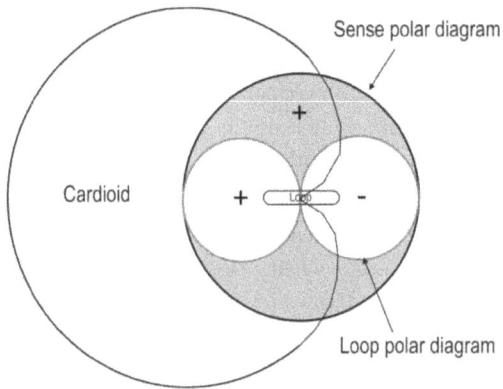

So, on one side of the loop, the polar diagrams are positive and combine, but on the other, one is positive and the other negative, so they cancel out, hence the null point on one side. The modern (and more stylish) equivalent of the loop antenna is a small housing with two coils at right angles to each other, wound on ferrite cores, one fore and aft and the other athwartships. The sense aerial resolves the two null points. There is another pair with a search coil in the middle that reacts to its influence and drives a needle as it searches for the null point.

THE HELICAL ANTENNA
A helical antenna, as used with GPS, allows you to use smaller equipment.

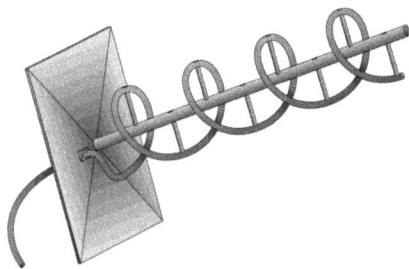

It can be used like a normal antenna, with maximum radiation at right angles to the axis of the helix. The radiation is linearly polarized parallel to the axis.

In the axial mode, however, the radiation comes out of the end (i.e. along the axis), and it works as a directional antenna radiating circularly polarized waves.

PARABOLIC
Parabolic dishes are used with radar systems and are described in that section.

THE SLOTTED PLANAR ARRAY
As used with most modern weather radar systems:

It is flat (i.e. a plane), with slots that act as waveguides (in fact, they have the same effect as a dipole antenna). By stacking them, as shown, the beamwidth of the E plane can be reduced. This gets round a problem caused by slotted waveguides which are long but thin, creating a wave that is wide in the E (vertical) plane but narrow in the H plane.

Sidelobes are also reduced.

GAIN
The ratio between the amount of energy propagated in a particular direction and that which would be propagated if the antenna were not directional is called antenna gain.

An antenna with a gain of 3 decibels, for example, could put out around double the power of a quarter wave antenna, which has no gain (referred to as *unity*). An antenna with a gain of 6 db hooked on to the back of an amplifier pushing 4 watts into it would put out the equivalent of 16 watts, or 80 if the gain were 13 db.

Note: Gain is not amplification, but making the best use of the energy available.

In an omnidirectional antenna, the gain can come from spreading the RF energy closer and flatter to the ground, creating stronger ground waves, as is found by using a five-eighths antenna, for a 3-4.5 db gain (i.e. the power is taken from the higher angles). The increase in range can be up to 10 km or more.

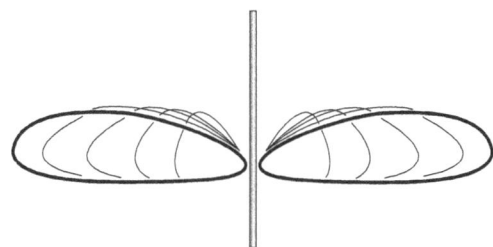

RECIPROCITY
This is the ability of an antenna to be used for transmitting and receiving.

TRANSMITTING SIGNALS
When an alternating current is applied to one end of a straight antenna, the wave travels to the other end, where it can go no further. This is a point of high impedance, so the wave bounces back towards where it came from. Although there is some loss from resistance, the wave is reinforced at the start point with more energy, which

results in continuous oscillations that are sustained with suitably timed impulses. There is also a high voltage at the *start* point, meaning the centre of the wire has minimum voltage. The maximum movement of electrons is also in the centre, so it has a low impedance there. The meeting of these two stresses sets up a standing wave which makes the particles oscillate all the time. Standing waves can be kept going with the minimum expenditure of energy.

The length of the antenna must allow the wave to travel from one end to the other and back within one cycle, and the wavelength is the distance travelled within that cycle.

RECEIVING SIGNALS

In simple terms, the antenna catches a radio wave and a small electrical current with the same waveform as the incoming signal is induced in it through an electronic tide. In practice a *selection* of frequencies is captured because an antenna is cut for the middle of the frequency band you want (half wavelength is good, but a quarter is often used).

The signal passed on to the radio set after being received is at the resonant frequency of the antenna, with a few on either side for good measure. This signal is amplified and selectivity improved with a tuned circuit, where capacitive reactance cancels out the inductive reactance. Some other signals do get through however, so filters eliminate them in later stages. In the end, all radio frequencies will finally be extracted, leaving only a low-level audio signal to be amplified and sent to your headset.

A receiver's ability to reject signals outside the relevant bandwidth is called its *sensitivity*.

Doppler

The Doppler effect is a change of frequency that comes from relative motion between the sender and receiver. It works on the principle that radio waves compress when directed to a station and elongate when going away (in other words, as two objects get closer together, the frequency of any radio wave between them will increase artificially because of their relative speed). The usual example given is listening to the change in the noise of a train approaching you, and passing by. The pitch is higher than normal at first, and becomes lower than normal when it has passed.

Picture: Doppler Effect

This is because the forward speed means that the sound waves have to fit into a smaller space, and therefore have shorter wavelengths, and a higher pitch, so the receiver will intercept more waves in a given time.

The opposite is true after the train passes - they have more room to fit into, and the wavelength becomes longer, to produce the lower sound. Apply that to radar, since both sound and radio travel as sine waves, and you have the basics of a good navigation system that can compute groundspeed and drift - in helicopters, it can provide auto-hover capabilities, amongst other things, although it has almost entirely disappeared, except for its use with GPS.

The change in frequency is called *Doppler Shift*, which is given a positive (+) quality when a closing relative velocity produces an increase in frequency, and a negative quality when otherwise.

Discharge Detectors

Otherwise known as *Stormscopes*, after one manufacturer, these detect lightning discharges and display them on a green screen in the cockpit. They work in a similar way to an ADF with its needle pointing towards a storm.

RADIO NAVIGATION
••

Most radio aids just give you information about your position - only landing aids tell you what to do with it. Your position can be given in four ways:

- As a relative bearing *to* a radio station relative to the longitudinal axis of the aircraft (ADF, VOR)

- As a radial *from* a station (VOR)

- As a distance from a station (DME)

- As an actual position (GPS, RNAV, INS)

For the first three, you need a chart with which to compute your position.

Note: As a point of airmanship, equipment not directly required for navigation should be tuned to ground stations to check accuracy or ground speed, so errors can be detected and the equipment be available in an emergency. Also, **do not rely on a beacon until it has been identified**.

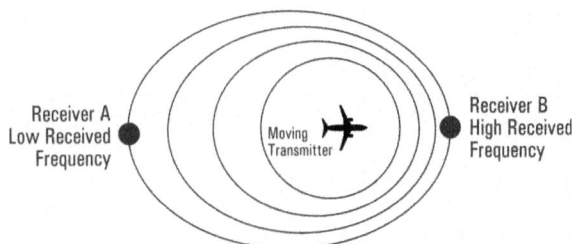

VOR

062 02 03

•••

Very High Frequency Omnidirectional Range is a ground-based short range navigational aid that broadcasts two signals on VHF, using the *phase difference* between them to signify your direction from the transmitting station as one of 360 radials *from* it. The usable frequency range is between **108-117.975 MHz**, which is just below aviation voice channels.

Low-powered VORs (as used near terminals) and ILS localisers occupy the space between 108-112, with 50 Hz spacing, so there is room for 40 ILS and 40 VOR channels. The VORs usually use even decimals, plus even tenths to prevent confusion with the ILS, which uses odd tenths. For example, an ILS might use 108.1, while a Terminal VOR might use 108.2.

136
Voice
720 Channels
118
117.975
Hi Pwr VOR
120 Channels
112
Lo Pwr VOR
ILS
80 Channels
108 MHz

Higher powered VORs, as needed for aircraft at higher altitudes, operate between 112-118 (112-117.975) on odd and even tenths, for another 120 channels. They can be received up to 100 nm away.

In total, there are 40 ILS and 160 VOR channels.

VORs represented on maps have a compass rose round them, aligned with Magnetic North. They are a pain to shut down and realign, which is why a VOR's variation will often be different from its aerodrome.

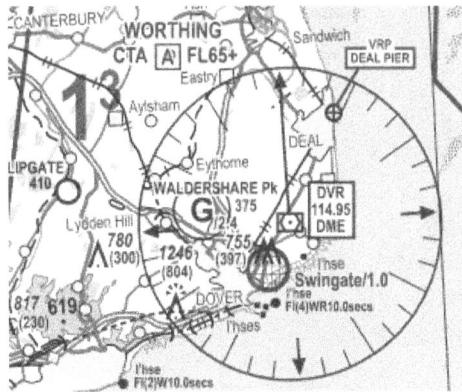

VORs are not sensitive to heading, as is the ADF (below), because they show *track*, although most pilots set the OBS to the heading anyway for neatness so that the left/right needle reads correctly. Neither do they suffer from many of the other problems associated with the ADF, especially night effect.

The *Station Identifier* is transmitted in Morse every 15 seconds (4 times a minute), and you must confirm the frequency and ID before using a VOR for navigation. If there is no ID, but behaviour is otherwise normal, the system is on maintenance (you may sometimes hear a Morse test code of ▬ ••• ▬).

Theory Of Operation

The equipment electronically measures an angle, having transmitted a signal with three components. There is a 30 Hz FM omniphase signal, received by all stations at a constant phase, and a variable phase (variphase) signal whose phase changes according to its bearing from North. The variphase signal is a 30 Hz tone that modulates the amplitude of the carrier, and its sidebands are used to make the phase angle of the modulation equal to the azimuth angle.

To make separation easier (or to detect which signal is which), the reference signal frequency-modulates a sub-carrier (at 9960 Hz), because the carrier is already modulated by the variphase signal. The result is that an apparently AM signal (rotating at 30 Hz) is eventually seen by the aircraft in terms of varying *power* (amplitude) levels. After demodulation, the signals have their phases compared to derive a bearing.

There is also a voice/ID channel that can carry 1020 Hz Morse and voice signals.

So, both signals are in phase when the "rotating" signal passes Magnetic North, but they get more out of phase by the number of degrees you go round the circle so, if the phase difference is 30° at your receiver, you are on the 030° radial from the VOR. Your receiver picks up the reference signal first and the maximum point of the variphase signal a little bit later. The time difference is indicated in degrees as your magnetic bearing *from* the VOR (which is actually called a *radial*).

All this produces a polar diagram called a *limacon*, which has been inherited from an earlier navigation system, and is similar in shape to the cardioid used by the ADF (later), but without an absolute null point, rotating electrically at 30 times/second.

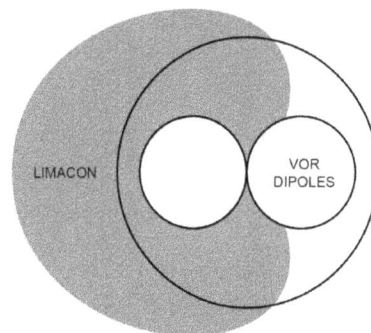

There is no null point because transmission is momentarily interrupted when the maximum point of the limacon passes through North. If it were otherwise, you would get a false North indication.

Because the signal is frequency and amplitude modulated, it is classed as an A9W signal (Doppler VOR, mentioned later, has its modulations the other way round).

In your aircraft, the signals are received by a horizontally polarised V-dipole antenna, then mixed, converted to an intermediate frequency, amplified, detected and demodulated. Then the audio part of the signal is fed into a low-pass filter which allows the reference signal to enter one part of the circuit and the rotating one to enter another, through a 10 KHz bandpass filter, eventually to become 30 Hz AC.

The rotating signal is also fed into a calibrated phase shifter which is controlled by the OBS on the front of the instrument in the cockpit. It is turned until the two signals are in phase and the Course Deviation Indicator (CDI) is in the centre.

The TO-FROM indicator is driven by another phase shifter and phase detector operating in parallel. Because of the nature of VOR transmissions and the way they are used for direction finding, there is a 180° ambiguity, so the CDI is equally sensitive to signals coming from either of two opposite directions (i.e. two radials, 180° apart, from the same VOR). To resolve this an additional circuit indicates TO or FROM with a flag. The reference signal is shifted by another 90° and compared again to the rotating one, to tell whether it is leading or lagging the rotating signal, to make the indicator show the relevant direction.

Diameter Around 9.5 nm

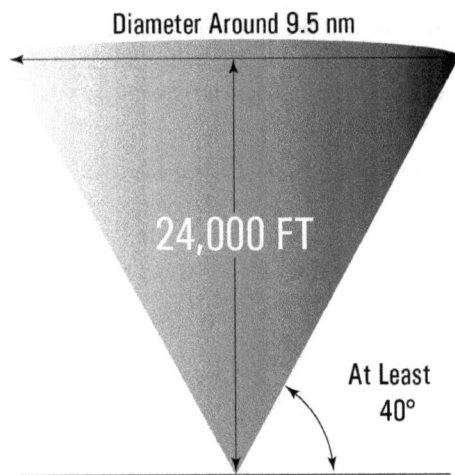

24,000 FT

At Least 40°

Over the beacon, you will be in a *cone of confusion*, the same as you would be with any antenna - this is an area where no signal is received, so the TO/FROM flags disappear and the alarm flag comes up. The ICAO limit for the cone is 100° across, and the width can be worked out by finding the tangent of the angle and multiplying it by your height, to get the answer in feet (FL 360 = 6 nm). During this *station passage*, just ignore the signal or use something else.

There are also ambiguities *abeam* the beacon - 90° either side of the selected radial there is a *zone of ambiguity* up to 10° across where the flag will not show at all, and the indications should therefore not be relied upon.

In the bowels of the aircraft will be a large black box, connected to a *remote indicator* in the cockpit, that might also double as an ILS display.

This one is a 5-dot display, using 4 dots plus a circle, so each one is 2°, for an overall width of 10°. For 3 dots plus a circle, each is 2.5°.

Once you select a radial by turning the *Omni Bearing Selector* (the knob under the dial), the *Course Deviation Indicator* (CDI) needle will be in the centre, or either side of it.

When the needle is in the middle, you will be on the selected radial, which is *from* the station when on the same side, shown by TO/FROM Flag, which, on later instruments, will be a small white triangle pointing in the relevant direction*. If the indicator shows *TO*, you are on the *reciprocal*, or going the other way. In the example above, the radial selected is S, or 180°, because the *To* flag is showing (as the needle is showing you are three dots left, you are on the 186° radial). Thus, when holding *inbound* on the 240 radial, your heading should be 060°. This is a common trap in exam questions (and check rides) - if you are tracking inbound on a radial, set the reciprocal at the top of the display, as radials go *from* a station.

*The changeover sector is within 10° either side of the abeam position. The TO/FROM indicator is independent of the heading. On the side of the radial you have selected, FROM is displayed. On the other side, you get TO.

All you have to do then is watch the needle - if the needle is pointing left, then you fly left until it centres.

The thing to remember is that the needle always points to *where the radial is*, which has *nothing to do with the heading of the aircraft* (on the RMI, the tail of the needle shows the radial), and you do not necessarily turn that way to get to it - sometimes, having the needle on the left means turn right! *Only if your heading is the same direction as the OBS will it be on the correct side.*

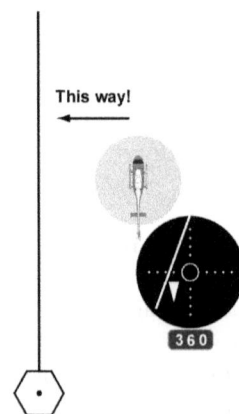

This way!

360

As an example, here is a comparison of the HSI against the OBI - you are heading 320°, and both have a setting of 120° *inbound*. Notice how the HSI presents the information clearly, but the OBI says something quite different - if you had no heading information, you might not realise you were going the wrong way!

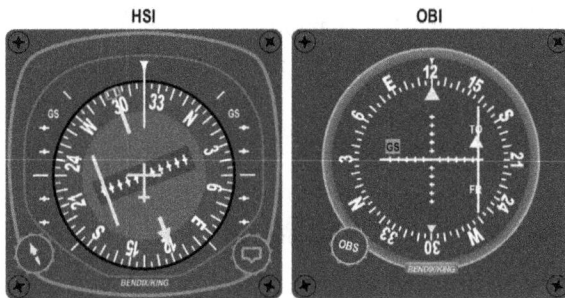

Thus, to get the best results, the heading should approximately follow the OBS setting.

The situation shown above is typically found during a procedure turn - it's not a normal tracking scenario.

For any radial, there are boundaries formed by the CDI and the TO/FROM indicator, creating quadrants around the station (that is, four distinct areas). You will be in one of them. In the picture below, which displays would the pilot see, and in what order, for a helicopter moving from A to B?

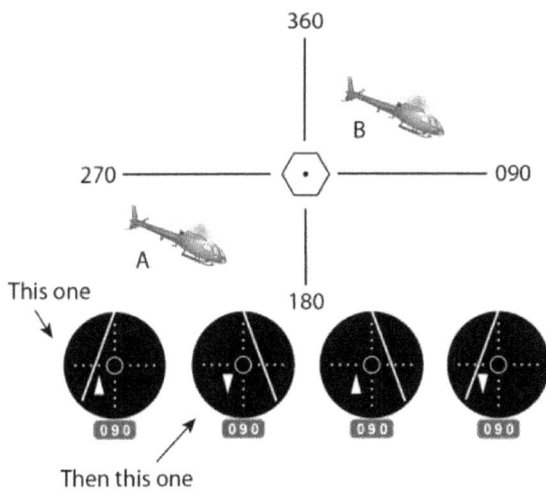

To intercept a radial inbound, tune and identify the VOR station, then select the reciprocal of the desired radial by turning the OBS until you get a TO reading. Fly to whichever side the needle is displaced, turning the shortest way to a heading 90° away from it, until the needle starts to move, at which point reduce the intercept angle to 45° (rather like 2-3 above). As the needle centres, reduce the intercept angle again and maintain the track with suitable adjustments for drift. Do the same outbound, except look for a FROM reading. A good rule (inbound and outbound) is to subtract the intercept angle if the needle goes left, and add if it goes right to find the heading to steer. For example, 280°-90°=190°.

Here are the needle movements and responses of an aircraft drifting off to the left and coming back on course:

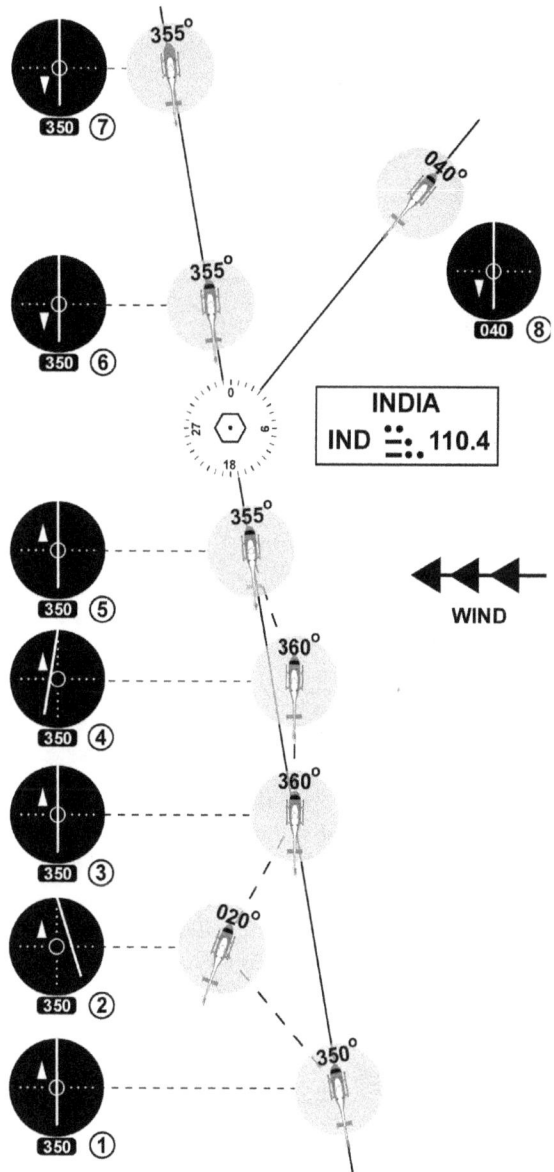

To bracket for drift, turn onto a zero wind heading and see what the drift actually is. Make a large correction the opposite way and see what happens. Then half the original correction. Keep going until the correct heading is found.

When tracking along an airway, tune and identify the station you are going from, track the selected radial until near the mid-point, then tune and identify the next station. The TO/FROM flag should change over.

If you have to use another VOR for a fix as a reporting point along the airway, select the required radial, and when the needle is centred you are over the fix:

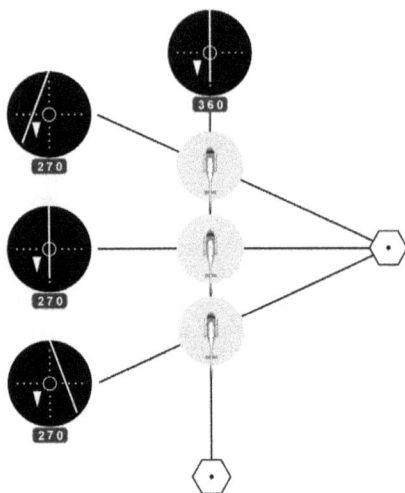

Range

As for standard VHF.

Time to Station

You often need to know the time it will take to get to a station (well, you will in the exam, anyway), which is simply found by turning 90° from the inbound radial and noting the seconds taken to go through a number of them. To get the time in minutes, divide the time just noted by the number of radials (degrees) gone through. All you need do then is use the groundspeed (or TAS in an emergency) to find your distance. It is a variation of the 1 in 60 rule, as explained in *Navigation*.

For time to station, the formula is:

$$\text{Time (mins)} = \frac{\text{Mins x 60}}{\text{Degrees}}$$

On the flight computer, set minutes on the outer scale, and the bearing change on the inner one. Read the answer on the outer scale opposite the 60 arrow. For the distance, just substitute miles for minutes, but you can also try:

$$\text{Distance} = \frac{\text{Mins x GS}}{60}$$

For example, your relative bearing to a fix is 315°, which 3 minutes later is 270°. What is the distance from the fix with a ground speed of 180 knots? On the flight computer, place the 60 marker against the time in minutes on the outer scale and read the answer (9 minutes) on the outer scale against the ground speed of 180 kts.

Tip: If you use a station 10-45° off the nose, the time taken to fly until the angle doubles is the same as the time to the station.

Airways

Question: If you are 100 nm from a VOR, and if 1 dot = 2°, how many dots deviation from the centreline of the instrument represent the limits of the airway boundary?

Airways are normally 5 nm wide either side of the centreline, so, applying a variation of the 1 in 60 rule:

$$\frac{5 \text{ x } 60}{100}$$

The answer is 3°, or 1.5 dots deviation.

At 200 nm you would be 3.5 nm off track, with a 1° error.

Question: An airway 10 nm wide is defined by two VORs with a bearing accuracy of ± 5.5°. To ensure accurate track guidance within the airway, what is the maximum distance between the transmitters? **Answer:** About 109 nm.

Tip: You change over halfway so there are two triangles.

The greatest acceptable cross track error is 5 nm off the airway centreline. If you fly out of one beacon and switch over halfway, the greatest error occurs at the halfway point, where the maximum distance off track is 5 nm, and the track error angle is 5.5°, so:

$$\frac{5 \text{ x } 60}{5.5}$$

Multiply by 2 to get 109 nm. Use this formula as well:

$$\frac{\text{airway width x 60}}{\text{accuracy}}$$

Testing

Some airfields have low power test equipment (2 watts) transmitting on 114.8 (usually, but you might get 108.0 from a repair station), identified with the ATIS, so have a pen ready to save you writing it down again later (the ID may just be a series of dots). The VOT is intended for ground use, although it can be used when airborne (there will be certified airborne check points), but you could always get to a position on a known radial and check the readings. As you move the OBS, you can expect the usual indications relating to the bearing selected (which is why two transmitters are used, to save you moving the aircraft to the radials). With the needle centred, the instrument should read 000° FROM or 180° TO at any point in the airport, with an accuracy of ± 4° (± 6° when airborne).

In fact, propagation error (or FM/AM synchronisation, at least) should be within ±1°. The system should shut down automatically if it gets outside that (the monitor will remove the ID once the measured bearing changes by more than 1°). Phase comparison (equipment) error should not be more than ±3°, and station (site) errors should be within ±1°. The nominal accuracy is ±5° within the published protection range, based on a 95% probability rate.

© *Phil Croucher, 2015*

CAPT

If this page is a photocopy, it is not authorised!

Problems

Although the VOR is less subject to static and other interference than an NDB (there is no night effect), and it is more accurate, the transmissions depend on line of sight, and there are suspect areas at 90° to a radial (zones of ambiguity), and overhead (cone of confusion), as mentioned above. In addition, certain rotor or propeller RPM settings can cause fluctuations up to ±6° (change them slightly before saying the instrument is not working!) Transmissions may be adversely affected by uneven propagation over irregular ground surfaces (scalloping), and if bearing information is used beyond published ranges, you may get interference from other transmitters.

Doppler VOR

Using Doppler allows the frequency of a signal to decrease when the distance between the beacon and aircraft increases, and *vice versa*. It removes site errors and allows you to use a VOR in hilly country (it also needs less of a clear radius around the station). Range is also improved. The reference signal is AM and the variphase signal rotates anticlockwise. The Doppler shift makes the transmitter look as if it is advancing and retreating 30 times a second. That is, the aircraft sees a varying frequency rather than varying power. The end result is signals that are the opposite way round to a normal VOR, but the equipment in the aircraft doesn't notice because the signals still have the right phase.

ADF/NDB   062 02 02
••

An *Automatic Direction Finder* (ADF), also known as a *radio compass*, is a device in an aircraft that picks up vertically polarised signals broadcast on the Medium wave band (LF/MF) by *Non Directional Beacons* (NDBs), so called because they radiate in all directions, using mainly surface waves as modified by indirect waves*. Medium frequencies are used because their range is good, and the aircraft dimensions are not similar to the wavelength.

*You can only depend on the range when the ground wave is dominant, as with low powered beacons that cannot manage a space wave. At higher powers, sky waves can reach the E layer of the ionosphere and make the readings inaccurate. If the needle is hunting and the signal gets louder and fades away, the ground wave is being contaminated by sky waves.

Although there are a few problems (see the next column), you can get 1,000 nm range over the sea and 300 nm over land if the power is high enough, but NDBs tend now to be used as *Locators*, or enroute navaids on airways, homing beacons for instrument approaches and markers for the Instrument Landing System (ILS), with a typical power of 15W and a range of about 10-25 nm.

A long range NDB could put out 200 watts for a range of between 50-60 nm. To help with the range, they could be N0NA1A, which uses less power but will require the BFO to be selected (see overleaf).

The approved ICAO frequency range for aeronautical NDBs is between **190-1750 KHz**, but that part of the radio spectrum also includes commercial radio stations, whose use in IFR work is not allowed because of the problems involved with quality control, and there are no guarantees of consistency of service. If there is no ID, but the system otherwise appears to behave normally, it is undergoing calibration or maintenance.

The minimum signal to noise ratio is 3:1. ICAO also requires ±7° accuracy for 95% of the time by day. Bearings in the published protection range should be accurate to within ±5° **by day**.

NDBs are dual systems, meaning that they have main and standby transmitters, plus two monitors to ensure continuous service. If the power falls by more than 50%, or a monitor or the ID fails, an automated telephone message creates an alarm. Standby transmitters have an E at the end of their identification so you know it is a standby. The ID is not transmitted when the system is being tested - instead you will hear T or TST (in Morse).

Errors

The most common error is failing to recognise *station passage* - if you are directly over the beacon, it will swing around all over the place and be confused with one of the above, or failure of the instrument, where the needle just rotates to the right. This is the same cone of confusion effect that VOR has (above).

Limitations*

Limitations of the system include:

- **static**, including local thunderstorm activity, which is likely to cause the greatest inaccuracy and make the needle point towards a storm.

- **night effect**, where the needle swings erratically, at its strongest just after sunset and before sunrise. The loop is designed to receive surface waves - any sky waves will be out of phase and distorted, because they energise the horizontal parts of the loop (waves change their polarisation when reflecting off the ionosphere). If the ionosphere is not parallel with the Earth's surface, they will also arrive from different directions. Low power beacons are virtually unaffected by this as they can only produce a ground wave. Check for an unsteady needle and a fading audio signal.

- **station overlap**, when NDBs have the same frequency. Because this is more pronounced at night, it can easily be confused with *night effect*, below (promulgated ranges are not valid at night for this reason). This will have the greatest effect on ADF accuracy, particularly at night.

- **mountain effect**, or variations caused by reflections from high ground, where two signals might be received at once from different paths.

- **quadrantal error**, or variations from the aircraft itself, in the same way as it might affect a compass. The signal is reradiated by the airframe and the receiver gets an additional (much weaker) signal to contend with. The greatest error lies at 45° to the fore and aft axis, hence the term *quadrantal*. Modern systems have corrector boxes for this.

- **coastal refraction**, from radio waves in transit from land to sea, because they travel slightly faster over water, which makes you aircraft appear closer to the shore. This effect is most noticeable at less than 30° to the coastline (i.e. an acute angle), and at lower frequencies, so expect errors if you are using an NDB inland directly in front of or behind you. With two NDBs, one 20 nm, and the other 50 nm inland from the coast, and if the coastal error is the same for both, the error seen by an aircraft will be greater from the beacon that is further away.

Picture: NDB Coastal Effect

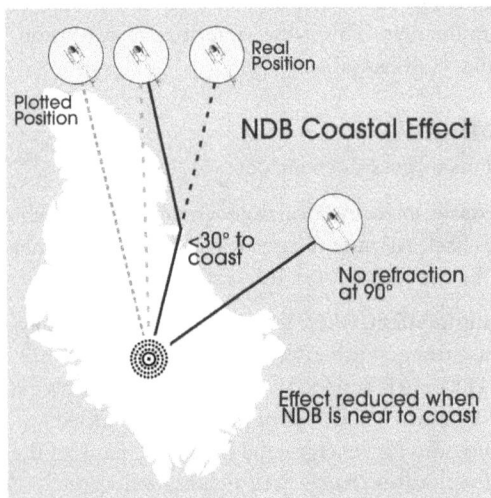

NDB Coastal Effect

- **Identification**. As there is no flag indication of failure, as there is with the VOR, you should continuously monitor the station ID when relying on the instrument. Aside from that, the only way of knowing about problems is seeing the needle rotate to the right if the signal is not received.

Use

The ADF is normally tuned with the function switch in the ANT position (it stands for *antenna*). This removes the needle from the loop (that is, receiving is done through the sense antenna) and saves wear and tear as it tries to point at every station you tune through - here, the sense antenna is used by itself to obtain the ID. Once there, return the switch to the ADF position.

As always, check - in this case, ensure that the needle points vaguely where you expect it to.

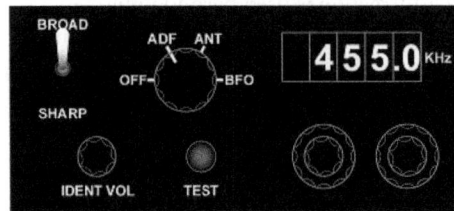

The TEST button spins the needle 90° from its tuned position, and back, to indicate a good signal. The BFO switch also uses the sense aerial by itself to detect the modulated Morse identifier.

While most NDBs use a modulated continuous wave, some use a plain carrier wave, which may be interrupted. The giveaway on a chart is an underlined frequency:

395

This requires the BFO (Beat Frequency Oscillator) to identify the station (it is used for A1A transmissions), but this is automatic on modern aircraft.

The fixed card display (*goniometer*) has a compass rose with 0° representing the nose of the aircraft at the top of the instrument, and a needle that points to where the signal is coming *from*, in this case a QDM of 165° (including thunderstorms if they are stronger than what you are tuned into).

Thus, if a station is ahead, the needle will point to 0°, or 180° if it is behind. However, if you made no allowance for wind, and just pointed the nose of the aircraft at the station (*homing*, as opposed to *tracking*), you would actually follow a curved path of pursuit towards it (also known as *bird-dogging*).

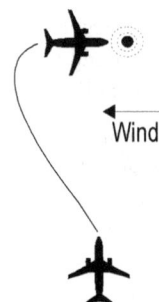

Wind

Allowing for drift lets you keep a straight track, which is needed for airways (see *Tracking*, overleaf). If you are heading to a beacon with a relative bearing of zero, and the magnetic heading decreases, you have some right drift, and *vice versa*. Unfortunately, working with fixed cards involves maths!

First of all, though, some definitions:

- **Magnetic Heading** - the angle between the aircraft's longitudinal axis and magnetic North

- **Relative Bearing** - the angle between the longitudinal axis and the NDB, which is what you read directly from a fixed card ADF

- **Magnetic Track** or **Bearing** - the angle between the aircraft position and the NDB, To or From

Take note of this formula (you will need it in the exam):

        MH + RB = BTS (MB)

The magnetic heading plus the relative bearing gives you the bearing to the station.

Taking the example below, the formula would read:

        324 + 46 = 010

MB = MH + RB

My **B**uddy
Must **H**ave
Red **B**lood

You can get the relative bearing like this:

        BTS - MH = RB

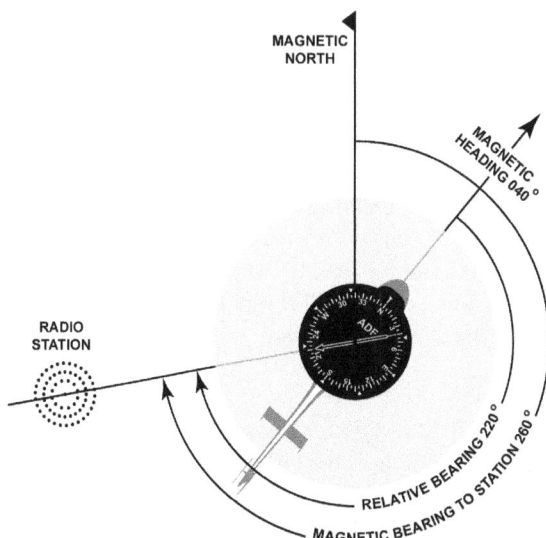

RMI

The *Radio Magnetic Indicator* is a combination of ADF indicator and slaved compass. The top of the instrument represents the aircraft's compass heading (which includes deviation) and the needle points to the QDM (or QDR, if you look at the other end), which saves you doing the calculations above in your head. In other words, it always displays the present heading and bearing, and does some of the work required by a fixed display. There may also be a repeater needle from the VORs giving you the same information relative to the stations they are tuned to.

In the picture, the heading is 139°, and the ADF QDM is 077°. The VOR needle is pointing to a QDM of 210°.

The RMI does not need a TO/FROM flag, as there is no 180-degree ambiguity. With the VOR, the tail of the needle on the RMI shows the radial. Change it to True by using the variation at the VOR.

As a point of interest, the VOR needle on an RMI will always read correctly if any deviation occurs, but headings and ADF readings will be in error by the deviation. This is because the ADF needle will naturally point towards the transmitting station, regardless of what the compass rose does. The VOR QDM, on the other hand, is created *within the instrument* by subtracting the aircraft heading from the QDM and applying the difference clockwise round the dial from the lubber line. Deviations are automatically applied because the number cruncher ensures that the VOR needle moves in the same direction for the same amount as the compass rose.

Put another way, the tail of the VOR needle always points to the radial even if the heading indication is wrong. The ADF needle always points to the station, so you will be on the wrong course if the Heading Indicator is not accurate, although you will always be able to find the station.

For either needle, however, if it is off to the left, you fly left, and *vice versa*.

Position Fix

For a fixed card ADF, find the relative bearing to each station and add them to your heading to get the tracks to the stations. Then find the reciprocals and plot them outwards (using variation at the aircraft). Along an airway, to find where you are in relation to an intersection, you will already know the bearing to station (BTS), because it will be on the map.

Time to Station

As with the VOR.

Tracking

When drifting, the needle will always point to the side of the aircraft the wind is coming from, so corrections should always be made that way, ensuring that the needle goes to the *other* side of the lubber line* once a corrected heading is established.

If needle moves right, aircraft is drifting left

Turn right to bring needle left of lubber line

*When tracking inbound.

For example, if the wind is coming from the left, you need the heading to be an equal amount of degrees the other side of the lubber line as the needle is, such as a heading of 350° (*minus 10 of the lubber line*), looking for a 010° relative bearing (*plus 10 of the lubber line*). If you just turned left enough to point the nose to the beacon, you would follow the curve of pursuit described above. Taking the needle across the lubber line means that you can make an attempt at regaining track as well. In other words, you are adding the drift to the track correction. If you were off track on the windward side, it may be possible to just turn to a heading that is equal to the track and let the wind do the work.

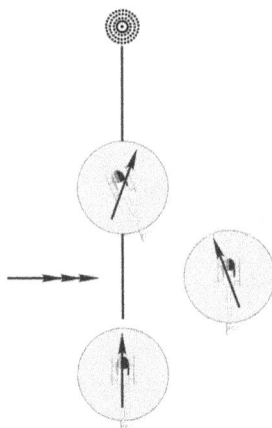

How far you are away from the beacon determines how large the intercept angle can be. It should be smaller as you get closer to the beacon. As you probably won't know how far away you are, the trick is to watch the speed of the needle as it moves - it rotates faster when you are close. In fact, it gets very sensitive in the overhead - you should not be correcting by more than 10° in that area, if any.

A good ploy is to allow the drift to happen until you get a positive reading, say 10° port, double it the other way (go 20° starboard), and when you are back on track, reduce it by half (10° in this case) to hold it. This is *bracketing*, and the process may have to be repeated several times in smaller amounts until you get it right. *Do not chase the needle* - hold it steady so you can see the effects of adjustments.

In fact, bracketing can be done simply with as few as two heading changes, and you should rarely need more than six. It is essentially a game between you and whatever needle you are using. Starting with your heading matching your track, at some point you will start to drift off if there is any wind at all. If you were heading 270°, your next heading could be 250° or 290°, according to the direction of the drift. Now you wait for the results, and your next heading change will be 10°. So, had we encountered left drift and turned onto 290°, if the needle moves to the right again, you would now select 300°, or if it moved left, you could select 280°. You should rarely need to go down to 5° changes.

Anticipation is the key! Do not wait until you have passed through your track until turning back on to it. Using 5° as a lead angle is good enough. The closer you are to the beacon the greater that angle will be.

When tracking *outbound*, you need the needle on the same side as the wind, so, although you are still looking for the plus 20, minus 20 equation, the needle would be pointing at 160° RB (when you make your initial turn, the needle looks like it's going the wrong way, but you get used to it).

If needle moves right, aircraft is drifting left

Turn right to bring tail further left of lubber line

In short, if the pointy end moves to the right of a line between 0° and 180°, fly right, as drift is to the left, and *vice versa*. This is true going to or from an NDB.

If you split the display into two halves, on a line between 0° and 180°, and call the right half plus, and the left minus (if going to a station), you can use the needle's position to find the track to a station. For example, if the needle is in the right half (the + segment), add the heading to the relative bearing to get the track. If it is in the left, take it away (work the needle back from zero). Whilst turning right, the aircraft heading will increase while the relative bearing decreases, and *vice versa*. If you remain on the same bearing, the heading change will always equal the change of ADF indication. When outbound, reverse the signs.

INTERCEPTION

To intercept a QDM or QDR, it's usual to use 90° inbound and 45° outbound, but 90° takes you no closer to the beacon, and involves large heading changes, and an angle that is too shallow takes you no closer to the track, so use what ATC and circumstances (or exam questions)

© Phil Croucher, 2015

If this page is a photocopy, it is not authorised!

CAPT

dictate. 30° is nice. In the picture below, to intercept the 090° QDM, you need to turn **the other way** (e.g. left), the same number of degrees the **other side** of the lubber line

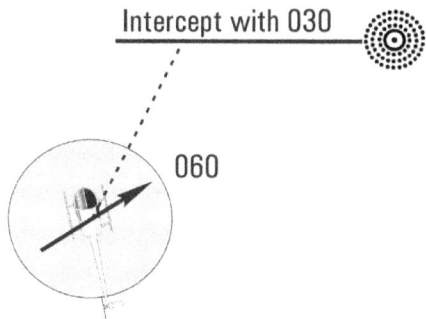

Intercept with 030

060

This is assuming zero wind conditions!

Remember: Going to a station, if the desired track is to the right of the QDM (in this case 090°), intercept to the left by the same difference in degrees, and vice versa.

Now the heading is 030°, and the ADF needle shows a relative bearing of 30°. The QDM is still 060°.

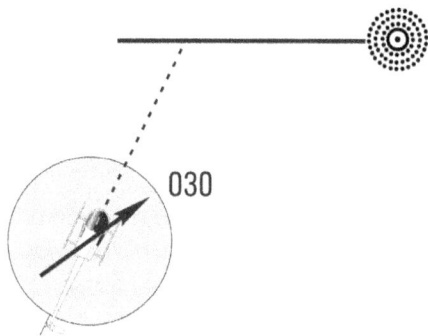

030

Now wait (on the same heading) until the needle moves a further 30°, which is double the original difference, or the sum of the angles either side of the lubber line.

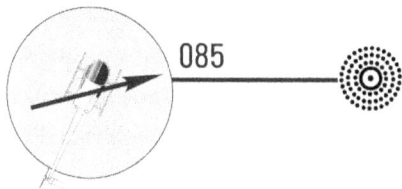

085

Start a rate one turn 5° before reaching the desired track, in this case at 085° Relative Bearing.

Going from a beacon, if the desired track is to the right, intercept to the right, and vice versa. In the picture below, the intercept heading is on the opposite side of the QDR to what the tail is showing, then turn the shortest way.

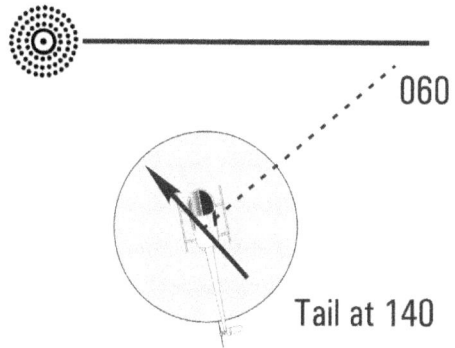

060

Tail at 140

EXAMPLES

1. An NDB bears 279° relative from an aircraft whose heading is 209°. If deviation is -7° and variation is 18°E, what is the bearing (M) of the aircraft from the NDB?

```
C = 209°C D = -7° M = 202°M
```

HDG(M) + RB = QDM:

```
202°M + 279° = 481° (-360°) = 121°M
```

QDR from NDB to aircraft = 121°M + 180° = 301°M. For a True Bearing:

```
C = 209°C
D = -7°
M = 202°M
V = 18°E
T = 220°T
```

HDG(T) + RB = QUJ

```
220°T + 279° = 499° (-360°) = 139°T
```

The QTE from NDB to aircraft = 139°T + 180° = 319°T

2. If the magnetic heading is 120°, and variation is 17°W, and there is an island 15° to the left, what is your True bearing from the island? The heading is:

```
120 - 17 = 103
```

And the relative bearing of the island is 345°:

```
103 + 345 = 448 - 360 = 008
008 + 180 = 188
```

AIRWAYS
•••

The information from navaids becomes less reliable the further away you get from them, so corridors are defined, within which the signals can be counted on.

For VORs, the corridor width starts 5 nm either side, diverging at 4° for 70 nm, until 20 nm wide. The width remains constant between 70-140 nm, where it diverges again at 4° until a width of 40 nm is reached at 280 nm out, at which point it remains constant.

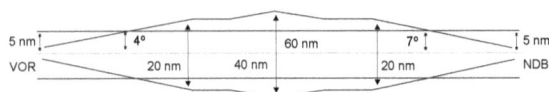

For NDBs, the corridor starts 5 nm either side, diverging at 7° until a width of 20 nm at 40 nm out, remaining constant between 40-80 nm out, thereafter diverging at 7° until 60 nm wide at 245 nm, then remaining constant.

TACAN
•••

This is a pulse-based military navigation system operating in the UHF band (*Tactical Air Navigation*), which can be used by the DME in your aircraft (*not* the VOR - military aircraft have a display which is not compatible). When a TACAN is co-located with a VOR, the VORTAC will show DME readouts automatically when you tune the VOR, as the frequencies are paired. Of course, a military machine can pick up the complete TACAN signal, which provides range, radial speed and bearing information.

The maximum distance between VOR and DME/TACAN ground installations if they share the same Morse ID is 600 metres.

RNAV   062 05
•••

Airways normally use ground-based navigation aids, but these days you don't necessarily need them to maintain an accurate track with aircraft-based equipment.

Area Navigation is a generic name for systems that allow navigation over wide areas - it was originally coined for a way of electronically moving navaids, VORs in particular, to other places enroute (they became *phantom waypoints*), which implies that you must be within the operating range of the navaids concerned. For example, you could tell the black box the distance and bearing of your house from the nearest VOR and it would present all the signals as if the aid was at your house. On a direct route with no specific navaids to aim for, you could shift all nearby ones to fit on your direct track for a series of phantom waypoints, typically displaying cross-track and along-track distance

with reference to the phantom, and not the navaid on which it might be based (1 dot represents 0.25 nm in approach mode on a 5-dot display).

The concept is illustrated in the picture below.

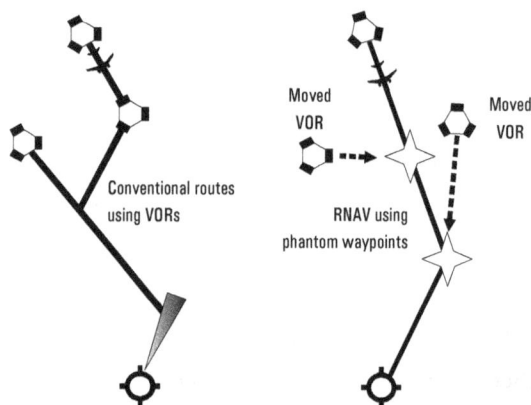

Thus, RNAV describes ways of flying directly across country without doglegging all over the place, or having to pass over radio fixes, which saves fuel and makes better use of airspace. You can also eliminate procedure turns because you don't care where the ground-based aids are (indeed, straight-in approaches can often be the norm, with arrival at the threshold in a specific time window). Lower minima and increased capacity are also available.

ICAO Annex 11 defines Area Navigation (RNAV) as "a method of navigation which permits aircraft operation on any desired flight path within the coverage of station-referenced navigation aids or within the limits of the capability of self-contained aids, or a combination." An RNAV waypoint could be a geographical position derived from a VOR radial and DME distance but, in the USA at least, RNAV is no longer VOR-based. Otherwise, RNAV can use VOR/DME, plus GPS and Inertial Reference Systems. It does not use ADF!

There are nearly as many RNAV standards as there are varieties of airspace. For example, B- and P-RNAV are used in Europe, MNPS over the North Atlantic and RNAV 1 and 2 in the USA (RNAV 1 = P-RNAV). *Performance Based Navigation* is an ICAO attempt to provide standardisation, where the emphasis is on specifications rather than equipment. You now just need the capability. When you meet the airspace requirements, you must include /R in Item 10 of the ICAO flight plan form. If you are not so equipped, ATC need to know, so in Box 18, insert STS/NONRNAV. Also mention it on your initial contact with them.

B-RNAV is the basic system, with an accuracy of ± 5 nm for at least 95% of the time, as for RNP5 (see below). B-RNAV is needed for flights in Europe above FL 95, using VOR/VOR or VOR/DME fixing. Precision Area Navigation (**P-RNAV**) has the same accuracy as RNP1, meaning ±1 nm on 95% of occasions, and will be controlled by the FMS (the FMC will automatically select and tune stations based on their relative accuracy). You need P-RNAV if you want to use DME/DME fixing, which gives you the best accuracy. P-RNAV requires a track-keeping accuracy of 0.5 nm standard deviation or better, referenced to WGS 84.

2D systems provide information in the horizontal plane only. 3D RNAV adds guidance in the vertical plane, and 4D has a timing function.

Lateral Navigation, and VNAV (*Vertical Navigation*) are used with custom routes stored in the navigation database. LNAV minima indicate a non-precision approach*, while LNAV/VNAV and LPV minima refer to APV approaches (RNAV approaches with vertical guidance).

*LNAV approaches use the usual minimum step-down altitude below which you may not descend. That is, without vertical guidance, you must remain at or above the MDA unless the required visual reference has been obtained, or you need to conduct a missed approach at the missed approach waypoint (MAWP).

RNAV equipment should at least be able to:

- Display the present position as latitude/longitude or a distance and bearing to a selected waypoint

- Allow you to select or enter the required flight plan through the CDU

- Allow review and modification of navigation data for any part of a flight plan at any stage of a flight and store enough to carry out the active flight plan

- Review, assemble, modify or verify a flight plan in flight, without affecting the guidance output

- Execute a modified flight plan only after positive action by the flight crew

- Where provided, assemble and verify an alternative flight plan without affecting the active one

- Assemble a flight plan, either by identifier or selection/creation of individual waypoints from the database, or defined by latitude/longitude, bearing/distance parameters or other parameters

- Assemble flight plans by joining routes or route segments

- Allow verification or adjustment of the displayed position

- Provide automatic sequencing through waypoints with turn anticipation. Manual sequencing should also allow flight over, and return to, waypoints

- Display cross-track error on the CDU

- Provide time to waypoints on the CDU

- Execute a direct clearance to any waypoint

- Fly parallel tracks at a selected offset distance (offset mode should be clearly indicated)

- Purge previous radio updates

- Carry out RNAV holding procedures

- Make available estimates of positional uncertainty, either as a quality factor or by reference to sensor differences from the computed position

- Conform to WGS-84

- Indicate navigation equipment failure

RNP

Certain standards must be met before a system can be a sole means navigation system for IFR purposes:

- **Accuracy** in terms of *position error*, or the difference between estimated and actual positions.

- **Integrity** - the measure of trust that can be placed in the information supplied by the system.

- **Continuity** (Reliability) - the system's ability (as a probability) to perform with a high probability that it will be available over a full approach procedure.

- **Availability** - the time during which the system can deliver for a specific phase of flight. Sole means navigation systems require 99% availability.

- **Coverage**.

Reduced Navigation Performance is a measure of the standards needed to operate within certain airspace. In common usage, this means the lateral accuracy in nautical miles that an aircraft is expected to maintain for 95% of the time, relative to a desired flight path (technically, a Total System Error* of X nm or less for over 95% of total flight time).

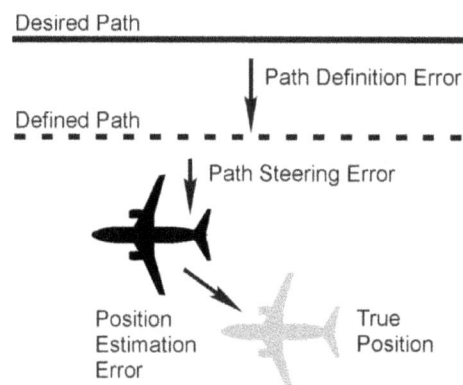

The system accuracy takes after the specification - for example, RNP4 means within 4 nm along or across track. This would typically be used en route, whereas you would need RNP 1 or 2 around terminals, which are busy. RNP is self-monitoring and can warn you if you are likely to stray outside airspace boundaries, which are equal to twice the RNP value - RNP4 means an 8 nm wide corridor.

*TSE is the vector sum of:

- **Path Definition Error**, or the difference between the intended path and the actual path

- **Path Steering Error**, from steering the course, either manually or by autopilot, not including human error (this is the biggest factor)

- **Position Estimation Error**, the combination of system or sensor errors and computation error

Short Range Systems (2D RNAV)

Traditional instruments display only one position line, such as an arc from the DME, or bearing from a VOR, and you have to combine several to get any meaningful information. They can now be combined on one instrument for ease of interpretation, and interfaced with other equipment. Short range systems are typically based on line-of-sight navigation aids, such as VOR or DME. For best results, the area you fly over must necessarily have a reasonable density of them (the FMC will have a database, including their frequencies, and it will tune those required for you). In normal NAV mode, with at least four stations (and position lines), the accuracy will typically be around 2 nm.

VOR/DME (RHO-THETA)

Here, you can get a fix from only one position line, so with the proper computer (such as the original KNS-80), this is the simplest form of RNAV. One of the functions of the Course-Line Computer is to transfer the information from a VOR/DME station into track and distance indications to any chosen phantom waypoint.

As mentioned above, the VOR/DME station can be offset electronically to any desired position within its range of promulgation. A VOR does not have to be in range when its details are entered into the system, but must be when used, otherwise erratic indications may be experienced when flying towards a Phantom Station at low altitudes close to the limits of reception. In fact, the system will go into DR (*Dead Reckoning*) mode when receiving only one VOR, or if there is no bearing and distance information, using whatever TAS is coming from the ADC, the heading from the compass and the last computed wind velocity (to calculate the wind, the system needs radials and distances from various VOR/DMEs, heading and TAS).

Filters limit the rate of change of VOR bearings, where they arise from multi-path reflections (site error). Close to the beacon, DME range sets the maximum rate, as the bearings change fast anyway, and errors might occur. On approach, 1 dot's deviation is equal to ¼ nm, and 1 nm en route, where 5 dots span half the airway.

Trivia: The Greek letter R (*Rho*) stands for range, and *Theta* is an angle, so a Rho-Theta fix involves a range and an angle, as you would get from VOR/DME.

DME/DME (RHO-RHO)

Also called *direct ranging*, DME receivers are used with a microprocessor to measure the distance from two DME receivers for a position fix. Some systems have their own tuners and can automatically set up DMEs, etc. according to signal strength for best position lines (the most accurate RNAV fixes come from DME/DME).

Long Range Systems

Long range systems do not rely on short-range navigation aids, such as INS/IRS, GPS, Loran, Omega, Decca, etc.

Inertial Navigation

Inertial systems can provide continuous information on your position, true track, heading, groundspeed and height without any outside help, allegedly first designed for the V2 rocket, but also extremely useful for submarines. With TAS information from the ADC, they can calculate wind velocity - being self-contained, they can work anywhere and, as a bonus for the military, are undetectable.

Although they can operate in True at any latitude, inertial systems can apply local variation (between 73°N - 60°S*) from a lookup table in a database, so a flux detector is not required, although there is an area between 90°W to 120°W and 70°N to 72°N (in Canada) where the variation table cannot update the output from true to magnetic. Some sets show HDG FAIL in that case and need manual switching to TRUE, which others can do automatically.

*At higher latitudes the variation is either unusable, unreliable, or has too high an annual rate of change.

Tip: INS/IRS navigation uses great circle tracks (i.e. the shortest - see *Navigation*), because they orient themselves in space (against the stars) and their data is converted into latitude & longitude through a mathematical model, typically WGS 84. When you see IRS/INS in a question, you know it involves a Great Circle. The differences between WGS 84 and the proper shape of the Earth are why Schuler tuning is needed, discussed later.

The data provided and the equipment used can be made available for other systems - the high quality gyros will typically drive the artificial horizons and allow for accurate heading maintenance, which is the real trick - once the initial heading is calculated from the Earth's spin rate, no corrections should be required.

The principles are simple enough. Starting from a known (usually precisely surveyed) point, your present position is calculated from the directions and speeds you have used since then, so you have a continuously running **dead reckoning** position that will drift over time. The drift should be around 1 nm per hour for a strapdown system, but it could be 3 nm for the older stable platform.

All this sounds wonderful, but as the accuracy degrades over time, you must supplement it with navaids or GPS, where it becomes subject to *bounded* errors based on the other system. Otherwise, in the dynamic situation (exam speak for *in flight*) the error normally continues to build, at differing rates as the velocity error varies, but it will never cancel itself. As the system error keeps growing, it is *unbounded*, and readings will therefore be inaccurate to some extent, especially at the top of the descent, because it has had the whole flight to drift off. It will also be inaccurate just after takeoff, because no updating takes place while you taxi (although the FMC position can often be updated on takeoff with the TO/GA button).

As a fix is obtained (say by being overhead a navaid), you can place the system on hold and tell it where it really is, or at least reset the drift to zero (*Map shift* occurs when the moving map changes position to show the updates).

However, manual updating is only allowed within 25 nm of a co-located VOR/DME, or above a visual fix below 5000 feet. Auto updating can take place within 200 nm of a DME when passing within 140 nm, or just within 200 nm of 2 DMEs (within 25 nm if receding). GPS, described elsewhere, is a lot more accurate, although it is actually a low bandwidth system, meaning that its update rate is very slow and will resemble a straight line between the start and end points of a journey. IRS and INS are high bandwidth systems that update a lot more often and will show a truer picture. Combining INS/IRS with GPS can therefore provide an accurate, drift-free system. The two can also provide redundancy, as INS can keep things going if GPS conditions are not ideal, say when less than 4 satellites are in view, or those that are have bad positioning (if GPS data is less than optimal, its signals are verified for accuracy before being incorporated into the system, which is why there are two receivers, but this is only possible with a strapdown system). The GPS can be used for alignment (takes 10 minutes) or navigation. The two systems can be *uncoupled, loosely* or *tightly coupled*.

There will normally be at least three INS/IRS systems on most modern aircraft to guard against error, working through the FMS. In the early days, they were standalone, so the only way to check for errors was to inspect each one against a position fix or your DR position (or readings from another aircraft), if you didn't have GPS. Errors would not necessarily be seen until the system concerned pumped out the codes, from which you could tell which one it was. Now, each one's output is compared in a voting system, from which inaccuracies are quickly detected.

Inertial systems have their own (28v DC) batteries which will run for 20-30 minutes, or they may switch into the hot bus. *If power is lost, you cannot realign for the rest of the flight.*

Older systems were called Inertial *Navigation* Systems because that was their main function, but more modern versions are fully integrated with other parts of the aircraft, hence the name Inertial *Reference* Systems.

Note: All INS/IRS systems depend on the right information being inserted in the first place, which is why it is so important in the checklist. *Both* pilots must check the entries (see *Flight Management Systems*).

ACCELERATION

Newton's first law of motion is the basis behind inertial navigation. Very loosely, it states that bodies at rest or in motion tend to retain their current state unless acted upon by an external force. Put another way, if you want to change the inertial state of a body, you must use a force. All that is obvious to us, probably, but apparently not so to Aristotle and other great thinkers before Newton. After Newton, however, Mr Einstein added his own views in his Special Theory of Relativity, which are relevant here.

In the wider scheme of things, it would appear that nothing is at rest! At least, a book on a table is "at rest" with regard to the table, but the book, table and the observer are actually sharing (curved) velocities in space, which brings us to Newton's second law which, in brief, states that the rate of change of velocity (acceleration) is directly proportional to the force making the body accelerate, and inversely proportional to the body's mass.

Acceleration is therefore a measure of how fast the speed of something is changing. More technically, it is the time rate of change of velocity, or the time rate of change of the time rate of distance. That is, it is measured in feet (or metres) per second, per second.

We know that velocity involves changes of distance over time, and acceleration involves changes of velocity over time. If you have a record of its history, an aircraft's accelerations in the vertical, horizontal and lateral planes in space can be integrated* over time to obtain the changes in its velocity, then again to determine how long it has been travelling at that velocity to find the distance travelled up, down or sideways.

*If you know how fast something is changing, you can find out by how much it has changed, in the same way that a fuel flow meter can work out how much has been used from the rate of flow, based on the measurement of infinitely small components. Thus, if you know by how much your speed has changed, you can find out what your speed is now, and from that deduce the distance travelled.

The data from the various integrations is used to calculate track and groundspeed and resolve distances into changes of latitude and longitude.

Starting with speed, which is the rate of change of distance with time:

$$S = \frac{D}{T}$$

It is also called the *differentiation* of distance over time. Acceleration is the differentiation of speed with time:

$$A = \frac{S}{T}$$

Since we know that S = D over T (see first formula), the above can be written as:

$$A = \frac{D}{\frac{T}{T}} \text{ or } A = \frac{D}{T^2}$$

Working backwards, you integrate acceleration once for your initial speed, then integrate speed for distance.

SYSTEM CONTENTS

A typical (early) system consists of:

- *Inertial Navigation Unit* (INU)

- *Mode Selector Unit* (MSU)

- *Control Display Unit* (CDU, or *Inertial System Display Unit*, ISDU, below) with a multi-line keypad. It is used for inputting information, such as your starting position and waypoints, as lat & long.

- *Battery Unit* (BU) as a backup

The MSU and CDU are on the flight deck, and the INU and BU in the depths of the aircraft, where only engineers touch them. The MSU (shown below) is used to switch the thing on in the first place, and select the mode of operation, such as STBY, ALIGN, NAV, ATT, etc.

Picture: INS CDU & MSU for a twin system

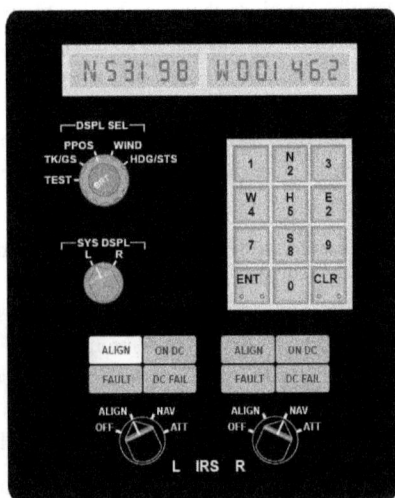

There are also a couple of warning lights. You get a red one when the battery is flat. An ALERT light may come on 2 minutes before a turn. The HOLD button, if you have one, freezes the display.

You turn the system on by moving the switch to SBY (if present), so the oil in the gyros can warm up to a specific viscosity, then ALIGN after you have entered your present position, time and date.

Note: The aircraft must remain stationary!

During alignment, the direction of North can be detected from which way the Earth is moving, and the rate of movement is used to provide the latitude. This process takes at least 2.5 minutes at the Equator and up to 10 minutes at 70° N or S.

Once everything is aligned, and before moving off, you must switch to NAV, which is the normal flight mode. The last point you can select NAV is just after pushback.

ATT mode is a backup which retains just attitude and heading information while realignment takes place, so if the navigation computer fails, you can still use the artificial horizon, etc. Once a stable platform INS loses power in flight, it loses its level and alignment references and cannot be re-aligned, because it cannot discriminate between motion of the aircraft and rotation of the Earth, although a strapdown IRS (below) might be able to provide attitude and heading information - the procedure then is to switch to ALIGN and fly straight and level for a minute or two. If the FAIL flags disappear the system may be used for attitude information. If you then input the aircraft heading it may be used as a heading reference.

STABLE PLATFORM

The *platform* (or *stable element*) is a gyro-stabilised cluster of linear accelerometers, in three circular gimbals (for the x, y and z axes), to keep them in the right position.

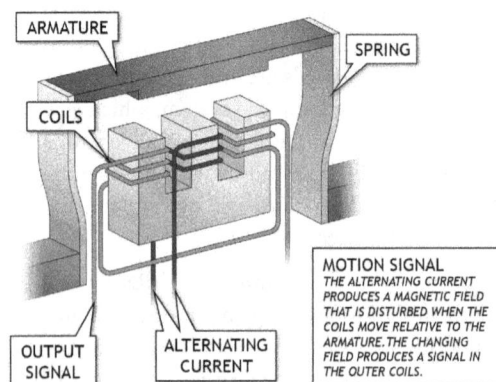

The basic system contains:

- **2 linear accelerometers** in the x and y axes (for LNAV sensing), with possibly another for the z axis. E & I bars may be used because they have minimal friction, otherwise some systems use pendulums. As with the arms on the flux detector, the bars are highly permeable, so a high flux density in proportion to the inducing field can be provided, with a rapid response to changes. The central arm is fed with 400 Hz AC, so the outer legs pick up a secondary induced AC voltage, which is affected by the gap between the bars. If there is no acceleration, the legs have the same voltage, but with opposite polarity. However, as the I bar moves away from the vertical (in the opposite direction to the acceleration), the secondary induced voltage is amplified, phase detected and rectified (to DC) so that a torque motor can try to restore the accelerometer to the null position - the amount of current involved is proportional to the acceleration experienced. The same signal also goes to the integrators.

Phase detection ensures that the DC is of the right polarity so the I bar can be moved the right way.

- A **stable platform** that keeps the x and y axes oriented N-S and E-W and the z axis aligned with local gravity, so that the x and y accelerometers do not mistake gravity for acceleration. This isolates the aircraft's movements from the Earth's.

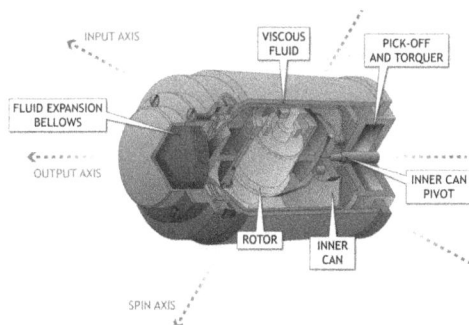

- **3 Rate Integrating Gyros** (for VNAV sensing) that measure and use changes in aircraft vectors to orient the stable platform (these have nothing to do with navigation - they are just there to keep the platform level). Rate integrating gyros provide a much higher response for a given movement than displacement gyros do. Their output also increases as a function of their rate of displacement, but they only act about a single axis, so three 3 are needed to cover all bases. They are surrounded with warm oil to eliminate friction and reduce bearing torques, and to stop the gyros precessing or toppling, as opposed to using a spring. They are mounted inside two cans, one inside the other. The outer one is fixed to the INS platform and the inner one is free to rotate within it, behaving like a gimbal.

When a tilt from the level position occurs, the spin axes of the gyros remain fixed in space, but their cases move, and an error signal is measured to determine the rate of this movement. Corrections are so quick that the platform does not rotate for more than 10 arcseconds before it is moved back to its original reference position. This also compensates for the local gravity vector being mistaken for an acceleration, which is what Schuler tuning is for (below). The RIG that senses the N/S axis is the *North Gyro*, the one for E/W is the *East Gyro*, and the vertical axis gyro (if there is one) is the *Azimuth Gyro*. Gyros are named for the sensitive axis.

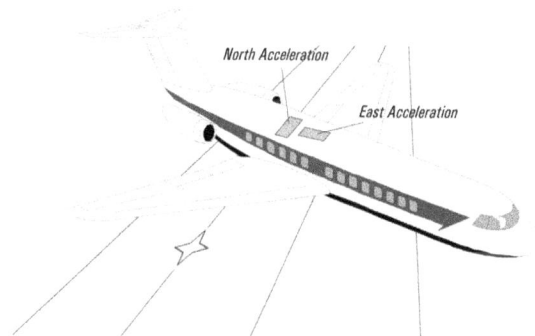

The platform is also forced to tilt (by torquing the gyros) in proportion to the Earth's rate of turn, based on the latitude. Transport wander is dealt with in the same way, and Coriolis and centrifugal force are also compensated for.

- **Integrators** to convert the acceleration data into velocity and distance information. The signals

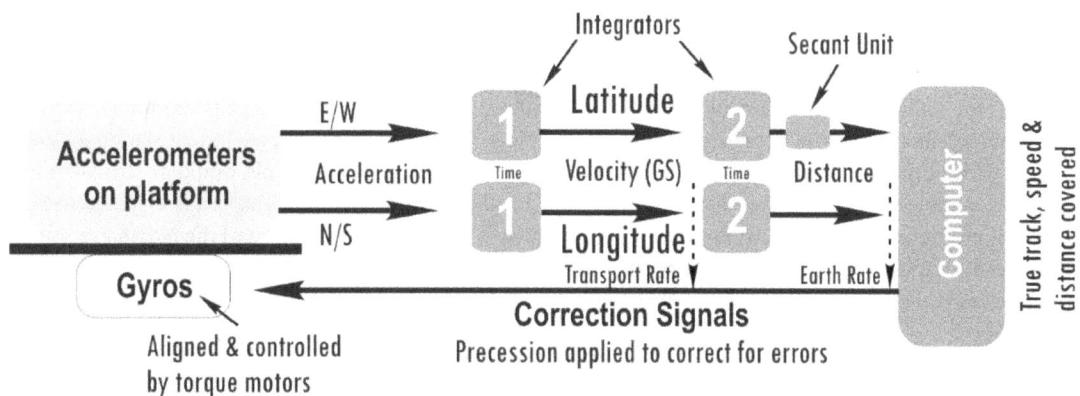

from the accelerometers go to the *1st stage integrators* which produce velocity information by multiplying the acceleration against time. The *2nd stage integrator*s multiply the resulting velocity against time to work out a distance. For N/S, as each minute is 1 nm, this is easily converted into change of latitude which can be added to the start point to find the present latitude. The E/W distance, where a nautical mile is not always a minute of longitude, has to be calculated with the aid of a secant unit.

- A **computer** to sort it all out and provide position information. Accelerometer signals are analogue, so there must also be an analogue-digital converter for the computer and displays.

SCHULER TUNING
If an INS is not moving, it assumes it is falling towards the centre of the Earth. If it isn't actually doing that, to register a zero change in position, gravity must removed from its calculations (you need it to measure acceleration).

However, the value of gravity changes with your position and height, what you are flying over, and even the weather. Only the latest systems can use a geometrically correct model of the Earth and its gravitational fields, so the INS must distinguish between the proper shape of the Earth and the mathematical one in its memory (WGS 84).

If the platform is only slightly away from the horizontal, there could be major errors in distance figures as gravity is mistaken for acceleration. If an accelerometer is out by just 1/100th of G, the error on a 1-hour flight would be 208,000 feet, or over 34 nm. Even when you are not moving, misalignment can produce similar effects, but as the velocity is in the system, the platform overcorrects, tilts in the opposite direction and senses a real acceleration to reduce the velocity back to zero. As the platform continues to apply the deceleration, the velocity increases in the opposite direction to produce correcting signals to stop the deceleration, and the increase in velocity. The process starts again because the system is now in full swing back to where it started.

The time taken for the disturbance to go from one extreme to the other (a pendulum effect) is the *Schuler period* of 84.4 minutes, named after Dr. Maximilian Schuler, who showed in 1923 that a pendulum whose length is the same as the radius of the Earth could help eliminate inadvertent acceleration errors because it will always point to the vertical (he was trying to figure out a way of stabilising sea compasses). Put another way, if you could build a pendulum the length of the Earth's radius, with its bob at the centre of the Earth, it would still point to the vertical wherever you moved the point of support (in our case, an aircraft).

If the aircraft accelerates, the bob should stay where it is and the pendulum "cord" should stay vertical for all motions of the pivot point (the aircraft). Schuler determined that, if the bob were disturbed, the pendulum would oscillate over 84.4 minutes, so if a system is built with an identical period, it would indicate the local vertical regardless of any acceleration of a vehicle carrying it. It is ironic that he thought it was impossible to build an INS!

An INS platform behaves just like an Earth pendulum in that, when it is disturbed, it takes 84.4 minutes to settle down again, during which time you may be a bit off course. The Earth wobbles, not the INS, but it appears to, relative to the Earth. In other words, it wanders, as can be seen in crosstrack readouts which may increase, then return, in a certain period. The wobble is the Schuler cycle.

The relationship between a circle's angle in radians and its circumference is $^1/_R$ (based on 2π divided by $2\pi R$)*. Multiplying this by V (from the first stage integration) gives you an angular velocity over a surface distance, or the transport rate, which is used to torque the gyro and make the platform precess at the same rate that is being moved over the Earth's surface. *Schuler tuning provides an undamped closed-loop corrective action to stop tilt errors, oscillating around a zero value over 84.4 minutes.*

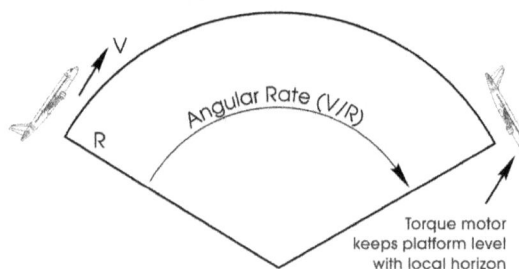

*To make allowances for altitude, $^1/_{R+H}$ is used.

Note: Although Schuler tuning prevents the accumulation of errors which would be caused by platform tilt and treating gravity as an acceleration, it will not compensate for errors from the precession of the steering gyro.

ALIGNMENT
You cannot use the system until two tasks are accomplished. The platform (or rather the accelerometers) must be levelled*, then lined up with True North, also known as *gyrocompassing*. This is done over about eleven minutes by motoring the (level) platform until there is no topple output from the East gyro (when stationary on the ground, the only cause of topple would be the rotation of the Earth, so if there is none, the axis is assumed to be aligned N/S). The topple output of the North gyro should now equal the Earth rate, which is 15° x cos latitude, so this is impossible at high latitudes because of the torquing rates. Also the cosine value would be near zero. However, the INS cannot do this unless it has a latitude input.

*Coarse levelling is followed by fine levelling, which is done by motoring the platform until no acceleration from gravity is sensed by the x and y accelerometers - this does not require lat & long input. This to take about 6 minutes.

Alignment is only done once, before the flight, because the outputs from the accelerometers and gyros are used differently, hence the separate ALIGN mode on the MSU. It takes about 17 minutes overall for a stable platform.

However, with such a North pointing system, things get interesting when you go over a Pole, because the platform would have to turn through 180° almost instantly (in fact, the problems start several hundred miles away). A workaround is to keep the platform level, but not worry about aligning it to North necessarily - just detect how far out of alignment it is, and include it in future calculations. In this case, the accelerometers would be offset by the *wander angle*. Yet another is not to bother even levelling (or aligning), but figure out how far out the accelerometers are at initialisation and monitor any changes.

During alignment the aircraft must remain stationary. If there is excessive movement, the ALIGN annunciator will flash and the fault indicator will come on. Switch the Mode Select switch off for at least 3 seconds then put it back to ALIGN. The ALIGN light will also flash if you do not enter the present position within the normal alignment time. Once aligned, the platform will be level, pointing along True North, and you can switch to NAV mode. If it is level, and the aircraft is not, the difference is measured and displayed as Pitch and Roll. The yaw difference between the longitudinal axis and the platform (North) is *Heading*. During alignment, most systems start passing attitude information to the FMS before being fully set up.

ERRORS
Bounded errors are constant over time, such as track or groundspeed errors that start off at a fixed rate, but these can lead to unbounded errors that get larger with time. Otherwise, accelerometers cannot tell the difference between gravity and acceleration, so you can get levelling errors. The estimated local gravity (from a database) can be subtracted from vertical accelerations to compensate. The usual stuff also applies, like Earth rate and transport wander, which are predictable, because the computer knows your position. Thus, Coriolis effect and centripetal acceleration can also be calculated, and Schuler corrections applied to compensate for Transport rate (using the velocity signal from the first integration).

Real wander is compensated for on the ground, but can occur in turbulence, etc.

STRAPDOWN
The *strapdown system* is strapped directly to the aircraft structure. It has no gimbals, because it uses ring laser gyros, so the outputs are *rate* sensitive, as opposed to being *displacement* sensitive. The "spinning mass" therefore follows the airframe and its alignment to true North is *calculated*. As there are no moving parts, the "stable platform" is maintained mathematically*, rather than mechanically. This provides more accuracy and reliability.

*The strapdown has a bias signal to compensate for Schuler drift applied to the readouts. You may notice position variations of about 1 nm between systems when they are not on the same points of the Schuler cycle. Other potential errors, such as Coriolis, are allowed for, but not mentioned here.

The IRS contains:

- two **Air Data Inertial Reference Units**, with:

  - a **power supply**

  - an **Inertial Reference** (IR). This senses and computes linear accelerations and turning rates around each axis, to feed pitch and roll displays and navigation calculations. The only other information needed is your start position, barometric altitude and TAS, which is obtained from the ADR, together with other useful information. Barometric altitude provides a reference for vertical navigation, and stabilises the vertical velocity and inertial altitude outputs. As an IRS doesn't need a platform, it needs three "accelerometers".

  - an **Air Data Reference** (ADR), which is separate on some aircraft.

- a **display unit**

- a **mode select unit**

Rotation about an axis can be sensed with fibreoptic or ring laser gyros, as described earlier.

ALIGNMENT
This is a much faster process than with the stable platform, because the system moves with the Earth, although levelling and alignment are still done while stationary, because the only acceleration is from gravity and the only angular movement from the Earth's rotation. From its direction and magnitude, the position of True North can be sensed and the latitude can be estimated.

However, you have to enter your whole position because present longitude cannot be worked out (the latitude input is used as a crosscheck for the calculated figure. Your longitude input is compared to the last stored one). Put more in exam speak, *you need to position the computing trihedron with reference to the Earth*. Well, of course you do.

CAPT

Without Earth rate compensation, the system would also think it is upside down after 12 hours at the Equator. Elsewhere, there would be pitch, roll and heading errors. If you put in the wrong latitude, the Earth rate calculations will be wrong and you won't be able to align to True North properly (if the ALIGN lights are flashing this is what has happened).

As with other systems, you must switch to ALIGN to set things up, although Boeing recommend selecting NAV directly if you're between the 70°S and 70°N latitudes (there is no STANDBY setting as there are no gyros to warm up). Alignment varies with latitude - 5 minutes at the Equator, 10 minutes at 70°N and 17 minutes between 70- 78°. Although, during turnarounds, it is best to turn the system off and allow it to realign completely, if time is tight (it usually is), a fast re-alignment can be done. Just switch to ALIGN and enter a new gate position. Reselect NAV once the ALIGN lights go out.

In NAV mode, the gyros measure the Earth's movement with respect to space, and your movement with respect to the Earth, in the form of Transport rate, because any movement over a sphere involves some sort of rotation.

Automatic Calibration

- **Auto cal** maintains the calibration of the gyros and the longitudinal and lateral accelerometers to improve performance and reliability.

- **Gyro autocal** measures the position error after the flight and estimates the gyro errors that would have caused it.

- **Accelerometer autocal** picks up lateral bias errors found during taxi, because movement is generally forward.

Errors

A strapdown system suffers from lock-in errors caused by imperfect mirrors, which are reduced by wobbling, or vibrating with the *dither motor* and *spring*.

Otherwise errors include:

- **Schuler Tuning**. Platform oscillations cause errors to be propagated over a 84.4 minute cycle.

- **Levelling & Azimuth Gyro Drift**. Real Wander possibly 0.01°/hour - the largest errors in the system, distance error unbounded.

- **Initial Levelling** (Tilt). The accelerometers sense gravity - velocity and distance errors unbounded.

- **Initial Alignment**. Accelerometers misaligned N/S & E/W - velocity error bounded, distance error unbounded.

- **Accelerometer Errors**. Small random errors throughout the system.

- **Earth Shape**. The computer's spherical trigonometry is in error.

- **Altitude**. Earth rate/transport wander gyro corrections are calculated for ground level, giving small unbounded errors on long flights.

- **Coriolis** (Accelerometer). Earth rotation and transport wander cause a curved track in space - very small random errors.

- **Centripetal Acceleration** (Accelerometer). A constant altitude creates a curved track in space and acceleration towards the centre of the Earth.

As the readings from the INS/IRS drift over time, you need to check that the system is working within certain limits. For this reason, after the flight, you check your real position with where the system thinks it is. The idea is to check the *radial error rate*. For this you divide the distance off by the time the system has been in navigational mode.

The error rate history can be checked on the *IRS Monitor* page of the Flight Management System. A probable error of 1 nm/hour is the maximum that is commonly accepted (0.3 nm/hr is considered normal), in addition to initial input errors, although you will usually see a spread of up to ½ nm. Vertical position is potentially not so accurate as horizontal position. If the end position is put in, some units can use it to self-correct for future flights (limits are 10° for base latitude and 30° base longitude).

```
Dist out (nm)
Time (hours)
```

The departure formula (see *Navigation*) can be used to find your distance E-W. Combine that with your N-S distance in a normal Pythagoras calculation to find the distance you are out, which is the hypotenuse:

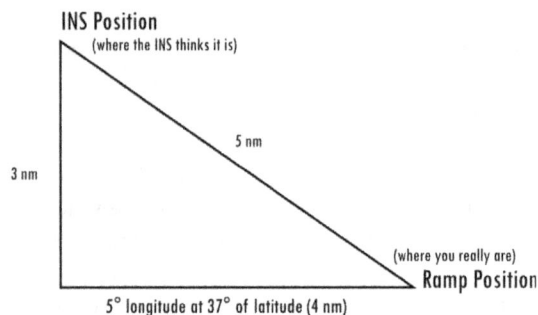

In the picture, the INS thinks you are 5 nm away from your real position, having flown for 2 hours.

Your radial error rate is 2.5 nm per hour (the cosine of 37° is 0.8).

EXAMPLE

With an azimuth gyro drift of 0.03° per hour, what will be the lateral position error after 5 hours at 500 knots?

© *Phil Croucher, 2015*

CAPT

After 5 hours, the error is 0.65° (0.13/2) for a 2.7 nm error, using the 1 in 60 rule.

AHRS

An AHRS (*Attitude and Heading Reference System*) replaces traditional gyros* and their problems, such as topple, drift or gimbal lock in aircraft that don't have a full IRS. It is a combination of inertial sensors in one package that can output attitude, heading and flight dynamics information to flight deck displays and other systems. A flux valve and Air Data Computer will be involved, and 3D orientation is obtained by integrating the gyroscopes with accelerometers and magnetometers (for the magnetic field vector). An AHRS also converts the raw data into standard units like feet or metres, etc., although it will not necessarily provide a True heading output, as this is associated with commercial and military inertial reference and flight management systems. Thus, an AHRS requires less power, less wiring, weighs less and has a smaller footprint, but it will probably cost a lot more.

*While fibreoptic or laser gyros provide very stable angular rate measurements, MEMS gyroscopes have the advantage of low power requirements and costs by using Coriolis Effect to measure an angular rate. MEMS stands for *Micro Electro-Mechanical System*. Most use a tuning fork configuration, where two masses oscillate and move constantly in opposite directions.

During linear acceleration, the two masses move in the same direction, so no change in capacitance will be detected. However, when angular velocity is applied, the Coriolis force on each mass produces a change in capacitance that is proportional to the angular velocity, which is then converted into output voltage for analog gyroscopes or LSBs for digital gyroscopes.

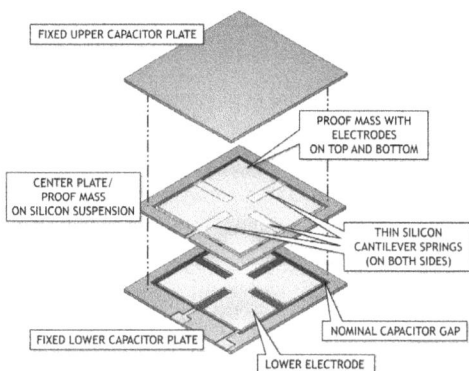

The magnetometer will usually be mounted remotely from the AHRS, where magnetic disturbances are minimal.

Global Navigation Satellite System

The original satellite systems were based partly on hyperbolic navigation aids such as Decca Navigator or LORAN, and Doppler. By measuring the distortions from Sputnik in 1957, it was realised that a satellite's position could be established with some accuracy. It wasn't too hard to reverse the situation.

There are two systems currently available, with another one coming. The USA one is **NAVSTAR/GPS**, and the Russian system is **GLONASS**, which is only just operational, so it is not approved even for B-RNAV, although smartphones can use it. Each can produce extreme accuracy at a much reduced cost compared to, say, Inertial Navigation, with better approach paths, etc.

These days, satellite signals are not only used for navigation, but also for specialised clock systems in various earthbound systems, such as cell phone networks and TV stations, since the satellites all have atomic clocks on board. ATC use it for this purpose as well (GPS is a legal source of accurate time).

A satellite system can calculate distance, track and speed from your changing position. It can also give your altitude, but such 3D readouts require 4 satellites. In any case, the datum for altitude information when under IFR or conducting approaches is **barometric altitude**, because the Earth is not a true sphere and there may be wide differences between its actual shape and the WGS 84 model inside the GPS receiver.

GPS reliability approaches 100%, within 100 m of the true horizontal position for 95% of the time and 300 m for 99%. However, it can be affected by atmospheric interference, satellite positioning and tuning inaccuracies.

GALILEO

Although the American GPS system is still usable, it is old technology and originally designed for military use so, for modern purposes, continual workarounds have to be employed, which often turn out to be more expensive than starting from scratch. *Galileo* is a European system whose first satellite was launched on the 28th December 2005. It will start with five types of signal - one being available to everyone, like the GPS C/A code, a more precise commercial signal, a *safety of life* service for critical applications, a *public regulated service* (PRS) for government use, and one combined with a distress signal, for rescues.

Galileo should use 30 satellites, with 9 plus a spare in each of 3 planes in a near circular orbit at 23 222 km inclined at 56° to the Equator. Each orbit will take 14 hours. The signals will be transmitted on two bands, 1164-1215 MHz and 1559-1591 MHz. The overlap with GPS will use *spread spectrum technology* to unscramble the mess.

062 06

NAVSTAR/GPS

The Global Positioning System was originally set up by the US military in 1977 to help submarines get lost more accurately, based on Doppler Shift, as one of six satellites passed overhead, although how they received the signals beats me. Now the system is managed by an executive board that ensures that all users' needs, including civilians, are considered. This was after flight KAL 007 hit a Russian missile that was on a peaceful mission.

GPS is supposed to use 24 (21 + 3) satellites, in 6 groups of 4 (60° apart), with at least 21 operational at any time, although there are now over 31 on line, to allow for orbital manoeuvres and maintenance. The idea is that the transmissions from as many satellites as possible, but at least 4 for best results, are received by a device that is permanently tuned to 1575.42 MHz, although there is another frequency used by the military for precision positioning. Satellite transmissions include atomic time in their signals so the receiver can calculate its distance from them. The phrase *Full Operational Capability* means that all 24 satellites are working. *All In View* means that a receiver is tracking all the satellites it can find (because it cannot find the ones that it wants), and can instantly replace a lost signal with another that is already being monitored. *Search The Sky* is a procedure that starts after switching on a receiver to check that no stored satellite data is available. It typically occurs after you move the GPS some distance since its last use.

A pseudo satellite (*pseudolite*) is a ground beacon that transmits information similar to that of a GPS satellite. The centre of the Earth can be used in the same way.

The satellites fly high enough to avoid the problems encountered by other navigation systems. They operate (at 7500 mph) between **6 circular planes, 20 200 km above the Earth, with 4 in each plane**, optimised for wide coverage. Each one should have a 28° view of the Earth, and at least 5 should be in line of sight from any point on Earth, provided they are more than 7.5° above the horizon (satellites are *in view* when over 5° above). The most satellites are visible round the Equator, but this varies, according to the time and your location.

Their orbits cross the Equator at a **55° angle** (or, rather, the inclination* of the satellite's orbit to the Equatorial plane is 55°), so you won't see a satellite directly overhead when North of 55° N or South of 55° S. This does not affect polar service, because, at high latitudes, receivers can see satellites over the other side, so more can actually be visible than elsewhere (they never go right over the Poles). Where the satellite goes South to North it is in the *ascending node*, and vice versa. The *mask angle* is the lowest angle above the horizon from where a satellite can be used, because of possible range errors.

*The inclination is the angle between the orbital and Equatorial planes.

The satellites move once around the Earth, from W-E, every 11 hours 58 minutes (that is, twice a day, getting 4 minutes earlier each day). That's 14 times faster than a 747! The height used gives the best coverage with the least number of satellites, though you could get a problem flying through the odd ravine, especially as their transmitting power is only around 50 watts, or rather less than the average light bulb, which allows you to use smaller antennae. The signals themselves have less strength than a Christmas tree light.

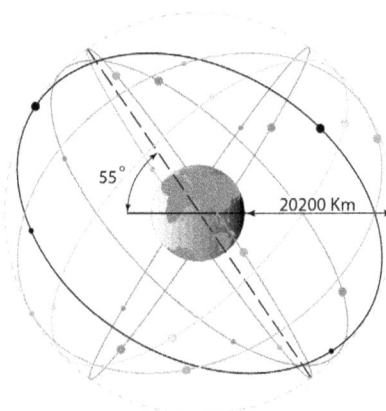

GLONASS, in contrast, uses 3 planes with 8 satellites equally displaced by 45° of latitude. To stop them hitting US satellites, they fly lower ,in a near circular orbit at **19 100 km** at an inclination of 64.8° to the Equator. Each orbit is completed in 11 hours, 15 minutes. The time reference is UTC Russian time, and the datum is PZ-90 Earth-centred, Earth-fixed. Navigation signals are transmitted on two frequencies on the L band (UHF), L1 at around 1.6 GHz and L2 around 1.2 GHz. The navigation message is 2 seconds long, with "immediate" data relating to the satellite transmitting the signal and "non-immediate" data relating to the other satellites.

Although it is guaranteed to be kept running for the foreseeable future, in (US) National Emergencies NAVSTAR may be unavailable, which is why you still need radio-based navigation aids, at least under EASA*. As well, the satellites are not always in an optimal position, and interference can affect their signals, including jamming, which can be done with minimal equipment.

*If a position fix from GPS differs from conventional systems by an unacceptable amount, the flight may be continued with those systems, so prescribed IFR equipment must still be installed and operational.

The system consists of three basic elements:

If this page is a photocopy, it is not authorised!

CAPT

• The **Space Segment**, which contains the satellites, transmitting signals that are used by the receivers.

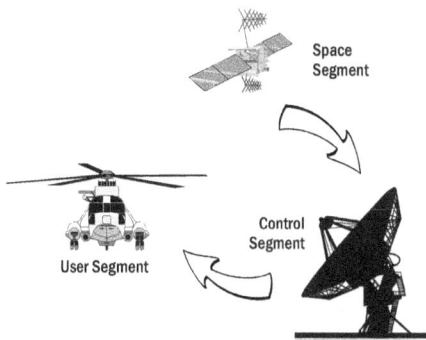

• The **Control Segment** has the ground stations and systems that track the satellites and monitor their status. It includes a Master Control Station in Colorado, its backup and 5 monitoring stations around the world. Their data is sent to and processed at the MCS, then used to refine and update satellite navigational signals. The main tasks of the control segment are:

  • to manage performance

  • to upload navigation data

  • to monitor satellites

• The **User Segment** includes the receivers that select satellites automatically, track their signals and calculate the time taken for them to reach the receiver. *Single channel* receivers move from one satellite to the next in sequence. Although this can be very quick, it is not fast enough for navigation. *Multi-channel* receivers (most suitable for aircraft) continuously monitor position data whilst locking on to the next satellites. *Continuous receivers*, with up to 12 channels, can eliminate GDOP problems (see *Errors*) by watching more than four satellites. GPS receiver antennae are semi-omnidirectional, and the active element is a quarter wavelength of 1.6 GHz, or approximately 2.5 cm.

GPS signals are line-of-sight, and will not pass through water, buildings or solid objects in general, although they do pass through clouds, glass and plastic (regardless of that, though, the best conditions for reception are in clear areas with open skies).

In essence, satellites transmit a **Coarse Acquisition** (C/A) code, with a **navigation data message** encoded in it. Navigation data is transmitted every 30 seconds as frames, that contain 5 subframes.

Clock	Ephemeris	Ephemeris	Almanac	Almanac

Because even atomic clocks can drift, the first frame tells the receiver the difference between satellite and true GPS time, as defined by the ground stations. Subframes 2 and 3 include details of that particular satellite's exact orbital path for the next 4 hours or so, which is called the **Ephemeris**, and unique to that satellite (it is used to correct for small disturbances). The last 2 subframes make up the **Almanac**, which has less precise positioning details of the other satellites, valid for around 6 months. Thus, the receiver knows which ones should be in view and searches for their C/A codes. It can then establish your range from them. The speed of light is assumed, as the signals come from space.

The C/A code is the ranging code used by the receiver to measure the distance (also called *Standard Positioning Service*, or SPS, as distinct from the military P code). It is a 1023-bit pseudorandom number (PRN) that is transmitted at 1.023 Mbits/second, so it is repeated every millisecond.

The receiver knows the PRN code of each satellite and is able to generate them internally. As the satellite includes a time tag (referenced to GPS time) in its signal, indicating when the PRN started, on reception, the receiver can compare when its own version started with the arrival time of the satellite's PRN. The difference in time (in nanoseconds) corresponds to the distance between the satellite and receiver. The result is a pseudo random range.

The system depends very much on precise timing between satellites and receivers. Although they generate time-codes together, satellite signals lag behind due to their distance. If they are out by 0.6 seconds, the satellite will be 11 160 miles away. 0.7 seconds will be 13 020 miles, and so on.

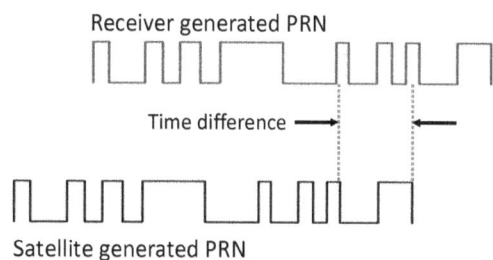

Time measurement therefore consists of:

• The transit time of the signal

• The time offset between transmitter and receiver

The timing accuracy is actually down to one billionth of a second. The General Theory of Relativity predicts that time runs slower with more gravity, and the atomic clocks in satellites indeed run slightly faster (2 seconds over UTC) than they would on the surface, so corrections have to be made continually.

If you are off by even 1 millisecond, your position would be in error by over 300 km, so, for 1 m accuracy, time measurement must be accurate to within 3 nanoseconds.

Satellites therefore use atomic clocks for high precision, and continuously transmit their positions, plus a code number in a set code, at exactly the same time. The signal is modulated with a pseudo-random code that allows the time of the transmission to be recovered by the receiver. Instead of trying to distinguish the signal from the Earth's background noise, it is sent as Pseudo Random Noise because it is not really as random as normal noise.

Although noise will change randomly, the GPS signal will have the same sequence. Over time, more matches will be found for the PRN than for the noise, so the GPS signal can be found. This technique allows all satellites to use the same frequency, with individual ones being identified by their Pseudo-Random Noise code (PRN).

The system thus works loosely like DME, except that is it passive - the time it takes for a signal to travel from a satellite to your receiver is multiplied by the speed of light to obtain a distance measurement, which gives you a *Line Of Position* (LOP). One, of course, is no good by itself, and you actually need 4 LOPs* to determine your position in terms of latitude, longitude and altitude.

*The job can actually be done with three satellites - the fourth is there to correct for timing errors by calculating the position a second time, and the results will differ by an amount equal to the timing error. As calculations are involved, and are therefore subject to error, the distance is called a pseudorange.

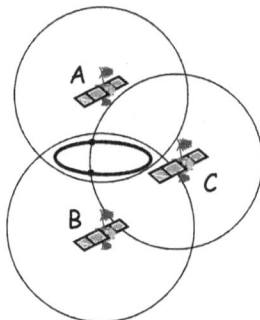

For example, you must be somewhere on the surface of a sphere centred on Satellite A, and similarly for Satellite B. In fact, you must be somewhere on the circle formed where they intersect. With Satellite C, the three spheres intersect at only two points, and you must logically be at one of them, which is where the fourth satellite comes in - there are techniques for deciding which one, using "bad mathematics" according to Garmin. Mostly the wrong one is discarded because it puts you somewhere completely weird, like 100 miles out in space.

The basic elements transmitted from a satellite are:

- clock offset from UTC
- ephemeris data
- almanac data
- ionospheric delays (see *Errors*, later)
- satellite health data
- satellite clock corrections

As each satellite contains **almanac** data for the entire constellation, a GPS receiver only needs to download it from one satellite to figure out the approximate location of them all. Almanac information is transmitted every 12.5 minutes and takes **12.5 minutes to download** (30 seconds per data frame), so it will take at least that time before accurate fixes can be determined (the initial setup is known as a *cold start*). This data becomes stale over time or if you move the receiver to another location more than several hundred kilometers away. The Almanac covers:

- Satellites that are operating normally
- The PRN codes of available satellites
- Predicted positions of satellites in their orbits

The receiver can then determine which satellites are in view and their relative geometry, then which are the four best ones to track for the best lines of position.

As each satellite transmits only its own **ephemeris** data, the receiver must get it from each one in view. Ephemeris data is transmitted every 30 seconds, and takes 12 seconds to download. It is valid for up to 4-6 hours.

Normally, when two PRNs are multiplied together, they give a value of near zero. A satellite's PRN is multiplied by the L1 carrier (described below) at different time shift intervals, until it finds a lock-on, when a particular time shift results in a high multiplication value. Thus, all the other satellites are filtered out and the time-shift required for the lock-on is used to calculate the satellite's range and extract the navigation message from the C/A code.

By decoding the navigation message, the receiver gets the data it needs to correct the pseudo range. When the two code patterns match, the satellite and receiver can be synchronised, which is the first step in finding an LOP (*initial acquisition*). The receiver in your aircraft can generate the same pseudo random code as the satellite because it has its own code book with them all in. The code sequence is started when the local clock says the satellite should have started transmitting its PRN.

The x, y, z position from the centre of the Earth is translated into latitude and longitude using the WGS 84 model, and GPS time is translated into UTC. Your velocity is calculated with a combination of your rate of change of position and Doppler shift from the L1 frequencies of different satellites, compared to the receiver's L1 oscillation frequency.

In fact, two UHF frequencies are used, L1 and L2*. The (higher) L1 frequency is 1575.42 MHz and L2 is 1227.60 MHz. Both are multiples of a base frequency of 10.23

MHz (L1 is 10.23 x 154) which is generated by a crystal controlled by an atomic clock. All satellites transmit on both frequencies, but their outputs are multiplexed so they can share the same carrier.

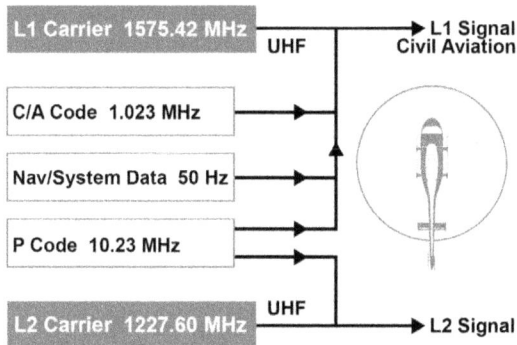

*L2C (and M for the military) was added in 2005 so that cheaper receivers could use proper signals instead of having to make do with the carrier, because they couldn't decrypt the military code. L5 is coming in 2015.

L5 is a civilian frequency that allows the avionics to compute ionospheric corrections without the need for a separate SBAS, like WAAS or EGNOS.

The (digital) information is superimposed on the carriers with BPSK modulation (*Binary Phase Key Shifting*), where code changes cause a 180° phase shift in the carrier. Being digital, the data exists as strings of 1s and 0s, which are simpler to transmit, more reliable, and less prone to jamming because redundancy checking can be used.

The P (Precise) code is transmitted on L1 and L2. As it runs at 10.23 MHz, it is ten times more accurate than C/A. It can be encrypted (as Y Code) and is therefore almost impossible to jam.

Comparing the L1 and L2 frequencies at the receiver can compensate for ionospheric propagation errors. In other words, differences between the frequencies tell you what the ionosphere is doing - radio waves change speed as they pass through it. As the delay is inversely proportional to frequency, it can be calculated and virtually eliminated.

SIGNAL AUGMENTATION
GROUND BASED
Ground Based Augmentation Systems (GBAS) are the practical application of Local Area Differential GPS*. Corrections are sent **directly to aircraft receivers** (over a data link in the VHF band) from ground stations at airports, typically within about 20-30 nm. A monitoring function in the ground station ensures the integrity of the broadcast. GBAS + GPS is also called *Local Area Augmentation System*.

*Differential GPS was a workaround (by the US Coastguard!) for the intentional errors in the C/A code for unauthorised (non-military) users of the GPS system.

It uses a fifth signal from a precisely surveyed ground based transmitter whose position can be compared against that of the receiver. The difference is the intentional error. The nearer the receiver is to a DGPS ground station, the more accurate is the fix.

A Loran data channel is used to provide Differential GPS.

GBAS can provide two services:

- Precision approach - down to 200 feet at Sydney

- Horizontal Positioning for RNAV operations in terminal areas

SATELLITE BASED
Here, Differential GPS is extended to cover a larger area. The idea is to measure the signal errors from the satellites and provide separate corrections for ranging, ephemeris, clock and ionospheric errors. Correction data is then transmitted directly to **geostationary** satellites, and re-transmitted to the user. The frequency band of the data link is identical to that of the GPS signals. Pseudorange measurements to the geostationary satellites can also be made as if they were GPS satellites. SBAS regionally augments GPS and GLONASS by making them suitable (as a standalone navigation aid) for safety critical procedures such as landing.

The FAA's **Wide Area Augmentation System** (WAAS) allows GPS to be used throughout a flight, including a Cat I precision approach. Satellite signals are received by precisely surveyed ground stations, which detect errors and send them to a Master Station (WMS), which in turn adds correction information based on geographical area (which is fairly constant) and uplinks a correction message to geostationary satellites (around the Equator and way above the other satellites) for rebroadcast, from which pseudorange measurements can be made, as with normal satellites. This improves the 95% signal accuracy from 100m to 7m, but it can be better than 2 m.

The term LPV stands for *Lateral Precision Vertical* guidance, with lateral accuracy as good as ILS, with vertical capability. Unlike BARO VNAV, SBAS vertical guidance is not subject to altimeter setting errors, or non-standard temperatures or lapse rates.

When SBAS integrity messages are used, the additional satellites that would be required for RAIM are not needed, because the messages are available wherever the satellite signal can be received. WAAS currently uses two satellites over the Atlantic and Pacific Oceans.

EGNOS, or the *European Geostationary Navigation Overlay Service* is the European equivalent to WAAS (there is also MSAS in Japan and GAGAN in India). It has INMARSAT satellites broadcasting GPS look-alike signals, so the coverage is limited to between 80N and 80S (EGNOS has a primary service area much further North than WAAS). It is designed to improve accuracy to **1-2 m**

horizontally and **3-5 m vertically**. Integrity and safety are improved by alerting users within 6 seconds of a malfunction, as opposed to the normal 3 hours.

AIRCRAFT BASED (ABAS)

This uses redundant elements (i.e. excess information that is not otherwise needed) within the GNSS constellation to develop integrity control (ABAS does not improve positioning accuracy, as you get with GBAS and SBAS). ABAS using GNSS information only is RAIM (*Receiver Autonomous Integrity Monitoring*), described below. A system using information from additional on-board sensors is AAIM (*Aircraft Autonomous Integrity Monitoring*). Typical sensors used are barometric altimeters, clocks and INS.

Although the ground stations monitor satellites and detect faults, it can take up to two hours for an error to be corrected. **Receiver Autonomous Integrity Monitoring** (RAIM) is a bit quicker than that. It is achieved within the receiver, which monitors satellites and verifies their signals, so an extra satellite is needed to detect corrupt information. For the bad signal to be isolated as well, you need one more. Without RAIM, accuracy is not assured, and you still need 4 satellites for a 3D fix. Thus, Basic RAIM (fault detection) needs 5 satellites in order to work, and 6 (with good positioning) to continue working after a failure is detected (*Fault Detection & Exclusion*, or FDE). If a satellite is excluded, the system works as Basic RAIM and can be used as an independent means of navigation.

If RAIM is available, the integrity limits are 4 nm for oceanic, 2 nm for enroute, 1 nm for terminal work and 0.3 nm for GPS approaches. If RAIM is not available, the GPS must be integrated with other systems, such as DME/DME fixing, with traditional equipment (VOR, etc.) as backup. If the GPS is the only equipment meeting the B-RNAV standards, RAIM availability must be confirmed before flight.

5 positions are calculated using 4 of the 5 visible satellites:

    ABCD
    ABCE
    ABDE
    ACDE
    BCDE

The signal is assumed to be reliable if they all agree within a certain tolerance.

RAIM can be assisted with *baroaiding* (barometric aiding), which uses barometric information from the aircraft's altitude encoder to reduce the number of real satellites required by one. Barometric altitude is the datum for altitude information such as MDA. The idea is to convert the aircraft's altitude to a range from the centre of the Earth, which can then be used for consistency checks with the pseudo ranges from the satellites that are used to create the fix.

Another technique is *clock coasting*, which uses atomic clocks in the user segment to reduce clock bias (below).

ERRORS

The effects of the errors below are smallest when the satellites are directly overhead and greatest when they are near the horizon, as the signal is affected for a longer time. Having said that, the most accurate fix comes from 3 satellites with a low elevation above the horizon, 120° from each other and a fourth directly overhead.

- **Clock Bias**. As the receiver's clock is not as precise as the atomic clocks in the satellites, there can be a large difference in the measurements, which can introduce a ranging error. When a receiver starts up, its own code is inaccurate by an unknown error called clock bias, or clock offset, against GPS reference time. In addition, the size of the atomic clocks in satellites are necessarily smaller than ground-based ones would be. The receiver corrects by running a series of simultaneous equations. It must be aware of the satellite's position, which is where the ephemeris comes in. Signals are monitored by control segment ground stations and the corrections sent to the Master station, which makes the necessary corrections then relays them to the satellites.

- Satellite **clock drift**. Although the orbital paths of GPS satellites could theoretically be predicted under Kepler's laws of planetary motion, the assumption that the Earth is a perfect sphere of uniform density is not correct, and gravity from other heavenly bodies (e.g. the Moon and the Sun) have their own effects on top of Earth gravity. There is also very slight atmospheric drag, because satellites are not travelling in a perfect vacuum, plus the impact of photons of light emitted by the sun both directly and reflected off the Earth and Moon. This solar radiation pressure is a function of a satellite's size and orientation, distance from the sun, etc., but the end result is that satellites headed towards the Sun are slowed down, and accelerated when headed away. This *clock drift* is virtually impossible to estimate accurately, and is the largest unmeasurable source of error.

- **Ephemeris** (position) **error**. This error is caused by the satellite not being where the receiver thinks it is. That is, there are errors in the satellite's calculation of its own position due to the gravitational effects mentioned above from the sun, moon and other planets. Ground monitoring stations check satellite positions every 12 hours, so the maximum error is 2.5 metres. The computers at the master control station can predict the satellite's future position at a specific time, which is

CAPT

compared with its actual position from the monitor stations. Updated information on future positions is then uploaded.

- **Ionospheric Propagation**. The ionosphere's effect on radio waves is proportional to their frequency. As the ionosphere changes the speed of the radio waves and therefore the pseudorange signal, by noting the time delay between the L1 and L2 signals, much of the effect of atmospheric propagation can be removed internally by the receiver. This is proportional to the inverse of the carrier frequency, squared. The corrections are imperfect, although they are slow and can be averaged over time. The model of the ionosphere is corrected by the ground stations every 12 hours, so the maximum position error is 5 metres.

- **Receiver noise**. Internal noise within receiver circuits can cause position errors of up to 0.3 m.

- **Signal noise**. Similar to Receiver noise.

- **Tropospheric**. Water vapour in the atmosphere affects refraction. The maximum error from tropospheric propagation is between 0.3 - 0.5 m.

- **Multi-path reflection.** Antennae should be fitted on the upper fuselage near the Centre of Gravity, as shadowing by parts of an aircraft may stop signals from being received or cause them to come from different directions. Some frequencies, such as 109.5 MHz, have been known to cause the GPS not to work if the antenna is not sited properly. The maximum error is 0.6 m.

- **C/A Selective Availability**. Now discontinued, but it used to be done by dithering satellite clocks.

- **Manoeuvring Errors**. Caused by aircraft attitudes and similar to Multi-path reflection.

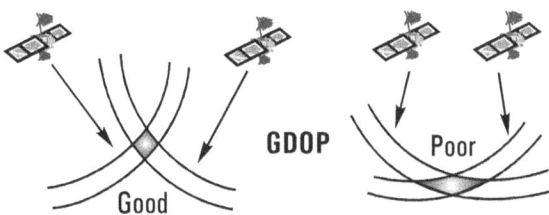

GDOP — Good — Poor

- **GDOP/PDOP.** When satellites are too close to each other, vertical and horizontal position accuracy is degraded, because the lines of constant range do not cut cleanly (the optimum is 60°) resulting in *Geometric (Position) Dilution of Precision*, where you end up anywhere inside a range of positions rather than just one. ICAO requires a PDOP/GDOP of less than 6 for en-route navigation, and 3 or less for non-precision approaches (4 is considered to be good). The

normal accuracy of 100 m for 95% of the time assumes a PDOP of 3 and a range error of 33.3 m (range errors are multiplied by PDOP to obtain stated accuracies). GDOP is minimised by RAIM.

OPERATION

Although it is tempting to use GPS all the time, remember that it is electrical, and therefore reserves the right to go offline at any moment, without warning. The antenna in a GPS is live as well, and equally liable to stop working. A GPS may also have a database of airspace and frequencies inside - although not so important for VFR use, it is still the mark of a professional to keep it up to date.

For GPS approaches, you use a CDI in the same way as you would for an ILS, except that the needle deflection is measured in terms of distance rather than degrees off course. This means that the instrument's sensitivity is fixed all the way down through the approach, and is not so sensitive in the final stages.

However, the sensitivity does vary according to the age of your receiver. For a non-WAAS capable one, you have three levels. In *en-route mode* (more than 30 miles from the destination or departure point), one dot is equal to 1 nautical mile. Inside those figures, it reduces to *terminal mode*, which is one fifth, so *full deflection* is now 1 nm. In *approach mode* (within 2 nm of the FAF), full deflection is 0.3 nm left or right of the centreline. At the MAP, the sensitivity returns to the terminal level.

WAAS capable receivers have a CDI sensitivity of only 2 nm in en route mode. The terminal level remains the same, but approach mode reduces to the *lesser* of 0.2 nm or 2°. The sensitivity of an LPV approach is 350 either side of the centreline at the threshold, or 70 feet per dot!

DIRECTION FINDING   062 02 01

Direction finding is the process of determining the straight line (Great Circle) along which a transmitter is located, so you need a chart that allows straight lines to represent Great Circles as closely as possible, so you can measure the angles correctly. For aviation purposes, this is normally a Lambert projection.

By using more than one transmitter, you can get a series of position lines with which you should be able to determine where you are. The accuracy is not brilliant, but it is enough to be a supplement for dead reckoning navigation, so it is useful when the weather is bad and you can't see much, assuming that you identify the correct station.

The most basic method is to turn a directional antenna round until the signal disappears.

VDF

The purpose of *VHF Direction Finding* is to provide directional assistance in times of difficulty, rather than for general navigation, so a typical frequency it might be used on is 121.5 MHz (the full range is between **118-137 MHz**). One or more ATC stations can get a bearing for you to steer (QDM) to get to their location from your transmissions, so the minimum equipment is a VHF radio. On its own, a direction-finding station can only find your position in relation to itself - for an exact position, you need two or even three more, who will all report to a Master Station. As well, you must work out the headings needed from the information given.

Being based on VHF, VDF is subject to the usual limitations (line of sight, multipath, etc.), so the higher you are, the better the results you will get. You must transmit for a few seconds for a bright line to spread from the centre of a screen to the outside which is marked with compass bearings.

The full range of services available could include:

- Emergency Cloudbreak
- Emergency No-compass Homing
- Homing
- Fix - only on 121.5 MHz
- Track-out Assistance
- Time & Distance Estimates

However, ICAO only recognizes homing, with no compensation for wind, which is actually the only element that most pilots are aware of, receive training on, or use.

The following services are available, assuming no wind:

- **QDM** - magnetic bearing *to* (with no wind)
- **QDR** - magnetic bearing *from*
- **QUJ** - true bearing *to* (to be steered, with no wind)
- **QTE** - true bearing *from*

The QTE & QDM are the only serious ones - a QTE allows you to plot a line on a map from the station and the QDM gives you a magnetic heading to steer.

When a position is given in relation to another point, or in lat & long, it is a **QTF**. When positions are given by heading or bearing & distance from a known point that is not the station making the report, the known point shall be from the centre of an aerodrome, a prominent town or geographic feature, in that order.

A series of bearings is a QDL (so QDL QDM means several QDMs). QGE is the distance from the relevant point. A VDF letdown exists where ATC give you QDMs, and you work out the headings to steer, so the responsibility lies with the pilot. A QGH is an approach based on VDF bearings, where a VDF unit is prepared to give you assistance, based on VDF bearings (the responsibility lies with the controller). Older equipment uses a cathode ray tube on which the line appears (like a radar sweep) pointing to where your transmission is coming from. More modern digital equipment uses a circle of LEDs at 10° intervals, which will show the same information, with a digital readout in the centre (see left). The controller can store the last transmission, if busy with something else at the time.

Accuracy comes in these classes, in relation to bearing or position, and will be included in the transmission:

Class	Bearing	Position
A	±2°	5 nm
B	±5°	20 nm
C	±10°	50 nm
D	<C	<C

The Adcock RDF Antenna

The Adcock antenna has been used for many years for Radio Direction Finding. It is basically an interferometer, and was originally developed to overcome Night Effect, which creates spurious signals in the horizontal parts of the ADF loop. With the Adcock, the top part of the loop has been dispensed with and the bottom part is sometimes shielded with an earthed metallic covering.

If the antenna is lined up on the four cardinal points, and an aircraft is to the North, the N-S poles will pick up the maximum signals, and the E-W ones will pick up none. As the aircraft moves to the East or West, the E-W poles will pick up a signal strength and move the needle accordingly (the N-S poles are connected to the upper & lower plates of a CRT and the E-W poles to the left & right ones). The system works on phase difference, and directionality can be changed electronically.

Since this antenna only responds to vertically polarized components, poor performance can occur when the signal is horizontal or nearly horizontal.

A series of such antennae is used for VDF operations, in a circle round a pole.

RADAR   062 03

• •

Although technology has improved matters, radar is still quite a crude instrument which requires an understanding of how it works in order to understand its information correctly, especially when you consider the speed of the waves against the ranges involved. Very short intervals of time in the order of millionths of a second have to be measured with considerable accuracy for the best results.

The use of radar improves aircraft spacing and safety - the word stands for *Radio Direction and Ranging*, but the system was called RDF (*Radio Direction Finding*) until 1943, when the name was changed to harmonise with the Americans (in those days it just about got the distance right). It works on the basis that microwave pulses can be reflected (or echoed) off suitable objects, and the time between transmission and reflection can be used to calculate the distance because the speed of transmission is known (the reflection of signals is called scattering. Reflections in the exact opposite direction are called *backscatter*). The "blips" representing the objects are displayed on a video monitor and a controller can see the relative positions of aircraft reflecting any pulses.

The radar beam is rather like that from a lighthouse, as the antenna focusses the pulses in one direction with the most energy concentrated in the centre. VHF does not provide the bandwidth required for the short pulses that allow good target definition*, so SHF bands are currently used. Thus, radar is limited to line of sight.

*For accuracy, the leading edge of the pulse must be sharp, so it needs to jump to its maximum value suddenly. This is a serious matter when using longer waves, because radio waves with different frequencies have to be mixed, so the process is better done with very short (centimetric) waves.

In most countries, outside of terminal control areas, radar is used more as a monitoring device but, in others, you are more or less under radar control all the time and you may very rarely follow a flight planned route. You will be given details of other traffic according to the clock system, such as "fast mover at 6 o'clock".

The word *pulses*, mentioned above, means that short bursts of electromagnetic energy are mixed with relatively long periods of silence (*relatively long*, in electronic terms, means less than a thousandth of a second). *Continuous Wave radar* is used in radio altimeters and the Doppler system.

Pulses were used originally because early radar sets used thermionic valves as opposed to the transistors of today. A valve small enough to produce the short waves required would overheat when used continuously, so it was allowed suitable periods to cool off.

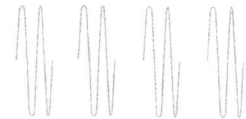

RF energy is created with magnetrons, which bunch together electrons that fly past alternately charged grids (essentially diodes that are influenced by a magnetic field). The energy is released at intervals (the PRF), which are determined by the range required, and discussed later.

The range of a target is determined by measuring the time taken for a pulse of energy to travel there and back. It takes around 3 microseconds for a wave to travel around 1 000 m, but it has to get back, so between transmission and reception there will be a time interval of around 6 m/s for every 1 000 m of (slant) range. This is *primary radar*.

Radio signals weaken over distance and, as the pulses must make two journeys (there and back), the range is necessarily limited. The blip on the screen is also quite large, and aircraft very close together cannot be told apart, unless the beam is narrow enough to pass between them

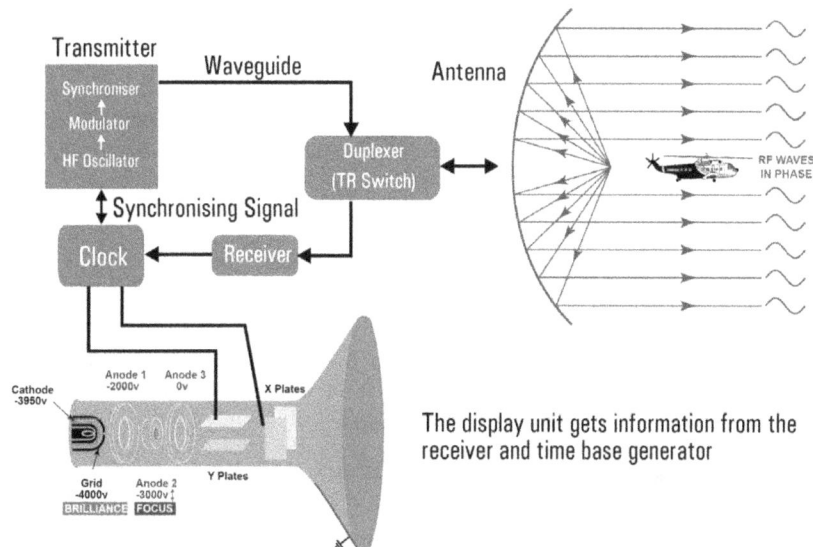

The display unit gets information from the receiver and time base generator

(a 1 millisecond pulse takes up 300 m of space). Finally, radio waves can be bent by the atmosphere or screened by mountains or buildings, and different aircraft return signals differently, in terms of shape or surface.

The strength of an echo received back at a radar set varies with the size of the target and its distance. As the returning pulse is not reflected, but re-radiated, it decreases in strength in the same way as it did on its way out, so the received signal in this case has one third of one third of its original strength, meaning one ninth. As power is proportional to the square of the field strength, echo power is inversely proportional to the distance of the target[4]. So every time you double the range of a target, you reduce the power of its echo by 2^4 or 16 times. Trebling the range reduces it by 3^4 or 81 times.

The transmitter has to:

• Generate very high power at high frequencies. The radio frequency (RF) energy is produced inside the **HF oscillator** by a *magnetron*, which is a piece of copper with cavities in surrounded by a strong magnet. The electrons are made to spin within the cavities and set up the microwaves, hence their use in microwave ovens.

• Be capable of being switched on and off rapidly to produce pulses. This is done by the **modulator**.

• Send out the pulses at regular intervals (as per the *pulse recurrence rate)* via the **synchroniser**, which regulates the rate at which pulses are sent (i.e. sets the PRF) and resets the timing clock for range determination for each pulse. Signals from the synchronizer are sent simultaneously to the transmitter, which sends a new pulse, and to the display, which resets the return sweep.

The generated pulses travel through either coaxial cable or a hollow, generally rectangular, metal tube called a *wave guide,* which prevents excessive power loss because it is tuned to the wavelength. The RF energy is injected into the waveguide by a probe, which is simply an antenna that only radiates into the waveguide.

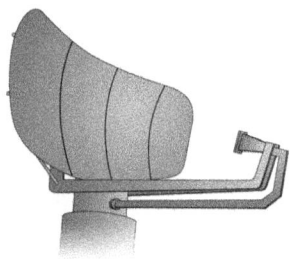

A waveguide is not required for weather radar because it uses slots on a flat (planar) array.

The clock drives the deflector plates of the screen used for the display. It oscillates at a very exact frequency, geared down by dividers. The clock also ensures that the spot of light that moves around the screen is cut off at appropriate moments to keep the screen clear (blacking out flyback -

by making the grid (brilliance) negative, the fly-back is suppressed, meaning that you won't see the lines where the pulse flies back from the end of one line to the beginning of the new line). Range markers are displayed with a saw-tooth wave.

The clock drives the deflector plates of the screen used for the display. It oscillates at a very exact frequency, geared down by dividers. The clock also ensures that the spot of light that moves around the screen is cut off at appropriate moments to keep the screen clear (blacking out flyback).

The problem is that the signals are very different - the transmitted signal is very strong, but the received one is very weak and the system must be sensitive enough to detect it. In other words, the receiver circuits must be protected against the high energy from the transmitted signals, otherwise they would be fried when the system is switched on. The solution is not necessarily to switch between transmit and receive, but to route the signals to the appropriate places, which is where the **duplexer** comes in. It is a routing device that directs outgoing pulses to the antenna and incoming pulses from the antenna to the receiver. The speed at which it returns to the receive position helps to determine minimum range.

The antenna is a parabolic dish, shaped according to its function. For example, the orange peel produces a wide narrow beam. A parabolic dish produces a focussed beam, but it spreads with distance. A phase array has a series of conducting elements like small dipoles that are arranged in a line and fed with signals that are in phase with each other. The interference patterns produce a pencil beam.

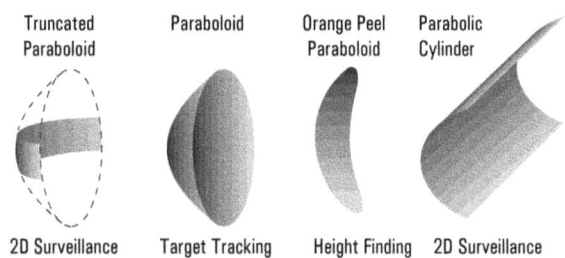

Truncated Paraboloid	Paraboloid	Orange Peel Paraboloid	Parabolic Cylinder
2D Surveillance	Target Tracking	Height Finding	2D Surveillance

There is a protruding radiating element (a probe) somewhere in the middle, which beams the signals to the face of the dish, to form the beam into the desired shape and go in the direction required.

The dish and element work in the reverse sense when receiving signals - the larger the dish, the more of the weak signal can be received. If the width of the main beam is taken from where the signal strength drops to half of what it is at the centre, you can find the beam width with this formula:

```
Beam Width° = 2 x wavelength in cm
                   diameter (ft)
```

try also:

```
Beam Width°  =  70 x wavelength
                   diameter
```

So a reflector 4 feet wide using 3 cm waves would have a beam width of around 1.5°. Here are some common sizes:

Dish Size	Beam Width
10″	9.5°
12″	7.5°
18″	5°

Advantages of a narrow beam are:

- getting bearings more easily

- greater concentration of energy

- more range

- target definition

A *short pulse length* with a *narrow beam* gets the best picture.

As the antenna is expected to work with a transmitter (horizontally) and a receiver (vertically), it should be able to produce a thin beam, and receive a wide one, respectively. A perfectly directional antenna would be very large and unwieldy so, to use small ones, we have to live with unwanted radiations known as sidelobes, which can show multiple targets for one aircraft at close range.

The advantage of using a slotted antenna is to virtually eliminate lateral lobes, and to concentrate more energy in the main beam. The receiver converts the microwave returns into electrical signals that are amplified, because they have only a fraction of the power that was sent originally. Thus, the receiver should have a high overall gain, with little random noise in its circuitry. Because of this high amplification capability, no RF stage is required.

Finally, the signal is sent to the *Plan Position Indicator* (PPI), which is called that because it displays the returns as if you were looking from the top, as opposed to the original display, which showed the returns from the side. The display's timebase (the frequency with which the picture is repainted) is linked to the antenna, in that when it passes through North, so does the beam painted on the display. As a pulse is fired off, a spot of light moves from the centre of the tube to the outside, reaching the circumference before the next pulse goes. The effect is a line of light rotating round the screen.

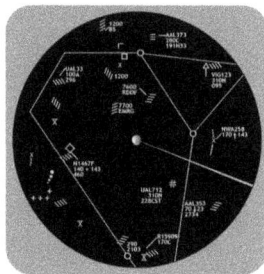

When a return is received, the electron flow is increased and the intensity of the display increases to a spot which fades away slowly as the line moves on.

Calculations

You can calculate the distance between the transmitter and the target because the speed of the radio wave is known, and the direction the antenna is pointing at the time supplies the bearing. It takes 12.36 microseconds for a radio wave to travel out and back for each nautical mile of range (radar mile), or 123.6 microseconds for each 10 nm.

Given that radar speed is 300 m per microsecond, the leading edge of the average pulse is already several hundred metres on its way when the transmitting stops.

Put more mathematically, if the time delay is Dt, then you can find the range (R) with:

$$R = \frac{cDt}{2}$$

where c = the speed of light, and it is divided by 2 because the pulse train has to get to the target and back again.

The maximum unambiguous range* will be determined firstly by the *Pulse Repetition Frequency* (PRF)**, because pulses have to return to the transmitter before the next ones are sent, plus the *Pulse Interval* (PI).

*If an echo is received from a long range target after the pulse following the one it relates to, the radar uses the very much shorter time between the second pulse and the echo, and calculates a shorter range. Range ambiguity occurs when the time taken for an echo to return from a target is greater than the Pulse Repetition Time. For example, if the interval between pulses is 1000 microseconds, and the return time of a pulse from a distant target is 1200 microseconds, the apparent distance of the target is only 200 microseconds.

To increase the unambiguous range, you have to increase the PRT, which means increasing the PRF.

**It is more correct to say that the PRF is limited by range. To see targets up to say, 25 nm, the maximum PRF is around 3000 pulses per second. It can be determined by:

```
Max PRF = 80 000
             nm
```

Simply replace the letters *nm* with the distance required. 80,000 represents half the speed of light in nautical miles.

In fact, the range is determined by the time *between* pulses (the *Pulse Recurrence Period* or *Interval*), which must be long enough for a pulse to go out to the target and return. It follows that, if it is too short, this cannot happen. As the number of pulses per second depends on the length of the interval, we say that maximum range depends on PRF.

The number of pulses per second is the Pulse Repetition Frequency (PRF), so the further the target is away, the longer must be the PRP and, by extension, the PRF. A shorter PRP means more pulses per second and a higher PRF. The two are related:

$$PRF = \frac{1}{PI \ (PRP)}$$

With this formula, make sure you use the right numbers!

In between pulses, you also need some dead (rest) time.

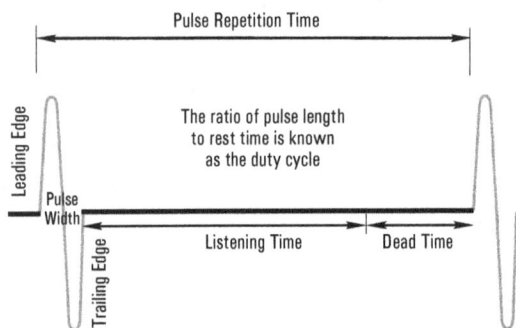

This is because a pulsed wave doesn't just stop when it hits a target, but carries on, and may be reflected from other objects way back. At 100 000 yards, for example, it would take around 610 microseconds to travel out and back from the target. If the time interval between pulses is only 610 microseconds, any reflected pulses from further away would be received after the next pulse and produce confusing results, such as a false echo near to the station.

Thus, the interval between pulses needs to be made a little bit wider to allow all possible echoes to be received. The sweep of the beam will still take 610 microseconds, but the spot on the screen will be held at the start during the dead time until the next pulse is ready.

MAXIMUM RANGE

Although it mostly affects the minimum range (see below), the pulse width can also affect the maximum detection range, as the energy depends on pulse width and output power (a long pulse has more energy and returns a stronger signal).

Maximum Theoretical Unambiguous Range (MTR) in km is found by:

$$MTR = \frac{C}{2 \times PRF}$$

PRF (if you know the range) is found by:

$$PRF = \frac{C}{2 \times Range \ (km)}$$

Example: Assuming transmission power is enough, the maximum range of a ground radar with a PRF of 450 pulses per second is 333 km.

MINIMUM RANGE

This (or, more technically, the dead zone at close range) is set by the pulse width (plus the recovery time of the duplexer), because a long pulse could still be receiving part of an echo from one target while starting to get the

information from a second, if they are close together (with continuous wave radar, the minimum range restriction is removed, so you can measure short distances, hence its use with radio altimeters). Put more simply, the receiver is switched off while the pulse is being transmitted.

The minimum range is around half the pulse width, as is range resolution. As a pulse width of a microsecond will cover over 300 m, two aircraft within 150 m of each other will appear on the screen as one, so the pulse width can also affect the ability to discriminate between targets that are close together. Based on the scale in the diagram above, if the duty cycle was 1:1000, and the pulse was 1 microsecond, the next one would be over 10 feet away. The transmitter is idle a lot of the time.

Moving Target Indication

Strong radar returns from stationary objects (e.g. terrain and buildings) can mask a primary radar return from an aircraft, especially if it is at low level. MTI uses Doppler to eliminate returns from fixed objects. That is, only returns that show a Doppler shift (moving targets) will be shown, but a target at a constant range would not show up.

Secondary Surveillance Radar

This is a development of a system introduced during the Second World War called *Identification Friend or Foe* (IFF), which was supposed to distinguish between friendly and enemy aircraft. Friendly aircraft had a small transmitter that produced a longer blip on the screen, so anything shorter was an enemy. It was codenamed Parrot (or Canary) by the British, which probably has something to do with the current use of the word *Squawk* to mean *transmit the relevant codes*, which you dial up on the transponder and which will appear next to your blip with your height readout, depending on the type of transponder you have.

SSR improves on primary radar by using double-pulse secondary equipment to provide more information, hence the name. Participating aircraft carry a *transponder* (for *transmitter/responder*) that receives the interrogation pulse from the transmitter (1030 MHz ±0.2 MHz), superimposes information on it and sends it right back on another paired frequency (1090 MHz). This means, first of all, that the range of operation can be doubled (the power of the echoed pulse has nothing to do with range, so is only subject to normal radio range limitations) and that the blip on the screen can be made much smaller, together with information that makes it more easily identifiable to ATC, because the pulses can be coded. As well, there is no storm clutter, as the principle of echo return is not used. Computer trickery can provide predicted tracks and collision warnings, amongst other things.

The following can be presented on the radar screen:

- Squawk Code
- Flight Level
- Flight Number or Registration
- Groundspeed

You cannot set the number 8! Watch for this in questions that ask you to choose between valid codes

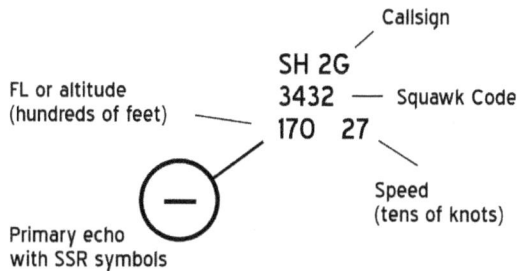

SH 2G — Callsign
FL or altitude (hundreds of feet) — 3432 — Squawk Code
170 27
Primary echo with SSR symbols
Speed (tens of knots)

There are standard numbers to squawk, when not otherwise instructed, which are:

- 2000 - from non-SSR area
- 7000 - conspicuity code

In emergency, squawk:

- 7500 - Hijack*
- 7600 - Comms failure
- 7700 - Emergency

*Absence of a reply is confirmation that the selection is not accidental

Note: When making routine code changes, you should avoid inadvertent selection of 7500, 7600 or 7700 (**do not** switch the transponder to standby during the change to avoid it, as senior pilots often do, because this removes your display from ATC's screen and creates all sorts of alarms). For example, when switching from 2700 to 7200, switch first to 2200 then to 7200, not to 7700 and then 7200. This applies to 7500 and all discrete codes in the 7600 and 7700 series (i.e. 7600-7677, 7700-7777) which will trigger special indicators in automated facilities.

When fitted, transponders should be used **all the time**.

Elementary Surveillance provides a controller with aircraft position, altitude and identification. It is based on ground initiated Comm-B protocols and needs a Mode S transponder with Surveillance identifier (SI) code capacity and automatic reporting of aircraft identification, known as ICAO Level 2s. SI codes must correspond to the aircraft ID in the flight plan, or the registration mark. On the other hand, *Enhanced Surveillance* extracts additional information from the aircraft, known as *Downlink Additional Parameters* (DAP).

Such information, being automatically extracted, reduces controller workload so that they can concentrate on safety. Because radio calls can be reduced, it also makes things easier for pilots.

MODES & CODES

Modes are used to ask questions, such as "Who are you?" (Mode A) or "How high are you?" (Mode C). The answer comes in the form of a code from the aircraft, of which there are **4096** (not Mode S, which has nearly 17 million).

The decoding of time between interrogation pulses determines the operating mode of the transponder (a spacing for transmission and reception is called a mode).

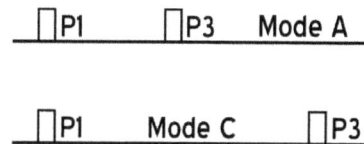

P1   P3   Mode A

P1   Mode C   P3

For modes A and C, a pair of pulses called P1 and P3 are sent out to the aircraft (the interval between them decides which one it is). An omnidirectional antenna sends out another one called P2, which is weaker than the others but stronger than any sidelobes so, if the transponder sees P1 and P3, it knows it is receiving the main lobe. If it sees P2, it's a side lobe. Mode S also uses a short P4 pulse.

A Special Position Identification (SPI) pulse is sent by using the IDENT switch.

MODE A/B

Mode A is the regular variety, based on the original IFF, which just displays the code you select in the aircraft - you get this just by turning the switch to ON. In other words, it is for basic identification (Mode B is occasionally used in place of Mode A in some countries).

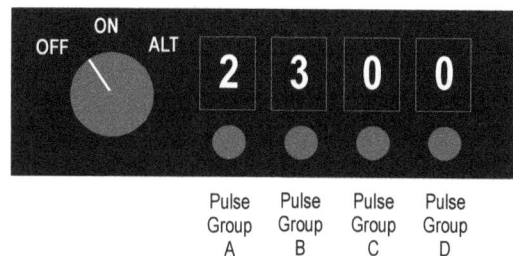

OFF ON ALT   2 3 0 0

Pulse Group A | Pulse Group B | Pulse Group C | Pulse Group D

In answer to an interrogation, a Mode A transponder will transmit up to 14 pulses 8 microseconds apart (17 for B), the first and last ones being *frame pulses* (F1 and F2), which are always there and enclose the whole signal so it doesn't get confused with others. The 12 that are left can be there or not in up to 4096 (2^{12}) combinations, from 0000 to 7777. The *ident pulse* is transmitted for up to 20 seconds, 4.35 microseconds after the last frame pulse when you press the button.

Each number selection knob controls 3 pulses (pulse groups A, B, C & D). 2300 (for example) produces the binary codes of 010, 110, 000 and 000. 0 means Off, or no signal, so selecting 2 means that only pulse 2 of Pulse Group A is transmitted. Selecting 3 requires pulse 1 plus pulse 2 of the B group (refer to *Binary Arithmetic* under *Computers, Etc.* for more information). There would therefore only be 3 pulses between the frame pulses, which saves on transmission bandwidth.

MODE C

Mode C is selected by switching to ALT, after switching on for Mode A, so it is separate (actually A + C). You should always use Mode C unless directed otherwise.

It will transmit altitude information alternately with the code information - a Mode C transponder is directly attached to an encoding altimeter (or, more precisely, an altitude digitiser, which selects a different code to that selected in the window), but only Pressure Altitude (or FL) information based on 1013.25 (or 29.92) information is sent from the aircraft (in 100-foot increments) - the conversion to local pressure, if required, is done inside the ATC computer. **Moving the altimeter subscale does not affect ATC's display**. In Mode C an air traffic controller's presentation gives information regarding your indicated flight level that is accurate to within ±50 ft. The tolerance is ±300 ft.

The pulses are 21 microseconds apart.

MODE S (DATALINK)

S stands for *Selective*, using pulses 25 microseconds apart. It allows aircraft to have unique codes, and respond only to requests directed to them (A and C transponders respond to all requests).

Mode S supplements Modes A & C with a 24-bit address allocated to each aircraft that allows nearly 17 000 000 possible codes. The aircraft address is allocated by the registering Authority, and is transmitted in any reply except Mode S only all-call (the SI code must correspond to Box 7 in the ICAO flight plan). This reduces mistakes and allows more capacity and efficiency, because the transponder does not have to transmit so often. For example, Mode S transponders have 20-foot resolution of altitude data, while Mode C has 100-foot resolution.

Mode A/C/S all-call consists of 3 pulses P1, P3 and the long P4. A control pulse P2 is transmitted following P1 to suppress responses from aircraft in the side lobes of the interrogation antenna. Mode A/C only all-call consists of 3 pulses P1, P3 and the short P4.

A Mode S transponder regularly delivers a *squitter*, which is a short transmission of basic data without receiving a request, simply to advertise your position for TCAA. *Extended Squitter* is additional data on the Mode S Squitter that carries position information from the GPS, so a device receiving the transmission knows the position of the transmitting aircraft without any bearing or range measurements. You can therefore have a pseudo radar service within range of a single mode S ground station (non-rotating antenna) simply by connecting a two-wire data cable from the GPS to the transponder.

Mode S can also provide a two-way data link on 1030 and 1090 MHz, used by TCAS for manoeuvre messages, but also as a backup for VHF voice.

Mode S equipped aircraft over 5 700 kg or with a max TAS over 250 kts must use *transponder antenna diversity*.

The two main design functions of Mode S are:

- air-ground and ground-air data link
- improved ATC aircraft surveillance capability

ERRORS & ACCURACY

Modes A and C can suffer from interference, otherwise known as *fruit* and *garble*. Garbling comes from other aircraft within line of sight range responding to the same interrogation - you could get overlapping returns within 1.7 nm (the transponder antenna is omnidirectional).

Fruiting comes from an aircraft at range responding to interrogations from another ATC. Defruiting involves removing random responses from the display.

Weather Radar

Although it shares the same name, this is not a good system for detecting other aircraft or ground returns because it is tuned to the average size of raindrops (when used for navigation, AWR is only a *secondary* means). In fact, the primary purpose of weather radar is to detect the sort of rainfall that would indicate thunderstorms and their associated turbulence. It therefore relies on your interpretation of the screen display for best results.

Note: Weather radar is required on aircraft that can carry more than 9 passengers under IFR or at night when current weather reports indicate that thunderstorms or other potentially hazardous weather conditions, regarded as detectable with airborne weather radar, may reasonably be expected along the route to be flown.

Two frequency bands are used, such as *C band* (4000-8000 MHz), and *X band* (8000-12500 MHz). C band illuminates storms beyond nearby precipitation better, but X band has more resolution, although its higher frequencies are subject to absorption, and scattering from smaller raindrops. The wavelength is about 3 cm (at 10 GHz, or maybe 9375 MHz), to detect a 1½ cm raindrop - ½ the wavelength is the optimum object size for detection. Larger droplets give good echoes and you can have a smaller antenna. Weather radar can detect volcanic ash, sandstorms and smog, but not clear air turbulence except with the use of Doppler. Cumulus clouds are most readily detected with the weather beam, but snow (or clear air turbulence) cannot be seen. At low altitudes, detection of turbulence may be difficult due to ground returns.

The antenna is inside a *radome* in the nose of the aircraft, with an RT box containing the transmitter/receiver, together with a scope in the cockpit. The antenna can be parabolic or flat, sweeping through 45-60° either side of the nose - the flat scanner reduces power demands and sidelobes. In *weather* mode, the beam is narrow (pencil) and cone-shaped. For mapping, it is wide and fan-shaped (effective up to 50-60 nm), but for long range mapping, use weather mode anyway, because the narrow beam goes further as more power is concentrated in it. The antenna is stabilised in pitch and roll, ±20° combined. It is not stabilised in yaw.

Weather radar detects rainfall to *avoid* (not penetrate) severe weather, as many large raindrops in a small area are a dead giveaway for thunderstorms or, rather, their activity is - turbulence is proportional to the rate at which rainfall increases or decreases over a given distance. Whether you want to go towards the area concerned depends on the intensity of the echoes received, the spacing between them, your capabilities and those of the aircraft.

Note: A clear area on the radar screen (say between significant echoes) does not mean there is no cloud or precipitation, as minute droplets, ice, dry snow and dry hail have low reflective levels, if at all. In fact, a clear area is more likely to indicate large water droplets, as they will totally absorb the energy as they approach the size of the radar wave, and the screen will not be able to display the remaining thunderstorm area behind the point of complete attenuation (absence of returns produces a use for the stray side lobes mentioned above, in that the downwards one produces a ring on the screen at the same range as your height above ground, so you can check if the equipment is working). The greatest echoes come from rain, and drop size is more important than their number.

Note: Because of attenuation, a weak return does not mean a less violent storm - you could just be too far away from it to get decent information.

Operation of weather radar is quite simple, but full use on the ground should be avoided (not below 500 feet, in fact, because the radiations will affect people or equipment). Naturally, you must check the equipment before departure, but most sets have an internal procedure for this. When you do switch it on, it should be set to *Standby* for at least 3 minutes first, to allow things to warm up. When not in use, the set should always be set to SBY to keep the (roll and pitch) stabilisation gyros running - it stops them crunching together as the aircraft moves. Ground testing requires *tilting up* in weather mode.

TILT

Once airborne, the tilt capability will point the antenna up or down so you can adjust for the aircraft attitude and get more detail about approaching storm cells, but don't expect to see the tops of a storm, because the crystals won't reflect the energy in the first place, and your beam focussing will be too narrow to include it (convective thunderstorms are much less reflective above the freezing level). The tilt control is an important key to a more informative display in moderate rain, and should be used often to get a better 3D picture. Tilt down until you see ground returns, then up until they disappear, then add 2° to cover for turns. The tilt should be higher at lower altitudes and lower at higher altitudes.

To see whether a cloud return on an AWR is at or above the height of the aircraft, subtract half the beam width from the angle of tilt. Thus, the tilt angle - beam width x 100 x range in nm equals the approximate height difference of the cloud tops (in feet) from your flight level.

MAPPING

In the same way, you will also get ground echoes, which are good for detecting the enemy coast ahead, but only because water will absorb the echoes and you will see a big black hole instead. Buildings and the like won't reflect properly at all - you might just see a mass of confusing colours (that's what the MAP selection is for, but that's not wonderful, either). MAP mode uses a *cosecant radiation pattern* with a *cosecant squared* antenna, so you can scan a large ground zone with echoes whose signals are practically independent of distance.

When looking at the ground for mapping purposes at fairly close range, the beam must be widened vertically as well as having its energy distribution controlled so that returns from longer range (the top of the beam) are of similar strength to those from shorter range (the bottom of the beam). The strength of the signal vertically within the beam depends upon the square of the cosecant of the angle of depression, so more energy is radiated in the upper part of the beam than the lower part.

You will have several scan ranges to choose from, possibly from 250 miles down to 5, but 80 is adequate, which is about what you would get with a 10 inch antenna, the usual fit in small aircraft. The smaller it is, the wider the beam and the dispersal of energy, which means that a lot of it will pass by whatever storm is around, giving you an indication very much less than the true hazard. You would be safe to assume that whatever you see on the screen is in reality one or two levels more severe.

MAP mode is effective up to 50 or 60 nm, but the pencil shaped beam is preferred for longer distances because more power can be concentrated in the narrow beam.

STORM PATTERNS

If you haven't got the luxury of colour and computer-controlled echo highlighting (and have to rely on steam), there are distinctive storm patterns to look out for:

- *The Hook.* These stick out from a cloud, suggesting strong wind circulations, like tornadoes, or hail, which has a wet surface and therefore reflects like a large raindrop. Both are found in thunderstorms with a marked windshear in the middle levels

- *The Finger.* This is like a spur out from a cloud, not quite as curled as the hook, and usually in the next intense colour, such as yellow. The trick here is to look at the edges - sharp contours mean a growing storm, while fuzzy ones mean a dissipating storm

- *The U-shape.* This is like a valley in a mountain, with strong updraughts surrounded on three sides by the sort of heavy precipitation associated with downdraughts

- *Scalloped edges.* When round a cloud outline, particularly at the back end of a storm, they signify severe attenuation due to heavy precipitation

Shapes can change quickly, so they need careful monitoring (hail shows up better when the gain is reduced). The heaviest precipitation, and the heaviest turbulence, will show up as black holes, or red when using colour, which is best detected in *Contour mode* (where high rainfall rates, or maximum cell activity, appears in Red).

Tip: Radar signals weaken, and might show the end of the weather falsely.

Iso-Echo (for mono screens) produces a hole in a strong echo when the returned signal is above a pre-set value. *It is used to detect areas of possible severe turbulence in cloud.* The edges of the hole that actually appears on the screen have the same rainfall rate, and is like a contour line, hence the name. When the lines are narrow, there is a strong intensity gradient, so avoid hooked echoes, especially rapidly changing ones. In fact, you should beware of thin lines of whatever colour.

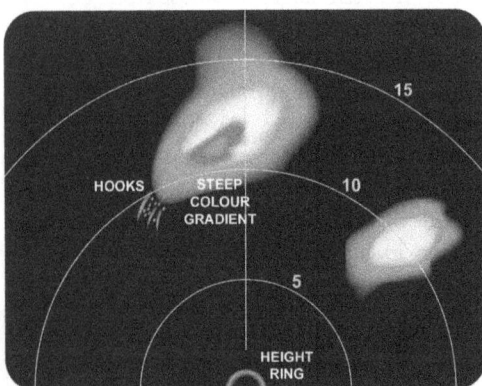

In the picture above, the line along the centre is your intended track, and the curved lines are your range markings, so there's something nasty lurking 10 nm away slightly on your port side, with a little finger (or hook) in front of you which may or may not be producing some rainfall. The colour zones closest together indicate the greatest turbulence. Note the colour progression from green to yellow to red, and possibly magenta for maximum severity. By changing the scale to 10 nm, the returns on the radar screen should increase in area and move nearer to the top of the screen.

Note: Targets separated by a distance less than the beam diameter will merge and appear on the display as one.

Avoid the brightest returns (i.e. those that are changing rapidly, or contouring, or coloured magenta or red) by at least 20 nm. Above the freezing level, make it 5 nm and 10 nm when below. If you see anything at all between 50-70 nm, keep well away from it. The minimum height above a storm should be 1,000 feet for each 10 kts of wind speed.

Ground Radar

Those used for longer range, such as those covering airways and larger airspace, tend to have lower frequencies and longer wavelengths, lower PRFs and larger pulses to get maximum range with as little attenuation as possible. Where shorter range is good enough, say, for use near an aerodrome, short frequent pulses provide better picture definition. In addition, antenna rotation will be higher because shorter range radar will be used when things are changing quickly.

A typical long range coverage will be up to 250-300 nm, with a preferred frequency of 600 MHz and a 50 cm wavelength. Shorter range coverage is provided by.....

AIRCRAFT SURFACE MOVEMENT RADAR

Otherwise known as *Airport Surface Detection Equipment* (ASDE), this operates in the SHF* band (16 GHz), using an antenna that rotates at around 60 RPM. Its definition is such that it is sometimes possible to determine the type of aircraft from the return on the radar screen.

*EHF is absorbed and scattered by moisture in the air.

SURVEILLANCE RADAR APPROACH (SRA)

With this system, ATC can normally talk you down to within 2 nm of the threshold (on QFE unless requested otherwise), but it can get as close as half a mile. As with PAR, below, the controller will give you the headings to fly, but *there is no height information* - just ranges with heights.

As for any approach, if you are using SSR only, non-radar separation standards will be used as soon as possible.

SRE (Surveillance Radar Equipment) can be used for an SRA, which is a form of GCA (Ground Controlled Approach) given in azimuth only, where corrections are given to the centreline in numbers of degrees, but heights are given in feet at ½ mile intervals on the approach corresponding to either a 2½° or 3° approach as required. (e.g. "5 miles 1500 ft, right of centreline correcting nicely....turn right 3 degrees heading 238, 4½ miles 1350 ft, slightly right of centreline correcting slowly.....check gear down....4 miles 1200 ft, [callsign] clear to land, surface wind 240/10 knots....slightly right of centreline correcting slowly..." etc.) Since the update rate on surveillance radar is slower and the centreline is not as accurate, the SRA is a non precision approach and minimum heights are correspondingly higher.

PRECISION APPROACH RADAR (PAR)

PAR is primarily used by the military.

It is high-definition in nature, because it uses the 9-10 GHz range and has a 3 cm wavelength, similar to weather radar, so weather clutter can be a problem (meaning you may be denied its use when you need it most!) It uses two radars (and antennae) to give horizontal and vertical guidance to aircraft on final approach up to about 9 nm within 20° of final track (azimuth) and 7° of elevation (i.e. relatively narrow beams).

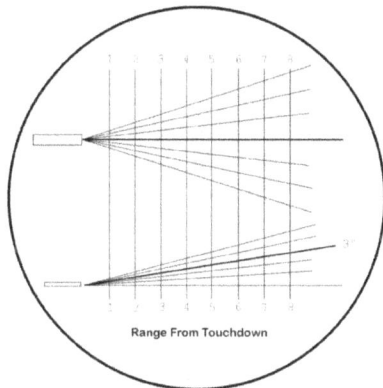

Range From Touchdown

It's supposed to be a landing aid, not one for sequencing or spacing aircraft. As the range is 9 nm, PAR is limited to the final stages of approach. The display is in two parts - the lower giving altitude and distance information, and the upper azimuth and distance. Most PAR decision heights are around 200 ft AGL.

The controller will give you headings to fly, plus position information with regard to the glidepath, but only if you are dangerously low will positive height information be given. In the final stages you will be told not to acknowledge the instructions as things will be happening hard and fast. As your height is monitored, the heights to which you can descend before overshooting will be lower.

PAR's usefulness lies in the fact that navaids are not required and neither is a compass, since the controller tells you to turn left, right, descend, etc. Also, as acknowledgments are not required, you can listen to instructions over an ADF or VOR.

While surveillance radar can be used for GCA applications if the update rate is quick enough, PAR doesn't really have the ability. There is also a PAR Azimuth Only Approach, using the PAR centreline to give a non precision approach more accurate than SRA.

DME   062 02 04

Distance Measuring Equipment is secondary radar, but in reverse. It measures the time difference between *paired pulses* being sent from an aircraft, and received back (on different frequencies). Then the distance is calculated.

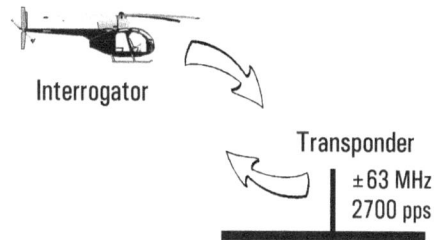

Interrogator

Transponder
±63 MHz
2700 pps

In other words, the aircraft is the first to transmit on UHF, then the DME transponder on the ground returns the signal (with the same PRF and pulse spacing) after a 50 microsecond delay which is subtracted during the number-crunching. The delay reduces the chances of uncoordinated activity when the interrogating aircraft is near the station. The pulses are 3.5 milliseconds wide.

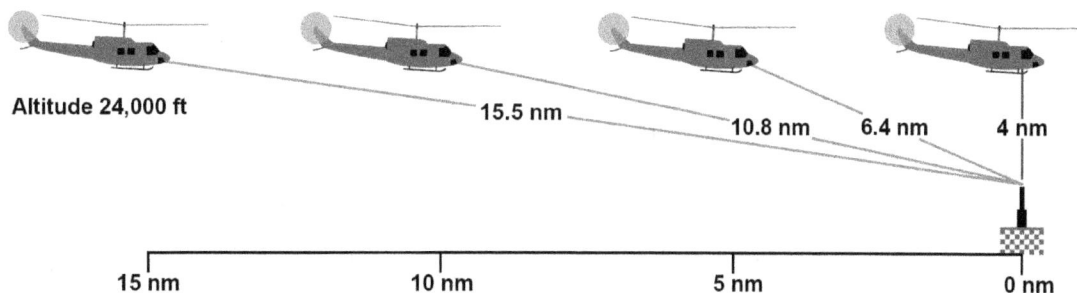

Altitude 24,000 ft   15.5 nm   10.8 nm   6.4 nm   4 nm

15 nm   10 nm   5 nm   0 nm

Two frequencies are used because, otherwise, the first pulse received would be the ground return from below (with normal radar, targets are relatively free from other objects. They are more difficult to distinguish the other way round). Similarly, the ground station could self-trigger from other sources, such as those being bounced off a building. *Jittering* is used to identify pulses. That is, only signals with the same jittering pattern (PRF) are replied to, because they are unique to each aircraft.

DME is UHF-based, between 960 and 1215 MHz, so a typical frequency is 1000 MHz.

Aircraft DME receivers do not lock on to transmissions reflected from the ground as they are not on the receiver frequency - the interrogation and reply frequencies differ.

The **Echo Protection Circuit** prevents lock-on to signals from the ground transponder that are reflected off a surface before reaching the aircraft, or signals from the ground transponder triggered by interrogation pulses from the aircraft that have reflected off a surface before reaching the ground transponder. Such a lock-on would cause an incorrect DME reading greater than the real slant range. It detects whether the transmitter/receiver has been locked by pulse pairs.

DME stations use channels rather than frequencies because they are normally co-located* with a VOR or ILS. The channel is paired with a frequency. When the demand for VOR/DME stations increased and the frequency spacing between VORs was reduced from 0.1 MHz to 0.05 MHz, the number of DME channels naturally doubled, which is not a problem when channels and frequencies are paired but, for those people who could use DMEs separately (i.e. the military using TACAN) a workaround was required. What they did was designate the old channels with an X and the new ones with a Y, reversing the 63 MHz interrogation and response frequencies. The information should be on the chart, but if you only see the frequency, X channels are linked with VOR frequencies ending in 0 (116.70 = 114Y) and Y channels are for those ending in 5 (116.75 - 114X). There are 252 DME channels.

Co-located means within 30 m and frequency paired within 600 m. *Associated* means that the DME callsign ends with a Z, and that they are more than 600 m apart (the maximum distance between VOR and DME/TACAN installations with the same morse ID is 600 m if used for enroute navigation).

DME is normally based with a VOR or TACAN and has a range of about 200 nm, ± 6, with an accuracy better than ½ nm or 3% of the distance, whichever is the greater (max range is determined by height). Thus, when the DME is co-located with a VOR, the two signals combined will give you a position based on a radial from the VOR and how far away on that radial you are.

Using X and Y Channels makes more efficient use of the bandwidth available and reduces interference. They are distinguished by the spacing between their pulses. On the X Channel (mainly UK), interrogation and reply pulses are separated by 12 microseconds. Y Channel interrogation pulses are separated by 36 microseconds, and replies are 30 microseconds apart. DME/P uses different figures. The reason for the spacing is that, in mode X, the received frequency is 63 MHz below the aircraft transmission frequency for channels 1-63 and 63 MHz above it for channels 64-126. This is reversed in Mode Y. The ground frequencies for channels 1-63 and 64-126 are 63 MHz above and below the aircraft frequencies, respectively, so the transmissions are in the air-to-ground band. X (126) + Y (126) = 252 channels.

VOR receivers with integrated DME normally select the associated Y channel (with two decimal places) automatically, while stand-alone receivers display X and Y channels separately.

Thus, signal discrimination depends on *frequency separation* and *pulse spacing*.

The ident is pitched higher than that of a VOR, so you can identify it between VOR idents on the same frequency (it is transmitted only once to the VOR's four).

Instruments in the cockpit will not only show your distance to a station, but will calculate the rate of movement and display the groundspeed (just multiply the distance flown in 6 minutes by 10 if yours doesn't). The reason it isn't completely accurate is because the distance measured is the *slant range* from the station, and not from your equivalent position on the ground, just as with primary radar, although at long distances and lower altitudes, this is minimised. The groundspeed readout reduces at an increasing rate when overflying an aid, to zero at the overhead. In practical terms, the difference is insignificant when you are more than 10 miles from the station, and the maximum error occurs overhead - at 12,000 ft, the instrument would read 2 nm, and 4 nm at 24,000 ft, and so on.

Simple Pythagoras will give you the real distance:

$$D = \sqrt{(S^2 - A^2)}$$

D is the ground distance, *S* is the readout (slant range) and *A* is your altitude in *nautical miles* (above the DME source).

The slant range itself is calculated by:

$$Range = \frac{Time\ (\mu s)}{12.4}$$

Don't forget to subtract a 50 m/s delay at the transponder.

Example: At FL 210, you will not receive any distance indication from a DME station approximately 220 nm away because you are below the line of sight altitude. If the

CAPT

time taken for an interrogation pulse to travel to the ground transponder and back is 2000 microseconds, the slant range is 158 nm (the ground transponder has a 50 microsecond delay, so total time is 1950 microseconds). The most accurate calculation of your ground speed will come from a DME on the flight route, meaning that you will be tracking directly to or from it.

The ground station can only respond to a certain number of interrogations in a given period of time. Normally, 30 pulse pairs are transmitted per second, but going up to 150 (for searching) allows up to 100 aircraft to interrogate the system before *beacon saturation* occurs. A DME experiencing difficulty with locking on will stay in search mode, but will reduce the PRF to up to 60 PPS after 15 000 pulse pairs have been transmitted. If too many aircraft are interrogating it, the receiver will automatically be desensitized so it can hear and reply only to the strongest. Busy airspace can result in shorter-than-normal DME reception range, particularly with lower-powered DME units. An aircraft DME in tracking mode that subsequently experiences a reduction in signal strength will switch in the first instance to *memory mode* so it has something to work on until the signal gets better.

Errors

Where the ground distance is less than or equal to 3 times the height, the inaccuracy is too much for the system. The difference is negligible for enroute navigation when the indicated distance in nm is more than the height of the aircraft above the DME in thousands of feet. Range errors should not exceed ± 0.25 nm plus 1.25% of the distance measured so, at 100 nm, the maximum should not exceed **± 1.5 nm**. The overall system error should be the greater of 3% of distance or 0.5 nm.

ILS

062 02 05

The Instrument Landing System is a pilot-interpreted *precision* approach aid because it includes tracking and slope guidance. It is currently the primary precision approach facility for civil aviation at all major airports, although no more will be installed in the US in favour of GPS approaches. The equipment is constantly monitored by ATC and calibration is carried out frequently by the authorities. If any limits are exceeded, transmissions will be stopped within 6 seconds The following components may be used to guide you down to a *Decision Height*:

- a **VHF transmitter** for **horizontal guidance** along the extended centreline (the *localiser*), with a 1.4° wide beam, at the far end of the runway (the upwind end), about 300m out, to stop it being an obstacle. The beam is about 700 feet wide at the threshold. If it does not go across the extended centreline within 30°, it is an *offset localiser*.

- a **UHF transmitter** for **vertical guidance**, which usually produces a 3° *glideslope,* within about 120m of one side of the runway, typically about 300m from the threshold. The touchdown area is a little way in from the threshold so you have concrete to land on if you have a problem. The *Threshold Crossing Height* (TCH) is where the glideslope antenna should be to ensure that the wheels don't hit the ground if they hang too far below the cockpit, otherwise you will get a runway-assisted go-around. *Glideslope signals are only valid down to the lowest authorised DH,* so if you bust minima, you need to be aware that following the needles will just take you along the runway at that height.

- Up to three 75 Mhz **marker beacons**

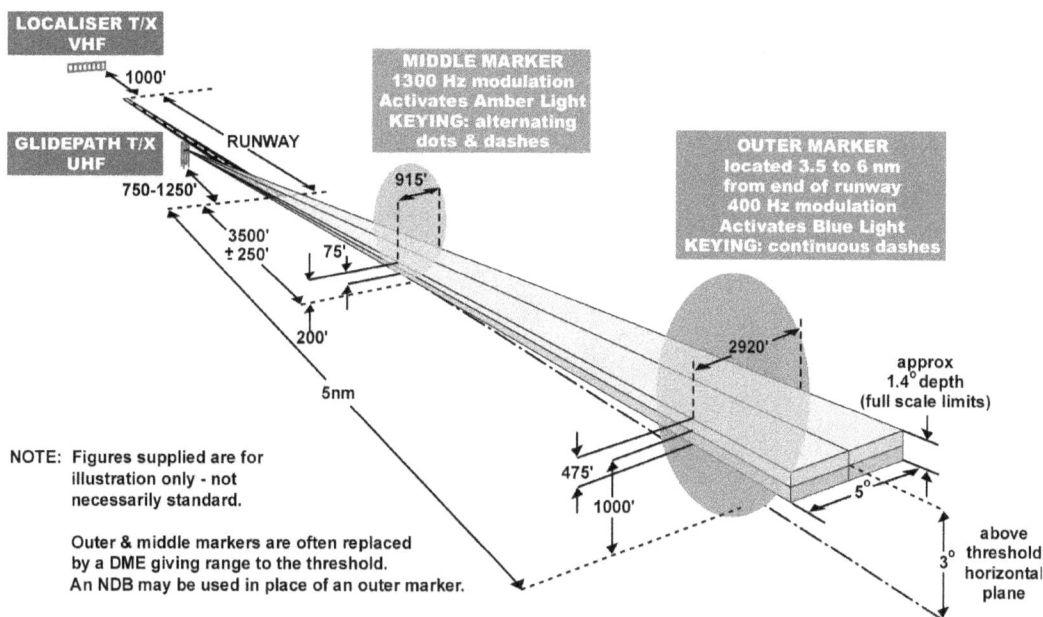

LOCALISER T/X VHF

1000'

GLIDEPATH T/X UHF

RUNWAY

750-1250'

3500' ± 250'

75'

200'

5nm

915'

MIDDLE MARKER 1300 Hz modulation Activates Amber Light KEYING: alternating dots & dashes

OUTER MARKER located 3.5 to 6 nm from end of runway 400 Hz modulation Activates Blue Light KEYING: continuous dashes

2920'

approx 1.4° depth (full scale limits)

475'

1000'

5°

above threshold 3° horizontal plane

NOTE: Figures supplied are for illustration only - not necessarily standard.

Outer & middle markers are often replaced by a DME giving range to the threshold. An NDB may be used in place of an outer marker.

- high intensity **approach lights** for better visual guidance in the latter stages (typically 100 feet apart, up to 3000 feet from the end of the runway)

- radar monitoring

Types Of Approach

Approaches are classified as to equipment on the aircraft and at the airport, plus pilot training and experience.

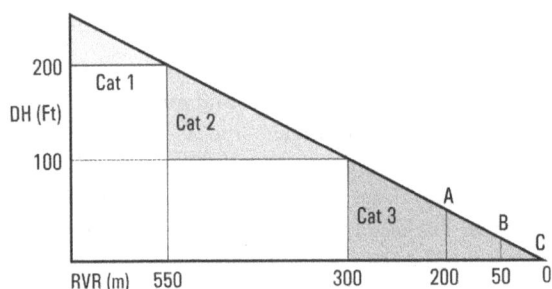

Note: This is the ICAO standard. PART OPS allows 75m for the Cat IIIb approach.

CATEGORY I

This is the least restrictive, and the one that most people in General Aviation will use. It uses a Decision Height* of at least **200 feet** and an RVR of 550 m, with a high chance of success. Ceiling is not a factor.

*Where the localiser intercepts the glideslope.

CATEGORY II

This takes you further down, to 100 feet DH and 300m RVR. It needs special training under an approved syllabus in the Ops Manual. Qualifications are specific to type.

For Cat II (and III - see below), the aircraft must be certificated for Decision Heights below 200 ft, or none, and equipped as per regulations. A suitable system for recording approach and automatic landing success and failure must also be established and maintained to monitor safety. There must be at least 2 pilots, with DH determined by radalt, and the aerodrome must also be approved. Low visibility takeoffs in less than 150 m RVR (Cat A, B and C) or 200 m (Cat D) need approval.

You also likely need the following to be up and running:

- **Lighting**: approach, threshold, touchdown zone, centreline, runway edge and end lights

- **ILS**: localiser, glidepath and middle marker

- **RVR**: two transmissometers, one at the threshold, and at the mid-point

- **Power** - airport emergency power as the primary source for essential elements, with commercial power available within one second

CATEGORY III

A Cat III ILS glidepath transmitter provides reliable guidance information down to the surface of the runway.

- **IIIa** - A DH of less than 100' with 200m RVR

- **IIIb** - Below 50' DH (or none), and 75-200m RVR

- **IIIc** - Zero-zero

Any precision more than Cat II needs a high accuracy radio altimeter.

The Localiser

The localiser comes from two overlapping lobes of radio energy (notes) on VHF, the one on the left (yellow) during approach being A2 modulated at 90 Hz, and the other (blue) also A2 at 150 Hz.

The principle of operation is that the *difference in depth of modulation*, or the ratio of the amplitude of the modulating waveform to that of the R/F carrier, determines the position of the needle. If the depth of modulation of both lobes appears to be the same, the receiver assumes you are on the ILS QDM in the centre, or following the *equisignal*. The greater the difference in modulation depths, the more the indicator needle is displaced. More 90 Hz than 150 Hz, for example, means fly right (and down).

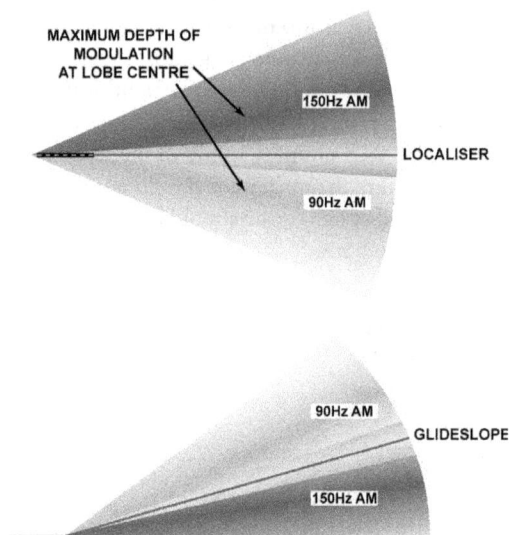

Note: The impression given is that two narrowly focussed beams intersect to provide the guidance but the "beams" are created electronically *by the equipment in the aircraft* (that is, voltages are produced from the radio signals - they have to be at a minimum level to keep the Off flag away). This means you can get on-course or on-glidepath indications regardless of your position, as was found by an Air New Zealand 767 in July 2000, which got down to 400', *6 miles short of the runway* (check your distance and altitudes, and do *not* use equipment on test! In ILS test mode, you always get an on-glideslope indication without warning flags, irrespective of your position). The warning flags are operated by voltmeters in the indicator.

Note: ICAO defines "established on course" as being within half full-scale deflection for an ILS or VOR/TACAN/RNAV/GPS procedure and within ±5° of the required bearing for the NDB. You are not established until you are within these limits.

Tip: When intercepting, double the track error, so if you are 4 dots off, turn by 4° until interception takes place, then turn on to the inbound track.

The frequency range for the localiser lies between 108.1-111.975 MHz (VHF), on *odd decimals* as this range is shared with the VOR, within which there will be 40 channels, so a typical frequency is 109.15 MHz.

The glidepath lies between 328.6-335.4 MHz.

A three-letter ID is transmitted at regular intervals in Morse Code (at 1020 Hz). If the localiser alignment exceeds 3° of the runway heading, the first letter will be *X*. If it is 3° or less, the letter is *I*.

The normal approach is called the *front course*, and is used with the other components of the system. The course line along the extended centreline in the opposite direction is called the *backcourse*. Unless your system has reverse-sensing capability (check for the B/C button on the autopilot), you have to do the opposite of what the needle says when inbound along the back course (as you would when outbound along the front course). Aside from the reverse sensing, backcourses are not used in UK because:

- There is no glideslope
- It is less accurate
- There are no markers

Disregard glideslope indications on a backcourse, unless one is shown on the chart.

ILS is 4 times more sensitive than the VOR, so full needle deflection is 2½°, as opposed to 10° (½° per dot). One dot means you are 300 feet off course at the Outer Marker or FAF, and 100 feet off at the Middle Marker.

Tip: When coming down the glideslope, don't forget to adjust your heading as the wind slows down and backs nearer to ground level (on an airfield near the coast, you will also be affected by sea breezes. At Southend, for example, you can suddenly get a tailwind halfway down the approach, followed by a headwind). This is particularly important for helicopters because the ILS was originally based on fixed wing characteristics. When very slow, large drift correction angles make it hard to follow a localiser.

Note: Localiser errors are due to ground reflections. *Scalloping* means that the beam direction varies from side to side of the intended approach path.

The Glidepath

Glidepath transmissions are done in a similar way, but on UHF (between 329-335 MHz), with the frequencies paired with localiser ones (i.e. the glidepath frequency is automatically tuned when the localiser frequency is selected). The upper lobe is the 90 Hz yellow one, but ground reflections from the lower lobe produce *side-lobes* which can give false indications*. These should be above the real glidepath, but you should still be aware of them. Watch for high rates of descent, and check altitudes against distances - full deflection is only 0.7°, and one dot means 50 feet at the Outer Marker (around 8 feet at the Middle Marker).

*The ILS is subject to false glidepaths resulting from multiple lobes of radiation patterns in the vertical plane.

The glideslope is captured from below to avoid false lobes.

The pattern is achieved through the interaction of directly radiated waves with those reflected from the ground. As the number of lobes increases with the height of an antenna above the ground, and the angle of elevation of the lowest lobe decreases with its height, two antennae, one above the other, are used to give the best effects. The lower one radiates at 90 Hz and the upper one 150 Hz. By adjusting the amplitude of the 150 Hz carrier, the lowest lobes of the two antennae can be made to intersect at the chosen glideslope angle (usually 3°). The first false equisignal should not be lower than 10°, so there should be a low risk of confusion.

Because they are offset from the runway (to stop aircraft hitting them), suitable phase adjustments must be made to keep you on the glideslope. This is achieved by moving the lower antenna a few inches further away from the runway.

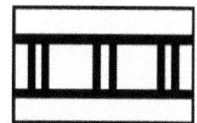

ILS transmitters are sensitive to vehicles, etc., around them, which is why there are *ILS Critical Areas*, in which no aircraft or vehicles are allowed to move during ILS operations. The same applies to *ILS Sensitive Areas* in low visibilities (Cat II/III). The reason why pre-takeoff holding areas are sometimes further from the active runway when ILS Category 2 and 3 landing procedures are in progress than during good weather operations is that aircraft manoeuvring near the runway may disturb the guidance signals. Look for the sign like the one left and above, and the *B Pattern* next to it on the taxiway.

The signals received in the cockpit are translated onto an instrument like the one on the left, below. The vertical needle shows whether you are left or right of the localiser and the horizontal one tells you whether you are high or low in relation to the glideslope. In the example, you are on the glideslope and *left* of the localiser, so you "chase the cross" to get back on, in this case, fly level to the right.

On the right is a picture of a *Horizontal Situation Indicator* (HSI). Glideslope indicators are on the side.

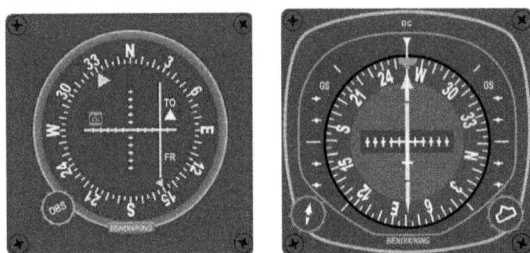

Note: The OBS doesn't work when the VOR instrument is used for the ILS, because it is only radiating one course, but it is usually set to the inbound course for neatness.

Note: *Glidepath* means any part of the glideslope intersecting the localiser.

Tip: When using an HSI, a smooth intercept can be obtained by keeping the top of the CDI bar next to the lubber line.

Markers & Beacons

Three beacons (radiating at 75 MHz as A2A) are used on the way down the glideslope to indicate that you are within the coverage of the localiser and glidepath, or to help with height, distance and equipment checks.

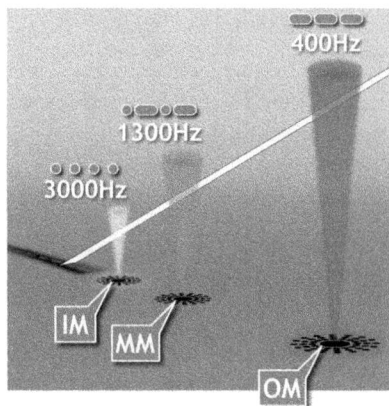

The Outer Marker is at about 4-5 miles (where you should be around 1500 feet, when the glideslope meets the minimum holding altitude), which often coincides with, or is replaced by, an NDB or DME. The Middle Marker is found at about ½ mile from the threshold (where you should be around 200 feet off the ground), using a quarter of the power of the Outer Marker, and the inner marker is just before the threshold, at DH, if it is there (it's mainly for Cat II approaches). It uses a tenth of the Outer Marker power. Vertical beams are used to stop interference.

The markers don't have to be tuned, as they have their own identification.

 The outer marker produces a blue flashing light within a few degrees of the overhead. Each vertical dot is about 50 ft.

 The middle marker is amber, where each vertical dot is equal to about 8 feet.

 The inner marker is white, if used.

The markers beep as well as flash, using different tones (400, 1300 and 3000 Hz if you really want to know) in Morse. The OM uses three dashes at two per second, the MM dot-dash-dot-dash at two per second, and the inner marker four dots at 6 per second. Markers have a sensitivity setting. *High* allows you to pick up the signals a bit sooner, but *Low* is a bit more precise on positioning.

CAPT

Lighting

These are meant to help with the transition from instruments to visual, although they are not actually a requirement for the system. However, if lighting is not present, the minima will be increased somewhat.

CATEGORY I

This is what you might see as you come out of the clag with a Cat I approach:

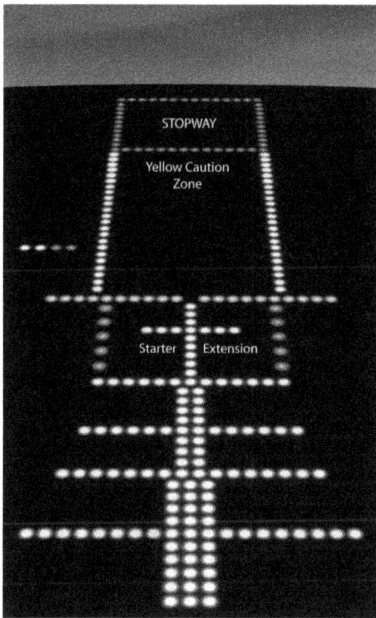

CATEGORY II

This would be the setup for a Cat III approach:

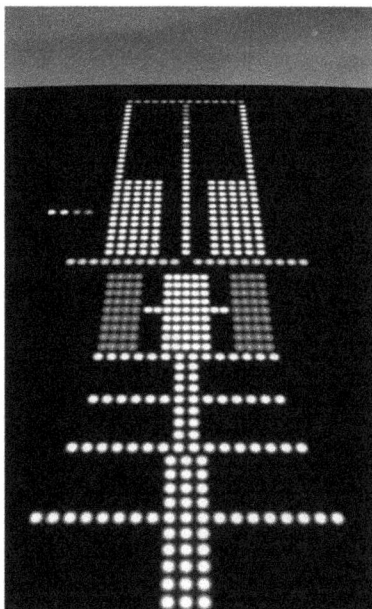

Gradients, Etc

You need to know how high you should be at particular distances from the runway as a gross error check. For example, you should be at the Middle Marker at about 200 feet, and the Outer Marker at 1400 feet. This ensures that you haven't hit a false glideslope (as long as you join the glideslope from below, you should be OK).

There is virtually no guidance below 100 feet - remember this if you bust minima at any time. The glideslope actually flares at around 25-30 feet, so if you follow the needle, you will start to climb at that height (autoland compares sink rate against radalt indications to cover for this).

RATE OF DESCENT

Radar will give you a distance to touchdown so you can calculate a smooth rate of descent. You don't want to be making sudden drops at the last minute to make the glideslope and risk spilling the coffee.

Glidepath gradient calculations are variations on the 1 in 60 rule - the standard 3° glidepath is an ROD of 300 ft per nm, or 100 feet per degree. 3° slopes can be calculated by multiplying your groundspeed by 5, as derived from:

$$ROD = \frac{GS \times 10}{2}$$

Note: At 60 kts, the ROC/ROD equals the gradient.

If the speed changes on the approach, a strong headwind causes a *decrease* in groundspeed and rate of descent, and a tailwind does the opposite. Every 10 kts decrease in groundspeed on a 3° glideslope means a decrease in ROD of 50 fpm, and *vice versa*.

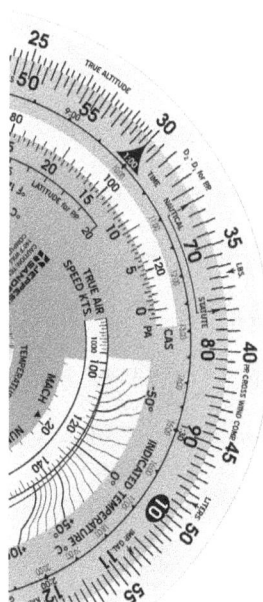

You can use the slide rule on the flight computer to solve these as a proportion problem. If you put the 60 kt index on the slide rule against 30 (3°) on the outer scale, you can read 450 fpm against 90 kts, and so on........

For a 2.5° glideslope, just put the index against 25, or 35 for a 3.5° glideslope. The rate of descent required to maintain a 3.25° glide slope at a groundspeed of 140 kts is approximately 800 ft/min.

HEIGHT ON THE GLIDESLOPE

Use the formula:

```
Height = GP Angle x dist to go in ft
                    60
```

Note: The formula refers to the touchdown point. If the distance is quoted from the threshold (like with DME) add 50 feet because you will be at the screen height.

If the glideslope is published as a percentage, place the 10 index on the inner scale of the flight computer and against the percentage value on the outer scale, reading the degree value on the outer scale against the 60 index on the inner scale. In the picture below, the gradient is 5%.

EXAMPLES

1. If an ILS has a glideslope of 2.5°, what height should you be at 6 nm from the touchdown point?

At 60 nm, you would be 2.5 nm high, which is 15,200 feet. 6 nm is a tenth of that, so you should be at 1520 feet (1500 in the exam).

2. The outer marker of an ILS with a 3° glide slope is 4.6 nm from the threshold. Assuming a glideslope height of 50 ft above the threshold, what is the approximate height of an aircraft passing the outer marker?

```
Range (ft) x GP Angle = Ht (ft)
        60
```

Substituting:

```
27968 x 3 = 1398.4
  60
```

Add the 50 ft above the threshold to get 1450 ft, in round figures. Another formula is:

```
Height = GS Angle x 100 x distance
```

where *distance* is in nautical miles.

3. With a minimum climb gradient of 200 ft/nm, at what altitude should you be 5 nm after departure to comply with the procedure?

This is simply a ratio, so:

```
200 = ?
 1    5
```

You should be at 1000 feet. How far will you be away from the departure point when you get to 2000 feet? 10 nm. If you set this up on the flight computer, you don't even have to move the wheel for the second answer.

4. If your groundspeed is 120 kts and your vertical speed is 500 fpm, what is your gradient? Again, a proportion problem. the answer is 2.5°.

Range & Coverage

Note: Outside the published range, you should not normally receive signals.

LOCALISERS

The localiser range and coverage is:

- 8° up to 10 nm
- 35° either side of the centreline up to 17 nm
- 10° either side of the centreline up to 25 nm

These may be reduced to 18 nm, 10° off the centre line if there is satisfactory alternate coverage within the intermediate approach area.

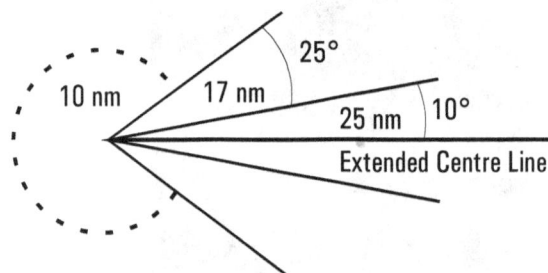

GLIDESLOPES

You should be able to receive the glideslope signal up to 10 nm. The approximate angular coverage of reliable navigation information for a 3° ILS glide path out to 10 nm is 1.35° above the horizontal to 5.25° above the horizontal and 8° each side of the localiser centreline. An aircraft tracking to intercept the localiser inbound on the approach side, outside the published ILS coverage angle may receive false course indications.

INDEX

trip-free 1-9
tropospheric wave 3-8
TRU 1-16, 1-26
True Air Speed 2-17
True Altitude 2-12
true height 2-48
True North 2-23
Turn And Bank Indicator 2-38
Turn Coordinator 2-6, 2-38
TV stations 3-33
Two-Frequency Simplex 1-50

U
UART 1-49
UHF 3-51

V
valence electrons 1-2
valency 1-2
Van Allen belt 3-9
variable capacitor. 1-30
Variation 2-23, 2-25
variometer 2-50
VDF 3-39
VDF letdown 3-40
Vertical Mode
    autopilot 1-58
Vertical Redundancy, 1-52
Vertical Speed Indicator 2-6, 2-20
VHF 3-41, 3-51
Virtual memory 1-41
VNAV 3-25
voltage depression 1-16
voltage regulator 1-14, 1-20, 1-36
voltage regulators 1-3
voltmeter 1-12, 1-16
Volts 1-5
VOR 1-27, 3-15, 3-19, 3-24
VORTAC 3-24
VOT 3-18
VSI 2-5

W
wander 2-28
wander angle 3-31
warning flags 2-43
wave guide 3-42
Wavebands 3-2
Weather Radar 3-46
weight on wheels switch 2-48
Wheatstone Bridge 2-4, 2-6
Wheatstone bridge 1-8
white noise 1-52
Wing Leveller 1-59, 1-64
wound rotor 1-39

Y
Yagi array 3-12
yaw damper 1-58

Z
Zener Diode 1-44
zone of ambiguity 3-16
zones of ambiguity 3-19

INDEX